BETWEEN
LANGUAGES

Sarah Lynn Higley

BETWEEN LANGUAGES

The Uncooperative Text
in Early Welsh and Old English Nature Poetry

The Pennsylvania State University Press
University Park, Pennsylvania

Library of Congress Cataloging-in-Publication Data

Higley, Sarah Lynn.
    Between languages : the uncooperative text in early Welsh and Old
English nature poetry / Sarah Lynn Higley.

        p.   cm.
    "Appendix: A selection of texts and translations": p.
    Includes bibliographical references and index.
    ISBN 0-271-00876-8 (alk. paper)
    1. English poetry—Old English, ca. 450–1100—Criticism, Textual.
2. Literature, Comparative—English (Old) and Welsh.   3. Literature,
Comparative—Welsh and English (Old)   4. Welsh poetry—To 1100—
Criticism, Textual.   5. Nature in literature.   I. Title.
PR217.H54   1993
829'.10936—dc20   92-8138
                                                                            CIP

Copyright © 1993 The Pennsylvania State University
All rights reserved
Published by The Pennsylvania State University Press, Suite C, Barbara Building,
University Park, PA 16802-1003
Printed in the United States of America

It is the policy of The Pennsylvania State University Press to use acid-free paper for the
first printing of all clothbound books. Publications on uncoated stock satisfy the minimum
requirements of American National Standard for Information Sciences—Permanence of
Paper for Printed Library Materials, ANSI Z39.48–1984.

For My Mother and My Father
with Love

Ræd biþ nyttost. *Maxims I*

Contents

Abbreviations   ix

Acknowledgments   xiii

BACKGROUND

Introduction   3

1 The Natural Analogy: Difficulties, Gaps, and Irritations   15

PART I. THE PHONETIC CONNECTION

2 Getting Around the Cipher: Translating the Uncooperative
   Text   29

3 Metrical and Stylistic Analyses   57

PART II. THE IMAGE AND CONNECTION

4   Grappling with the Gnomic: Modern and Medieval Concepts
of Image and Connection   97

5   The Vanishing Point: Deixis and Conjunction   119

6   The Third Thing: Context as Connection in Gnomic and
Nature Poetry   149

PART III. THE PRIVATE CONNECTION

7   Intentional Difficulty in Early Welsh Poetry   187

8   Clarity and Obscurity in Old English Poetry   221

Afterword: Between Worlds   251

Appendix: Selected Texts and Translations   255
Laments: 1. *The Seafarer*   256
                2. *The Sick Man (Leper) of Abercuawg*   263
                3. *The Song of the Old Man*   268
Gnomes and Nature Poems:
                4. *Maxims II*   271
                5. *Let the Cock's Comb Be Red*   275
                6. *Keen the Wind*   278
Enigmas: 7. *Wulf and Eadwacer*   282
                8. *Angar Kyfyndawt*   284

Textual Commentary   293

Name and Title Index   303

Subject Index   310

Abbreviations

The primary editions for the most commonly cited poems are (for the Old English) *The Exeter Book*, vols. 1 and 2, published by *The Early English Text Society*, and (for the Welsh) *The Red Book of Hergest* and *The Book of Taliesin*, edited by J. Gwenogvryn Evans. I give column (or stanza) and line numbers for the Welsh texts and line numbers (and page numbers where a short text is cited in full) for the English texts. These editions have the advantage of being the least altered by modern punctuation and emendation. Other editions, manuscripts, and dictionaries are listed below for the more occasional reference and are used primarily in the footnotes and the Appendix.

ASMP   *The Anglo-Saxon Minor Poems*, ed. Elliott Van Kirk Dobbie (New York: Columbia University Press, 1942).
BL Addl. Ms British Library Additional Manuscript.
BBC   The Black Book of Carmarthan (Ms). Also: *Llyfr Du Caerfyrddin*, ed. A. O. H. Jarman [Caerdydd: Gwasg Prifysgol Cymru, 1982]).

BT	The Book of Taliesin (Ms). Also, *The Book of Taliesin Facsimile and Edition*, J. Gwenogvryn Evans (Llanbedrog: Issued to Subscribers Only, 1910).
CA	*Canu Aneirin*, ed. Ifor Williams (Caerdydd: Gwasg Prifysgol Cymru, 1938).
CLlH	*Canu Llywarch Hen*, ed. Ifor Williams (Caerdydd: Gwasg Prifysgol Cymru, 1978).
CTB1	Cotton Tiberius B.1 (Ms).
EB1	*The Exeter Book*, vol. 1, ed. Israel Gollancz (London: Early English Text Society, 1985).
EB2	*The Exeter Book*, vol. 2, ed. W. S. Mackie (London: Early English Text Society, 1934).
ECNP	*Studies in Early Celtic Nature Poetry*, Kenneth H. Jackson (Cambridge: Cambridge University Press, 1935).
EECL	*The Early English and Celtic Lyric*, P. L. Henry (London: Allen and Unwin, 1970).
EETS	*Early English Text Society.*
EWSP	*Early Welsh Saga Poetry: A Study and Edition of the Englynion*, Jenny Rowland (Cambridge: Boydell and Brewer, 1990).
G	*Geirfa Barddoniaeth Gynnar Gymraeg*, ed. J. Lloyd-Jones (Caerdydd: Gwasg Prifysgol Cymru, 1931–63).
GM	*Geiriadur Mawr: The Complete Welsh-English English-Welsh Dictionary*, ed. Evans H. Meurig (Aberystwyth: Aberystwyth Press, 1960).
GPAS	*Gnomic Poetry in Anglo-Saxon*, Blanche Colton Williams (New York: AMS, 1966).
GPC	*Geiriadur Prifysgol Cymru: A Dictionary of the Welsh Language*, ed. R. J. Thomas et al. (Cardiff: University of Wales Press, 1950–).
JEGP	*Journal of English and Germanic Philology.*
Jes 3	Jesus 3 (Ms).
LlH	*Llawysgrif Hendregadredd*, ed. John Morris Jones and T. H. Parry Williams (Caerdydd: Gwasg Prifysgol Cymru, 1971).
LlT	*Llyfr Taliesin: Astudiaethau ar rai agweddau*, Marged Haycock, Doctoral Dissertation (University of Wales at Aberystwyth, 1983).
NLW	The National Library of Wales.
Pen	Peniarth 111 (Ms).

PLlH	*The Poetry of Llywarch Hen,* Patrick K. Ford (Berkeley and Los Angeles: University of California Press, 1974).
PMLA	*Publications of the Modern Language Association.*
PT	*The Poems of Taliesin,* ed. Ifor Williams and J. E. Caerwyn Williams (Dublin: Institute for Advanced Studies, 1968).
RB	The Red Book of Hergest (Ms). Also: *The Poetry of the Red Book of Hergest,* ed. J. Gwenogvryn Evans (Llanbedrog: Issued to Subscribers Only, 1911).
VB	*The Vercelli Book,* ed. George Philip Krapp (New York: Columbia University Press, 1932).
WB	The White Book of Rhydderch (Ms).

Acknowledgments

This book would never have come to fruition without the kind help of several people. It is the work of a decade, beginning where it left off as a University of California doctoral thesis and completed in Wales under the auspices of a Fulbright-Hays Grant in 1983/84. *Between Languages* is thus an apt title for it, shaped as it is by the ideas and input of mentors on both sides of the Atlantic. In the ten years since then, many new influences have affected my reception of medieval poetry. From the beginning I had found that I was excited not merely by ambiguous and obscure poems but by the very effects of ambiguity and obscurity on the modern scholar of old poems. The philological training I received from my instructors here and abroad allowed me to undertake the daunting task of reading Taliesin, and yet the fascination (and the doubt) in the cultural and historical process of reading and translating still persisted. These preoccupations were being investigated enthusiastically in areas far removed from Early Welsh or Old English literature, but I soon discovered that I had fallen between war zones. I was a philologist interested in "deconstruction" (that hazy and incendiary term): too speculative for my colleagues in Wales, too conservative for my colleagues in Switzerland. So I turned to my earlier manuscript and rewrote it. There is much in this new book, I think, to please—or displease—most of the people I thank here.

I am hardly the first scholar of insular literature to find myself in this liminal position: Allen Frantzen, Gillian Overing, John Hermann, and others have attempted to bridge traditional and contemporary theories in Anglo-Saxon Studies, and I hope that the Welsh sphere will reap the benefits that such investigations, controversial as they are, have brought to the study of Old English. Frantzen's recent anthology of essays on medieval literature, *Speaking Two Languages*, which aims to bring "contemporary criticism to parity with traditional methodology," offers a useful trope in its title, and it is in this sense of the enlightening analytical stance which two discourses give us that I offer *Between Languages*.

I would like to thank my teachers at Berkeley for their instruction over the years in Early Welsh, Old English, and other medieval languages, and who helped send me to Wales: Carol Clover, Joseph Duggan, Kathryn Klar, Dan Melia, the late Brendan O Hehir, Ray Oliver, Annalee Rehjon, and especially Alain Renoir, to whom I am most grateful for the formative hours and years he has given me as a professor, director, and friend. I am also grateful to John O. H. Harrington, of the United States/United Kingdom Educational Commission, for welcoming me to Great Britain and arranging my stay there. I thank Gerallt Harries at the University College of Swansea and Marged Haycock at the University of Wales at Aberystwyth for their assistance. But special thanks must go to my academic director Brynley Roberts (then at the University College of Swansea), whose instruction, encouragement, open-mindedness, patience, and personal kindness helped me over the rough areas of my first year abroad.

I have also garnered assistance and suggestions for this book from numerous friends and colleagues: Derek Brewer, Harry Butler, Mary Cappello, Patrick Ford, Orin Gensler, Ken Gross, Thomas Hahn, George Lakoff, Seth Lerer, Françoise Le Saux, Laura Morland, Russell Peck, Eve Salisbury, David Sewell, Brian Stock, Nancy Porter Stork, and Paul Beekman Taylor. I am especially grateful to Nick Doan, Jim Earl, Allen Frantzen, Alexandra Olsen, Eve Sweetser, and Maria Tymoczko for the detailed care and attention they have given the manuscript in its various final stages. Thanks must go as well to the patience, encouragement, and scrupulous vigilance of the editorial staff at Penn State Press, especially Philip Winsor, Wilma Ebbitt, and Cherene Holland. My mistakes are my own, but my inspiration and courage have found much assistance from others—inside and outside of America, inside and outside of the field.

BACKGROUND

Introduction

All written records are to some degree uncooperative. The written utterance does not present the advantages of a spoken utterance and its immediate exchanges. Its voice is silent, it is deaf to our responses. If it is an ancient text, its author has died centuries ago along with the informing discussions that surrounded its original recitation, including a familiar and usable language. The difficult ancient text adds an extra layer to its native uncooperativeness: to all the problems cited above we must add faulty scribal transmission, contextual ellipses, *hapax legomena*, generic anomalies, and (in the case of the hermetic text) the nearly impenetrable ramparts of esoterica and private discourse. We have countered with the machinery of critical scholarship, and though deeply aware of its limitations I will attempt a discussion of certain difficult Old English and Early Welsh nature poems, wisdom poems, and enigmata.

A comparative study of early English and Welsh poetry invokes a host of interpretive problems, not the least of which is how we are to read these texts, how we are to read them together, and, more important, through which literary tradition we are to read the other. This book, then, will be as much a study of the developing criticism of the material as it is of the material itself. It questions what it means to respond to likeness or otherness in texts that are removed from us linguistically, culturally and temporally, and which bear the *aegis* of obscurity. It examines the perilous quality of *translation*, the "carrying across" of cultural meaning, on several levels: not only across two contemporaneous cultures (the Anglo-Saxons and the Early Welsh in their handling of certain common themes), but also across a millennium where time puts us out of touch with old contexts and encourages a kind of literary ethnocentrism in the form of English scholarly discourse; thus its title, *Between Languages*, which is meant to imply yet a third form of mediation, that of finding a middle ground wherein conservative and innovative theoretical approaches can combine to bring this sequestered poetry into a new light. I take as my starting point the connection of natural image and emotion, "the natural analogy" as I term it, a worldwide poetic phenomenon whereby external nature is connected to internal mood, and one which is employed differently by these two traditions. I show how the Old English elegies, long thought to be disjointed and cryptic, are actually invested in explanation and disclosure to a degree that the comparable Welsh poems are not; and how the Welsh "omissions" might be better understood as dynamic juxtapositions wherein other poetic aspects (metrics, imagery, obscurantist traditions) serve to link ideas and to fulfill or frustrate our expectations. My argument revolves around the plight of lonely people depicted in these poems in a precarious state of connection with the rest of the world and the different registers they employ to describe their placelessness; it will move on to a discussion of imagery and intentional difficulty in the maxims and gnomes, and in certain poems thought to be hopelessly obscure. I offer texts and translations in the Appendix.

The cold war between medievalists and the contemporary academy (in America and Europe) has been keenly felt by many recent scholars who expose the "constructions of meaning" in the allegedly objective approaches to medieval texts. Allen Frantzen and Charles Venegoni challenged the "disinterested claims of scholarship" in their ground-breaking 1986 article;[1]

---

1. "The Desire for Origins: An Archaeology of Anglo-Saxon Studies," *Style* 20.2 (1986), 142–56, locates the resistance to contemporary theory expressed by many traditional medievalists in a need to maintain a "fiction of origins" that is political in its basic impulses but concealed in a Foucauldian discourse of power (143). Frantzen has expanded his study into a book-length work (*Desire for Origins: New Language, Old English, and Teaching the Tradition* [New Brunswick: Rutgers University Press, 1990]).

James W. Earl uses the psychoanalytic terms "resistance" and "transference" to describe a similar process of occlusion whereby we re-create the medieval text in the image of our own desires.[2] Other scholars of Old and Middle English and Old French have challenged traditional methodologies,[3] but Celtic studies still remains one of the last bastions of what Donald Howard has called the "Third Medievalism."[4]

If the "Second Medievalism" (following "the antiquarianism of the Renaissance" that comprises the First) is "a sounding board" in the eighteenth and nineteenth centuries "for nationalism, liberalism, [and] sentimentalism,"[5] then the Third Medievalism sets out in the twentieth century to challenge its constructs and to ascertain the medieval world through a rigorous appeal to authenticity and definition. It seeks to focus the lens sharply on the medieval world and translate it into terms that are culturally intelligible. I have no intention of arguing that all readings are meaningful because all lenses are opaque (the stereotypical—and simplistic—objection to postmodern theory). Clearly there are more informed and less informed textual examinations. Nor do I intend to belittle the vast amount of philological work that has made these poems critically available to us. Sir Ifor Williams and other fine scholars have cleared away many obstacles. What this book seeks to expose, however, is the tendency, too long unquestioned, to read the Welsh from a distance through the Old English, to repair its gaps, smooth out its differ-

2. "Beowulf and the Origins of Civilization," in Speaking Two Languages: Traditional Disciplines and Contemporary Theory in Medieval Studies, ed. Allen J. Frantzen (Albany: State University of New York Press, 1991), 65–89.

3. Suzanne Fleishman and Howard Bloch contribute controversial articles to the January 1990 issue of Speculum (65.1) on the "New Philology" (respectively, "Philology, Linguistics, and the Discourse of the Medieval Text," 19–37, and "New Philology and Old French," 38–58); Lee Patterson's Negotiating the Past: The Historical Understanding of Medieval Literature (Madison: University of Wisconsin Press, 1987) examines the contradictions implicit in concepts of historicism practiced by medievalists and how these have affected—and retarded—study of Middle English literature. See also his article "On the Margins: Postmodernism, Ironic History, and Medieval Studies," in Speculum (65.1), 87–108. Books by Gillian Overing (Language, Sign, and Gender in Beowulf [Carbondale: Southern Illinois University Press, 1990]) and John Hermann (Allegories of War: Language and Violence in Old English Poetry [Ann Arbor: University of Michigan Press, 1989]) challenge the intellectual stranglehold that the philological heritage has had on the study of Anglo-Saxon. In "The Premodern Text and the Postmodern Reader," Thomas Hahn adds to and elucidates many of these arguments in his introduction to the special issue on Chaucer published by Exemplaria 2.1 (1990), 1–21.

4. "The Four Medievalisms," University Publishing (1980), 7.

5. Howard, "Four Medievalisms," 7. C. S. Lewis's The Allegory of Love (1936) is "a great monument of the Third Medievalism." So, too, are Ifor Williams's painstaking and invaluable editions of Canu Llywarch Hen (1935), Canu Aneirin (1938), and The Poems of Taliesin (1975). Challenges to his authority are "handled with tongs," as Howard might have said (7).

ences by means of the long-standing hegemony of *anglocentrism*, which ensures that an unreadable text be critically resolved in such a way that it becomes readable within the ideological contexts established by traditional English academic standards. In looking at poetic connection and intelligibility, I examine a deep-seated modern desire to correct the unintelligible and the unconnected. In particular, I examine a group of poems that insist on the precarious situation of sufferers caught between society and wilderness, inside and outside, sacred and secular, meaning and nonmeaning. Scholars have noted the obvious similarities in mood and imagery between some of the Old English elegies and the early Welsh "saga" verses. The outcast bewailing his solitude, the descriptions of indifferent nature, the mournful cuckoo, the inclusion of gnomic materials, and the troubled issue of spiritual consolation have led to the standard theory that both traditions derive from a genre of "penitential lyric." The case is far from being settled definitively, and the sheer amount of argumentation, retranslation, revision, and juggling of verses points to a kind of uncooperativeness in the texts in question—some quality of unreadability by which they evade being stretched or amputated to fit our procrustean interpretations.

Produced in adjacent areas of Britain, English and Welsh poems of the ninth and tenth centuries offer a particularly appropriate opportunity to use two medieval traditions (and their ensuing scholarship) as foils to each other, yet few comparatists have taken advantage of the contiguity. An early inspiration for this book was Peter Schroeder's plea for a "Northern medieval aesthetic,"[6] one that could offer comparative examinations of Norse and Irish material in efforts to explain the mysterious disruptions and flatnesses in Old English poetic narrative. Disappointingly, Schroeder makes no mention in his plea of the Welsh—Anglo-Saxon England's closest and perhaps most inimical neighbors. Only a handful of scholars have done comparative work in Anglo-Saxon and Early Welsh, yet reexamination shows how blithely the Welsh is interpreted by means of the valorizing tradition of the Old English. The holes in the Welsh are filled in and made coherent by using the English (or the Latin Christian tradition) as a template for its silences. The English is explicit, the Welsh is not. I offer not only a new reading of texts that have been relegated to the realm of the specialist; I also speculate on the ways we read and translate insular (and insulated) literature. Important differences have collapsed in the search for sameness; the Welsh mode has been overpowered by the English academy, even in the hands of Welsh scholars. Indirection and private dis-

6. "Stylistic Analogies Between Old English Art and Poetry," *Viator* 5 (1974), 197.

course have been treated as embarrassments rather than strengths (academic discomfiture about the "mythological Taliesin" being a case in point), ambiguity as a condition that needs explaining. The expressed need to rescue Welsh lyric poetry from the feminizing tendency of enthusiasts (the sentimental Celt, the Celtic Twilight, the passive Celt in contrast with the resolute Anglo-Saxon) is itself fraught with unexpressed anxieties about gender and critical power. If medieval Welsh poetry—rich, various, in full tune with the many moods of medieval European literature—has been kept in its parochial Celtic Studies box throughout much of the twentieth century, it is due less to the problems posed by its language and more to the covert privileging of anglocentric methods of appropriation and textual study that need to be reevaluated.

Certain poems of lament from *The Red Book of Hergest* and *The Black Book of Carmarthan*[7] show a lonely figure pitted against impersonal nature, such as we find in some of the poems from *The Exeter Book.* These Welsh poems have been gathered and edited many times, and they are known to us most frequently as *Canu Llywarch Hen* ("The Songs of Llywarch Hen").[8]

---

7. Respectively, Jesus College cxi and Peniarth 1. These two manuscripts are the most important sources for the poems of this study. *The Red Book* is probably late fourteenth to early fifteenth century (D. Simon Evans, *A Grammar of Middle Welsh* [Dublin: Institute for Advanced Studies, 1976], xxi); the age of *The Black Book* is less clear, but traditionally put in the thirteenth century. A. O. H. Jarman discusses the various arguments in his "Brwydyr y Cymerau ac Ocd Llyfr Du Caerfyrddan," *Bulletin of the Board of Celtic Studies* 14 (1951), 179–86. Variants of the *Canu Llywarch Hen* can be found in other manuscripts, primarily *The White Book of Rhydderch* (the estimated date being 1325–50, copies of which are to be found in Peniarth MSS 4 and 5 and part of Peniarth MS 12). The poems themselves are dated earlier. How much so is disputable, but conventional thought places them around A.D. 900.

8. Editions of the poems have been sundry, but are not of much help until Ifor Williams's exhaustive work in the twentieth century. William Owen Pughes was the first to gather most of the corpus in his *Heroic Elegies and Other Pieces of Llywarç Hen, Prince of the Cumbrian Britons* (London: Owen and Williams, 1792); then comes *The Myvyrian Archaeology of Wales*, ed. Owen Jones (London: S. Rousseau, 1801–7, rpt. Denbigh: Thomas Gee, 1870); followed by *The Four Ancient Books of Wales*, ed. W. F. Skene (Edinburgh: Edmonston and Douglas, 1868). *Canu Llywarch Hen*, ed. Ifor Williams (Cardiff: University of Wales Press, 1935, 1978), is entirely in Welsh and thus inaccessible to the novice. More accommodating, if more controversial, is Patrick K. Ford's *The Poetry of Llywarch Hen* (Berkeley and Los Angeles: University of California Press, 1974), which includes facing-page translations. His notion that the figure of Llywarch is the construction of a Welsh dynasty interested in resurrecting an "ancestor figure" (he translates Llywarch "the Ancestor" rather than Llywarch "the Old") has won him the disapproval of some scholars. Jenny Rowland's *Early Welsh Saga Poetry: A Study and Edition of the Englynion* (Cambridge: Boydell and Brewer, 1990) takes him to task at almost every juncture, rescuing the received opinion of the Llywarch corpus, and speaking on behalf of "modern critics" against Ford's iconoclasm: "Ford . . . is alone among modern critics in denying any sort of narrative framework for the poems, seeking rather to force all the verse into other genres"; he also seems "deliberately distant from usual interpretations," she writes, and refers us to her dissertation for even fuller indictment of his theory and practice (p. 4).

They revolve around the vague persona of "Llywarch the Old," who possesses tenuous historic legitimacy.[9] It is still uncertain which cycle of poems can be grouped among the "Llywarch" corpus, or exactly where certain poems begin and end. Is *Claf Abercuawg* ("The Sick Man (Leper) of Abercuawg") part of the tradition of Llywarch? It is followed in the manuscript by a *planctus* (*Can yr Henwr*, "Song of the Old Man"), the first text to name Llywarch, wherein a speaker laments his age and his losses. Even this poem has uncertain closure, and in *The Red Book* it seems to segue at the top of column 1037[10] into a poem that Ifor Williams entitles *Gwen ap Llywarch a'i Dad* ("Gwen son of Llywarch and His Father") and prints first in his edition.[11] What of the gnomic and nature poems that precede it in *The Red Book*? What, too, of *Llym Awel* ("Keen the Wind"), verses in *The Black Book* that are traditionally incorporated with the Llywarch Hen poems? The sequence in which these poems were recorded then is not the sequence in which we like to record them now. Is this sequence irrelevant, this palpable textuality dismissible? Or can we credibly reconstruct these poems, using the variants in *The White Book*,[12] as we would like to think their original composers intended them in oral form? And when, finally, were any of these originally composed? Before or after Alan's *Anticlaudianus* with its vicious Old Age? Before or after the Old English elegies with their mournful cuckoos, so similar to the ones given voice in the sad Welsh poems?

Like the Welsh poems, the Old English elegies are linked in a ghostly and mysterious fashion. The Old English poems are also without titles, leaving us to guess at their contextual relationship. And also like the Welsh poems, the bulk of the Old English elegies appears in a manuscript that includes a medley of different genres (elegies, maxims, religious poems, riddles, narratives, and esoterica), allowing us to locate them a little more precisely in the late tenth century. A number of scholars have sought to find a link between the English

9. Reference to "Llywarch hen m. Elidyr Lydanwyn m. Meirchawn m. Gorust ledlum m. Keneu m. Coel" is to be found in the *Early Welsh Genealogical Tracts* (ed. Peter C. Bartrum [Cardiff: University of Wales Press, 1966]) where he is listed among the sixth-century Men of the North.

10. As represented in Evans's diplomatic edition, *Grammar of Middle Welsh*, 11.

11. *Canu Llywarch Hen*, 1–3. These titles that Williams has made standard do not appear in the manuscripts. While he creates a potential context for the poems by rearranging them, he misses opportunities to show up manuscript contexts; Ford offers an alternative grouping of the poems that is closer to the manuscript order and refrains from conferring titles, but a drawback to his edition is his modernization of the Welsh, which, while helpful to the student, is considered too interpretive by some.

12. See note 7 above.

and the Welsh. Ernst Sieper,[13] Ida L. Gordon,[14] Nora Chadwick,[15] J. J. Conybeare,[16] P. L. Henry,[17] Herbert Pilch,[18] and more recently Jenny Rowland[19] have suggested the possibility of cultural influence and/or similar generic origin to explain the likenesses in mood and imagery between the Welsh and English traditions. Eager to note similarities, however, they gloss over distinct differences in style which reveal important differences in intentionality and poetic strategy. These differences are significant, as is the critical impulse to diffuse difference by reading the Welsh through the English, as though they are all of a color: the hard, alien edges of *The Sick Man (Leper) of Abercuawg* are softened when compared to *The Wanderer*, or when shown to have influenced *The Seafarer*, or when proved to have derived from the same genre.

Every English-speaking scholar knows *The Wanderer*, at least in translation; it is English and marginally recognizable. *The Sick Man* hides behind the veil of its unfamiliar semiotics. It seems full of gaps, one of the most glaring being the absence of a didactic or spiritual message that would put the longing of the sufferer in recognizable context with the familiar tradition of medieval Christian *consolatio*. The received theory of the Llywarch poems, challenged by Patrick Ford in *The Poetry of Llywarch Hen*[20] and reinstated recently by Jenny Rowland in her exhaustive *Early Welsh Saga Poetry*,[21] is to find the missing pieces of the Welsh puzzle in other neighboring poetic traditions and to reconstruct a poetry of penance through comparison with more explicitly didactic poems that share with the Welsh certain details of imagery, structure, and mood.[22] Instead of asking why there are these gaps at

13. "Keltische Einflusse," in *Die altenglische Elegie* (Strassburg: Trübner, 1915).

14. *The Seafarer* (London: Methuen, 1960).

15. "The Celtic Background of Early Anglo-Saxon England," in *Celt and Saxon: Studies in the Early British Border*, ed. Kenneth Jackson et al., (London: Cambridge University Press, 1963), 323–52.

16. *Illustrations of Anglo-Saxon Poetry*, ed. William D. Conybeare (London: Harding and Lepard, 1826).

17. *The Early English and Celtic Lyric* (London: Allen and Unwin, 1970).

18. "The Elegiac Genre in Old English and Early Welsh Poetry," *Zeitschrift für celtische Philologie* 29 (1964), 209–24.

19. Rowland, EWSP, "*Claf Abercuawg* and Penitential Lyrics," 190–228.

20. Ford, PLlH, 34–37.

21. Rowland, EWSP, 190–228.

22. Rowland is more irate with Ford for his emphasis on the heroic and antiquarian aspects of the texts. "This approach among other things," she writes, "makes the poetry far less comprehensible" (p. 4). Ford's theory may be unorthodox; it is still no *more* theoretical than the standard notion of a missing prose saga background from which the verse has been excerpted, a notion that until Ford's book has remained unchallenged since Ifor Williams expounded it in his Rhys Lecture "The Poems of Llywarch Hen" (*Proceedings of the British Academy*, 1932).

all in the Welsh verses, the prevailing theory is to fill them in. I attribute this to a need to rescue the Welsh from accusations of difference leveled at it by readers steeped in an anglocentrism that valorizes the Welsh by comparison with the argumentatively "clearer" English poems.

Anglocentrism has little to do with writing in English; rather, it is inextricably tied up with the thorny problems of translation and connection in its attempt to ascertain texts that are incomplete, palimpsistic, and ambiguous within an academic tradition that demands wholeness. The distinction is important: If my point is misunderstood, this book will only seem to contradict itself, for it is filled to the brim with translations. I use the term *anglocentrism* in a manner reminiscent of "logocentrism," not so much in the original Derridean concept of "centered upon the spoken word," but in its more expanded meaning as "centered upon the clear word," the disambiguating word, the word that can substitute for the opaque words of a foreign language; in short, the modern English—and even the modern Welsh— word. Anglocentrism assumes that the norm in poetry lies in clarity, explicitness, organic development, seamlessness, diaegesis, low context, clear opening and closure, and other well-known features that signal familiarity and logical progression. The anomaly is opacity, implicitness, nonorganic development, omissions, disruption of chronology, modular or discrete elements, high context, unclear opening and closure, all of which signal foreignness and "defy analysis."

Readers of Julia Kristeva and Luce Irigaray and their theories of language will undoubtedly find in this dichotomy evidence yet again of the distinction between what is routinely called "masculine" and "feminine discourse"—the *yin* and *yang* of the heterogeneous and fluid language (which Kristeva refers to as the feminine "semiotic") congealed, explained, and made "other" by the coded and prescribed language (which she calls the masculine "symbolic").[23] In fact, critical theory has had much to say about the Self that is always casting its shadow on the Other, but medievalists have been alert to this issue early on: For the past twenty-five years they have repeatedly counseled us to abandon our neo-Aristotelian prejudices when we read medieval poems and to retrain ourselves in a different system of signifying. Textual emendation is

23. Julia Kristeva, *Desire in Language: A Semiotic Approach to Literature and Art*, ed. Leon S. Roudiez; trans. Thomas Gora, Alice Jardine, and Leon S. Roudiez (New York: Columbia University Press, 1980), 133–34. Luce Irigaray, *This Sex Which Is Not One*, trans. Catherine Porter and Carolyn Burke (Ithaca: Cornell University Press, 1985), 29: "Hers are contradictory words, somewhat mad from the standpoint of reason, inaudible for whoever listens to them with ready-made grids, with a fully elaborated code in hand."

therefore taken up more reluctantly than it used to be and studies in orality and literacy in the Middle Ages, along with contemporary criticism and its emphasis on margins and disruptions, have contributed to the now common understanding that reading itself is deeply informed by the ideologies of our time and the desires of our editors. The act of reading privileges vision as the dominant sense,[24] and my efforts to find a "new reading" of poems that were probably meant to be heard have just one more layer of contradiction to deal with. For no matter how we polish our pronunciation, the fact remains that it is through the eye and not the ear that we have any contact at all with these texts. Their marks remain on the vellum; their voices, along with the cadences peculiar to their era, faded a millennium ago.

Nevertheless, Anglo-Saxon and, even more, Celtic Studies have resisted deconstructive trends in criticism, unlike Old French, Middle English, and medieval Latin Studies—languages that have suffered neither the obliterating changes that Old English endured nor the obscurity and indifference that all of Welsh did and does endure. Late twentieth-century critical theory has grown up around texts and contexts familiar enough to their critics that their unacknowledged ideological assumptions called out for exposure. "How can we do the same to an Old English or an Early Welsh poem before we can be sure what it means?" is a protest one often hears. It lies behind Bloomfield and Dunn's recent pronouncement that "the poems [of Taliesin and Aneirin] may stir the critic's heart and excite his analytical faculties, but the critic's comments can scarcely be considered relevant until he has discovered why the poems were composed."[25] We must face up to the possibility that we may *never* discover why these poems were composed and that thoughtful critical and even aesthetic response to mysterious texts is and remains relevant. Of equal relevance is the discomfort felt in the presence of poetry that resists being subdued: Many scholars of medieval Welsh (who write in both English and Welsh) have been affected by the need to explain their poetry. Criticism of *Canu Llywarch Hen* has been largely concerned with finding the underlying narrative that will make it hold together, with rearranging and titling its poems, with surrounding it with glosses; in short, reconstructing it along lines more suited to a modern readership in efforts, paradoxically, to uncover a medieval intentionality.

These efforts are understandable and completely human. First, the pro-

24. See Walter Ong in "Orality, Literacy, and Medieval Textualization," *New Literary History* 16.1 (1984), 2.

25. Morton W. Bloomfield and Charles W. Dunn, "Primal Poetry and the Modern Audience," in *The Role of the Poet in Early Societies* (Cambridge: D. S. Brewer, 1989), 159.

nounced *alterity* of these poems has invited scholars to focus on translation, appropriation, and familiarization. The Linguistic study of Middle Welsh has more ground to cover than that of Latin or Greek; lexical and pedagogical aids lag behind even Old English;[26] and the gappy and imperfect quality of its transmission has bothered many a scholar eager to find in it a classical standard of completeness. The result has been the production of a number of editions that not only punctuate the texts according to modern norms, thereby making decisions on word and clause divisions, but balance out uneven or imperfect verses by analogy with the variants. A prominent case in point is A. O. H. Jarman's translation of *The Gododdin*, which omits interpolations and conflates numerous A texts with their variants among the B texts to produce a single corrected version.[27] While claiming on the one hand that it is a popularization, Jarman declares on the other hand that his edition tries to present the famous Welsh epic "as it appeared to those who preserved it in the thirteenth century and to their fairly immediate predecessors."[28] This goal is optimistic but anachronistic. In his comments about an "écriture de la variance," Bernard Cerquiglini proposes a fresh editorial philosophy, one that sees medieval writing not as a production of variant texts, the main or best one of which must be chosen for an edition, but variance itself.[29] Straddling both vigorous oral and burgeoning literary traditions, early insular writing and its variants tell us much about medieval attitudes toward the written transmission, interpolation, and attribution of texts that may have had a strong oral life. This interplay between scribe and tradition is masked by the modern urge to locate or affix the single text, and it does little justice to the qualities of ambiguity with which this study will concern itself.

Second, Early Welsh and Old English poetry (along with many other areas of medieval culture in general) have appealed to the romantic; they have too

---

26. The urge to clarify is a symptom of the cloistered and inaccessible nature of this poetry: Neither Early Welsh nor Old English is frequently taught in universities because of the linguistic demands both make. Middle Welsh scholars are at more of a disadvantage than Old English scholars in not having either a concordance (whereby one can check the use of a word against other uses without having to rely on the abbreviated information provided by lexicographers) or a complete, updated Middle Welsh dictionary. *Geriadur Prifysgol Cymru* ("The University of Wales Dictionary," R. J. Thomas et al. [Cardiff: University of Wales Press, 1950–]) is now up to the letter *p*. There is also *Geiriadur Mawr: The Complete Welsh-English English-Welsh Dictionary*, ed. H. Meurig Evans (Aberystwyth: Aberystwyth Press, 1960), which is of limited use for medievalists. *Geirfa Barddoniaeth Gynnar Cymraeg* ("Early Welsh Bardic Vocabulary"), ed. J. Lloyd-Jones (Caerdydd: Gwasg Prifysgol Cymraeg, 1931–63), is helpful to the medievalist who can read modern Welsh.

27. *Y. Gododdin: Britain's Oldest Heroic Poem* (Llandysul: Gomer Press, 1990).

28. Jarman, *Y Gododdin*, lxviii.

29. *Éloge de la variante: Histoire critique de la philologie* (Paris: Seuil, 1989), 111.

easily fallen prey to the popular cult following that has grown up around the antiquarian movement and the Celtic Revival of the eighteenth and nine-teenth centuries with their spurious translations.[30] Celtic Studies in particu-lar has a vigorous following among students and enthusiasts interested in fantasy and science fiction, mysticism, folklore, folk music, magic, gaming or "role-playing," and the Society for Creative Anachronism. In the eigh-teenth and nineteenth centuries it expressed itself in a flurry of forgeries, Macpherson's *Ossian* being one of the most famous. Scholars of Welsh and Irish are still fighting off embarrassing reactions to popular concepts of "the "Sentimental Celt" or the "Celtic Imagination";[31] which insist on celebrating an "otherness" that has grown tiresome, obstructive, and condescending to actual Celts. No other medieval literature has attracted quite such a fringe group except, perhaps, for Old English and its Lewis and Tolkien fans. Consequently, there has been an especially urgent need to keep the study rigorous, the subject matter pure, pinned down, and firmly on the track it ought to be on. In the history of both Old English and Welsh studies, emphasis has been no less enthusiastically centered on archaeology, on recov-ering the true origins, the *Ur*-text, and the authenticating wisdom of tradi-tional philology, which has subtly favored patristics and source and linguistic studies at the expense of equally interesting and fruitful examinations in the areas of folklore, anthropology, and critical theory.

I offer various new ways of examining these texts that I hope will incorpo-rate both the traditional and the innovative. Exposing Old English and Welsh together to more contemporary hermeneutical approaches, we might see how each tradition throws into sharp relief quirks of the other that are normally taken for granted; hearing both together we might detect harmonies or dissonances that go unheard in isolation. We also understand something about the values we attach to clarity, obscurity, imagery, and difference. My goal, ultimately, is to see difficulty as the norm instead of the anomaly, as the

30. Robert Graves's *The White Goddess: A Historical Grammar of Poetic Myth* (New York: Farrar, Straus and Giroux, 1948, 1966, 1974) perhaps did more than any other single book to harden Welsh scholars against interpretive or imaginative examination of the Taliesin corpus and its mythic under-pinnings. His approach was a poetic study of material that he did not himself translate and that he felt free to rearrange when it suited his purposes. In so doing, he incurred the silent contempt of Celtic scholars, and he writes ruefully in the foreword to his 1966 edition that since his book's first printing in 1946, "no expert in ancient Irish or Welsh has offered me the least help in refining my argument, or pointed out any of the errors which are bound to have crept into the text, or even acknowledged my letters" (p. 9).

31. See Patrick Sims-Williams, "The Visionary Celt: The Construction of an Ethnic Preconcep-tion," *Cambridge Medieval Celtic Studies* 11 (1986), 71–96.

locus of power and significance, and as central to the intentions of some of these texts instead of attributable to the failings of their transmission. To be sure, obstacles arise from our temporal and critical distance from this poetry, and an understanding of medieval conventions and theories is essential. To insist, though, that there can be no connection between new readers and old words because our information is incomplete or the texts uncooperative is unnecessarily nihilistic. I intend to explore the semiotic possibilities that lie under the surface of these ancient texts.

To this end, I divide my study into three general sections, each of which approaches the issue of "connection" from a different angle. Part I focuses on translation and the phonetic connection: how we struggle to make sounder what seem to be unsound connections and how metrical and stylistic requirements of the different poetic styles may affect the use of conjunctions or juxtapositions that give meaning. Part II focuses on the image and point of view as a kind of analogy to the conjunction: how person, tense, and other deictic markers put the speaker into visual and spatial relationship with the landscape that affects him and how "context" serves to make sense of images that seem unrelated to the modern reader. Part III examines the problem of "intentional difficulty" and the private connection; it looks at traditions that exclude the reader (or hearer) from privileged access to the poem. Many of the aretalogies or "revelation discourses" of *The Book of Taliesin* have a tenuous link with gnomic and nature poetry; their disjunctions seem deliberate, intended to offer a "vatic" as opposed to a sententious catalogue of the world and its elements. I suggest that the concept of poetic discourse as one that works to keep hidden rather than to make manifest, that suppresses the deictic references which show specificity, and that tests the perspicacity and knowledge of its hearers is an ancient one in Wales and has exerted far more influence on the style of other types of Welsh poems than scholars are perhaps willing to admit. I contrast this impulse in Welsh with the prevailing impulse in Old English—continually revealed in the elegies, the maxims and even the riddles—to explain, to clarify, to control, to preach, and to bring mysteries into relationship with common human experience.

We shall start in Chapter 1 with a recurring pattern in Old English and Welsh poetry—the "Natural Analogy"—which involves connection on a more minute level and which will narrow my focus while not severing it, I hope, from more theoretical issues of reading and context.

1

The Natural Analogy:
Difficulties, Gaps, and Irritations

The lack of a sign can itself be a sign.
> —Maurice Merleau-Ponty

Wea bið wundrum clibbor   wolcnu scriðaþ
("Misery is marvelously tenacious. The clouds glide.")
> —*Maxims II*

As a focus for this analysis I have chosen a pattern that involves the connection between statements of mood and the natural image, in the use of which Old English and Welsh differ significantly. This book takes as its paradigm and starting point the universal link between the physical world and a state of mind, present in many different literary traditions and in many permutations, involving a loner—an exile, a pilgrim, or a poet/seer—pitted against the wide open spaces of the world. I call it the "natural analogy" because of the worldwide understanding of nature or any external as an analogue of the poetic mood. Its special feature, one that makes it appropriate to this study of connection, lies in its mediation between private and public, internal and external, human and nonhuman. The narrative impulse is to "translate" from one area to another by making the outer relevant to the inner and vice versa (confession does the same, by externalizing verbally what is internal and inchoate). The hermetic and lyric impulse is to complicate translation, to blur the distinction between inner and outer. Thus the natural analogy can range from a complex delineation of relationships that set the parameters for our understanding to a bald juxtaposition of statements where connection is not explicated on the level of verbal code. Consider these two examples from the English and the Welsh, respectively:

All pleasure has perished. Therefore he knows, he who must long forego the counsel of his dear lord, his beloved lord, that when sorrow and sleep together often oppress the wretched lone-goer, it seems to him in his mind that he embraces and kisses his liege lord and on his knee lays his hands and head as sometimes earlier in days of yore he enjoyed the gift throne.

Then the friendless man awakens again, sees before him the fallow waves, the bathing seafowl, the spreading of feathers, the falling hoarfrost, and snow mingled with hail.

Then will the wounds of the heart be from that the more grievous, sorrowing after the beloved one.

(*The Wanderer*)

Clamorous the birds, wet the beach,
bright the sky, broad the wave,
withered the heart with longing.
(*The Sick Man of Abercuawg*)

The translation into modern English prose, especially of the Old English poem, gives my argument an unfair advantage, but even so the difference between the two styles is not so superficial as it might at first seem. By virtue of the archetypal and highly suggestive background provided by nature in these poems of lament, all sorts of questions are raised about function, motive, and intentionality, about contextual information and what is assumed or "spelled out." The Old English frames our expectations in ways that the Welsh does not; its explicitness is therefore less inclined to be questioned. Old English has a narrative and didactic form of poetry not belonging to the Welsh, wherein events and ideas are put in a temporal and logical progression that further masks rifts in explicitness and renders us all the more surprised when we come upon them. Even in the notoriously ambiguous *Wife's Lament* a kind of diaegesis unfolds. Images seem to be given orientation with respect to the narrator more often than they are in the Welsh: deixis abounds in the Old English and is notably lacking in the Welsh. The language of orientation in general, such as conjunctions and adverbs (which connect one idea to the next, link events in space and time, and unite the speaker to his surroundings) proliferates in the English and not in the Welsh.

We could turn this argument around and see the "lack" from the Welsh perspective: What is lacking in the English is a "discrete" mode of poetry that imposes an obvious pattern of disruption, repetition, and condensation on Welsh expression. What is lacking in the Old English is an intricacy of poetic requirement and a play of sounds that is absolutely required in Welsh poems. Much of the emotional impact of *The Sick Man* and *Song of the Old Man* (for modern readers, at any rate) derives from the ambiguity and laconism created by their highly stylized form, which assist the point that the Welsh poet might be making about bereavement: just as the bereft one is cut off from everything that gives the world meaning and continuity, so is the personal utterance cut off grammatically from the observation about nature. The Old English *Seafarer*, however, is ultimately concerned with mending or at least finding solutions to human estrangement; thus we have the proliferation of conjunctions, especially the repeated *forþon* that has caused so much controversy. In both, the message finds expression in the diction. It is easy to chart the similar uses of nature in these poems; it is harder to chart the different ways in which each tradition employs it.

Examples and Analogs

In Early Welsh and Old English, the natural analogy appears most prominently in the elegy, or "poem of lament," as opposed to the epic. Compare the following passages taken, respectively, from *Claf Abercuawg* of *The Red Book of Hergest* and *The Wife's Lament* from *The Exeter Book*:

Neus e[n]deweis i goc ar eidorwc brenn.
neur laesswys vyg kylchwy.
etlit a gereis neut mwy.
                       (RB: 1034.39–40)

[I listened to a cuckoo on an ivy-covered branch.
Loose is my shield-strap;
Grief for what I loved is greater.]

heht mec mon wunian   on wuda bearwe
under actreo   in þam eardscræfe·
eald is þes eordsele   eol ic eom oflongad
sindon dena dimme   duna uphea
bitre burgtunas   brerum beweaxne
wic wynna leas

(EB2: 27–32, 152–54)

[One bade me dwell in a forest grove
Under an oaktree in this earth cave.
Old is this earth hall. I am all oppressed with longing.
Dim are valleys, high the hills,
Harsh the habitations overgrown with briars,
dwellings empty of joys.]

In Middle English the pattern tends to appear in the love lyric or the carol. The following Middle English poem bears such a strong resemblance to some early Welsh verses that I include it:

Foweles in the frith
The fisses in the flod
And i mon waxe wod.
Mulch sorwe i walk with
For best of bone and blood.

Gordyar adar gwlyb neint.
llewychyt lloer oer deweint.
crei vym bryt rac gofit heint.

(RB: 1035.1–2)

[Birds loud; streams wet.
Moon shines; midnight cold;
Raw my heart from the torment of illness.]

Finally, the pattern appears in the seemingly irrelevant nature references of many English ballads, and we have a similar instance of seeming irrelevancy in some of the Middle Welsh dialogue poems:

She laid her back against a thorn,
  Fine flowers in the valley,
And there she has her pretty babe born,
  And the green leaves they grow rarely.

Gwalchmei: Abrwysg vydd tonn aneddfawl
             pan fo mor yn y kanawl;
             pwy wyt filwr anianawl?
Tristan: Abrwysg fydd tonn a tharan
             kyd boed brwysg a gwahan;
             ynydd trin mi yw Trystan.
                          (Jackson, ECNP: 184)
[Gwalchmei: Huge is the ungovernable wave when the sea is
             in the midst;
             Who are you, spirited warrior?
Tristan: Huge is the wave and the thunder
             though it be vigorous and dissimilar;
             in the days of combat I am Tristan.
                   (Jackson's translation, ECNP: 184)

In each of the cases cited above, the pattern is employed differently. In the first two the speaker makes clear his involvement in the scene, which adds to his sorrow. In the remaining four the nature reference is more stereotypical and is removed from the direct experience of the speaker; the last two seem to employ nature reference purely for phonic or metrical reasons. While I am not so concerned in this study with charting the origins of the Natureingang as I am with its rhetorical and psychological effects, some awareness of the textual tradition and its requirements is obviously essential to interpretation.[1]

The natural analogy is not unique to Britain. World poetry throughout the ages has enhanced the expression of mental or emotional turmoil by juxtaposing it with references to nature. We know this best, perhaps, in the French reverdie, but it is present in Old Irish poetry as well:

1. For theories about origins, see J. E. Caerwyn Williams, "The Nature Prologue in Welsh Court Poetry," Studia Celtica 24/25 (1989–90), 70–90. Williams deals primarily with the gogynfeirdd, court poets composing in the twelfth and thirteenth centuries.

Is aicher in gáeth in-nocht,
fo-fúasna fairrge findfolt;
ní águr réimm mora mind
dond láechraid lainn ó Lothlind.

[The wind tonight is bitter;
it tousles the sea's white hair;
I have no fear that gentle seas
will bring fierce warriors from Norway.][2]

And translated from third-century Chinese:

A single swan shrieks past the fields,
hovering birds cry in the northwoods,
pacing round, what is it that awaits me?
Anxious thoughts alone that hurt the heart.[3]

Many Japanese *haiku* poems bear, in translation, striking similarities to the
early Welsh *englyn* ("stanza"):

A falling leaf:
the moment it touches the ground
time slows down.[4]

This leaf, the wind snatches her away;
alas for her fate!
Old she, born this year.
(RB: 1036.29–30)

In his comparative study of early English and Celtic poetry, P. L. Henry
has called this pattern the "man-nature synthesis,"[5] and others might recog-
nize in it a specialized form of the pathetic fallacy. Not to be confused with

2. Text and translation by Ruth P. Lehmann, *Early Irish Verse* (Austin: University of Texas Press, 1982), 10.
3. Hsu Kan, second century A.D., translated by Ronald C. Miao in *Sunflower Splendor: Three Thousand Years of Chinese Poetry*, ed. Wu-Chi Liu and Irving Yucheng Lo (Garden City: Anchor Press, Doubleday, 1975), 40.
4. Kato Shūson, in *Modern Japanese Haiku: An Anthology*, ed. Makoto Ueda (Toronto: University of Toronto Press, 1976), 226.
5. EECL, 70.

the Wordsworthian or Romantic concept of nature, it is, rather, a basic and universal element of the lyric impulse. It is a "mood" device, so widespread among our contemporary lyrics about lonely people and so taken for granted that it nearly escapes notice, but it fills today's records.[6] One could talk endlessly about the part that references to the external world play in creating a mood or offsetting an emotion in popular literature. Atmosphere in films is heightened by focusing on some apparently unrelated image, a device we encounter in Hitchcock, Bergman, Polanski, Lynch, Altman, and other mood producers: The man makes a private disclosure to the woman, a personal revelation of deep significance; the camera cuts abruptly to a shot of the restless fir trees sighing in the wind. Had he been a filmmaker, Shakespeare might have used such a technique:

> Come, seeling Night,
> Skarfe up the tender Eye of pitiful Day
> And with thy bloddie and invisible Hand
> Cancel and teare to pieces that great Bond
> That keepes me pale.
> *Light thickens, and the Crow*
> *Makes Wing to th' Rookie Wood.*
> Good things of Day begin to droop and drowse,
> While Night's black agents to their Preys do rowse.
> (*Macbeth* III.ii.50–58)

Commenting on this "device of particular irrelevance," William Empson remarks that "a dramatic situation is always heightened by breaking off the dialogue to look out the window, especially if some kind of Pathetic Fallacy is to be observed outside."[7] Its visual properties are self-evident. Sergei Eisen-

6.   Broken windows empty hallways.
      Pale dead moon in a sky streaked with gray.
      Human kindness, overflowing,
      And I think it's going to rain today.
      ("And I Think It's Going To Rain Today," Randy
      Newman, Warner Brothers, R6459)
7. *Seven Types of Ambiguity* (New York: New Directions, 1947), 19. The italics are Empson's. It is uncertain whether Shakespeare is having Macbeth refer to an offstage crow—one that we are to pretend has flown by—or whether he is using a rhetorical figure. If the latter, the device has relevance. If the former, its relevance is complicated by the assumed presence of a world outside the mind of the speaker where unrelated events go on and to which one can refer. These things of the natural world become relevant in an act of reference: for one moment, forlorn crow and forlorn man become fused in a mysterious way.

stein compares the Japanese lyric to montage effects in film.[8] Unlike the
"pan," which moves slowly across a scene to give a sense of vista and dimen-
sion, the montage is the sharp and sometimes unexpected juxtaposition of
images that serves to isolate them from an orienting environment or context,
illustrating "an absence of the sensation of perspective." In comparing mon-
tage to the "fusion of images" in Japanese poetry, Eisenstein enters into
complicated territory that would take us down paths we cannot pursue in our
study of medieval Western poetry; namely, the element of the visual in both
the film and the haiku. In the one, the signifying elements involve visual and
aural as well as verbal modes, along with movement and apparently in-
discrete sections; and in the other, the use of Chinese ideographs, literally
"pictures," makes the haiku a good deal more visually complex than can be
expressed in a translation. Analogies of this nature are tricky. What they do
highlight is the degree to which we have dismissed uses of juxtaposition in
medieval British poetry while we search to fill gaps. Scholars have recently
addressed this prejudice: Carol Braun Pasternack points to the deliberately
"disjunct" sections of The Dream of The Rood which may emphasize the
fallen nature of man and his separation from the divine;[9] Fred Robinson
examines the poetic device of "apposition" (or "variation") in Beowulf which
gives it, he offers, its spiritual double perspective.[10] Gillian Overing's notion
of metonymy resembles these arguments in her observation that images and
ideas "are placed side by side in a text but remain essentially discrete, con-
nected only by association and proximity."[11] She further remarks that "film is
especially useful in illuminating the metonymic [as opposed to the meta-
phoric] process" wherein "associations are made by contiguity rather than
comparison."[12] Bearing these notions in mind, I shall focus on the formal
expression of the "natural analogy" in poetry, in its range from a simple
juxtaposition to a complex grammatical delineation of the effect of the envi-
ronment on one's mood. In its most basic form it keeps the analogy "open,"
"appositive," "metonymic," and preserves the complexity and ambiguity of
the connection through the leap, unassisted by explanatory grammar, be-
tween image and expression. It lends itself particularly well to the aural and
oral instead of the visual and literate. It is a perceptible lull.

8. Film Form, trans. Jay Leyda (Cleveland and New York: World Publishing Company, 1967),
32, 26.
9. "Stylistic Disjunctions in The Dream of the Rood," Anglo-Saxon England 13 (1984), 167–86.
10. Beowulf and the Appositive Style (Knoxville: University of Tennessee Press, 1985).
11. Language, Sign, and Gender in Beowulf (Carbondale: Southern Illinois University Press,
1990), 24.
12. Ibid., Language, Sign, and Gender, 24.

Gap or Juxtaposition?

Christine Brooke-Rose classifies metaphors according to their syntax of con-
nection, which she terms "pointing formulae."[13] Parallelism, she writes, is
"the loosest and most implicit" syntactical expression of metaphor, and in its
extreme form "it becomes mere juxtaposition, which is effective, but it takes
us further away from metaphor than any other method."[14] Michael Riffaterre
states that "one factor remains constant" in poetic language: It "expresses
concepts and things by indirection."[15] Take, for instance, the English version
of a poem by Nakamura Kusatao:

> The metaphors are
> Gone and so is my faith.
> Sun over a moor.[16]

While lamenting the loss of metaphoric power, this poem challenges us to
find a metaphor for depression and despair in its final line. Despite the
evocativeness of the image and its powerful emotional overtones, we can only
conclude that the message of a poem such as this amounts to more than the
sum of its parts. Much the same could be said of medieval Welsh poetry:

> I am not nimble, I keep no host.
> Nor can I get about.
> As long as it likes, let the cuckoo sing.

In both, the natural images have much less *explicit* or systematic connection
with the emotional utterance than Brooke-Rose's concept of metaphor al-
lows. They help to induce a mood, and their relationship to human experi-
ence has an intriguing ambiguity.

Within the last hundred years, British and American poets have become
self-conscious about this looseness of connection, and after centuries of a
poetic tradition where necessary syntactic links were made, the "modernists"
adopted the effect that we find in English translations of haiku and some
Welsh *englynion*. In the following extract from William Carlos Williams we
find the natural analogy in its tersest form:

13. "Pointing Formulae," in A *Grammar of Metaphor* (London: Secker and Warburg, 1958),
68–104.
14. Ibid., 26.
15. *Semiotics of Poetry* (Bloomington: Indiana University Press, 1978), 1.
16. In *Modern Japanese Haiku*, ed. Ueda, 198.

Thirty-five years I lived with my husband.
The plum tree is white, today, with masses of flowers.
("The Widow's Lament in Springtime")

Theories of poetry, language, and the visual arts have likewise seen a soaring interest in the philosophy of absence: "No level of language or aspect of literature is immune to the pervasive power of the absent," writes J. Lee Magness in his examination of the Gospel of Mark.[17] "Verbalization," writes Tzvetan Todorov, ". . . does not change the nature of the material objects but establishes their absence rather than their presence."[18] The "gap" or the "silence" of the text have become central concepts in philosophy and critical theory: Wolfgang Iser gives the term "blanks" to these "suspensions of connectability"[19] that are peculiar to literature where there is no *dyadic* interaction as in other forms of social communication, no "face to face situation" that will allow the text to accommodate each reader with whom it comes in contact.[20] As a consequence, such blanks "initiate an interaction whereby the hollow form of the text is filled out by the mental images of the reader."[21]

Where these mental images are incompatible with the information given in the texts, a certain failure ensues, and may account for the frequently baffled reception of both Old English and Welsh poetry in general. This confusion has stemmed, I believe, from an unacknowledged assumption that has permeated medieval criticism until recently—that poetry is to be measured and understood by a standard of explicitness; that underlying a stark juxtaposition is a grammar of relationship which has been left out for artistic effect but can be resupplied if needed:

Although the wave is wide, my heart, for which the
wave is metaphor, is withered . . .

Interpretability becomes that much more challenging in certain Welsh texts where the connection between image and mood is even less obvious, where it appears that aphoristic formulae have intruded:

17. *Sense and Absence: Structure and Suspension in the Ending of Mark's Gospel* (Atlanta: Scholars Press, 1986), 16.
18. *The Poetics of Prose* (Ithaca: Cornell University Press, 1971), 101–2.
19. *The Act of Reading: A Theory of Aesthetic Response* (Baltimore: Johns Hopkins University Press, 1978), 195.
20. Ibid., 167.
21. Ibid., 225.

Na wisc wedy kwyn. na vit vrwyn dy vryt.
llem awel achwerw gwenwyn.
amgyhud vy mam mab yt wyf.

(RB: 1037.1–2)

[Do not arm after a feast, let not your mind be sad.
Sharp the wind, poison bitter.
My mother proclaims that I am your son.]

Explicitness is not a substantive quality of any given poem or utterance, but is a problem of the hearer, and for this reason it is hard to discuss. Like pi, it is never to be counted out in full. To do so would be to threaten not only poetry but all language. It undoubtedly varies among different languages and cultures; what comprises a logical or emphatic link between ideas in Malay might prove unintelligible to a German or an American. When we read early Welsh poems in English, and even when we read them in the Welsh, we often respond to our sense of something having been omitted, some step in reasoning, some linking idea. This accounts, it seems, for the number of times English-speaking scholars (myself included) have spoken of the "mannered," "pointed," "highly fused," "abrupt," "cryptic," "oblique," "impressionistic," and "inexplicit" qualities of Welsh poetry, and in so doing have indirectly revealed our response to something foreign:

> Some early Irish lyrics . . . are commonly more explicit and descriptive where the Welsh are highly fused and cryptic.[22]

> . . . certain Norse poems are mannered and pointed like the Welsh *englyn*.[23]

> And in the Welsh elegies, nature description, though stylistically abrupt, plays an important part in the elegiac theme.[24]

> But even granting this oblique form of expression, many of the lines and stanzas are susceptible to various interpretations.[25]

22. Henry, EECL, 70.
23. Ibid., 121.
24. Ibid.
25. Ida L. Gordon, *The Seafarer* (London: Methuen, 1960), 17.

It was supposed . . . that the sketchy, "impressionistic" phrasing was taken from the Irish; but on the contrary, the Irish poems do full syntactic justice to every thought . . .[26]

[Gwalchmai's poem] defies analysis on account of its seemingly disjointed character.[27]

Rarely has an Old English scholar found much occasion to call attention to the "connectedness" of Old English poetry; on the contrary, complaints about its departure from this expected standard are legion, all the more so because of its illusion of continuity. I suggest that we abandon the *topos* of the gap, or "absence," in our explanations of the natural analogy and see it instead as a juxtaposition or parataxis which sets up a triangulation: Two contiguous items are given dimension by a third thing that might be grammatical or situational context, or the projections of the reader, or the effect of a juxtaposition.[28] This "third thing" is the most speculative aspect of my study but absolutely central to it, and I will pursue it from its various angles. The concept of betweenness naturally involves three elements, not two; looking at Old English and Welsh poetry likewise allows us to see both traditions in three dimensions, like stereoscopy, not two. In the next chapter we will see how the history of Anglo-Saxon and Early Welsh scholarship records this essential struggle of translation.

26. Patrick K. Ford, PLlH, 177.
27. J. E. Caerwyn Williams, *The Poets of the Welsh Princes* (Cardiff: University of Wales Press, 1978), 37.
28. Semioticians are indebted to Charles S. Peirce's complex discussion of "Thirdness" in the construction of signification (*Collected Papers*, ed. C. Hartshorne and P. Weiss [Cambridge: Harvard University Press, 1931–58], 1: 23, 353), what Overing refers to as "an analogue for the metaphorizing reader who collocates and resolves meaning." Overing's discussion of Peirce's *semeiosis* is quite helpful to any medievalist interested in contemporary sign theory ("Swords and Signs: Dynamic Semeiosis," *Language, Sign, and Gender in Beowulf*, 33–67), and she has arrived at an application of triangulation to the reading of medieval insular poetry that I have been struggling with for years. See also Kaja Silverman on Peirce: *The Subject of Semiotics* (New York: Oxford University Press, 1983), 14–25.

PART I

THE PHONETIC CONNECTION

Getting Around the Cipher:
Translating the Uncooperative Text

> Do not forget that a poem, even though it is composed in the language of information, is not used in the language-game of *giving* information.
>
> —Ludwig Wittgenstein, *Zettel*

Translation of these poems into modern English prose, while it remains really the only solution left to us as explicators, sometimes occludes the text we are trying to understand. Of great importance is a frank recognition that our desires for the text will shape our interpretations of the text, a truth well known to scholars; that even the employment of the so-called disinterested mechanisms of scholarship (philology, linguistics, source studies) can be bent to the powerful forces of our theories. They *are* theories. And between our theories and the original artifact, a third thing is fashioned. This book offers no exception.

The Problems in Welsh Poetry

In 1911, W. P. Ker made the following comment about the Welsh in his book *The Dark Ages*, voicing what seems to have been a widespread feeling of bewilderment and semi-irritation on the part of English scholars toward Celtic verse:

> One can make out pretty surely that the Welsh refused to write intelligible poetry. . . . The difficulty is something like that of the Icelandic court poetry. But the Icelander always has a clear idea: he knows the fact before he starts coating it with professional epithets. In the Old Welsh poetry, there is apparently vagueness of thought as well as ingenuity of words to be got over.[1]

Ker is probably grumbling about poems like *Angar Kyfyndawt* in *The Book of Taliesin* (see Texts no. 8 in Appendix) or some of the more convoluted poetry of the *gogynfeirdd* ("the not-so-early bards"). These poems tax the interpretive abilities of our most learned Celticists, and will be dealt with later. But Ker reveals assumptions about "clarity" in poetry that are symptomatic not merely of his era, but of English hermeneutics for a long time: Not only is the word a transparent vehicle of meaning through which the clear idea must shine, but facts stand distinct from the words that define them; poetic words are "facts" dressed up. Any artist who deviates from this prescription is being obstinate, is *refusing* "to write intelligible poetry."

Complaints like Ker's have been directed to the *Canu Llywarch Hen*. The history of Welsh criticism shows an expectation that imagery in poetry serves a clear function, either as a mimetic device which depicts the natural world or as an expressive device which suitably illustrates the emotion of the speaker. While these assumptions have largely been discredited by later scholarship, it has been hard to shake off the damning judgment leveled by the academic outsider. To W. P. Ker and a body of anglocentric scholars, "there is vagueness of thought and ingenuity of words to be got over" in Early Welsh poetry. Because it does not adhere to criteria established by English tradition (criteria that much contemporary poetry would fail to meet, incidentally), Early Welsh poetry is viewed as a curiosity, and it has not only been marginalized; it has been apologized for in all sorts of subtle and damaging ways. This tendency should be exposed and resisted.

A non-Welsh reader might be perplexed, for instance, by the imagery in *Claf Abercuawg* (Texts no. 2). The poem begins with descriptions of summertime that seem vivid and lifelike and that have a discernible relationship to the speaker. As the poem progresses, this verisimilitude breaks down, and we

---

1. *The Dark Ages* (New York: Charles Scribner's Sons, 1911), 335.

encounter images apparently chosen at random from a "floating" perspective: cattle in a shed, slippery paths, the merriment of men over beer, the bitter tips of the ash. These seemingly dislocated images are juxtaposed to independent statements of sententious wisdom: "The boundary of knowledge is patience." This mixture seems to be the prevailing motif in the poems preceding *Claf Abercuawg* in the *The Red Book* (*Mountain Snow*, RB: 1028–29; *Winter's Day*, RB: 1031.30–1032.4; *Lovely the Tops of the Ash*, RB: 1033.1–1034.23). Here is an admirable example of the "natural analogy" from the first of these:

> Eiry mynyd gwynn keunant.
> rac ruthur gwynt gwyd gwyryant.
> llawer deu a ymgarant.
> a phyth ny chyfuar uydant.
> (RB: 1028.3–4)

> [Mountain snow, white the ravine.
> Before the onslaught of wind trees bend.
> Many a couple love each other
> who never get to be together.]

The *Biddiau* ("Let the Cock's Comb Be Red") and the *Gnodiau* ("Typical Is Wind from the South") of *The Red Book* are catalogues of proverbial wisdom strung together by the anaphoric use of "typifying" modifiers: "Let the debt-collector be accusing; let the contestant be savage." Or: "Typical a handsome man in Gwynedd; typical depression after drinking." The verses from *The Black Book* ("Keen the Wind"), traditionally included in the Llywarch Hen corpus, offer a similar mixture of description and proverb, but to add to its deictic confusion it features temporal and personal references: "This is not like a summer day," "Care has long been in my heart."

These verses have been identified as *gnomes* or *quasi-gnomes* and will be discussed at length in Chapter 4. Taken for what they offer us in the way of everyday life in medieval Wales, their charm is undeniable: They are poignant, vivid, cynical, panoramic, and earthy; they offer a wide variety of juxtapositions that are often humorous in their incongruity; and their unique quality lies in the way they elevate personal and general observations to the same tonal level. By the same token these features often strike us as disturbingly flat and monotonous in their endless amplification. Their makers seemed to revel in the ludicrous combination. Not only are the lovely tips of the ash juxtaposed with the hurts of the heart; in the following stanza we have a blithe disregard for temporal continuity:

kalan gaeaf kein gyfreu adar.
byrr dydd ban cogeu.
trugar daffar duw goreu.
(RB 1031:41–42)

[Calends of winter, fair the songs of birds.
Short the day, loud the cuckoos.
The merciful provision of God is best.]

There is a discrepancy here if the poet meant to portray the characteristics of winter (as the cuckoo is a summer bird), but this is one of the main vexations to early scholars struggling with these texts.

In his 1912 lecture to the Honourable Society of the Cymmrodorion,[2] Glyn Davies searches for verisimilitude in *Llym Awel* of *The Black Book* (see *Texts* no. 6). In his attempts to take it as a description of a real place at a particular time, he is at pains to straighten out what he considers its inconsistencies: "mention of a short twilight" in stanza 4 "suggests December," he notes,[3] but the detail about the frostbitten buds in stanza 6 suggests "a snowstorm in spring." He is puzzled by the litotes in stanza 9: "It is not the nature of a summer day today." "The line . . . would be pointless if summer-like days had not begun again," he writes.[4] Davies is trying to impose a logic on these stanzas they do not possess, and he concludes that they represent "a debris of poetry" recited "by one who could remember fragments only."[5] He was not alone in his assumptions; the theory that the verses of Llywarch Hen belonged to a lost saga was first expounded by Ifor Williams, who proposed that the remaining poems are the "verse elements" in "a cycle of stories now missing."[6] Presumably the narrative elements of the story were preserved in prose, as was the custom in Old Irish narrative, while the poetry took care of artistic embellishment and expressions of sentiment. Just why the poetry and not the prose should be left to us is a problem not easily resolved, though

2. "The Welsh Bard and the Poetry of External Nature: From Llywarch Hen to Dafydd ap Gwilym," *Transactions of the Honourable Society of the Cymmrodorian*, Session 1912–13 (London: Chancery Lane, 1914), 84–88.
3. Ibid., 85.
4. Ibid., 86.
5. Ibid., 84.
6. *Lectures on Early Welsh Poetry* (Dublin: Institute for Advanced Studies, 1970), 35.

mitigated by the more convincing theory of an oral story context.[7] It was undoubtedly seen as an effective way to unify these disparate Welsh poems as well as to dispel criticism of their lack of "internal unity" and "organic progression."[8] This feature of Welsh poetry is made more obvious in the following stanzas from *Canu Llywarch Hen* than it perhaps has appeared in the previous selections:

Redegawc tonn ar hyt traeth.
ech adaf torrit aruaeth.
kat a[g]do gnawt ffo ar ffraeth.

(RB: 1037.11–12)

[A wave runs along the shore.
By chance does resolution break.
(Under) battle cover, typical is flight with braggarts.]

Yssit ym a lauarwyf.
bri[w]aw pelydyr parth y bwyf.
ny lauaraf na ffowyf.

(1037.13–14)

[I have what I speak of:
Spears will shatter where I shall be.
I shan't cry out nor shall I flee.]

Medal migned kalet riw.
rac carn cann tal glann a vriw.
edewit ny wnelher ny diw.

(1037.15–16)

[Soft the swamps, hard the hill.
The stream bank breaks with the horse's hoof.
A promise not performed is no promise.]

---

7. See Jenny Rowland, EWSP, 11.

8. Idris Bell, *The Development of Welsh Poetry* (Oxford: Clarendon Press, 1936), 5: "[Early Welsh poetry's] attention to form has too often been directed to the detail rather than to the whole. . . . The poets of Wales . . . frequently neglected the task of so organizing and correlating the various parts of a composition as to give it an internal unity of design. Very many longer poems in Welsh literature, and not a few even of the shorter ones, might aptly be described as 'variations on a theme' . . . but in which we feel the want of any organic progression or feeling."

Gwasgarawt neint am glaud caer.
a minneu armaaf.
ysgwyt br[w]yt briw kynn techaf.

(1037.17–18)

[Streams spread about the banks of the fortress.
And I'll prepare on my part
for a shattered shield before I flee.]

Here we have a dialogue between Llywarch and his son Gwen. Llywarch expresses skepticism about Gwen's valor, and Gwen defends his promise to stand firm on the battlefield. The old man's poetic comments are punctuated by gnomic utterances—"by chance does resolution break," "a promise not performed is no promise"—and are understandable in a context where an older man is giving advice to a younger one. But the comments about nature are harder to understand in connection with Gwen's utterances, for they are not so clearly gnomic. Streams do tend to spread around the castle moat, but it is not clear how this information connects with Gwen's resolution to have a shattered shield. The same problem occurs in most of these verses where the imagery seems to have only marginal association with its attendant expression of feeling. The unclear relationship of natural image to emotional statement continues to puzzle scholars, and here are two different punctuations of one verse from "Marwnad Gwen" ("Elegy on Gwen"):

Tonn tyruit toit eruit.
Pan ant ky[n]vr[e]in ygovit.
gwen gwae ryhen oth etlit.

(RB: 1037.39–40)

["The wave is tumultuous, it covers the strand;
when warriors go out to battle,
Gwen, woe to the old man who grieves for you."][9]

["A wave thunders, breaks over the coast,
when warriors engage in battle;
Gwen, alas! the ancient one grieves for you."][10]

9. Kenneth Jackson, *Studies in Early Celtic Nature Poetry* (Cambridge: Cambridge University Press, 1935), 185.
10. Patrick K. Ford, PLlH, 89.

The sense of these translations is entirely different, and each depends on the translator's sense of the autonomy or subordination of the natural element. In the first, Kenneth Jackson has put the two human referents together and allowed the natural referent to stand alone, in which case it bears some resemblance to the nature tags in the "Dialogue Between Tristan and Gwalchmai," a poem that Jackson groups under "Problems of Welsh Nature Poetry" (Huge is the ungovernable wave / when the sea is in the midst; / who are you, spirited warrior?)[11] In the second, Patrick Ford ascribes martial associations with the breaking of waves, taking his cue from countless other juxtapositions wherein waves and war are associated, as they are in the "Dialogue." But when we read these verses, cut off from the voices that would have removed our doubt, it is hard to shake off the feeling that the nature references are only embellishment, and Ifor Williams advises us to pass over the "irrelevant padding" and go on to the "significant lines."[12] Williams ascribes the "padding" in the poetic dialogues to a problem of style. He writes that Welsh poets "found considerable difficulty in fitting question and answer, the thrust and parry of lively talk, into a metric frame," and he compares them to an illuminated manuscript (*italics mine*):

> Brevity is the soul of wit. Even a three-line stanza is too long for a neat reply; one line is ample in most cases. So they *framed* their dialogues in nature poetry and proverbs, which provided them with just the *material* required to *fill up* what was left of the line or englyn or poem. There was no chance of their listeners mistaking the *frame for the picture*, for this padding had no relevance whatsoever to the dialogue. *It was like the scrollwork decorating the initial letters in manuscripts.* The more irrelevant it was, the less likely it was to mislead.[13]

The analogy between the visual and verbal arts is long-standing in medieval scholarship and has some compelling arguments. Accretion, modularity, and "filling up" are entrenched aspects of medieval aesthetics, but I disagree with Williams's assumption that neatness of reply was sought after. The look of the decorative initial with its flattened floral and animal shapes is analogous to the sounds of *cynghannedd* verse, which flatten and stretch out its statements,

11. Jackson, ECNP, 183–84.
12. *Lectures*, 39.
13. Ibid., 21.

putting them in the same pitch with the ornaments. To excise the one is to do violence to the whole.

Jackson believes these "nature tags," as he calls them, to have originated in the elegies, where they had more application to the substantive matter in the englyn; that is, they served to offset and create a mood of sorrow.[14] But because of the discrete structure of each englyn, they became detachable, easily manipulated and repeated. In the following stanzas, from the *Claf Abercuawg* ("The Sick Man [Leper] of Abercuawg"—see Texts no. 2), Llywarch laments his old age, contrasting the vigor of spring with his feebleness, but even here the relationship between image and message seems loose, arbitrary, and devoid of explanation:

> 11.   Gordyar adar gwlyb neint.
>   llewychyt lloer oer deweint.
>   crei vym bryt rac gofit heint.
>   (RB: 1035.1–2)

[Clamorous are birds, wet the streams,
moon shines, cold is midnight
raw is my mind from the torment of illness.]

> 13.   Gordyar adar gwlyb gro.
>   deil cwydit divryt divro.
>   ny wadaf wyf claf heno.
>   (1035.5–6)

[Clamorous the birds, wet the gravel,
a leaf falls, despondent is the exile,
I do not deny that I am ill (a leper) tonight.]

> 14.   Gordyar adar gwlyb traeth.
>   eglur nwyvre ehalaeth
>   tonn. gwiw callon rac hiraeth.
>   (1035.7–8)

[Clamorous the birds, wet the beach,
bright the sky, broad the wave,
withered the heart with longing.]

---

14. Jackson, ECNP, 21.

The sentiment expressed in these verses is unmistakable. The very birds seem to have a virility the speaker has lost. The wave is broad, but his heart is withered. This much can be inferred from the juxtapositions. Nevertheless, we want an explanation of the relationship and seek evidences of analogy.[15] How, we ask ourselves, are we supposed to hear these poems?

Three general assumptions reveal themselves in the critical comments of the first half of the twentieth century about this poetry. The first is that poetic images of nature are inferior unless they are literal descriptions. Thus we have Davies's puzzlement over the winter verses, and the dissatisfaction he later expresses with the formulaic repetition of certain nature images in Gwalchmai's *Gorhoffedd*, possessed of a stereotyped prologue, many deflections and lacunae, and full of "stupid," "stutter[ing]," "tiresome," "irritating" "debris," and "bad break[s]."[16] "This is not the expression of a love of nature," he exclaims, "but of prosody."[17] While contemporary critics are more tolerant of the prosodic, Davies's anger over the use of natural imagery as mere embellishment reveals in 1913 a buried prejudice that medievalists started to challenge only twenty years ago.

The second assumption is that if natural imagery is to be incorporated for some other reason than "love of nature," if it is to be functioning figuratively, then the analogy should be manifest. Jackson and Ifor Williams prefer to see the illogical juxtaposition of image and statement as a quirk resulting from the exigencies of style. The issue of figurative imagery has inspired loud arguments in critical response to Old English poems, primarily because the style of the poetry does not allow for the neat explanations of Jackson and Williams. Old English "continuity" portrays a seemingly realistic imagery which may be functioning as figuratively and ornamentally as it is in the Welsh.

The third assumption is that translation and emendation can solve all defects; it can fill in the gaps, smooth the perceptible lulls, render periodic what is paratactic and abrupt. With translation one can provide connections (in parentheses); with emendation one can rearrange words and stanzas; and with conflation one can solve the troublesome problem of loose variants and make the text single and monologic. This assumption is actually a failure of recognition: It fails to recognize that translation has become dominated by

15. Ford offers a tentative paraphrase of stanza 11 that resembles a kind of gnomic *Priamel*: "Just as birds sing on high, and just as streams are wet, as the moon is wont to shine and as the middle of the night brings cold, so has disease ravaged me" (PLIH, 38).
16. Davies, "The Welsh Bard," 101–2.
17. Ibid., 102.

the eye. No longer a province of the ear, it has become a synoptic impulse and a province of the written. The problems of translation are especially apparent in debates about the Old English elegies.

The Problems in Old English Poetry

In 1955 Eric G. Stanley forced a gap in the entrenched views about "realistic" treatment of imagery on the one hand and the uncompromising views of the allegorist on the other.[18] He finds fault, for instance, with H. C. Wyld's understanding of the Old English nature references as he expressed it thirty years earlier:

> The old poets are fond of using the processes of
> nature as symbols of moods; it might indeed almost
> be said that for them
>   the meanest flower that blows can give
>   Thoughts that do often lie too deep for tears.[19]

Such a generalization, Stanley objects, proceeds out of the "lingering notion that the Old English poets were 'sons of nature,' a part of the 'Gothick' conception of the Dark Ages."[20] Wyld expresses discontent with the unreality of certain passages of natural description and comes close to saying about the Old English very much what Davies has said about the Welsh:

> The vocabulary for describing the milder aspects of nature is rich enough, but it cannot be said that these pictures are very convincing. They resemble too much a stage landscape, bathed in eternal sunshine, with trim cottages nestling by pastures forever green, woodlands which "never bid the spring adieu," and gleaming brooks meandering through the fields and groves.[21]

---

18. "Old English Poetic Diction and *The Wanderer, The Seafarer,* and *The Penitent's Prayer,*" *Anglia* 73 (1955), 413.
19. H. C. Wyld, "Diction and Imagery in Anglo-Saxon Poetry," *Essays and Studies* 11 (1925), 69.
20. Stanley, "Poetic Diction," 427.
21. Wyld, "Diction and Imagery," 70.

However much we are jarred by this anachronistic description of the deficiencies of Old English, we must keep in mind that both Wyld and Davies were writing at a time when naturalism was the norm, when "pictures" were to be convincing, palpable, and immediate. The assumption in these and many other critical responses to the basic alterity of medieval poetry is that the particular, the "you-are-there" image is good and the figure is bad. Wyld's critique is based entirely on a metaphor that is inapplicable to Old English poetry, and that is the stage or the framed painting. Stanley counters by reminding us of the "scholastic" tradition of Old English poetry and exposing an important misconception in the critical separation of *icon* and *figura*.[22] The blurring of fact and figure is characteristic of Old English, and Stanley declares that with much of its figurative diction, "it is not possible to be sure if the figure was not as real to the Anglo-Saxons as the reality that gave rise to the figure."[23]

The Seafarer and Forþon

The poem that has inspired the most polemic is *The Seafarer*. The literal and figurative registers of this poem are not clear, and there is also a special problem with the connection of ideas. The speaker's tone seems inconsistent, switching back and forth between lamentation over a wretched lot at sea and yearning for the life of wandering that will give redemption. M. Rieger accordingly developed the "dialogue theory" in 1869 that split the narrative into two speakers: an old man and a headstrong youth.[24] The second half of the poem, largely taken up with religious didacticism (starting line 64[b]), was looked upon by F. Kluge in 1883 as a later addition.[25] Both these theories were discarded, but the need to reconcile the two halves of *The Seafarer* remained a major concern for a long time.[26]

22. Stanley, 427: "Few will deny that with the old poets the processes of nature may be symbols of their moods: but it is not the flower that gives the thought; with the OE. poets it is the thought that gives the flower. And the flower that is born of the mood may take on sufficient concreteness to appear capable of existence without and outside the mood."

23. Ibid., 414.

24. M. Rieger, " 'Der Seefahrer' als Dialog hergestellt," *Zeitschrift für deutsche Philologie* 1 (1869), 334–39.

25. F. Kluge, "Zu altenglischen Dichtungen: I. 'Der Seefahrer,' " *Englischen Studien* 6 (1883), 322–27.

26. See, for instance, S. Olof Anderson, "*The Seafarer*: An Interpretation," K. *Humanistika Vetenskapssamfundets i Lund Arsberättelse* 1 (Lund: Gleerups, 1937–38); Ida L. Gordon, Introduc-

The first hint of a change of mind in *The Seafarer* comes in line 33^b, where the speaker tells us that his heart's thoughts urge him to wander the high seas. The lines that follow are clearly taken up with spiritual matters whereas up to this point the seafarer appears to complain of the physical and psychological traumas of a life at sea. The allegorical interpretations were marshaled as an obvious way of reconciling the spiritual and secular aspects of the poem,[27] and the history of this debate reveals not only the "concrete" quality of the natural imagery in this poem but an urge in Anglo-Saxon studies to eliminate ambiguities. The polemic starts in earnest with Dorothy Whitelock's objections to S. Olof Anderson's view that ships, rocks, storms, and waves have obvious biblical and homiletic significance as *figurae*. She writes that "we are given no hint of any kind that the beginning of the poem is anything other than a realistic description."[28] Stanley cautions us that "the poem is neither realism nor allegory. It is an imagined

---

tion, *The Seafarer* (London: Methuen, 1960); Robert D. Stevick, "The Text and Composition of *The Seafarer*," PMLA 80 (1965), 332–36; Roy F. Leslie, "The Meaning and Structure of *The Seafarer*," in *The Old English Elegies: New Essays in Criticism and Research* (Toronto: Associated University Presses, 1983), 96–122.

27. The allegorical debate has too many contributors for me to do justice to. I cite the following: G. Ehrisman (in "Religionsgeschichtliche Beiträge zum germanischen Frühchristentum," *Beiträge zur Geschichte der deutschen Sprache und Literatur* 35 [1909], 209–39) wrote that *The Seafarer* is the expression of "monastic asceticism" [*monklische Ideal*], whereby the dangerous voyage represents the afflictions of life which the man of God willfully embraces for his soul's sake; his opposition is the fortunate man on shore given to worldly materialism. L. L. Schucking (review of Sieper's *Die altenglische Elegie*, in *Englischen Studien* 51 [1917], 105–9) and S. Olof Anderson ("*The Seafarer*: An Interpretation," *K. Humanistika Vetemskapssamfundets i Lund Arsberättelse* 1 [1937–38], agree that the sea voyage of lines 39 to 46 is to be taken symbolically, but not necessarily as a symbol of monastic life. Anderson speculates that the voyage may stand for "the life of the pious on earth . . . as well as the road to Eternity," through death, and he notes the high degree of figurative diction in the poem, which recalls "venerable sentences used in every homily book; the rocks of life, the fetters of existence, the hunger for the life to come, the coldness and loneliness of life, etc." (5) G. V. Smithers cites the metaphors of the *peregrinus* in medieval ecclesiastical writings, especially Augustine's *De Civitate Dei* ("The Meaning of *The Seafarer* and *The Wanderer*," *Medium Ævum* 26 [1957], 147). Here, he writes, we have the idea that there are two *civitates* of men who live *secundum Deum* and *secundum hominem*. The *peregrinus* in *The Seafarer* has made himself an alien on earth in order to be a member of the City of God. It is in this sense, then, that Smithers takes the *elpeodigra eard* of line 38, which he believes to be a symbol for Heaven, "The land of 'aliens in this world' " (151). The original *topos* for this idea comes, of course, from Adam's Fall and his exile from Eden. In its discourse on this subject, Blickling Homily 2 substantiates Smithers's argument (*We synd on þisse worlde ælpeodige*; in *Blickling Homilies*, ed. Richard Morris, EETS, o.s., no. 73 [1880], 23).

28. "The Interpretation of *The Seafarer*," in *The Early Cultures of Northwest Europe*, ed. Cyril Fox and Bruce Dickens (Cambridge: Cambridge University Press, 1950), 263.

situation, invented to give force to the doctrine which forms the end of the poem and is its purpose."[29]

A persistent source of difficulty is the vague notion that many have brought to this term *image*; Whitelock and Stanley use it to mean "figure of speech"; others use it to mean a reference. I take up this issue in more detail in a later chapter. Another persistent source of difficulty is the covert privileging of the "monologic," the unquestioned assumption that the voice and the message of a poetic text be consistent, one, untrammeled by contradictions or intertextuality. Eric Stanley and more recently the late Stanley B. Greenfield have done much to take the edges off this bias, but for years a popular subject of debate among medievalists was whether or not a text had "unity"[30] (a term which in itself marked the prejudices of those trying to remove prejudice— why not "plurality" as a viable aesthetic?) Nowhere has this preoccupation been more evident, though, than in the arguments over connections in *The Seafarer*.

The Old English word *forþon*, especially as it appears in *The Seafarer*, has posed a problem to an audience looking for explicit connections. Some of the major links between image and message, including the important transition from secular to spiritual concerns, are enigmatic and vague. *Forþon* appears to mean a number of things. It most often expresses causality, as we have seen in Blickling Homily 2, but in both directions; that is, it can refer to the cause ("because," "on account of," "since"), or it can refer to the effect ("therefore," "for this reason," "the reason why"). S. O. Andrew gives us a rule for this difference: "When the principal sentence [the clause containing the effect] comes first, *forþon (forþi)* shows that stress is laid not so much on the action predicated by the verb as on the reason for it."[31] Here is his example: "*Forþon heo fæmne cnede forþon heo wæs fæmne geacnod*, 'The reason why she brought forth as a virgin was that she had conceived as a virgin.' "[32] According to S. B. Liljegren, *forþon* can express adversative sense ("yet," "however,"

29. "Poetic Diction," 453. Rosemary Woolf has suggested that we take *The Seafarer* as an example of *planctus*, where the use of the first person is employed by the poet to make a point ("*The Wanderer, The Seafarer*, and the Genre of *Planctus*," in *Anglo-Saxon Poetry: Essays in Appreciation for John C. McGalliard*, ed. Lewis E. Nicholson and Dolores Warwick Frese (Notre Dame: University of Notre Dame Press, 1975), 192–207.

30. Ralph Baldwin, *The Unity of the Canterbury Tales* (Copenhagen: Rosenkilde and Bagger, 1955); R. MacGregor Dawson, "The Structure of the Old English Gnomic Poems," *Journal of English and Germanic Philology* 61 (1962), 14–22.

31. *Syntax and Style in Old English* (Cambridge: Cambridge University Press, 1940), 32–33.

32. Ibid., 33.

"but"), and he arrives at this conclusion from an examination of Old and Middle English translations of biblical passages, and from his own opinion that an adversative meaning is the only one whereby *forþon* will make sense in line 33 of *The Seafarer*.[33] Another meaning gives it intensive quality ("assuredly," "forsooth"), yet removes from it the burden of connection. We could retranslate Andrew's line, "Indeed she brought forth as a virgin; for she conceived as a virgin," and still have the general sense of the statement. Having the context for the sentence, however, would significantly affect our interpretation of it; analyzing it in isolation seems wasteful.

Forþon appears seven times in *The Seafarer* in the sense in which I want to examine it. The first (line 27[a]), ordinarily translated "indeed," introduces the comment about the fortunate landlubber who has no understanding of the torments that the mariner must endure. The second (line 33[b]) introduces a seemingly contradictory utterance about the speaker's desire to experience the high seas, and the third (line 39[a]) returns us to his negative attitude toward seafaring and is commonly translated as "nevertheless." Here we have the proud man who is fearful of what the Lord will bring him on his voyage. Then we have the reference to the cuckoo which inspires the wanderlust in the heart of the seafarer and the fourth *forþon* (line 58[a]), normally translated as a solid "therefore," introduces the account of a spiritual transmigration in the form of another bird that urges his heart over the "whaleroad." The fifth (line 64[b]), translated as "because" by most, affirms the seafarer's decision to make a voyage—"for the joys of the Lord are dearer to me than this dead life"—and ushers in the didactic second half of the poem. The sixth (line 72[a]) is a fairly uncomplicated transitional conjunction and could be translated as either "therefore" or "indeed," and the seventh (line 108[a]) is crucial to the logical connection with the thoughts expressed in lines 107–108[a]. If translated as "therefore," we have "Blessed is he who lives humbly; to him comes the grace of heaven. / God establishes that disposition in him; *therefore* he believes in His might." If translated as "because," then the lesson is altered, the theology turned on end: "Blessed is he who lives humbly; to him comes the grace of heaven. / God establishes that disposition in him *because* he believes in His might." And if adversative sense could be applied to it we might conceivably have "God establishes that disposition in him; *yet* he believes in His might." Context is a powerful guiding tool.

But when the context itself is ambiguous, we are left to swim in deep water. Those instances of *forþon* which have caused the most debate are to be

---

33. "Some Notes on the OE Poem *The Seafarer*," *Studia Neophilologica*, 14 (1941), 145–59.

found in lines 33[b] and 64[b]. In his translation, W. S. Mackie makes both conjunctions begin a new section, which he designates by skipping down a space to indicate the transition.[34] In this way he maintains the schismatic nature of the poem which originally led early scholars to endorse the dialogue theory and the "spurious" ending. Whitelock eliminates the schism by taking the *forþon* in line 64[b] as correlative with that in line 58[a]. We would then have, awkward as it is, something like Andrew's construction:

> *The reason why* my mind passes over the enclosure of my heart, my spirit passes wide with the ocean over the home of the whales, the expanse of the earth—it comes back to me, eager and greedy; the solitary flier yells; it irresistibly incites my heart onto the whale-way over the waters of the deep—*is because* the joys of the Lord are dearer to me than this dead life . . .

Whitelock argues that the seafarer "states unequivocally" his reason for embracing "the hardships he has described so forcibly," and she opposes rendering *forþon* as "assuredly" or "indeed" or any other such "vague word."[35] Obviously, this interpretation supports her belief that the narrator is relating a factual experience which has given impetus to his desire to become a *peregrinus*. It is difficult, however, to see how the one *forþon* could be correlative with the other without producing the ugly and confusing translation that we see above. Three complete statements about the *anfloga* intervene between the two appearances of *forþon*, and it is reasonable to surmise that the conjunctions are serving more loosely as connectives than scholars of Old English trained to admire the periodic, Latinate, and finished sentence find comfortable.[36]

Stanley Greenfield approves Whitelock's attempts to reconcile the two parts of the poem but criticizes the rigidity of her interpretation.[37] It does not allow for the ambivalent feelings of the seafarer, he argues, whose complexity and fluctuation add greatly to the depth of the poem and are reinforced time and again in the ambiguous diction (*dryhten, dream, blæd, duguð*). He too, however, seeks to tighten up the meaning of the word *forþon* and adopts the adversative theory in order to interpret the seafarer as one who is fraught with

34. Mackie, *The Exeter Book*, 2, EETS (London: Oxford University Press, 1934). 4

35. Whitelock, "Interpretation of *The Seafarer*," 266, 249.

36. Bruce Mitchell and Fred Robinson shed some sensible light on this tendency in their study of Old English grammar, *A Guide to Old English*, 4th ed. (Oxford: Basil Blackwell, 1986), 100.

37. "Attitudes and Values in *The Seafarer*," *Studies in Philology* 51 (1954), 17.

conflict. Here is his translation of line 39, *forþon nis þæs modwlonc mon ofer eorþan:* "And yet there is no man in the world so high-hearted."[38] He continues to insert adversative sense where it is not indicated in the text:

> The woods blossom, the cities grow fair, the plains become beautiful, the world hastens on; all these (it is true) urge the man eager of heart on his journey, urge onward him who so thinks to depart far on the floodways. (But) also the cuckoo urges with sad voice, the herald of summer sings, forbodes sorrow bitter in the heart. *That* the man who is prosperous does not know, what some suffer . . . , those who set their exile steps the furthest.
>
> [48–57][39]

Greenfield offers this translation as a means of clarifying a distinction that is not made by the syntax, yet one he senses exists in the conflicting nature of the mariner: the youthful exuberance belonging to "the eager of heart" and the spiritual sobriety of one who knows that some day he will die. This last is expressed by the sad voice of the cuckoo. But *swylce* (line 53) does not offer adversative sense; rather, it emphasizes a comparison. Greenfield is responding to what seems like an omission to him, and he supplies the missing link.

Both the Old English and the Welsh inspire anxieties over the inconsistency of their signs, their floating signifiers and unfilled gaps, and the widespread response on our part to the feeling that something has been omitted makes us scramble around to nail down its language. Perhaps the most eloquent plaints have been voiced by T. A. Shippey over the vagueness of the famous line 33b *forþon* in *The Seafarer.* "In the middle of a line and without pretence of warning," he writes, "[the poet] expresses sudden desire for what he has been given every reason to loathe:

> The shadow of night grew dark, it
> snowed from the north, frost bound the
> earth, hail fell to the ground, coldest
> of grains. / / So the heart's thoughts
> impel me to make trial myself of the
> deep currents, the salt waves' tumult.

38. Ibid., 18.
39. Ibid.

The juxtaposition is a shock for the wariest of readers [he continues].
No wonder that a dialogue theory sprang into being! or that the loose
connective *forþon* has been wracked with scrutiny in an attempt to
make it seem something firmer.[40]

Shippey here touches on a primary problem: the degree to which our own
translations govern our interpretations of difficult poetry.[41] In illustration of
his point, he has given us his *prose translation*, which emphasizes the
disjunction and which obscures the aural and intellectual connection be-
tween cold seeds beating the earth and the heart's thoughts beating the
mariner that is obvious in the original Anglo-Saxon poem but not so obvious
in a translation. Instead of the vivid verb *cnyssað*, Shippey gives us the pale,
Latinate "impels." Prose is a medium which is understandably more given to
eliminating ambiguity than is poetry, and as the tool for the homilist and the
historian, it has had from the beginning in English a didactic and informative
purpose. While poetry can also be didactic and informative, its artistic and
expressive functions allow it to make ambiguity work for it in powerful ways.
Our utilitarian translations of Old English poems will be prose translations
most of the time, containing all the explanatory diction of prose, and then we
try to wrest from them exactitudes their originals do not provide. Shippey, for
instance, is irritated with Old English elegies, finding them "shapeless, drop-
ping into familiar scenes without preamble . . . their corresponding virtue
[being] to maintain in tension disparate but loosely related elements of
thought and emotion, forcing the reader or listener to supply his own interpre-
tation, if he feels the need."[42] He makes this comment about a passage from
Maxims I:

> Styran sceal mon strongum mode.   Storm oft holm gebringeþ,
> geofen in grimmum sælum;   onginnað grome fundian
> fealwe on feorran to londe,   hwæðer he fæste stonde.
> Weallas him wiþre healdað . . .
>
> (lines 50–53)

40. T. A. Shippey, *Old English Verse* (London: Hutchinson University Library, 1972), 68–
69.
41. Alain Renoir makes this point effectively in "*Wulf and Eadwacer*: A Non-Interpretation,"
Franciplegius: Medieval and Linguistic Studies in Honor of Francis Peabody Magoun, Jr., ed. Jess B.
Bessinger and Robert F. Creed (New York: New York University Press, 1965), 147–63.
42. Shippey, *Old English Verse*, 68.

"A man must control with strong mind. The
sea often brings a storm, the ocean in grim
times; the fierce grey waves begin to strive
from afar to the land, whether it may stand
fast. The walls hold them back . . ."

[Shippey's translation]

Here [Shippey writes,] human control and the chaos of the sea are
brought into a startling but quite undeveloped juxtaposition, and,
oddly associated with both, the image of the walls resisting, found in
similar contexts in *Juliana* and *The Wanderer*. Verse like the *Maxims*
is bad and not immediately purposeful. But in its curt oppositions,
one might say, many poems lie in embryo; from this unformed state
some are developed, even though they never shake off entirely the
tone of mystery and association.[43]

A "mature" poem, he implies, should be free of mystery and association.
To be sure, there is no conjunction linking the two thoughts syntactically,
only a caesura bridged by the alliteration on *styran*, *strongum*, and *storm*,
which in itself yokes these words and their images together. But an analogy of
some sort is being made through the word *styran*, origin of our word "steer."
Shippey has given it its equally correct but more abstract meaning, "control,"
and consequently misses the link with the sea: a man "steers" through experi-
ence as well as through the stormy sea, which holds literal as well as symbolic
force. Both kinds of steering, however, require courage and control, and we
are given the sturdy walls as a corresponding figure, holding back the waves.
The Anglo-Saxon metaphor blurs the edges between fact and figure, but far
from being an undeveloped juxtaposition, this connection is complex and
involves a visual image, the effect of which would have been diminished by a
conjunction or other such linking word.

The Celtic "Connection"

A number of scholars have argued that the Anglo-Saxon elegies are "of Celtic
Inspiration."[44] There is first of all the shared subject matter of the wanderer or

---

43. Ibid., 62.
44. Nora Chadwick, in *The Heritage of Early Britain*, ed. M. P. Charlesworth et al. (London:
Bell, 1952), 125. See also her comments in "The Celtic Background of Early Anglo-Saxon England,"

pariah who must face the elements alone. There is also the juxtaposition of "gnomic wisdom" with the plaints uttered by the speaker, the similar treatment of nature, always seen in connection with the speaker's emotions and reflections, and the notable motif of birdsong, especially the sad voice of the cuckoo. Ernst Sieper has pointed out the curious fact that the cuckoo as a bird of lament appears nowhere else in Western European literature of the ninth century except in two Old English poems, *The Seafarer* and *The Husband's Message,* and in some Welsh and Irish poems.[45] Along with the geographic proximity of the Welsh and Anglo-Saxon peoples, this fact leads Ida L. Gordon to suggest in her introduction to *The Seafarer* that "we have in the West Midland region of the mid-tenth century, and possibly a little earlier, an environment, both poetic and homiletic, in which *The Seafarer* might well have had its origins."[46] Nora Chadwick believes in a sphere of interchange, what P. L. Henry has termed the "Cymro-English" tradition of southern Britain.[47] Gordon protests, however, that while the English and the Welsh elegy "strike off from what seem to be the same conventional topics" and while they both come out of a generally Christian tradition, "the overall result is quite different in form and spirit."[48]

Nevertheless, efforts to place Anglo-Saxon and Welsh elegies within a British genre of religious or penitential poetry have made some scholars downplay the differences in form and spirit and emphasize the similarities. Herbert Pilch's premise that the "elegiac genre in Old English was created in imitation of a similar Welsh genre known to us through 'Claf Aber Cuawg' " calls upon the weakest elements of source hunting and stylistic comparison.[49]

---

in *Celt and Saxon: Studies in the Early British Border,* ed. Kenneth Jackson et al. (London: Cambridge University Press, 1963), 340.

45. See Ernst Sieper, *Die altenglische Elegie* (Strassburg, 1915), 70; and Gordon, *The Seafarer* (London: Methuen, 1960), 17.

46. Gordon, *Seafarer,* 31.

47. EECL, 69.

48. Gordon, *Seafarer,* 340.

49. Herbert Pilch, "The Elegiac Genre in Old English and Early Welsh Poetry," *Zeitschrift für celtische Philologie* 29 (1964), 209–24. Pilch notes the occurrence of stanzas and refrains in *Deor* and *Wulf* and *Eadwacer* and cites as evidence the similarities already noted above—the subject matter, the gnomic asides, the imagery, and the stress laid on the transient character of the world in general; he adds to these items the "anti-chronological," "erratic," and "inconsistent" order of elements along with a "difficult" and "obscure" narrative construct in both the English and the Welsh (212, 219). His final suggestion is that the Old English poet, "hard put to invent a stanzaic pattern as closely knit as the Welsh englyn," sought to bring about similar effects with the Germanic alliterative line (220). For this reason, he suggests, we find throughout *The Seafarer* the frequent introduction of a new subject in the second half-line, which reproduces the Welsh device

Pilch's most interesting contribution, however, lies in his attempt to read the Old English through the Welsh, instead of the other way around. He puts a positive value on the stylized "silences" in the Welsh poem, but fails to convince us that the English poets were imitating this mode. More persuasive is P. L. Henry's book, which seeks to relate a wide body of European literature, primarily Old English, Early Irish and Welsh, and Scandinavian, within a common generic category—the "penitential lyric"—in which the wanderer seeks exile for the salvation of his soul. Henry draws many very intriguing comparisons between the Old Irish *ailithre* ("exile") tradition and the Old English poetry of exile, focusing particularly on *The Seafarer, The Wanderer,* and *The Penitent's Prayer* or *Resignation A* and *B.* He lays heavy emphasis on the motif of the bird-soul, such as we find it in the *anfloga* (line 62[b]) of *The Seafarer* and notes the occurrences through Irish legend and literature of souls becoming birds. He strains a little in his discussion of the Llywarch-Hen corpus, which does not emphasize religious consolation in the way that the English or the Irish do, and he relates *Canu Llywarch Hen* to the rest by insisting that "outcast" poetry is a branch of the penitential genre. He observes that a few of the *englynion* in *Claf Abercuawg* speak of prayer in an oratory, but such religious references are overwhelmed by the predominantly negative attitude of the speaker and his *Angst:*

29.   ny at duw da y diryeit.

(RB: 1035.38)

[God does not allow good to the unfortunate.]

30.   Da y diriei ny atter.
namyn tristit a phryder.
nyt atwna duw ar a wnel.

(1035.39–40)

[Good to the unfortunate is not allowed,
only sadness and anxiety.
God does not undo that which he does.]

---

of enjambment. The "continual shifting between narrative, gnomic, and nature elements" in the Old English is a device borrowed from the Welsh as well, and its erratic nature in both *The Wanderer* and *The Seafarer* is due to the fact that "the Old English poet could hardly succeed in integrating [these elements] in a close structure" (221).

31.   Oed mackwy mabklaf. oed goe[w]in   gy[n]ran
       yn llys vr[e]nhin.
       poet gwyl duw wrth edein.

(1035.41–42)

[The poor sickman was a youth, was a daring nobleman
in the court of the king.
May God be gentle to the outcast.]

32.   Or a wneler yn derwd[y].
       ys tiryeit yr ae derlly.
       cas dyn yman yw cas duw vry.

(1035.43–44)

[Despite what is done in a house of prayer,
wretched is he who reads it.
An enemy to man below is an enemy to God above.]

Such statements would not be made in *The Seafarer*, where the wretched are expected, by embracing wretchedness, to escape the damnation decreed for those who have their "heaven" on earth. But in *Claf Abercuawg* there is no sense of heaven's rewards, no expiation of sins, no *consolatio*, aside from a prayer expressed in stanza 31 (*poet gwyl duw wrth edein*, "may God be gentle to the outcast"), which has the earmarks of an interpolation because it breaks up a triad of concatenated verses. Patrick Ford challenged Henry's identification of *Claf Abercuawg* as a penitential lyric, suggesting that the elegiac tradition in early Wales developed out of "the native tradition of eulogy" wherein the poet is not concerned with the "topos of mutability" so much as with the "loss of valor, protection and generosity, for which God can give no compensation."[50] Among conservative circles, this interpretation was viewed as an attack upon the Christian underpinnings of the text. In her study of the saga englynion, Jenny Rowland devotes an entire chapter to *Claf Abercuawg*, reversing the order of stanzas 31 and 32 "contrary to [her] usual practice," as it is "crucial to [her] interpretation" of the text as a penitential poem.[51] She takes as her evidence the wrongness of the interrupted triad, but her strategy is not so much to restore the broken concatenation as to rescue the poem from spiraling down at the end as it does. In her reading, the saving statement concludes the poem and turns it in the direction of the genre she wants to fit

50. Ford, PLlH.
51. "Claf Abercuawg and Penitential Lyrics," EWSP, 190–228.

it into. Instead of asking why the leper does *not* counsel penance as a remedy for sickness and anomie, Rowland explains and corrects the uncooperative lacuna, rewriting the text to conform to her notion of genre.

Mindful of the echoing silence in the text itself, she asks "Is it justifiable . . . to call a poem which ends on such a note of despair and severance from God a penitential poem about the expiation of sins?" She answers her question by an appeal to other related traditions in Old Irish and Latin where hardship and leprosy are looked upon as spiritually healing conditions, returning again to the Old English elegies as a gauge for the "explicit" material that is left out of *Claf Abercuawg*:

> The leper knows his position of *direit daear* ["hapless one of earth"] cannot be reversed but he is not yet aware that he need not remain *direit new* ["hapless one of heaven," i.e., "damned"]. The poet's interjection . . . is senseless if the leper's own assessment of hopelessness is correct. The poem leaves the impression that the process of repentance already begun by the leper will eventually bear fruit.[52]

Appealing as this interpretation is, it is nevertheless an *extension* of the poem, a gloss; it is not so much penitence that we are made to see in the Sick Man's verses as it is Rowland's desire for his penitence, a standard critical response to poetry which privileges unity and classifiability. It is not unusual to find texts in this period that have been copied incompletely from other sources with frequent scribal interpolations. Trying to locate the original poem will always be an extension of our anglocentric reading habits, our prejudices in favor of completeness, *wholeness* in translated form. In approaching these texts we should be mindful of their plurality. Silences and perceived omissions are as concrete in shaping the extant text as the words themselves, and it must be recognized that the Welsh poems, like the English, do not exhibit a pure generic form, but seem to be an amalgam of many different traditions which blend spiritual and secular values in a perplexingly ambiguous way. They are palimpsests, of sorts, in which the motif of an outcast in the wilderness may originate in part from native Celtic concepts of poetic initiation, a tradition that naturally lent itself to Christian overlay. The gnomic material and the natural description may have other origins. As guides for generic placement, we really only have the poems themselves. It is a fact that the Llywarch *englynion* omit mention of what one

---

52. Rowland, EWSP, 200.

must do to gain salvation, stressing instead what one has lost. This emphasis does not make them unchristian; it marks them, though, as different in rhetorical intent from those Old English poems wherein penitence and Christian consolation are explicitly counseled.

Song of the Old Man, following upon the heels of *The Sick Man* and the first poem to mention the name Llywarch, is a litany of the griefs of age. Were it not for the lateness of Alan's text, one might see in it shades of the *Anticlaudianus*, where *Senectus*, portrayed as a Vice and injurious to the New Man, is beset with all the miseries that plague Llywarch:

> Morbid, sad, trembling, weak Old Age, full of years, leaning on a staff, without the support of strength of mind, stirs up wars and in the heat of a new war grows young again. Weakness, Disease, Weariness, Boredom, Failure accompany Old Age on his way: they are afire with love of war and wish to live the life of the camp. Grief is inflamed as he rushes into arms, clad in a rent mantle, bedewed with tears, he furrows his face with his nails. Gloom, Lament, Sorrow, Depression, Disaster are enthusiastic in his service, profess their military allegiance to their master: ministers and king together are hot for war.[53]

Equally bellicose and mindful of honor, Llywarch laments the deaths of his sons whom he urged to war. There are also the sadness, the weakness, the morbidity, and the staff in *Song of the Old Man*; both these verses and those of the "Sick Man" would seem to fit into a medieval tradition of the *senex* and the pariah that emerges in medieval tradition, often within a Christian context as in Ireland's *Old Woman of Beare*. However, their strong suggestions of a heroic story, which has inspired the "saga" interpretation of the Llywarch Hen corpus, make it unlikely that they are a comment on the *topos* of old age, but rather a moving account of the plight of an old man. Again, genre eludes us.

The Problems of Genre

Defining the nature of "genre" has always been a vexed task, no less so the defining of "elegy" in Old English. "Penitential lyric," as it has been applied

---

53. Alan of Lille, *Anticlaudianus*, Book 8, trans. James J. Sheridan, (Toronto: Pontifical Institute of Medieval Studies, 1973), 218–19.

to the diverse texts of the Llywarch-Hen corpus, is a vague term, and I would counsel finding some other rubric that does not carry overtones of the confessional, that is, the vocal realization of one's sins. Old English "penitential" poetry has attracted its fair share of critical attention, but few can decide on what it is exactly. Allen Frantzen writes that there is no specific Old English poetic genre that obviously derives from confessional or penitential practice.[54] "It is worthwhile," he says, "to investigate poetic themes and images which recall penance or confession and to distinguish poems which contain explicit exhortations to repent from those which do not."[55] Frantzen briefly outlines the various criteria that scholars have marshaled in their definitions of "penitential" literature and that have been applied to both the form and the content of the texts.[56] Prose works containing homilies, catechisms, rules for daily living and praying, modes of confession and penance are more directly related to the sacramental practice and include such works as *Judgment Day II*, *The Exhortation to Christian Living*, *A Summons to Prayer*, *The Lord's Prayer*. Classifying the content of poems such as *The Wanderer*, *The Seafarer*, *The Wife's Lament*, and even *Resignation A* and *B* is more problematic, as most of these poems neither name a sin nor speak directly of penance or confession. Their connection with the more explicitly religious literature has been made through the *topos* of the pilgrim and the exile, to which both the Old English and some of the poems of *Canu Llywarch Hen* clearly apply. But are they penitential poems? And if not, do they stem from the same genre?

More pertinent to my particular topic are Frantzen's comments about disclosure and the distinction he makes between two poetic "modes" in Old English poems of lament, the "penitential" and the "stoic," and their dissimilar emphasis on speaking. For obvious reasons, the penitent must unburden his heart through a speech act. His salvation is contingent on his making known and heard to the world and to God that which he sought to keep unknown and unheard, and these poems abound with stock images and expressions of disclosure.[57] The Old English "wisdom" poems operate differently. Secrecy is coun-

---

54. Allen Frantzen, *The Literature of Penance in Anglo-Saxon England* (New Brunswick: Rutgers University Press, 1983), 180.

55. Ibid., 180. "It is time not to redefine the term but to recognize the disadvantages of pigeonholing Old English poems, many of which fall into several categories and hence defy the labels fixed to them. Poems which refer to confession and penance intersect with these generic classifications; they do not form a self-contained or cohesive group. They make specific use of the materials of penitential practice and should be separated from those poems which merely express sorrow for sin and stop short of naming confession or penance" (182).

56. Ibid., 180–92.

57. Ibid., 193: "The subject matter is evident in their vocabulary, which consists of stock expressions (the medical metaphor, words meaning 'confess,' 'repent,' and so forth), the arrangement of these traditional materials into a motif, and sometimes direct exhortation."

seled in *The Wanderer*. We never hear just why it is that the mariner has taken to sea in *The Seafarer*. In *The Wanderer*, the speaker's "stoicism dignifies circumstances which poems about penance seek to transcend":

> . . . the wise man does not share the secrets of his heart. Penitential practice demanded confession from the recesses of the heart, leaving no evil undisclosed. In wisdom poems, the unknown is sacred; in poems about penance, the known is potentially fatal. The wisdom poems would be destroyed by the revelation of their mysteries, while without systematic and full disclosure, penitential poems would have no resemblance to either confession or penance. Poems which refer to penance and confession teem with images of revelation—wounds are opened, thoughts unveiled, bodies seen through—and abound with references to speech. They are poems about disclosure. In wisdom poems it is enough that the speaker contemplate his unhappiness and formulate a resolution in his mind. [58]

Though mysterious and secretive as Frantzen rightly claims them to be, the Old English elegies are nevertheless paragons of explicitness when compared to the Welsh. We can hear in these two traditions the sound of two different types of discourse—that of the lament with its perceptible lulls, its omissions, its pregnant pauses, and that of the homily with its periodic phrases, its connections, its lessoning information and exhortations. And yet, for all their verbosity, *The Wanderer* and *The Seafarer* are much less deeply personal in tone than *Claf Abercuawg*. Unlike the sufferers in *The Wanderer* and *The Seafarer*, we know exactly what it is that bothers the leper and the Old Man in the companion poem *Can Yr Henwr*. They are verbose when it comes to a litany of their earthly sufferings, but about divine counsel for their souls' sake, they are silent. Nor is there nearly as much discourse on futurity in *The Sick Man* stanzas as there is in *The Seafarer*. While also plaintive, *The Wanderer* and, even more, *The Seafarer* set out to persuade, explain, and impart wisdom; they are more like dramatic monologues than lyrics. Nevertheless, we hear the absence of saving counsel in the Welsh poems, and this is distressing. Thus Rowland's hopeful plea: "The poem leaves the impression that the process of repentance already begun by the leper will eventually bear fruit." But there is no "eventually" in this poem. To all intents and purposes, it deals bluntly with the here and now of the leper's unhappiness, and is followed by a poem of marked secular misery in *The Song of the Old Man*,

---

58. Ibid., 196.

which in turn is followed by a history of Llywarch's tragic *hubris* in dealing with his sons.

What does it mean when a text does not say what we want it to say? What is at stake in our filling in—which is what we often resort to in our translations and critical interpretations? Partially at stake, I believe, is the preservation of the translator—"the middle-man," the "third thing"—who understands and elucidates, but who must necessarily remain invisible as the transparent conductor of the text. This is one reason, perhaps, why scholars have been reluctant to comment at length about the more difficult poems attributed to Taliesin which seem designed to put our ignorance on display. But also at stake is the covert privileging of certain poetic *topoi*: activity, clarity, and purpose are good, their opposites bad. The historical is "good," and so are arguments attesting to the residue of the sixth century among the *cynfeirdd* poets: the "historical" Taliesin gets press, the "mythological" Taliesin does not. [59] In other words, what is at stake in much conservative Welsh scholarship is a political impulse that seeks to confirm time-honored myths about heroic Welsh figures whose early panegyric and warlike deeds lend solidarity to Welsh poetic history. This impulse is to be respected. But until its subtext is deconstructed or squarely faced, it can blind. The attempts to read the Llywarch-Hen *englynion* through the English or the Irish penitential tradition stem from another covert privileging of the Latin scholastic tradition over evidences of indigenous or Indo-European roots. The one has a certain respectability that has been in vogue since Robertsonian criticism and the fascination with the Patristic tradition. The other seems to smack of the trendier anthropological studies. Less obvious is the need to rescue Llywarch and/or the leper from an unflattering contrast with poems that appear to show more *masculine* spiritual virtues of activity, clarity, and purpose; left to themselves their secular despair (especially that in *Song of the Old Man*) seems to diminish them, whereas the penitential or heroic context sets them right again. The Old English poems that most markedly resemble *The Sick Man* in tone and style are *The Wife's Lament* and *Wulf and Eadwacer*,

---

59. Ifor Williams's book, *The Poems of Taliesin* (Dublin: Institute for Advanced Studies, 1975), omits all the mantic poetry associated with the mythological figure from the sagas and prints only the texts assumed to have been written by the historical sixth-century figure mentioned along with Aneirin by Nennius in his *Historia Brittonum*, ed. Ferdinand Lot (Paris: H. Champion, 1934), 201. A. O. H. Jarman, in *Y Gododdin, Britain's Oldest Heroic Poem* (Llandysul: 1990), argues vigorously against the supposition put forth by "the American scholars" Kathryn Klar, Brendan O Hehir, and Eve Sweetser ("Welsh Poetics in the Indo-European Tradition: The Case of the *Book of Aneirin*," *Studia Celtica* 18/19 [1983–84], 30–51) that *The Gododdin* of *The Book of Aneirin* postdates the *gwarchanau*, traditionally considered to be later and corrupted additions.

texts wherein the speaker is not only unempowered and mired in private worldly griefs, but a woman, and cryptic and incoherent to boot. Some Anglo-Saxon scholars have gone to lengths to change the sex (and the grammar) of the speaker in *The Wife's Lament*, arguing that Old English is predominantly a literature by and about men; clearly, this is hardly an impartial observation, much less solid grounds for emendation.[60] In contrast, Patricia Belanoff's elegant application of Kristevan language theory to both these women's songs shows us the energetic and positive light in which a feminine "semiotic" can be read,[61] and with her I see no reason why this category must be confined to natural gender.

I do not intend to argue that the Sick Man is effeminate, as that would be ludicrous; but he is certainly "feminized" by our embarrassment. His verses show him to have been pushed to the edges, sheltering against the wide open spaces of the world which men and warriors move through with intent, and his inability to take his situation into his hands even on a spiritual level and make the world and God connect with him has inspired an extraordinary amount of polemic and retranslation which says intriguing things about our preferences. I suggest that poems that are cryptic, contradictory, unreadable, poems whose connections are "unsound," poems that talk of passivity, disenfranchisement, and the disabling effects of terrible grief and old age, such poems have a power and pathos that need no excuses.

60. Witness Rudolph C. Bambas's article, "Another View of the Old English *Wife's Lament*," *JEGP* 62 (1963), 303–9, which emends the feminine endings of *geomorre* and *minre sylfre* (lines 1–2) to masculine ones on the grounds that an Old English scop reciting this poetry would be hard-pressed to do so impersonating a woman, and these must therefore be "scribal errors."

61. "Women's Songs, Women's Language: *Wulf and Eadwacer* and *The Wife's Lament*," in *New Readings on Women in Old English Literature*, ed. Helen Damico and Alexandra Hennessey Olsen (Bloomington: Indiana University Press, 1990), 193–203.

3

Metrical and Stylistic Analyses

a gwedy elwch tawelwch vu.
("And after rejoicing there was silence.")
—*The Gododdin*

Before we can come to any new conclusions about the connection of ideas in these poems, a discussion of the metrical and grammatical styles of Old English and Early Welsh poetry is called for. Both languages are Indo-European, and presumably their poetic traditions have an origin in the Indo-European "long" and "short" line that we find in Greek, Sanskrit, and Slavic traditions.[1] Both feature alliteration, and it has been recently shown that the distinct syllabic stress characteristic of Early Welsh poetry might have devel-

1. See Calvert Watkins, "Indo-European Metrics and Archaic Irish Verse," *Studia Celtica* 6 (1963), 194–249; also James Travis, *Early Celtic Versecraft: Origin, Development, Diffusion* (Ithaca: Cornell University Press, 1973), 2, 13. The matter of Welsh origins in Indo-European poetry has been a polemical topic, with the "nativists" arguing for the indigenous development of Old Welsh poetic forms and the "Indo-Europeanists" arguing for its development in pre-Celtic tradition. For the former, see Ifor Williams, *Canu Aneirin* (Caerdydd: Gwasg Prifysgol Cymru, 1938, 1970); for the latter see Kathryn Klar, Brendan O Hehir, and Eve E. Sweetser, "Welsh Poetics in the Indo-European Tradition: The Case of the *Book of Aneirin*," *Studia Celtica* 18/19 (1983–84), 30–51.

oped credibly from earlier accentual Indo-European forms which became stress-metrical in later Latin verse, early Germanic, and Old English.[2] The most obvious difference, however, is the occurrence of the stanzaic or "discrete" style in the Welsh and the continuous or "epic" style in the Old English.[3]

The Discrete Style

The discrete style of Welsh poetry, along with its history, is sufficiently unknown among scholars of English that it warrants special observation in itself. The historic categorization of Welsh poetry is a difficult and contested task. In his Cerdd Dafod,[4] John Morris-Jones divides medieval Welsh poetry into the following categories: (1) the cynfeirdd ("early bards") included the Llywarch-Hen poet along with Taliesin and Aneirin (author of The Gododdin); their period lasted presumably from A.D. 550 to 1075. (2) The gogynfeirdd ("somewhat early bards") wrote between A.D. 1120 and 1300. These poets modified the poetic devices already being developed by the cynfeirdd, and they perfected a complicated system of embellishment called cynghanedd, noted for its difficulty and technical brilliance. (3) From about 1330 to 1640, we have the period of "strict cynghannedd," when poetic embellishment flourished among the cywyddwyr ("men of the cywydd," a special type of meter). Among these, we find Dafydd ap Gwilym, contemporary of Chaucer.

My concern in this chapter is primarily with the poems of the cynfeirdd, which present a particularly frustrating problem to those who wish to date them. We simply do not have manuscript evidence of poems existing earlier than the eighth century, and the fragments found in eighth-century manuscripts such as the Juvencus exhibit a form of Welsh that is linguistically and orthographically earlier than the poetry of Aneirin, Taliesin, and the Llywarch-Hen poet. Learned tradition, however, places these poets in the

---

2. See Eve E. Sweetser, "Line Structure and Rhan-Structure: The Metrical Units of the Gododdin Corpus," in Early Welsh Poetry: Studies in the Book of Aneirin, ed. Brynley F. Roberts (Aberystwyth: National Library of Wales Press, 1988), 139–54, especially 141–46.

3. I borrow the terms from J. E. Caerwyn Williams, The Poets of the Welsh Princes (University of Wales Press, 1978), 55.

4. John Morris-Jones, Cerdd Dafod (Oxford: Clarendon Press, 1925).

sixth century[5] while their poetry is preserved in thirteenth-, fourteenth-, and fifteenth-century manuscripts respectively. It is presumed that they are either copies of earlier texts now lost to us, which would explain their archaisms, or the written forms of older, orally composed poems.[6] A conservative estimate for the original date of *Canu Llywarch Hen* is ninth to tenth century.

The Englyn

The eighth-century Juvencus poems are written using *englynion* ("stanzas"), a fact which suggests that the *englyn* (singular) is one of the oldest of poetic forms in Wales. It offers us a clear example of the discrete style of poetry and is amply illustrated in *The Elegy on Cynddylan*, a poem or series of poems of the *cynfeirdd* period found along with those of Llywarch Hen in *The Red Book of Hergest*. The verses are spoken by Heledd, sister to Cynddylan, Prince of Powys. She surveys his ruined hall at Pengwern (possibly Shrewsbury) and keens over his death at the hands of Saxon warriors:

1.   Sefwch allan vorynnyon afyllwch
      werydre gyndylan
      llys benn gwern neut tande
      gwae ieuienc a eidun brotre.

                                    (RB: 1044.9–11)

5. This notion stems primarily from Nennius's *Historia Brittonum* (Paris: F, Lot, 1934, 201), where Taliesin and Aneirin are listed as contemporaries under the sixth-century king Outigern (or Eudeyrn, according to Ifor Williams, *The Poems of Taliesin* [Dublin: Institute for Advanced Studies, 1968], xi).

6. This matter of the "archaisms" of Early Welsh poetry has been in much dispute. David Greene, in "Linguistic Considerations in the Dating of Early Welsh Verse," *Studia Celtica* 6 (1971), 1–11, refutes claims made by Jarman, Jackson, and Morris-Jones that *cynfeirdd* poetry exhibits features of the sixth century. Both John T. Koch ("The *Cynfeirdd* Poetry and the Language of the Sixth Century," in *Book of Aneirin*, ed. Roberts, 17–41) and A. O. H. Jarman (Preface to *Y Gododdin* [Llandysul, Gomer Press, 1990]) have rebutted, proposing further linguistic argument in favor of the earlier origins. For a detailed summary of the problems of dating the Llywarch corpus and other saga *englynion*, see Jenny Rowland, *Early Welsh Saga Poetry* (Cambridge: Boydell and Brewer, 1990), 367–89.

[Stand out, maidens, and look upon
the land of Cynddylan.
The court of Pengwern is on fire.
Alas the youths who long for a beard(?)]

5.   Kyndylan befyr bost kywlat.
      Kadwynawc kildynyawc cat.
      amucsei tren tref y dat.

                                              (1044.18–19)

[Cynddylan, bright support of the borderland,
wearing a chain, stubborn in battle.
He defended Tren, his inheritance.]

17.   Gan vyg callon i mor dru.
      kyssylltu ystyllot du. gwynn gnawt
      kyndylan kyngran canllu.

                                              (1044.42–43)

[How sad to my heart:
the union of the black planks (i.e., coffin or burnt rubble) [and?] the
    white flesh
of Cynddylan, leader of a hundred hosts.]

19.   Stavell gyndylan ystywyll heno.
      heb dan heb gannwyll
      namyn duw pwy am dyry pwyll.

                                              (1045.2–3)

[The Hall of Cynddylan is dark tonight,
without fire, without candle.
Save God, who will give me steadiness?]

21.   Stauell gyndylan ystywyll y nenn.
      gwedy gwen gyweithyd.
      gwae ny wna da aedyuyd.

                                              (1045.6–7)

[The Hall of Cynddylan, dark its roof
after the bright gathering.
Alas for him who does not do the good that may come to him.]

22.   Stavell gyndylan angwan y gwelet.
       heb doet heb dan.
       marw vyglw. buw ma hunan.

                                                    (1045.8–9)

[The Hall of Cynddylan, it wounds me to see it,
without roof, without fire;
my lord dead, myself alive.]

The above is not the entire poem, obviously. The term "poem," in fact, is problematic, as a series or "cycle" of Welsh verses may contain a number of "poems" as we understand the concept. A contemporary reader might have the impression that the order in which the stanzas proceed could be re-arranged without significant damage to the whole. This notion is belied by the fact that *englynion* are sometimes connected by a device called *cymeriad* ("concatenation"), whereby a word or phrase in the last line of an *englyn* is repeated in the first line of the next *englyn*, as in *Claf Abercuawg*:

ny at duw *da y diryeit.*

Da y dirieit ny atter.
namyn tristit a phryder.
nyt atwna duw *ar a wnel.*

Or a wneler yn derwd[y].
ys tiryeit yr ae derlly.

The device is not used with any great consistency; we have seen how the scribe himself missed this triad and inserted an extraneous verse, which merely shows how the poem, as an architectonic unit with beginning, middle, and end, seems to be largely the *englyn* itself, repeated with complex and demanding variations. Whereas a few Old English poems, *Deor* and *Wulf and Eadwacer* for instance, are divided into stanzas, in no way do they exhibit the stricture and rigidity of form that is a feature of the Welsh *englyn*, and no Welsh poetry of this early period demonstrates the continuity and flow of the Germanic epic style that we find in *Beowulf* and even in poems as short as *The Ruin*. In medieval Wales poetry did not seem to be adapted to sustained narrative. Its purpose, as far as we can tell, was to give a series of succinct vignettes. A poem was lengthened incrementally—stanzas added to stanzas—and for this reason it is difficult to cite any Welsh poem in its entirety; the *englynion* for the Cynddylan section in *The Red Book* number over a hundred. Often groups of stanzas are written in "blocks" in *The Red Book*, set off from each other by a capital, but we are still uncertain whether or not these groups of *englynion* are to be looked upon as single poems. Sometimes the added ornamentation in an *englyn* will indicate the reciter's commencement or closure, and some of the Welsh poems exhibit the Irish custom of closing a cycle of verses by repeating a word or a phrase in the opening line. Verses 2–16 of *Elegy on Cynddylan* seem to comprise a single unit, with prologue and epilogue in verses 1 and 17, and closing repetition in 12 of an opening image (*vn prenn*) in 2:

> 2.   Vn prenn [ygwydvit] a gouit arnaw
>   o dieinc ys odit.
>   ac a uynno duw derffit.
>
>   (RB: 1044.12–13)
>
> [One tree (of the woods), hardship upon it.
> If it escapes, it is a rarity.
> What God wishes, may it happen.]

> 16.   Kyndylan kae di y nenn.
>   yny daw lloegyrwys drwy dren.
>   ny elwir coet o vn prenn.
>
>   (1044.40–41)
>
> [Cynddylan, protect the breach
> where the Englishmen come through Tren.
> One tree is not called a woods.]

Consider also verse 21 from *Llym Awel* in *The Black Book* with its pyrotechnic display of alliteration, assonance, and consonance:

> Bronureith breith bron.
> breith bron bronureith.
> briuhid tal glan gan garu carw culgrwm cam.
> goruchel awel gwaetvann.
> breit gwir orseuir allan.

This verse seems to be a closing one, especially as it echoes phrases in one of the opening verses noted for its equally elaborate alliteration (*Tonn tra thon toit tu tir*). Nevertheless, discussion of the division of sections into individual poems, as well as the organization of verses within such poems, is ongoing and controversial.[7] In recording these perhaps aural experiences and transmitting them into visual artifacts, the scribes undoubtedly introduced confusions that we are still grappling with, and this act of "translation" should be kept in mind.

The origins of the *englyn* are obscure. Latin and Irish influences have been suggested, as has indigenous development.[8] It may have its origin in the *awdl* ("song," "ode," "stanza"), a fairly general term given to a poem that employs "the same rhyme throughout, or a long poem containing a series of connected poems, having a single rhyme throughout each of the same."[9] *The Gododdin* consists of a number of *awdlau*, which vary in length from about six to thirty lines and for the most part exhibit *unodl*, or one terminal rhyme—as with "-an" in the following example:

> Kaeawc kynhorawc bleid e maran.
> gwevrawr go/diwawr torchawr am rann.
> bu gwervrawr gwerthvawr gwerth gwin vann.
> ef gwrthodes gwrys gwar dis grein.
> ket dyffei wyned a gogled e rann.
> o gussyl mab ysgyrran
> ysgwydawr angkyuan.[10]

In *The Book of Taliesin* we find longish poems of various metrical styles.[11] *Preideu Annwn* is divided into *awdlau*, which function rather like stanzas, exhibiting a unifying refrain that marks them as members of the same long poem. *Angar Kyfyndawt*, however, consists of relatively short lines that maintain a rhyme for three or four lines before introducing a new rhyme. Kathryn Klar, Brendan O Hehir, and Eve Sweetser coined the term *rhannau* ("parts") for such sections of rhyme within the *gwarchanau* of *Canu Aneirin*, propos-

---

7. Ifor Williams's divisions and titles in CLIH have been generally taken as standard. Patrick Ford offers an alternative means of division in PLIH, and he omits formal titles. Rowland retains most of Williams's titles but presents the poems in a different role in EWSP, 404–67.

8. For a lucid summation of these arguments, see Rowland, EWSP, 305–8.

9. *Geiriadur Prifysgol Cymru* (Caerdydd: Gwasg Prifysgol Cymru, 1950), 1:239.

10. *Canu Aneirin* no. iv, ed. Ifor Williams, (Caerdydd: Gwasg Prifysgol Cymru, 1938), p. 2.

11. For a discussion of Taliesin's metrics, see Marged Haycock, "Metrical Models for the Poems in the *Book of Taliesin*," in *Studies in The Book of Aneirin*, ed. Roberts, 155–78; also her dissertation, *Llyfr Taliesin: Astudiaethau ar rai agweddau* (Aberystwyth, 1983), 524–85.

ing that the *englyn* may have been a highly technical development of a certain type of *rhan*.[12]

The *englyn* as we know it in *Canu Llywarch Hen* and *Elegy on Cynddylan* is characterized by three lines with end rhyme. In brief, there are two main kinds of *englyn* among the *cynfeirdd*: *englyn milwr* and *englyn penfyr*.[13] The former is the more common; in it, each line has seven syllables, or thereabouts, and a consistent end rhyme, as we can see from *Elegy on Cynddylan*:

> 5.   kyndylan befyr bost kywlat.   (8)
>   kadwynawc kildynnyawc cat.   (7)
>   amucsei tren tref y dat.   (7)
>   (RB: 1044.18–19)

Compare this stanza to the following *englyn penfyr*, which has a long first line of ten syllables, a second line of five or six syllables, and a final line of seven syllables:

> 18.   Stauell gyndylan ys tywell heno   (10)
>   heb dan heb wely.   (5)
>   wylaf wers. tawaf wedy.   (7)
>   (1044.44–1045.1)

Here, now, is what looks like *englyn milwr*, but with a variation:

> 17.   gan byg callon i mor dru.   (7)
>   kyssylltu ystyllot du.   gwyn gnawt   (9)
>   kyndyllan kyngran canllu.   (7)
>   (1049.38–39)

Were we to discard the final two words in the second line we would have a perfect *englyn milwr*, seven syllables per line with end rhyme on "-*u*." The additional two syllables are what is known as the *gair cyrch*, or supplemental foot. Ordinarily the *gair cyrch* occurs in the first line of an *englyn penfyr*, and

---

12. (Klar, O Hehir, and Sweetser, in "Welsh Poetics." See also Eve Sweetser, "Line Structure and *Rhan*-Structure: The Metrical Units of the *Gododdin* Corpus," in *Studies in the Book of Aneirin*, ed. Roberts, 139–54.

13. The respected authority on *cynfeirdd* metrics is John Morris-Jones's *Cerdd Dafod*; for the most minutely thorough discussion of the *englyn* and its various ornamentations, see Rowland, *EWSP*, 305–55.

its ultimate syllable must rhyme with the second or third syllable of the
following line:

21. Stauell gyndylan ys tywyll y *nenn.*
     gwedy *gwen* gyweithyd.
     gwae ny wna da aedyuyd.
                            (1045.6–7)

27. Stauell gyndylyn amgwan y gwe*let.*
     heb do*et* heb dan.
     marw vyglyw. buw ma hunan.
                            (1045.8–9)

Rhyme is an important and complicated factor in Welsh poetry. Not only
is terminal rhyme a fixed requirement, there are quite often multiple internal
rhymes within the line as well:

marw vyglyw buw ma hunan
gwae ny wna da aedywyd . . .

kyssylltu ystyllot du
kyndyl*an* kyn*gran can*llu.
     (stanza 17, 1044.42–43)

These last two lines illustrate another perhaps less obvious but no less effec-
tive feature of Welsh poetry: the superb sense of the Welsh poets for asso-
nance. Not only syllables, but vowels rhyme in intricate ways, and frequently
high and low vowels are contrasted. When isolated, the vowels in the entire
stanza 17 create their own distinctive rhythm:

Gan vyg callon i mor dru.
Kyssylltu ystyllot du. gwyn gnawt
kyndylan kyngran canllu.

[a] [ʌ] [a] [o] [i] [ɔ] [i]
[ʌ] [ʌ] [i] [ʌ] [ʌ] [o] [i]   [I] [aU]
[I] [I] [a] [I] [a] [a] [i]

Skaldic poetry features stanzas very similar to those found in Celtic poetry,
and because Skaldic poems also exhibit patterns of consonance, internal

rhyme, and end rhyme, we might consider the possibility of some exchange between the Irish and the Scandinavians. I cannot hope to go beyond the most superficial observations in this matter. We might, however, speculate about the effect that a discrete or a continuous form may exert on the connection of ideas in the text.

The obvious difference, of course, is that a stanzaic structure such as the *englyn* requires that utterances be compressed within the boundaries of the stanza, whereas Old English has allowed itself room to expand an utterance indefinitely by having shorter, less complicated poetic units. The Welsh *englyn* is a highly technical and mannered development in this period, showing a predilection among the Welsh for patterns and embellishment, instead of the narrative devices employed in Old English poems. If we look ahead to the *gogynfeirdd* and the *cywyddwyr*, we see how the poetic structures of the earlier Welsh poets were already anticipating the *cynghannedd* patterns employed later, whereby alliteration, rhyme, and consonance were used in highly artful and rigid combinations. Because of the demanding metrical and phonic requirements of the poem, liberties were taken by the "not-so-early bards" with quotidian Welsh syntax, and for this reason their poems enjoy a notoriety not generally extended to the "early bards." It would be safe to say, then, that the general movement of medieval Welsh poetry until the end of the thirteenth century was toward an increasingly greater degree of artificiality.

The Continuous Style

Within the small corpus of Old English poems, styles differ considerably, but stanzaic structure is notably rare. *Deor* and *Wulf and Eadwacer* exhibit stanzas of a sort marked off by a refrain, which have moved some scholars to suggest Scandinavian or Celtic influence.[14] The proliferating form, however, is the "continuous" narrative style; Old English seems especially adapted to telling stories: *Beowulf, Elene, Juliana, Andreas, Guthlac, The Battle of Maldon*. Old English poetic form gives itself room to expand an utterance indefinitely—the type of verse that Eduard Sievers calls "stichic."[15] That Old English is unflaggingly stichic has been challenged recently by scholars who argue for a Carolin-

---

14. W. W. Lawrence, "The First Riddle of Cynewulf," PMLA 17 (1902), 247.

15. Eduard Sievers, "Old Germanic Metrics and Old English Metrics," in *Essential Articles on Old English Poetry*, ed. Jess B. Bessinger, Jr., and Stanley J. Kahrl (Hamden, Conn.: Archon Books, 1968), 267.

gian aesthetic of modularity, linearity, and decoration; and in the case of Old English poetry it has been argued that it is far more deliberately disjunct than it has appeared to be to those of us who think of it as "rolling, recitative."[16] Certainly, Old English has stylistic breaks that mark off sections of verse; but by the same token, a poem containing distinct sections or stanzas can have narrative continuity—as *The Song of Roland* and the English ballads amply demonstrate. All that a stanza really does is put phonetic boundaries around a section of utterance and discourage continuation into the next marked section, thereby making it natural to begin a new "paragraph" with the next stanza. It should be stressed, too, that our contemporary notions of stanzas, paragraphs, lines, and enjambment are vigorously influenced by visual standards that, since the invention of cheaper printing materials than parchment, have given us the spaces throughout and around the poem, very often without affecting the way it is to be recited. Very often, too, editors' decisions to punctuate medieval poems, to decide where sentences end and begin, are made from a predominantly visual (read "logical") sense of grammar. We have no records of scops reciting their poems. They may very well have used cadence and rhythm and silences to indicate gaps that are not visible on parchment.

The only clue we have that Welsh has a stanzaic system at all is the way it sounds. Rhyme, meter, anaphora, and other repetitions tell us that a section is a discrete unit; punctuation in the medieval manuscripts is notoriously unhelpful. Sometimes the Welsh scribe marks the beginning of an *englyn* with a capital, and the custom seems to have been to mark the ends of phrases with a *punctum*. This device is not reliable, for we often find *puncti* in the middle of a phrase, perhaps to indicate a *diaeresis*. If the Welsh lyric is over-punctuated, though, the Old English elegy is under-punctuated, making it doubly difficult to find textual evidence of dividing points in the poetry.[17] In

---

16. See Carol Braun Pasternack, "Stylistic Disjunctions in *The Dream of the Rood*," *Anglo-Saxon England* 13 (1984), 167–86. See also Peter R. Schroeder, "Stylistic Analogies Between Old English Art and Poetry," *Viator* 5 (1974), 195–97; and Charles W. Jones, "Carolingian Aesthetics: Why Modular Verse?" *Viator* 6 (1975), 309–40. W. P. Ker (*The Dark Ages* [Chicago: Charles Scribner's Sons, 1911], 233–34) wrote: "The Old English type agrees in much of its grammar and rhetoric with the practice of blank verse. It makes paragraphs where the sentences are distributed unequally, and where rhetorical swell and cadence are freely varied. The Icelandic type . . . , more emphatic and formal, is not adapted for the long, rolling recitative of the other school; it is quicker, more alert, more pointed."

17. In her chapter "Reading and Pointing in the Major Poetic Codices," Katherine O'Brien O'Keefe comments on the use of pointing in the *ne*-constructions of *The Wanderer* and *The Seafarer*, and remarks that the amount of pointing differs from poem to poem within the Exeter MS (*Visible Song: Transitional Literacy in Old English Verse* [Cambridge: Cambridge University Press, 1990], 158–60.)

Deor, each stanza begins with a capital, but it is of the same kind used to mark the beginnings of individual poems. The unclear function of the initial capital has inspired some debate about the relationship of *The Husband's Message* to the riddle that precedes it.[18] Interestingly, the "sections" of *Wulf and Eadwacer* are unmarked.

Therefore, Pilch's suggestion that the reputed use of enjambment in Old English elegies is due to deliberate borrowing from the Welsh[19] tumbles into the same visual fallacy that results when one views Old English poetry as contemporary conventions print it: a single numbered line with a caesura in the middle. In truth, we don't really know exactly where in either the Old English or the Welsh we are to begin a new line. Presumably, Welsh lines end in a rhyme; Old English lines end with a completed alliterative unit. This unit is, in effect, a couplet of two-stressed lines. Sentences frequently begin in the *b*-verse of the line indicating that the focal unit to the Old English poet was the half-line, not the line. The liberties that Old English poets felt they could take with such half-lines is demonstrated by the hypermetric lines, and the extra (or missing?) half-lines.

Narrative and Lyric

My distinction, then, rests not so much on the division of poetry into sections as it does on the logical relationships presented which may be affected by divisions. Joseph P. Clancy makes a distinction between "associative" and "logical sequence" in his description of Welsh poetry;[20] J. Caerwyn Williams sees both types of poetry (narrative and declarative) as following a kind of logic, the one "sequential," the other "associative."[21] For both scholars the difference seems to be that in the one type of poetry the connections are pointed out, and in the other assumed or implied—a shadow, perhaps, of Kristeva's more complex "symbolic" and "semiotic."

In a traditional narrative, the unfolding of events in time presents us with a built-in sequential logic: first A, then B, then C happened. Despite the many

18. For a summary of this discussion, see Craig Williamson, *The Old English Riddles of the Exeter Book* (Chapel Hill: University of North Carolina Press, 1977), 315.

19. "The Elegiac Genre in Old English and Early Welsh Poetry," *Zeitschrift für celtische Philologie* 29 (1964), 221.

20. *Medieval Welsh Lyrics* (New York: St. Martin's Press, 1965), 9.

21. J. E. Caerwyn Williams, *Poets of the Welsh Princes*, 55.

literary variations on this structure (the flashback, beginning *in medias res*, the frame tale, and so on), traditional narrative depends on some kind of chronology to be effective as a story. Lyrical or declarative literature is not so dependent on a sequential logic, for it often serves to voice ideas that its audience already shares, and in this group I put eulogy, elegy, praise, and all those poems which serve to confirm or declare a society's emotional or aesthetic inclination. Associative logic can be used very effectively in this category because the denotative meanings of words and phrases are less important than their connotative meanings—what shared associations they call up in hearers (and readers), what aesthetic reactions they inspire.

This is not to say that narrative or declarative types of poetry never overlap, or that their distinctions are as simple as I may have suggested. Certainly, many narratives contain eulogy, elegy, and praise, and very often they do not have the function of "informing" an audience which has heard the story they tell time and again, just as lyrical or elegiac poetry can have elements of the sententious and the didactic. Nevertheless, the degree to which the Old English "elegies" narrate or argue is of crucial concern. Saunders Lewis offers a brilliant explanation for the logic of Welsh praise poetry where words have musical value within a line of *gogynfeirdd* poetry depending on their *aura* (contextual associations), and their sound. Poetry is for the ear, prose is for the intellect, he argues, and if one tries to translate one into the other, one "sets upon it the logical fetters that are not natural to it."[22]

Grammatical Disjunctions

The conjunction in Old English poetry has been hotly contested, given the strong prescriptive tendencies of earlier grammarians. Literary theorists have occasionally spoken of poetry as doing "violence" to language by defying its logical fetters. Acts of translation, especially those that seek to turn poetry back into the discourse of prose by filling in its gaps, wreak a similar violence: meaning is not easily separated from form.

In the Welsh texts, the disjunction and sense of association are heightened by the repetitive features of the *englynion*. Argument does not progress

---

22. Saunders Lewis, "Beirdd y Tywysogion," in *Braslun o Hanes Llenyddiaeth Gymraeg* (Caerdydd: Gwasg Prifysgol Cymru, 1932), 1:27, quoting M. Vendryès on the *gogynfeirdd* (*La poésie galloise des XIIe et XIIIe siècles dans ses rapports avec la langue* [Oxford: Clarendon Press, 1930]).

through different stages, but is restated like a "variation on a theme," and its lyrical qualities are marked.[23] In medieval Wales, poetry was known as *cerdd dafod*, "tongue craft," and distinguished from other types of craft such as that produced by stringed instruments—*cerdd dant*. With most of our ancient forms of poetry it is unclear whether they were recited or sung.

Old English poetry tends toward the argumentative and sequential. We should not deny its possible origins within a tradition of song,[24] and it is certainly not without its poetic strictures. Like Welsh, its framework is based on the unit: a half-line of paired stresses. Paired half-lines give us our familiar Old English line with caesura and linking alliteration:

> Wrætlic is þes wealstan / / wyrde gebræcon
> burgstede burston / / brosnað entageweorc
> *(The Ruin, EB2: 1–2)*

We might look upon the alliterative "couplet" as the basic building block of Old English verse, where the presence of a caesura creates a kind of parataxis superficially similar to the juxtapositive nature of the Welsh *englyn*. As we have seen in the Heledd and Llywarch Hen verses, statements stand next to each other like dominoes; the diction of connection or subordination is missing:

> The Hall of Cynddylan is dark tonight,
> without fire, without bed.
> I shall weep awhile; I shall be silent after.

In the "Hearth Stanzas" from Llywarch's *Elegy on Urien Rheged*, the contrast between past and present is effectively expressed by this parataxis and incremental repetition:[25]

> Yr aelwyt honn neuscud glessin.
> ym myw owein ac elphin.
> berwassei y pheir breiddin.
> (RB: 1041.20–21)

---

23. Idris Bell, *The Development of Welsh Poetry* (Oxford: Clarendon Press, 1936), 5.

24. See especially Sievers, "Old Germanic Metrics," 267–68, and Watkins, "Indo-European Metrics," 214.

25. Kenneth Jackson, "Incremental Repetition in the Early Welsh *Englyn*," *Speculum* 16 (1941), 309.

[This hearth, turf conceals it.
When Owain and Elphin were living
its cauldron boiled booty.]

    Yr aelwyt honn neuscud kallawydyr llwyt.
    mwy gordyfnassei am y bwyt.
    cledyfual dyual diarswyt.
                    (1041:22–23)

[This hearth, gray moss conceals it.
It was more accustomed to fierce and
fearless swordplay about its food.]

The similarities between these stanzas and *The Ruin* have not gone un-
noticed.[26] The Old English poem provides us with a fitting analogue, as it too
makes the contrast between past glory and present decay its major poetic
feature:

    Wrætlic is þæs wealstaon   wyrde gebræcon
    burgstede· burston   brosnað enta geweorc
    hrofas sind gehrorene   hreorge torras
    hr[un]geat berofen   hrim on lime
    scearde scurbeorge   scorene gedrorene
    ældo undereotone   eorðgrap hafað
    waldendwyrhtan   forweorone geleorene
    heard gripe hrusan   oþ hund cnea
    werþeoda gewitan
                    (1–9)

[Wondrous is this wallstone   by fate broken,
city buildings shattered, decays the work of giants,
roofs are fallen,   ruinous towers,
barred gates plundered,   frost on stone,
sheared shower-town   shorn, fallen,
by age undermined,   earth's grip holds
the masterbuilders,   perished, passed away
by the hard grip of the ground   until a hundred generations
of people depart.]

26. John Josias Conybeare, *Illustrations of Anglo-Saxon Poetry*, ed. William D. Conybeare
(London: Harding and Lepard, 1826), 250–51.

It is also a grammatically "simple" poem in comparison with some other Old English poems in confining many of its statements to the half-line, a feature that brings us to a discussion of parataxis.

Parataxis

The paratactic style of much Old English narrative has inspired furious linguistic and stylistic analysis.[27] Generally defined as the juxtaposition of related grammatical elements without the coordinating or subordinating conjunctions found with hypotaxis,[28] it has given rise to a number of variant terms: *asyndeton* is a construction wherein a coordinating element is missing that would normally be there (sometimes called asyndetic coordination) as in the famous example from *Beowulf: he þe æt sunde oferflat, hæfde mare mægen* ("he overcame you in the sea; he had more strength," lines 517b–18a).[29] *Adversative asyndeton* juxtaposes two contrasting statements without benefit of an adversative conjunction:

> Sund is geblonden
> grund wiþ greote;   God eade mæg
> headoliþendum   helpe gefremman.
> (*Andreas*, VB: 424b–26)[30]

> [Sea is stirred up,
> deep with grit. (But) easily may God
> to sailors send help.]

Roy F. Leslie has commented in his edition that "the *Ruin*-poet has a penchant for asyndetic parataxis,"[31] where the coordinating conjunction has

27. For a thorough discussion and bibliographical citation, see Bruce Mitchell, "Parataxis and the Multiple Sentence" in *Old English Syntax* (Oxford: Clarendon Press, 1985), 693–767.

28. Following E. P. Morris's definition, W. P. Shepard writes that parataxis is "any form of sentence structure in which two finite verbs are brought into close connection without a subordinating word to define their relation." "Parataxis in Provençal," PMLA 21 (1906), 520.

29. *Beowulf*, ed. Fr. Klaeber (Lexington: D. C. Heath, 1950), 20. Further references to *Beowulf* are to this edition.

30. Claes Schaar, *Critical Studies in the Cynewulf Group* (Lund: Haken Ohlssons Boktryckeri, 1949), 176.

31. *Three Old English Elegies: The Wife's Lament, The Husband's Message, The Ruin* (Manchester: Manchester University Press, 1961), 70.

been repeatedly omitted, and elsewhere in the poem the process of excision is marked, the diction of relationship tightened up and stylized in a manner reminiscent of the Welsh. The copula, for instance, is often dropped out or made to serve double duty in another form of juxtaposition that requires the omission of a linking element; this is known to medieval grammarians as *zeugma*:

> hrofas sind gehrorene   hreorge [sind] torras
> hrungeat [sind] berofen   hrim [is] on lime
> scearde scurbeorge   [is] scorene [ond] gedrorene
> (*Ruin*, lines EB2: 3–5)

> eald is þes eordsele   eal ic eom oflongad·
> sindon dena dimme   duna uphea
> bitre burgtunas   brerum beweaxne
> wic wynna leas . . .
> (*Wife's Lament*, EB2: 29–32ᵃ)

While it cannot really be equated with this technique of gapping in parallel elements, the Welsh use of nominal sentences with zero-copula superficially resembles the *zeugma* of the Old English:

> Kintevin keinhaw amsser
> dyar adar glas callet.
> Ereidir in rich. ich iguet.
> Guirt mor brithottor tiret.
>
> [Maytime fairest season.
> Birds loud, trees green.
> Ploughs in furrow, ox in yoke.
> Sea green, fields dappled.][32]

Some important distinctions need to be made here; namely, whether we are observing a desired stylistic effect or whether these structures result from normal grammatical means of expressing connection. If the former, we should consider whether this apparent "tightening" is meant to accommodate the mechanical requirements of the poetic form. In so doing, we fall back

32. From *Llyfyr Du Caerfyrddin*, ed. A. O. H. Jarman and E. D. Jones (Caerdydd: Gwasg Prifysgol Cymru, 1982), 15.

into "anglocentric" expectations: explicitness, "gaplessness," is the norm, merely violated by language anomalies like poetry. In Middle Welsh, zero-copula structures are common in prose: *a chorn canu am y uynwgyl, a gwisc o urethyn llwytlei amdanaw yn wisc hela* ["And a hunting horn about his neck, and a garment of fawn-colored material about him as hunting garb"].[33] In most discussions of Anglo-Saxon parataxis it is assumed that the juxtaposed statements have a causal or adversative link, which would require that we add something in translation. For instance, S. O. Andrew suggests that much of what we call "parataxis" in Old English is actually a grammatical norm that has become an idiomatic means of expressing coordination in Old English.[34] Paratactic sentences introduced by *wold, wende,* and *cwæd* are equivalent to adverbial clauses of reason or purpose, he writes:

> Heo eode of ðam stæðum to ðam halgan cyðere, wolde heo gebiddan.
>
> "She went from the steps to the holy martyr in order to pray."[35]

As in Old English, hypotactic constructions in Middle Welsh clearly develop from juxtapositions. The affirmative particle that precedes verbs is also used to introduce noun clauses and improper relatives: *y brenhin y kiglef y glot a'e volyant* ["The king, I have heard of his fame and renown," i.e., "The king of whose fame and renown I have heard"].[36] Examining the Cynewulf poems,[37] Claes Schaar is particularly interested in "the extent of which logical relations between sentences get their formal expression. We must not underestimate the difference between a style in which this extent is great, and a style in which it is inconsiderable," he writes.[38] It seems to be inconsiderable in the Welsh:

> Crutch of wood, this is winter.
> Men will be talkative over drink.
> Inhospitable my bedside.

33. *Pwyll Pendeuic Dyuet*, ed. R. L. Thomson (Dublin: Institute for Advanced Studies, 1957), 1.
34. S. O. Andrew, *Syntax and Style in Old English* (Cambridge: Cambridge University Press, 1940), 72.
35. Ibid., 87–88.
36. Example given in *A Grammar of Middle Welsh*, D. Simon Evans (Dublin: Institute for Advanced Studies, 1976), 65.
37. *Critical Studies*, 153–372.
38. Ibid., 143.

In the Welsh the repetition calls attention to the adversative asyndeton, and the *englyn* structure seems to supply what we might require of a conjunction. Because Old English poetry is without such a distinct signaling framework, its use of similar juxtapositions is confusing to readers expecting more syndesis. Schaar looks upon this kind of connection as clumsy, and he makes efforts to illustrate the *Andreas*-poet's basic lack of refinement by noting the high incidence of adversative asyndeton.[39] Neither is the *Andreas*-poet very good at hypotactic constructions, Schaar concludes. *Essential hypotaxis* is a term he gives to a construction found most frequently in *Andreas*; he defines it as "the introduction of an episode, vital to the plot, in a subordinate clause."[40] Presumably the *Andreas*-poet diminishes the dramatic power of his narrative when an asyndetic or paratactic construction would have been more effective: having been made invisible to the heathens, Andreas suddenly reappears, and they seize him. The detail of his visibility, however, is left to be mentioned after the fact:

> Æfter þam wordum com   werod unmæte,
> lyswe larsmeoðas   mid lindgecrode,
> bolgenmode;   bæron ut hræde
> ond þam halgan þær   handa gebundon.
> Siþþan geyþþed wæs   æþelinga wynn,
> ond hie andweardne   eagum meahton
> gesion sigerofne . . .
>
> (VB: 1219–25)[41]

[After these words came an immeasurable crowd,
false teachers with a shield troop,
angry hearted, (they) bore him out quickly
and there bound the hands of the holy one
after the best of noblemen was revealed to them
and they might with their own eyes
see the brave one in their midst.][42]

39. Ibid., 183–84, 325: "The result of our analysis of adversative asyndeton testifies to some inability to differentiate divergent matter on the part of the *Andreas* and the *Guthlac* A poets." Schaar notes that adversative asyndeton most often occurs in "passages of marked vividness and emotion" (175).

40. Ibid., 154.

41. Ibid., 162–63.

42. George Philip Krapp has "emended" the sense of the passage by putting a semicolon after *gebunden* in line 1222 and starting a new sentence with *siþþon* (which he construes adverbially) in

Schaar concludes that "an examination of causal parataxis demonstrates various degrees of logical sensitivity in the poets, the lowest degree being represented by the authors of *Andreas* and *Guthlac* A."[43] He shows a decided aesthetic preference for poetry with a high degree of syndesis, and his notion that poetic style evolves from the "primitive" paratactic construction to the more "sophisticated" hypotactic one has come under attack by Alarik Rynell.[44] Schaar's theory is that poetry can be dated according to the use it makes of parataxis or hypotaxis,[45] and while he is not the first to argue that hypotaxis develops from parataxis in the English language in general,[46] his notions about the evolution of poetic style seem simplistic to Rynell, who expresses skepticism that the mere addition of a formal grammatical feature such as a conjunction has [the] power to change a relationship.[47] Rynell differentiates between "loose" and "close" relationships, which are determined by psychological rather than formal factors, and he notes the possibility that there may be means of expressing relationship that are not grammatical or syntactical, such as "musical or phonetic means."[48] Indeed, the psychological factor in "close" and "loose" relationships might contribute to our sense that "wide the wave, withered the heart with longing" has the quality of parataxis, whereas "men will be talkative over drink, inhospitable is my bedside" is a more enigmatic connection. Both are "paratactic" in the purest sense: insubordinate, both set two ideas next to each other without explanation. Rynell concludes his study by taking issue with Schaar's assumption that parataxis is a more primitive form than hypotaxis, which is generally "more natural to poetry" and "particularly so at a time when poetry was largely founded on oral tradition and intended for oral delivery."[49] This issue I shall take up presently, after a brief discussion of explicitness.

---

the following line: "They bore him out quickly, and there bound the hands of the holy one. Then the best of noblemen was revealed to him." In this way, the heathens have presumably been wrestling with an invisible man who appears to them after they've bound him. Schaar objects that not even the *Andreas*-poet could have committed such a glaring "hysteron proteron" (58).

43. Schaar, *Cyneulf Group*, 325.
44. *Parataxis and Hypotaxis as a Criterion of Syntax and Style, Especially in Old English Poetry* (Lund: C.W.K. Gleerup, 1952).
45. Schaar, *Cynewulf Group*, 172.
46. See George W. Small, in *The Comparison of Inequality* (Baltimore: 1924), 125: "It may be laid down as a general principle that in the progress of language parataxis precedes hypotaxis."
47. Ibid., 3–6.
48. Ibid., 4, 9.
49. Ibid., 47.

The Later Grammarians

The definition of the sentence has been a source of polemic for centuries. Aristotle, Boethius, and Abelard grappled mightily with the subject.[50] In keeping with these earlier scholars, later prescriptive grammarians have stated that a subordinate clause cannot be a sentence because its structure indicates that a complete thought has not been expressed.[51] Noam Chomsky has stated that a sentence is "a finite sequence of phonemes."[52] There has been a certain congruence over the centuries, but just what do we mean by a "complete thought"? What we often call "hypotaxis" in Old English is simply the insertion of one word—*ac, forþon, þeah*—between sequences of phonemes that would be "finite" without it. The difference occurs in what transformational grammarians have termed the "surface structure" of the utterance.[53]

We get into a real linguistic snarl as soon as we raise the subject of "explicitness." The term evades definition, for concepts of explicitness vary from language to language. If we are to accept Chomsky's original premise about an abstract semantic level and a concrete phonetic level, we might attempt to define "explicitness" as a condition whereby every nuance of the idea in the deep structure finds full semantic expression in the surface structure. This task reminds me of Abelard's "infinite" sentence, the one wherein "no statement is linguistically or meaningfully complete while anything which can contribute to the sense remains unsaid."[54] Chomsky offers a definition in his explanation

---

50. *De Interpretatione*, by Aristotle, with translation and commentary by Boethius in *Peri Ermeneias*, ed. C. Meiser (Leipzig: Teubner, 1880); Abelard, *The Dialectica* 68.34–69, ed. L. M. de Rijk (Assen: Van Gorcum, 1970).

51. L. Ben Crane et al., *An Introduction to Linguistics* (Boston: Little, Brown, 1981), 103.

52. Noam Chomsky, *Syntactic Structures* (The Hague: Mouton, 1957), 2.

53. The notion of deep structure and surface structure was originally devised by Chomsky as an alternative to the traditional structuralist view of grammar, which dealt primarily with sentence patterns rather than semantics, with the results of an utterance rather than with the speaker's ability to generate new utterances out of a basic set of rules. Acknowledging his debt to Ferdinand Saussure's distinction between *parole* and *langue*, Chomsky redefines the latter concept as the "universal" or "generative" grammar that lies at the basis of every particular utterance (*Aspects of the Theory of Syntax* [Cambridge: MIT Press, 1965], 16). The intention or the idea behind the utterance is an abstraction that he calls the Deep Structure. The actual utterance is the Surface Structure. The first determines the semantic content of an utterance, the second its phonetic content. Thus, the generation of grammatical utterances involves a series of "transformations" which mediate between the two, changing the semantic level into phonetic terms. In his efforts to dispel our prejudices about the simple nature of Old English syntax, S.O. Andrew is in fact concerned with this very dynamic.

54. Brian Stock, *The Implications of Literacy: Written Language and Models of Interpretation in the Eleventh and the Twelfth Centuries* (Princeton: Princeton University Press, 1983), 376, paraphras-

of "generative grammar": a grammar that is "perfectly explicit" is one that "does not rely on the intelligence of the understanding reader but rather provides an explicit analysis of his contribution."[55] This explanation suggests that the reader's contribution to the text requires the least effort possible as the level of explanation in the text becomes more perfectly congruent with her expectations. It opens up obvious theoretical problems pertinent to my own study. Deconstructive theory has had serious impact on literary and linguistic analysis in its distrust of the notion that language is simply a mirror, a glassy vehicle of some deep structure of meaning which grows more visible as the vehicle becomes more transparent, or that there can be anything approaching a perfect congruence between text and reader. Both reception and reader-response theory posit that text and reader/hearer provide a symbiotic relationship whereby "meaning" is never perfectly fixed in either the utterance or the hearer of the utterance but that acts of interpretation work to establish one's conception of the text as much as the text does on its own.[56]

With good reason, generative grammarians have questioned the original premises made about deep and surface structure. No one sentence can really be analyzed in isolation; sentences function properly only in context with other sentences and with a hearer, an issue which has been taken up with fervor by students of the philosophy of language.[57] The nature of poetry

---

ing Abelard on "oratio," in the *Dialectica*, 68.34–39. My quotation is taken somewhat out of context: Abelard is arguing that hearers will not know when a verbal statement is complete until it has come to an end. It is only at the end, then, that meaning arises in a meaningful utterance, and it is dependent upon the memory and reason of the hearer. Abelard's thought, Stock claims, "takes him in the direction of a distinction similar to that between *parole* and *langue*." In one sense, he argues, the meaning is not established until the last instant of utterance (*in ultimo puncto prolationis*). Yet the parts of the discourse which do not physically exist at a given instance do not on that account lack potential significance. Meaning, it would appear, arises equally from that which exists in spoken sound and from that which does not" (*Implications*, p. 375). If we put these notions together, we come up with the almost Borgesian notion of an utterance that can never be rendered completely explicit. Explicitness, in Abelard's terms, would require an unending sentence.

55. *Aspects of the Theory of Syntax*, 4.

56. Wolfgang Iser, *The Act of Reading: A Theory of Aesthetic Response* (Baltimore: Johns Hopkins University Press, 1980), 107: "Textual Models designate only one aspect of the communicatory process. Hence, textual repertoires and strategies simply offer a frame within which the reader must construct for himself the aesthetic object. Textual structures and structured acts of comprehension are therefore the two poles in the act of communication, whose success will depend on the degree in which the text will establish itself as a correlative in the reader's consciousness."

57. J. L. Austin gives us the notion of the "speech act" and examines the effect of intention and result in *How to Do Things with Words: The William James Lectures Delivered at Harvard University*, 2d ed., ed. J. O. Urmson and Marina Sbisà (New York: Oxford University Press, 1975); John Searle extends his analysis in *Speech Acts: An Essay in the Philosophy of Language* (Cambridge: Cambridge University Press, 1969). Others have applied discourse analysis and pragmatics to the study of

imposes special limitations on discourse. Attempts on the part of earlier Old English scholars to dispel the "oddness" of Old English poetry by translating paratactic phrases into acceptable hypotactic constructions lose sight (or should I say "sound"?) of the poetic texture of Old English.

Scholarship in the aesthetics of medieval art has done a great deal to shed some of these Aristotelian biases by locating the linear, modular, and disjunct nature of medieval narrative in a preoccupation with number and accretion as opposed to organic imitation.[58] And the recent discussions of the New Philology as it applies to medieval texts stress the prominence in medieval experience of the "voice" along with the variant nature of the "text."[59] There is an area of study that calls for fuller examination before this discussion of the differences between the Early Welsh and the Old English poem can continue—the polemic over the formula.

Oral Formula and The Orality and Literacy Debates

It may be assumed that close adherence to traditional prosodic and metric requirements adapted over centuries to aid oral recitation will in many cases govern the expression of grammatical relationship; in fact, such a system appears to lend itself naturally to juxtaposition and paratactic construction. The search for the oral formula as an end in itself has fallen out of favor in current critical interest, but mention of its many-faceted applications and their contribution to an understanding of medieval texts is relevant here.

---

literature and poetic style. See in particular Mary Louise Pratt, *Toward a Speech Act Theory of Literary Discourse* (Bloomington: Indiana University Press, 1977); Teun A. van Dijk, "Pragmatics and Poetics," in *Pragmatics of Language and Literature*, ed. Teun A. van Dijk (New York: North-Holland, 1976), 23–58; R. A. York, *The Poem as Utterance* (New York: Methuen, 1986); Raymond Chapman, *Linguistics and Literature: An Introduction to Literary Stylistics* (London: Edward Arnold, 1973); also Dan Sperber and Deirdre Wilson, especially chapter 4, in *Relevance: Communication and Cognition* (Cambridge: Harvard University Press, 1986).

58. Eric Auerbach, "The Arrest of Peter Valvomares," in *Mimesis: The Representation of Reality in Western Literature*, trans. Willard R. Trask (Princeton: Princeton University Press, 1945, 1974); Ernst Curtius, "Numerical Composition," in *European Literature and the Latin Middle Ages*, trans. Willard R. Trask (Princeton: Princeton University Press, 1953, 1973), 501–9; and Charles W. Jones, "Carolingian Aesthetics," 309–40.

59. See the January 1990 issue of *Speculum* (65.1) for articles by Stephen G. Nichols, "Philology in a Manuscript Culture," 1–10; Siegfried Wenzel, "Reflections on (New) Philology," 11–18; Suzanne Fleishman, "Philology, Linguistics, and the Discourse of the Medieval Text," 19–37; R. Howard Bloch, "New Philology and Old French," 38–58. See also Paul Zumthor, "The Text and the Voice," *New Literary History* 16.1 (1984), 67–92.

Though the issue of "Homeric unity" is still controversial, scholars have long suggested that *The Iliad* and *The Odyssey* were the result of the collected redactions and interpolations of editors of varying ability; in this way they could account for the "lapses" attributed to the legendary Homer. Even though the stylistic devices in Greek poetry had come to be recognized as metrical aids, the assumption was that a poem and its style were the result of the moment: a synchronic phenomenon. The poem was composed at a certain point in time and its text was fixed. Milman Parry challenged this assumption in 1923, and the ensuing theory of the oral formula, which was to become a popular and polemical branch of Anglo-Saxon studies for the next fifty years, postulates the stylistic development of a familiar poem over generations. It is a diachronic phenomenon, without fixed text or single author. This theory served to move the unquestioned emphasis on writing to an emphasis on declaiming; it replaced the visible document with the voice, paving the way for contemporary preoccupations with "orality and literacy."

The formula, as defined by Parry, is "a group of words . . . regularly employed under the same metrical conditions to express a given essential idea."[60] The *oral* formula was a mnemonic aid which assisted rapid extemporaneous composition and easy assimilation by successive hearers. The theory met with approbation and challenge, the complexities of which I cannot hope to do justice to here.[61] Those who objected to the theory did so on the grounds that it robbed the talented poet of poetic discretion[62] and that the

---

60. "Studies in the Epic Technique of Oral Verse-Making, I: Homer and Homeric Style," *Harvard Studies in Classical Philology* 41 (1930), 80.

61. Several important contributions should be mentioned: Francis P. Magoun applied the theories developed by Milman Parry to the study of Old English poetry ("The Oral Formulaic Character of Anglo-Saxon Narrative Poetry," *Speculum* 28 [1953], 446–67); and Albert B. Lord, in *The Singer of Tales*, applies them to medieval epic (*The Singer of Tales* [New York: Atheneum, 1978]). For bibliography and discussion, see Alexandra Hennessey Olsen's articles: "Oral-Formulaic Research in Old English Studies: I," *Oral Tradition* 1 (1986), 548–606, and "Oral-Formulaic Research in Old English Studies: II," *Oral Tradition* 3 (1988), 138–90; also Alain Renoir, *A Key to Old Poems: The Oral-Formulaic Approach to the Interpretation of West-Germanic Verse* (University Park: Pennsylvania State University Press, 1988), and John Miles Foley, *Oral-Formulaic Theory and Research: An Introduction and Annotated Bibliography* (New York: Garland, 1985), 3–77, particularly his contributions in *The Theory of Oral Composition: History and Methodology* (Bloomington: Indiana University Press, 1988) and "Texts that Speak to Readers Who Hear: Old English Poetry and the Languages of Oral Tradition," in *Speaking Two Languages: Traditional Disciplines and Contemporary Theory in Medieval Studies*, ed. Allen J. Frantzen (Albany: State University of New York Press, 1991), 141–56. Scholars interested in the history and theory of literacy should also consult Walter J. Ong, *Orality and Literacy: The Technologizing of the Word* (London: Metheun, 1982).

62. See especially Larry D. Benson, "The Literary Character of Anglo-Saxon Formulaic Poetry," *PMLA* 81 (1966), 334–41.

presence of formulae is no indication that a poem has been orally composed, for it stands to reason that writers of poetry can easily imitate the conventions of their predecessors. Those who have taken the middle road argue for a combination of oral and literary technique in Old English.[63] I shall return to some of these notions presently, after a discussion of the relationship of the metrical and the grammatical unit.

Study of oral formula in ancient Greek poetry has revealed what Gregory Nagy refers to as the "intimate relation between metrical blocks (cola) and syntactical blocks (formula)."[64] The colon is a rhythmical section of verse within a poetic line that measures from two to six feet and is divided from other cola by a caesura or diaeresis. It is generally assumed that the metrical length of the colon corresponds with the length of the phrase or clause provided by the formula.[65] Nagy's view runs counter to the prevalent understanding of meter as a "container" or a "frame" into which words can be fitted. He suggests that the formula, the "fixed phrase conditioned by the traditional themes of oral poetry," generates meter, not the other way around, and, in fact, *is* meter.[66]

The requirements of a poetry grounded in formulaic techniques and the need to fit words and phrases into a structure would affect the use or disuse of connecting syntax and explain some of the problems noted by Schaar in *Andreas*. Adversative asyndeton may very well have been a function of the strikingly formulaic nature of that poem. If we look again at the "storm" passage and its startling juxtaposition of the blithe heart of the sufferer next to the black floodpaths of his tormenting vision, we see that both phrases are formulaic:

> blæc brimrade   bliðheort wunode
> eorl unforcuð . . .

The rhythmic demands of the type-A verse require that *bliŏ* begin the first syllable of the second half-line. The poet could have inserted a monosyllabic conjunction such as *ac* or *þeah*, at the expense of the drumroll effect created

63. Ibid.; also Donald K. Fry, "Some Aesthetic Implications of a New Definition of Formula," *Neuphilologische Mitteilungen* 69 (1968), 516–22.

64. Gregory Nagy, "Formula and Meter," in *Oral Tradition and the Formula*, ed. Benjamin A. Stolz and Richard S. Shannon III (Ann Arbor: Center for the Co-ordination of Ancient and Modern Studies, 1976), 253.

65. Joseph A. Russo, "The Structural Formula in Homeric Verse" *Yale Classical Studies* 20 (1966), 217–40.

66. Nagy, "Formula and Meter," 251.

by the troches. These require a strongly accented syllable at the beginning of each half-line that would have been ruined by the intrusion of another syllable, especially following two unaccented syllables in *brimrade*. It is not merely formula, then, that invites asyndeton, but an ear for felicitous patterns. It is very unlikely that the *Andreas*-poet was an illiterate. But in his verse adaptation of the Latin text, his ear may have been trained by vernacular poetic patterns that were centuries in the making. A formula does not need to signal oral composition to be "formulaic."

The presence of the formula as we know it in Old English is harder to detect in the Welsh and does not have the backing of an entire critical movement to bring it to light. A phrase such as *gordyar adar* seems to be conventional in nature. It appears in both *Kintevin* and *Claf Abercuawg* in the same metrical place within the line, leaving room for a similar formula with suppressed copula to complete the line:

> *dyar adar* glas callet
>   (BBC: 33.1)
> *gordyar adar* gwlyb naint
>   (RB: 1035.1)

Like the Old English, the Welsh seem to have some standard phrase-types, such as the pattern *lwyd gwarthaf mynyd* ("gray the mountain-top") which, when analyzed, can be summed up as *color* plus "top of" plus *high object* such as a hill or a tree: *gwyn gwarthaf bre* ("white the hill-top"). While there is a great deal of repetition of phrase types, however, the majority of these occur in groups, such as the stanzas in *The Red Book* beginning *gorwyn blaen* ("radiant the tops of . . .") or the *stavell Kyndylan* stanzas that we have already examined. Kenneth Jackson describes a decidedly formulaic feature of Welsh poetry—the progression by increments of a variable element with an invariable.[67] Here is one of his examples from *The Black Book of Carmarthan*:

> Accursed be the *white* goose
> that plucked out his eye *from his head*,
> Gallawg, son of Lleinnawg *the chieftain*.

---

67. Jackson, "Incremental Repetition," 310. The term "incremental repetition" was coined by F. B. Gummere to describe the repetition and parallel structure of certain variables in the refrains of English and Scottish ballads (*The Beginnings of Poetry* [New York: Macmillan, 1901], 194).

Accursed be the *gray* goose
that plucked out his eye *when a youth,*
Gollawg, son of Lleinawg *the distinguished.*

Jackson finds examples of this device in Portuguese, Turkish, and Chinese ballad verse, and he concludes that "the evidence of all these other instances set beside the Welsh shows that incremental repetition is a feature common to several literatures in widely separated parts of the world, having presumably a similar origin everywhere; so that to explain the others would be to explain the Welsh type, too."[68] It seems likely that the device here in the Welsh is grounded in some technique of formula which originated independently in these different literatures. The term *formula* is a dangerous one, though, and subject to much misinterpretation and controversy.

For one thing, the study of formulas has been applied almost exclusively to narrative poetry, except, for instance, in the work conducted by Jeff Opland[69] of African praise poems, and its connection with the metrical unit stresses its function as a narrative device to keep the story in motion. Welsh poetry is not narrative, and it lacks the linking or action formulas of the *Beowulf madelode* variety which give it a sequential framework. Furthermore, the tight poetic form of the *englyn* with its complex metrical and prosodic requirements makes it difficult for us to distinguish the formulaic from the individual and the artistic. A line like the one in stanza 2 of *Llym awel*—*ton tra thon toid tu tir* ("Wave after wave washes the shore")—seems particularly self-conscious in its alliterations. Oral formula is predicated on the flexibility of its text; it is difficult to see how the individual englyn with its tight correspondences can be modified, and for a number of reasons the theory has never been in vogue among scholars of Welsh poetry. First, as I have said, oral formula has been turned primarily to the study of narrative poems. Second, the terms *formula* and *oral formula* are too often identified with the popular and the improvisational, a romantic preoccupation with the bardic craft. The pleasing picture of the poet composing *extempore* has extended to the term *formulaic* despite the many and sundry arguments that have insisted upon the vestiges of oral styles in poems that are written or precomposed. Third, there is an apparent class distinction drawn between the bardic poets and the *cyfarwyddiaid* of Middle Welsh, and, as is hinted in *The Maginogion*, "storytelling was one of

---

68. Ibid., 313.

69. *"Scop* and *Imbongi*: Anglo-Saxon and Bantu Oral Poets," *English Studies in Africa* 14 (1970), 161–78; *Xhosa Oral Poetry: Aspects of a Black South African Tradition* (Cambridge: Cambridge University Press, 1983).

the roles of the lower grade of poets (or apprentices) and the master-poet would become storyteller only on special occasions or perhaps for certain categories of narrative."[70] Because oral formula is associated with telling stories instead of composing non-narrative poetry, and especially because it connotes extemporaneous performances and a lack of premeditation, it is crucial that it not taint the highest bardic tradition. What is operating here is a modern aesthetic of literacy that occludes wholehearted reception of a tradition that was not as engaged in literacy as we know it.

The theory of the oral formula in Old English has undergone many revisions and modifications. Most important, the facile assumption that the formula replaces individual creative artistry like a computer program has long been a defeated argument: over twenty years ago, Stanley Greenfield suggested that without denying the contribution of oral formula to the style of these poems it is possible to grant the poet some literary discretion in his choice and placement of traditional phrases.[71] In his exploration of reception theory and the medieval formula, John Miles Foley advises us to rethink our own aesthetic criticism of oral and literary works. Does it make such a difference whether poetic phrases are traditional or not? he asks. What limitations are imposed on our enjoyment of these texts "by saying yes to art but no to tradition"?[72]

It seems clear that the search for evidence of oral formulas in either the Old English or the Welsh poems leads us to a *cul de sac* if that be the final point of the search, for it is eventually reductive and contradictory given the highly complex relationship of orality and literacy by the tenth century. On the other hand, one must not discount the contribution this theory has made to understanding something of what Walter Ong calls "oral residue"[73] and "the historical origins of literature out of oral verbalization."[74] Along with other philosophical and poetic theories, it has opened up room for discussion of "the phenomenon of the human voice as a dimension of the poetic text,"[75] a dimension too often overlooked in our highly literate dissections of chirographic poetry. The handwritten codices of the Middle Ages were more

---

70. Brynley F. Roberts, "Oral Tradition and Welsh Literature," *Oral Tradition* 3 (1988), 63.

71. Stanley Greenfield, "Grendel's Approach to Heorot: Syntax and Poetry," in *Old English Poetry: Fifteen Essays*, ed. Robert P. Creed (Providence: Brown University Press, 1967), 283. See also Greenfield, "Syntactic Analysis and Old English Poetry," *Neuphilologische Mitteilungen* 64 (1963), 373–78.

72. "Texts that Speak," 148.

73. "Oral Residue in Tudor Prose Style," *PMLA* 80 (1965), 145–54.

74. "Orality, Literacy, and Medieval Textualization," *New Literary History* 16.1 (1984), 1.

75. Paul Zumthor, "The Text and the Voice," 67.

intimately associated with the voice than the mechanically printed books of today. Reading was a social, not a private activity; *legere* meant to read aloud, not silently, and even "silent" reading was conducted under one's breath.[76] Medieval literature is saturated with an orality that we find hard to understand today, and Suzanne Fleishman finds in it a major source for the "idiosyncrasies and incoherences," the "gaps in the text," the inconsistent word boundaries and orthography, the "clauses strung together, with little or no formal connective tissue" of the sort that often characterizes the Old French corpus.[77]

This is not to say, however, that these features were undesirable to their makers—a necessary evil and accidental by-product of orality; the abruptnesses of Carolingian poetry were the style and undoubtedly sought after. One could assume that matters of style were equally important in the British Isles and if its written literature bears the marks of the orality that affected so much of its culture, the obverse could be equally true. Poems composed orally and transmitted verbally could bear all the marks of a finished, literate composition, mulled over in leisure, recombined, erased, polished, and varied before recitation. One need not have the luxury of a word processor to produce premeditated and deliberate texts in an oral culture. The "formula" was obviously not the only resource for oral poets.

Message and Studied Effect

The skillful Old English poets were not confined to the formulas of their poetic trade, and I believe they may conceivably have attempted imitating non-English stylistic forms in order to enhance the effect of certain phrases and the impact of their message. *The Rhyming Poem* shows a departure from conventional Old English form by its inclusion of end rhymes, and the author of *Wulf and Eadwacer* may have adopted a Scandinavian poetic line. As we have seen, Pilch notes the similarly "erratic" order of details in *Canu Llywarch Hen* and *The Wanderer* and *The Seafarer*, arguing for stylistic

76. Ong, "Orality, Literacy and Medieval Textualization," 1; also Jeffrey Kittay, "Utterance Unmoored: The Changing Interpretations of the Act of Writing in the European Middle Ages," *Language in Society* 17 (1986), 209–30, and Fleishman, "Philology, Linguistics," 20–22, who suggest that the many elisions and abbreviations in manuscript spelling forced the reader to "sound out" the words.

77. Fleishman, "Philology, Linguistics," 21.

influence. The problem with his argument is that neither the Welsh nor the English poem is erratic; the style of each is grounded in strict poetic conventions. Another problem with his argument is that it challenges us to ask why, in the first place, an Old English poet would have been interested in imitating the style of a Welsh poem that ran counter to his message. All the comparisons made of *The Seafarer* and *Claf Abercuawg* fail to note the striking difference in attitude present in these poems. The one is an ambiguous meditation that leads to a spiritual discovery of salvation; the other is a cynical and self-pitying plaint on the part of an outcast who laments the loss of his sons, his youth, and his health. The one is *consolatio*, the other *planctus*, and the styles of these two poetic traditions do much to underscore their philosophic content. Furthermore, if the Old English poet were truly interested in adapting the style of an early Welsh poem, he could have done a far better job, and other Old English poems feature disjunctions and juxtapositions that are more strikingly "Welsh" in nature than either *The Wanderer* or *The Seafarer.*

The Ruin, for instance, gives us neither an argument nor a consolatory message; it is a description and a lament for an age that has passed. In both *The Ruin* and *The Wife's Lament* we find passages where the caesura gets extra emphasis, not only by the confinement of self-contained phrases within the half-line, but by a chiastic pattern made by the syntax; in a number of lines the verbs or participles are put together on either side of the break and their subjects made to flank them:

> burgstede burston   brosnað entageweorc
>
> (2)
>
> [The buildings collapsed, decays the work of giants]

The pattern here is subject, verb, verb, subject. Further on, the same pattern is made with subjects and accompanying modifiers:

> beorht wæron burgræced   burnsele monige
> heah horngestreon   heresweg micel
>
> (22–23)
>
> [Bright were cityhalls, bath-houses many,
> high host of gables, martial noise much.]

In line 20 the datives are put next to each other in the center:

weallan wirum   wundrum togædre

[walls with wire with wonder together]

Chiasmus is not an uncommon device in Old English heroic poetry. We frequently find direct or indirect objects grouped in the middle of a line and flanked by the verbs, a construction that automatically creates a kind of asyndeton:

wand wacne æsc   wordum mælde

[shook the spear, with words spoke]
(*Battle of Maldon*, 40)

The term *chiasmus* is inadequate for what is happening aurally, calling up as it does a *visual* image of the line having been severed, its halves pasted one over the other and a cross drawn to the corresponding sections. A more appropriately aural image is a pulsation, like a sound wave, with peaks and valleys of similitude. This effect lends a stateliness and symmetry to Old English poetry that is one of its most prominent features, and its development out of the alliterative requirement is obvious. Those items which alliterate are most frequently the nouns. Where a verb alliterates, then it holds prominent position in the *b*-verse:

Het þa haleþa hleo   healdan þa bricge
(*Maldon*, 74)

This pulsation in *The Ruin*, however, seems especially distinct, with its peculiar emphasis on verbs of decay and destruction which echo each other in their symmetrical placement within the line. The effect survives even the ruined parts of *The Ruin*:

ofstonden under stormum   steap geap gedreas·
wonað giet se   . . . num geheapen
felon . . .
grimme gegrund . . .
                . . . scan   heo

[stood under storm   tall, broad, it perished,
it crumbles still   . . . ?? heaped (hewn?)
by files . . .
fiercely ground . . .
                    . . . shone it]

                                        (11–15)

   Daniel Calder remarks that *The Ruin* is a poem about spatial and temporal "motion,"[78] and his ideas are vindicated by the plethora of verbs, even among the remaining words of the damaged section. This singsong arrangement also lends a certain kind of artistic sonorousness to the poem which underlines the aura of inevitability that is a thematic concern throughout. Yet there is a constant sense of interruption created by putting two verbs next to each other, one ending a syntactic unit, the other beginning it. It creates the effect of point and counterpoint that finds its visual analogy in the symmetrical mirror images of Northern Medieval interlace designs where disjunctions and discretions are emphasized. Likewise in the poetry: it is hard to believe that this effect was not intentionally created by a poet with skillful control of his medium.

   The notion of inevitability or man's weakness in the face of time and change is a powerful and prevalent theme in Welsh poetry, and it seems to find especially apt expression in the stark, uncompromising juxtapositions of *Canu Llywarch Hen* and other works. We hear a similar kind of point-counterpoint rhythm with internal rhyme and consonance in Welsh poetic lines:

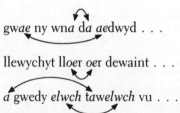

The strong spondee in mid-line draws our attention to a juxtaposition of unlike items, and middle rhymes are often made with words of contrasting meaning, as in this famous passage from *The Gododdin*:

----

78. Daniel G. Calder, "Perspective and Movement in *The Ruin*," *Neuphilologische Mitteilungen* 72 (1971), 442.

gwyr a aeth gatraeth oedd fraeth eu llu.
glasved ei hancwyn a gwenwyn vu.
trichant trwy beiriant yn catau.
a gwedy elwch tawelwch fu.

(CA: 8.A, 1–4)

[Men went to Catraeth—was ready their host.
Pale mead their *drink* and *poison* was.
Three hundred through command (were) fighting.
And after *rejoicing silence* was.]

In a manner tantalizingly reminiscent of the Old English *ealoscearwan*, the Welsh *glasved* (pale mead) is both "drink" and "poison" to the warriors who enjoy it before battle. The rhyme on *elwch* and *tawelwch* caps the grim association by yanking out of chronological order two separate events and juxtaposing them, namely the feasting and frenzy that accompanies war preparations, and the stillness of a field strewn with corpses. The battle has been neatly omitted; the sad and heroic inevitability of warfare receives effective expression in this terse, contrastive manner.

Far more prevalent than chiasmus is the parallel construction within the Old English line. This device also emphasizes the caesura by repeating the same or similar syntactic patterns in each half-line. The passage previously cited from *The Wife's Lament* draws much of its power from the use of parallelism:

eald is þes eorðsele   eal ic eom oflongad
sindon dena dimme   duna uphea
bitre burgtunas   brerum beweaxne

(29–31)

We have already noted the asyndeton and suppressed copula which give this passage its "Welsh" flavor. Also strikingly Welsh is the repetition of sound patterns that surpass mere alliteration—*eald, eal, dena, duna*. This last configuration is remarkable for its emphatic consonance and its "squinting" adjective *dimme*, which for a split second after the pause also seems to modify *dunne* and to play upon the meaning of a homonymous word: *dunn*, "dark-colored."

Line 29 of *The Wife's Lament* contains a subtle chiasmus—*eald is þes eardsele; eol ic eom oflongad*—masked by the intervention of the adverb *eol* in the second half-line, which gives an additional sense of parallelism. The subjects are actually grouped together between the two copulas, and their modifiers lie at either end of the line:

Old is this earth-hall; all I am oppressed.

The structure of the line brings out an association of speaker and earth-hall which is grammatically unstated by juxtaposing the two subjects—*eordsele, eol ic*—while the predicates have a natural association by occupying initial and terminal positions, *eald, oflongad*. What seems like a non sequitur is actually a perfect example of the natural analogy, the leap of association between image and personal utterance unassisted by a conjunction. The "conjunction" is tonal. The visible gap on the page is an audible lull, accentuated and turned into a connection.

Logically, the oldness of the cavern has nothing to do with the woman's longing, and yet it does, in the strange way that all external objects absorb and come to life with our projected feelings. We are also dealing here with an enormous issue that I shall address in a later chapter—the role of context in the connection of ideas. The connotations that certain objects have for certain peoples, perhaps for whole societies, should greatly facilitate the relationships of certain images with ideas, and this is part of the logic behind the theory of the oral formulas and themes. To an estranged and expatriate Anglo-Saxon woman, then, a cave is a sad and ironic reminder of the hall. We find the echo in the figure of speech, *eordsele* ("earth-hall"), which closes her in as darkly as her own longing. Whatever the intended effect may have been, it increases in ambiguity and power through an asyndetic juxtaposition.

Style and Latin Influence

We have not as yet turned full attention to the argumentative, narrative and "connected" nature of much Old English elegy, which affects its form, its disclosure of ideas, and its use of imagery in ways that are distinctly non-Welsh. One of the most important differences is the use to which Anglo-Saxon poets may have put their exposure to Latin poetry, as we may see by an examination of *The Wanderer*. The syntax of this poem is far more periodic than that of *The Ruin*. An analysis of a single sentence in *The Wanderer*[79]

79. Conducted originally by Stanley Greenfield in "Syntactic Analysis and Old English Poetry," *Neuphilologische Mitteilungen* 64 (1963), 375.

reveals a high degree of subordination and complexity of thought, not matched by the sentences in the other poem:

> swa ic modsefan   minne sceolde·
> oft earmcearig   edle bidæled
> freomægum feor   feterum sælan
> siþþan gearu iu   goldwine mine
> hrusan heolstre biwrah   ond ic hean þonan
> wod wintercearig   ofer waþema gebind·
> sohte seledreorig   sinces bryttan
> hwær ic feor oþþe neah   findan meahte
> þone þe in meoduhealle   mine wisse
> oþþe mec freondleas[n]e   frefran wolde
> weman mid wynnum
>
> (EB1: 19–29)

> [Thus, I my heart must—]
> often miserable, deprived of homeland,
> far from noble kinsmen—seal with fetters,
> since long ago my gold-companion
> the darkness of earth covered and downcast I then
> went winter-desolate over the binding of the waves,
> sought out, homesick, a dispenser of treasure,
> wherever, far or near, I might find
> who in the mead-hall would know my people,
> or would console my friendless self,
> entertain with pleasure.]

Stanley Greenfield notes the Chinese-box effect of clauses within clauses here, which contributes, he writes, to the extraordinary "majesty and sweep" of this line.[80] The remarkable amount of syndesis in the form of conjunctions and adverbs continually places ideas in relation to each other: *swa* in line 19a links the reason for the speaker's self-repression with the gnomic wisdom that precedes in lines 15–18. *Siþþan* in line 22a gives the cause for his sadness, the death of this "gold companion," and *þonan* in line 23b describes the effect of this loss on his life. *Hwær* and *þone þe*, in lines 26a and 27a respectively, restrict the concept of the "dispenser of treasure" in the matter of his where-

---

80. Ibid.

abouts and identity, and throughout the poem we find a good deal more dislocated syntax and enjambment than we do in *The Ruin*, as in the following passage where the adjective is divided from the noun that it modifies by a half-line:

swimmað oft onweg
fleotendra ferð·   no þær fela bringeð
cuþra cwidegiedda . . .

(53^b–55^a)

> [Literally: "Swim often away of the floating ones (the) spirits; they do not there many bring of familiar things (the) utterances"; i.e. "Often the spirits of the floating ones swim away; they do not bring there many utterances of familiar things."]

The phrase *no þær fela bringeð* is not clearly formulaic as are many of the Old English phrases that fill and are bound by the half-line; neither does it stand on its own as a self-contained phrase. The question, then, is whether this high degree of subordination and hypotaxis is a result of exposure to Latin. Being an inflected language, Old English could conceivably adapt devices like *tmesis* or abnormal syntax, and we find sentences of this sort in *Judith*, *The Dream of the Rood*, and *Beowulf*, among others:

nymðe se modga hwæne
niðe rofra   him þe near hete
rinca to rune gegangan

(*Judith*, 52^b–54^a)

[Literally: "Unless the arrogant (one) any in wickedness bold him nearer should summon of (the) warriors to council to come," i.e., "Unless the arrogant one should summon any of the warriors bold in wickedness to come nearer him to council."][81]

The English poems that we are examining were recorded by clerics and scribes learned in Scripture and Latin religious literature, and it is a little difficult to believe that they were unimpressed by Latin syntax and style. Other scholars have argued for the origins of the Old English elegy within

---

81. Frederick G. Cassidy and Richard N. Ringler, *Bright's Old English Grammar and Reader*, 3d ed. (New York: Holt, Rinehart and Winston, 1971), 273–74.

Germanic and Celtic traditions, but a trend in scholarship today is to look to Latin models for influence in shaping the final products that have been recorded in *The Exeter Book*.[82] In finding Latin source material for these poems, scholars have given as much attention to Latin prose as poetry,[83] a circumstance which suggests the prominence, to modern readers at least, of the argumentative and narrative nature of *The Wanderer* and *The Seafarer*. Although Rynell refers to the influence of the Latin "periodic structure" on Germanic poetry, he cites no examples. Nor does he make a distinction in his study between the influence of Latin prose syntax and poetic syntax. Medieval Latin poetry takes many different forms. It can be pithy and abrupt and divided into discrete sections, such as the poetry of Thomas of Celano or of St. Columba; or it can be flowing and "continuous," like the poetry of Boethius or Venantius Fortunatus. The point, then, seems to be not that Latin poetic syntax per se has affected Old English poetic syntax, but that Old English poetry was particularly suitable for adapting to the didactic, homiletic, and argumentative form which its writers found in Latin Christian prose. One must remember that the Welsh had been exposed to Latin Christianity longer than had the English, and while we find many Latin borrowings in Welsh vocabulary, we find little didactic homiletic poetry in Welsh; the tradition would not allow it.[84] The requirements of Old English poetry permit a certain flexibility and rearrangement of phrase that we do not find in the poetry of the *cynfeirdd*. This circumstance may be due to the fact that the Anglo-Saxons had developed a poetic narrative form early on while the Welsh did not. Nonetheless, the Latin model and the privilege scholars have

82. See Michael J. B. Allen and Daniel G. Calder, *Sources and Analogues of Old English Poetry: The Major Latin Sources in Translation* (Cambridge: D. S. Brewer, 1976). Latin source material represents a major critical enthusiasm in Anglo-Saxon Studies. Two projects are now being undertaken in Britain and the United States respectively: *Fontes Anglo-Saxonici* has been described as "a large collaborative project aimed at identifying all written sources which were incorporated, quoted, translated or adopted anywhere in English or Latin texts which were written, probably or certainly, in Anglo-Saxon England" (Allen Frantzen, *Desire for Origins* [New Brunswick: Rutgers University Press, 1990], 85), and *Sources of Anglo-Saxon Literary Culture*, "a 'collaborative project that aims to produce a reference work providing a convenient summary of current scholarship on the knowledge and use of literary sources in Anglo-Saxon England' " (Frantzen, 86).

83. Allen and Calder, in *Sources and Analogues*, 146–53, cite the Latin Homilies of Pseudo-Augustine and Cesarius of Arles as analogues for the Old English elegies.

84. The possibility of the influence of Latin verse upon the Welsh *englyn* is yet another polemical issue, J. Glyn Davies torturing the *englyn penfyr* into a Latin "long-line" ("The englyn trisectual long-line in early Welsh metrics," *Zeitschrift für celtische Philologie* 17 [1927–28], 113–28), John Morris-Jones arguing that all subforms of the englyn derive from the native *englyn milwr* (*Gerdd Dafod*, 313–18). See Gerald Murphy for the influence of early Christian hymns on Irish stanzaic verse (*Early Irish Metrics* [Dublin: The Royal Irish Academy, 1961]).

given to it over the centuries has monumentally affected our understanding of wholeness and explicitness, so that it is no wonder that we have expressed perplexity over the departures from this rhetorical standard in many native medieval situations. The following chapters will examine these differences from another angle, that of the "image" and its implicit contexts.

PART II

THE IMAGE AND CONNECTION

4

Grappling with the Gnomic: Modern and Medieval Concepts of Image and Connection

Gnawt nyth eryr ym blaendar. ac yg kyfyrdy gwyr llauar. golwc vynut ar a gar.

("Typical an eagle's nest in the top of an oak, and in the tavern talkative men. Courteous the glance upon one who is loved.")
—*Gnodiau*, RB

I have discussed the oral and aural aspects of early English and Welsh poetry, and here I will examine the controversial nature of the image. As readers today we are predominantly visual in our approach to reading poems, and there is consequently a special relationship between our desire for grammatical cohesion and the importance we place on visual point of view in any artistic depiction of supposedly "visual" things. W. J. T. Mitchell writes of the hegemony of artificial perspective in the visual arts in "the way it denies its own artificiality and lays claims to being a 'natural' representation of 'the way things really are.' "[1] I maintain that our privileging of grammatical cohesion follows the same lines of hegemony and denial, in that both conjunction and hypotactic construction lend a hierarchy and system of relationships to the statement that is paralleled in the arrangement of images and events around a first-person point of view.

1. W. J. T. Mitchell, "What Is an Image?" *New Literary History* 15.3 (1984), 524.

The problems scholars have had with the laments is magnified significantly with the gnomes, to which they are closely related. I have given an entire chapter to gnomes because so much of Welsh and to a different extent Old English "nature" poetry is saturated with them in ways that are perplexing to modern readers. Because the poem that speaks of nature most often does so with what we think are "images," the overwhelming urge is to regard it imagistically, but the insular gnome is one of the most uncooperative of all our medieval poetic modes because it denies us the subjectivity we want to attach to seeing. To demonstrate how this is so, I will briefly discuss the various ways poets and critics of poetry have conceptualized "imagery," as well as make a few remarks about medieval concepts of the image.

The History of the Image

One of our most controversial issues in poetic and visual theory is tied up with arguments over metaphor, semiotics, and the nature of perception and representation, and it has profoundly affected how we react to medieval poetry. At the root of it is this confusing term *image*. The idea of the mental image as something intrinsic to the poetic image is relatively new, but it lies at the heart of much of the early to mid-twentieth-century critical exasperation that we have already seen.

The root meaning of the word "image" in Latin (*imago, imaginem*) is "copy" or "likeness," stemming from the same root as *imitare*, "to imitate," and it was commonly used to refer to statues or visible representations of gods or saints. In this sense, it is akin to the Greek term *eikon* or "icon," a word that was quick to develop pejorative connotations. In the Middle Ages, *imago* had the more abstract meaning of similitude: man is made in the spiritual (not physical) likeness of God (*imago Dei*); so, too, are all the concrete things of the universe symbols of the furnishings of God's house.[2] The term is related to Greek *mimesis*, but whereas Aristotle's use of the word seems to have more generally meant "the imitation of reality," *image* in Latin, and consequently in English, took on specific connotations of a single symbolic figure (*figura*), hence its associations with "metaphor." It described an equa-

2. For a "handlist of medieval imagery, of things that attract meaning," see Hugh of Saint Victor (*De arca Noe morale*, 1:4–6, in *Selected Spiritual Writings*, translated by "a religious of C.S.M.V." [London: Faber, 1962], 49–51), cited by V. A. Kolve, *Chaucer and the Imagery of Narrative: The First Five Canterbury Tales* (Stanford: Stanford University Press, 1984), 61–62.

tion between signifier and signified, rather than a triangulation, which comes about by introducing the effect of the signifier on a perceiver, so essential to modern conceptions of art.

We find no single rhetorical term in the Middle Ages for the literary creation of mental images: *enargia* was the term used by Renaissance grammarians for "the process of making the reader seem to see something," but it was not one that caught on.[3] Poetic "imagery," as we are inclined to think of it, is invariably described by early grammarians and rhetoricians as "ornament," "trope," "decoration." Geoffrey of Vinsauf likens the use of such techniques to the "clothing" and "doctoring" of a word.[4] "Imagery" is most often refered to as *descriptio*, and again it is only one of many garments of style in which a rhetorical text is dressed. In the following passage, Geoffrey comes as close as any rhetorician of his day to linking the use of such tropes with the mind's eye and ear, or mouth, even, "refreshed" by the food of the descriptive word:

> See that the words with due ceremony are wedded to the subject. If description is to be the food and ample refreshment of the mind, avoid too curt a brevity as well as trite conventionality. Examples of description, accompanied by novel figures, will be varied, that eye and ear may roam amid a variety of subjects.[5]

Composed in the early thirteenth century, Geoffrey's *Poetria Nova* is a little late for our purposes, but his precepts stem from a long-standing tradition in classical and medieval Latin rhetoric.[6] The Welsh Bardic Grammars,[7] preserved in the fourteenth-century *Llanstephan* 3 and in the sixteenth-century manuscript *The Red Book of Hergest*, offer the same problems in chronology (despite the fact that later manuscripts often record earlier texts)

3. Ray Frazer, "The Origin of the Term Image," *English Literary History* 27.2 (1960), 149.

4. *Poetria Nova* 4:757–65, trans. Margaret F. Nims (Toronto: Pontifical Institute of Medieval Studies, 1957): "In order that meaning may wear a precious garment, if a word is old, be its physician and give to the old a new vigour. Do not let the word invariably reside on its native soil—such residence dishonours it. Let it avoid its natural location, travel about elsewhere, and take up a pleasant abode on the estate of another. There let it stay as a novel guest, and give pleasure by its very strangeness. If you provide this remedy, you will give to the word's face a new youth" (43).

5. Nims, *Poetria Nova*, 36.

6. See Nims, 10, 12.

7. *Gramadegau'r Penceirddiaid*, ed. G. J. Williams and E. J. Jones (Caerdydd: Gwasg Prifysgol Cymru, 1934). I am especially grateful to W. Gerallt Harries at the University College of Swansea for bringing these texts to my attention.

and are largely unhelpful in understanding images, aside from their repeating suppositions put forth by Plato, Aristotle, Isidore, and other philosophers and rhetoricians.[8]

Throughout medieval and Renaissance thought one finds the poem consistently regarded as *tekhne*, an artifact, and its poet an artificer, a maker, a craftsman whose tools are words. One's private, mental experience of the crafted thing is rarely elucidated in the early treatises although there is plenty of commentary in antiquity and Latin learning about the imagination, the power of the mind to create images, the possibility to be moved to sensation and private feeling.[9] V. A. Kolve based his book *Chaucer and the Imagery of Narrative* on the visual contexts of *The Canterbury Tales*, exploring the fundamental premise that "literature can offer an experience that is in some sense 'visual,' " a traditional conception of the verbal arts, he says, that goes back to the ancients.[10] Nonetheless, the vocabulary for describing the tools of this process remained centered, then and throughout most of the Renaissance, on the rhetorical trope and not the mental representation, the artifact and not the perception.

In the seventeenth century we find a decline in prestige of "rhetorical tropes"—metaphor, synecdoche, metonymy, apostrophe—as emphasis shifted away from the "devices" of language toward the veracity of sensory perception.[11] The terms *image* and *description* replaced the term *figure*, that deceptive and lifeless ornament of rhetoric which recalled the now unpopular scholasticism.[12] The *image* had more to do with what the eye saw and the mind re-created, and it allied poetry with the visual arts and the Horatian notion of *ut pictura poesis*. Thus it was that Joseph Addison could write in 1712 that "words, when well chosen, have so great force in them that a description often gives us more lively ideas than the sight of things them-

---

8. *Gramadegau'r Penceirddiaid*, p. 6: *Mydr neu brydyat yw kyuansodyat ymadrodyon kyfiawn o eireu adurn arderchawc a deckaer o eireu gwann adwyn kymeredic, a arwydockaont moliant neu ogan, a hynny ar gerd dafawt ganmoledic* [A metrical or poetic composition is a composition of expressions derived from decorative, excellent words which are made fair with gentle, acceptable weak words (adjectives and adjectival phrases) which signify praise or censure, and that in praiseworthy "tongue music."]

9. Aristotle compares the process of mental imagery to wax imprinted with the signet ring (*De Anima* 2.12.424a). See Peter Clemoes's discussion of Alcuin's *De Ratione Liber* and other texts that describe the power of the mind to "think on things absent" ("Mens absentia cogitans in *The Wanderer* and *The Seafarer*," *Medieval Literature and Civilization: Studies in Memory of G. N. Garmonsway*, ed. Derek A. Pearsall and R. A. Waldron (London: Athlone Press, 1969).

10. V. A. Kolve, *Chaucer and the Imagery of Narrative*, 9.

11. Mitchell, "What Is an Image?" 515.

12. Ibid.

selves."[13] And in 1819 Abraham Rees defines "imagery" (or *hypotyposis*) in the *Cyclopedia of Arts, Sciences, and Literature* as a figure whereby a thing is described or painted in such strong and bright colours that it does not seem to be read, or heard, but actually seen, or presented before the eye."[14]

Thereafter, the use of the term *image* by critics becomes vague. Having acquired the meaning of mental picture, it never lost the meaning of "symbol" or "figure of speech"—a circumstance that charges it with a peculiar duality. Thus a statement like "the silent moon is the constant image of the world's inconstancy"[15] clearly draws a figurative comparison, and speculation about the sensorial evocativeness of this "silent moon" is beside the point until we begin to conjure images that are grotesque or distracting:

> Love's not Time's fool, though rosy lips and cheeks
> Within his bending sickle's compass come.

The obvious images here are Time, represented as the Reaper and his scythe, and Youth, represented as a lovely face, both standard rhetorical figures. But if allowed any visual force at all, the mental representation is horrible: lips and cheeks coming within range of the swinging knife. One wonders if Shakespeare intended us to visualize a scene of mutilation; the juxtaposition has the effect of the conceits denounced by Johnson. Elizabethan satiric pictures drawn of maidens with naturalistic roses for cheeks reinforces a suspicion of conventional tropes already raised by Spenser with his false Florimel, whose body, automaton-like, is materially constructed from the hackneyed metaphors of poets.[16]

The notion that verbal tropes deceive because they cover up nonverbal "truths" persists into the twentieth century with George Orwell's "Politics and the English Language," wherein a "dead metaphor" is that which overuse has

13. Joseph Addison, *The Spectator*, no. 416, 27 June 1712, in "The Pleasures of the Imagination, 6," *Eighteenth-Century Critical Essays* 1, ed. Scott Elledge (Ithaca: Cornell University Press, 1961), 60.

14. Cited by P. N. Furbank, "Do We Need the Terms 'Image' and 'Imagery'?" *Critical Quarterly* 9 (1969), 344.

15. Cited in the entry under "image," *The Compact Edition of the Oxford English Dictionary*, (Oxford: Clarendon Press, 1971), 1:1376.

16. *The Faerie Queene*, III. viii. 6–7. An Elizabethan portrait inspired by John Davies's *The Extravagant Shepherd*, an "anti-romance," gives "the beloved mistress a complexion white as snow, two branches of coral at the mouth opening, a lily and rose for each cheek, two suns for eyes, and hair like chains of gold" (*Shakespeare's Sonnets*, ed. Louis B. Wright and Virginia A. LaMar [New York: Washington Square Press, 1972], 130.)

robbed of *enargia*, the power to call up a vivid mental image in its readers. Imagery should be "immediate," free from all taint of the conventional (synonymous today with "trite").[17] Immediacy of imagery was of course given tremendous importance by the Romantic poets, but one of the more significant impacts upon the conception of poetic imagery in this century was made by the Imagists and their notion of the "sensuous apprehension of thought."[18] In William Pratt's words, "it is the visual content of language . . . which makes it communicative, and it is the visual accuracy of poetry which makes it more communicative than prose."[19]

Despite its visual "accuracy," the Imagists still did not seem to be agreed on the extent to which a poetic image can in fact be visualized. Sometimes it is a description of an object, like William Carlos Williams's "A Red Wheelbarrow"; at other times it is a metaphor, like Pound's "In a Station at the Metro." The association of the poetic with the mental image has created a host of cognitive problems, and P. N. Furbank declares the term to be unhelpful when applied to poetry.[20] Can we rightly call a figure of speech like "a Forest huge of Spears" an *image* as in the sense of a picture?[21] Furbank exposes a major problem with analyses that look for "word pictures" in texts which predate the concept,[22] and he questions the ability of the visual imagination to see one thing in terms of another: "You cannot present something to your mind's eye as being both a forest and spears. . . . You cannot *actually* think of something in terms of something else."[23]

However much we might object to such a statement, it is true that from the mid-twentieth century on we have seen a growing distrust of this term

17. "Politics and the English Language," in *A Collection of Essays* (Garden City: Doubleday, 1957), 162–77.

18. T. S. Eliot, *Selected Essays* (London: Faber and Faber, 1951), 286.

19. *The Imagist Poem* (New York: Dutton, 1965), 28.

20. Furbank, " 'Image,' " 344.

21. Ibid., 342, 341–42; "People still tend [in 1969] to think of mental images as having an actual optical reality—as if seeing things in the head were fundamentally different from seeing them in the world outside. They believe that mental images are presented to them, and they contemplate them. . . . It can never happen with a mental image, as it happens all the time when you look at the world outside, that there is something in your field of vision that you can't identify—making you ask yourself, 'Is it a bush or a rabbit?' "

22. For instance, Furbank takes Caroline Spurgeon to task for her analysis of "a little word-picture" in *Love's Labour's Lost* depicting the charm of young Berowne, able to make "aged ears play truant at his tales" (*Shakespeare's Imagery and What It Tells Us* [Cambridge: Cambridge University Press, 1935], 9). "What," asks Furbank, "are we meant to visualize?" (ibid). His criticism is sound; Spurgeon has shown us a *figure*, an example of synecdoche, and has misled us by calling it a picture.

23. Furbank, " 'Image,' " 335, 341. George Lakoff and Mark Turner argue differently in their exploration of the mapping of image structures in *More than Cool Reason: A Field Guide to Poetic Metaphor* (Chicago: University of Chicago Press, 1989), 57–139.

"imagery" at the very time that cognitive scientists have been zealously investigating the concept of "mental imagery." While debates rage in the field of psychology and philosophy of mind about whether the mental image is more like a picture or more like a sentence,[24] literary critics have lost confidence in the mental image as a guarantor of intelligibility, as an "epiphenomenon" that is somehow separate from the poetic mechanism which triggers it. Nevertheless, it is an entrenched modern tendency both to associate the poetic image with a point of view and to call this association into question. Theater, film, the photograph, the framed picture, theories about the spectator and the "gaze"—all reflect a modern obsession with "looking." A disruption of *deixis* bothers us in the same way that ambiguous juxtapositions do, but our inquiries into artistic effects and our experimentation with new effects arise from what disturbs us, as we are a body of readers and writers who find pleasure in alterity.

In the midst of all this inquiry, mid-twentieth-century medieval scholarship grappled with the alterity of medieval poetry, and the disjunct images and statements in ninth- and tenth-century texts. And yet, as Stanley says, let an Old English figure start to become too concrete and we are thrown off base. Old English scholarship has wanted to keep the figure in one niche and the image in another. It has been confused by a blending of modes. And especially so with the Welsh. What are we to make of lines like these?

> Bit las lluarth. bit diwarth eirchyat.
> bit reinyat yghyuarth.
> bit wreic drwc ae mynych warth.
>
> (RB: 1030.31–32)

[Let the vegetable garden be green. Let the beggar be shameless.
Let the (?) be in battle.
Let the woman be bad and her many shames.]

[Or: Green is the garden, shameless is the beggar.
The (?) is in battle.
Bad is the woman and her many shames.]

> gnawt deil agwyeil agwyd.
>
> (1031.14)

[Typical (are) leaves and saplings and trees.]

24. Daniel Dennett, "Two Approaches to Mental Images," in *Imagery*, ed. Ned Block (Cambridge: MIT Press, 1981), 88.

We have labeled these verses gnomic because of their gnomic tags (*bid*, "let be," "is customarily," and *gnawd*, "typical," "usual") but are these poetic images in either of the two senses of an image as (1) a description of something or (2) a figure of speech? Despite the fact that they are written in appropriate *cynghannedd*, their status as poetry has been repeatedly questioned.

The "Specificity" Spectrum

To put poetry aside for the moment, let me address a question that pertains to language in general, and that is whether or not we can refer to the nouns in the following sentences as "images": "a wheelbarrow carries dirt" or "birds of a feather flock together." The one offers information about the function of wheelbarrows, and the other is a proverb meaning "like seek out like." Both express general truths, the latter having a metaphor embedded in it. But are these images? For those who associate image and metaphor, then the latter example gives us an "image." The former example is harder, because up till now we have dealt with poetic utterances, not prosaic observations where the rhetorical intention is to say something *about* a wheelbarrow, and not present it sensorially. The very term *image* implies artificiality, for one can hardly call a verbal reference to an actual thing an "image"; it is indexical. One cannot hear one's spouse say "your study is untidy" and reasonably answer with "I don't like your image."

Traditional aesthetics has not attached artistry to aphorisms like "a wheelbarrow carries dirt"; these differ from the observation about the untidy room only in that they refer to a generic type, not a specific object. In intent, the two are the same: they make a factual observation. The sensorial effect of the statement is irrelevant, its "truth factor" dependent on what one knows about wheelbarrows. But if someone who has a bent for the metaphoric uses "wheelbarrow" to mean a loutish person who spends his time reading pornography and corrupting children, then the statement "the wheelbarrow carries dirt" takes on new connotations—it becomes an "image" because (1) it associates a relatively simple object with a more complex object or idea, and (2) it does so by calling that object to mind in a more specific way than if we were simply to consider its function. We need the sensorial impact in order to confirm the truth of the analogy. Furthermore, it can only become such an analogy if hearers/readers have understood this to be its purpose or if they endow it with this purpose. In the first instance, we don't really know how the referents or images in Welsh gnomic and nature poetry were meant to be understood, and in the second we find ourselves stretching mightily to make most of these gnomic comments into analogies.

"The Wheelbarrow Carries Dirt" is a poor illustration of an ambiguous analogy, but the questions it raises pertain as well to "the vegetable garden is green." I suggest that the term *image* as it appears in these poems be regarded as a reference to a concrete thing that is capable of being perceived by the senses within the conventional concepts of a given culture and that, through its relationship with other elements of the poem or the revealed intention of the poet, does one or both of two things: (1) it appeals in some way to our collective sensory knowledge of this object, and (2) it associates attributes of this object with something else—another object, a concept, an emotion, again collectively understood.

Each function has its various degrees of "specificity" or "explicitness" as these properties are revealed in language. In the first, for instance, the sensorial quality of a poetic image can range from the bare mention of something to a complex description. In the second, the explicitness of the analogy can range from a bald juxtaposition to the complex use of explanatory diction, which brings us back to the pivotal point of this study: The more the author adds informative or connective diction to an analogy, the more "explicit" it becomes and the more a reader's perception of it is *controlled*; the more the author qualifies an image with effective description, the more "concrete" it becomes. Through language it acquires perspective and relationship. Taste, an ever-changing thing, decides where it likes its poetry on the specificity spectrum or what it is that makes a poem effective. The twentieth century seems especially wary of art that controls our imaginative perception, especially appreciative of the silences in poetry that allow us to think feelingly, as Alcuin puts it, "upon things absent." Consider this famous line from *The Gododdin*:

> seinnyessyt e gledyf ym penn mameu
> (CA: 27.A, 7)

> His sword rang in the heads of mothers.

Two isolated events—the sharp sound of sword on metal and the anguished shock that the woman (absent from the battlefield) must feel when later told of her son's death—are here brought together in a kind of conceptual *zeugma* that pivots on the verb. Our shopworn simile, "She took it like a physical blow," suddenly comes to life in this Welsh image, and it reminds us vividly that poetry, if not the mind, is perfectly capable of hearing one thing "in terms of another."

There are, however, a number of verses in Early Welsh and English where the objects named are lists of observations about human life and natural phenomena very much on the order of "the vegetable garden is green"; as such, they do not seem to have a perceptible sensorial or associative function. Scholars have reacted to these *gnomic* poems with baffled curiosity or dismissal. The designation of poetry has even been denied the Old English *Maxims*, and in the Welsh poems it is unclear whether the stereotyped images are meant to have sensorial or associative effects or merely to offer sententious observation. Following is an outline of these poems and their critical reception.

Gnomes and Descriptions

The two Old English gnomic poems, *Maxims I* and *II* are to be found respectively in *The Exeter Book* and *The Cotton Manuscript of the Anglo-Saxon Chronicles* (for the latter poem, see Texts no. 4). Those verses of the Welsh that are most obviously gnomic occur as the *Gnodiau* and the *Bidiau* in *The Red Book of Hergest* (for the latter, see Texts no. 5). In *Peniarth* MS 102, we have *Bidiau II*, which repeat some of the verses in the *Bidiau* of *The Red Book*. Then, throughout *The Red Book*, we find a collection of nature or seasonal poems, some of them associated with the Llywarch-Hen cycle, which have gnomic elements; and in *The Black Book of Carmarthan* a poem called *Llym Awel* (see Texts no. 7) has been frequently designated as gnome. These are the controversial poems.

This matter of the gnomic, its relationship to epigram and its aesthetic value in both the Old English and the Welsh verses, has been in much dispute. Gnomes constitute some of the oldest literary expressions in the world and are to be found among Sumerian and Egyptian writings. Proverbs in the Old Testament partakes of this genre. In a sweeping generalization, one could say that gnomes "celebrate phenomena of the natural world."[25] A great deal of work has been directed at defining and classifying them: Aristotle defines a gnome or an apothegm as "a statement not relating to particu-

25. Blanche Coulton Williams, *Gnomic Poetry in Anglo-Saxon* (New York: Columbia University Press, 1914), 11–12.

lars . . . but to universals; yet not to all universals indiscriminately as, e.g., that straight is the opposite of crooked, but to all such as are the objects of (human) action and are to be chosen or avoided in our doings."[26] H. Munro Chadwick and Nora Chadwick qualify his definition by dividing the gnomes of the world into three categories: (1) those which exhort one to moral behavior by listing human virtues, (2) those which observe human activities or the workings of the gods or of Fate but which pass no judgment on those observations, and (3) all other gnomes, that is, observations of the processes of nature.[27] Patrick Ford writes that gnomes are "catalogues of wisdom" related to the proverb,[28] but Kenneth Jackson distinguishes them from the proverb: "A gnome need not be, and usually is not, a current popular saying with an implied moral, as the proverb is . . . and it need contain no advice or exhortation like the precept."[29]

Jackson would make a distinction, then, between "A rolling stone gathers no moss," which is popular and proverbial and seeks to "lesson," and "The vegetable garden is green," which is gnomic and seeks to categorize. The latter is not a description: the use of the Welsh verb *byd*, the imperative and/ or consuetudinal of *bod* ("to be"), renders "Let the vegetable garden be green," "the vegetable garden tends to be green." This, says Jackson, is a "nature gnome"; "Let the woman be bad and her many shames" is a "human gnome."[30]

One can understand why scholars have been reluctant to view the gnome as poetry. An originally *oral* product, the gnome is unconcerned with iconic depictions of the perceptible world. It is very low on the "specificity spectrum," its images stereotypical and common (this, indeed, seems to be its point) and it calls upon a particularly medieval predilection for categorizing, list making, and moral instruction, all of which bores and confuses the contemporary reader. There is nothing really comparable in contemporary English poetry. Our aphorisms are parodied or put on bumper stickers: "A good man is hard to find," "Life's a bitch and then you die." Even our more poetic gnomes—"Birds of a feather flock together"—are exiled from serious poetry.

26. *The Rhetoric*, II.xxi.2 (1394a).

27. *The Growth of Literature* (Cambridge: Cambridge University Press, 1932), 1:377.

28. *The Poetry of Llywarch Hen* (Berkeley and Los Angeles: University of California Press, 1974), 9.

29. Kenneth Jackson, *Early Welsh Gnomic Poems*, 3d ed. (Cardiff: University of Wales Press, 1973), 1. See also N. Barley, who makes the distinction in "A Structural Approach to the Proverb and the Maxim" (*Proverbium* 20 [1972], 737).

30. Jackson, EWGP, 1.

An additional problem lies in the unclear purpose of these obvious statements, mixed in as they so often are with narrative or bits of what seem more like real description. If they are literal, they are not purposeful;[31] but if they contain some hidden significance, then they are not gnomic but proverbial. Shippey compares a passage from Proverbs to lines from *Maxims II*:

> The conies are but a feeble folk,
> yet make they their houses in the rocks.
>
> (26:30)

> A dragon must live in a barrow,
> old and proud of his treasures.
>
> (26[b]–27[a])

The remark from Scripture is "either a banal statement or else a proverb, meant to be taken as a metaphor for the general truth that shelter may compensate for weakness," and the remark from the Old English poem may be one of several metaphors illustrating the general truth that there is "a place for everything and everything in its place."[32]

The function of the Welsh gnomes is similarly ambiguous. As with the English, it is hard to differentiate the sententious from the descriptive comment, and, further, its relevance to the first-person utterances or other "human interest" elements in the passage. This oddity has accounted for most of the controversy over Welsh poetry and what is to be looked upon as the important part of each verse. The gnomic passages have been described as interpolations made by later sententious poets who simply appropriated poetry that was originally descriptive of nature.[33] To others, it is the natural description that is irrelevant in a group of poems devoted to producing sententious sayings;[34] and Ifor Williams, as we have seen, suggests omitting the references to nature altogether in his edition of *Canu Llywarch Hen*.[35]

Even if one were to approve such editorial emendation, we can hardly condone Williams's amputation of the nature references in the *Llym Awel*

---

31. T. A. Shippey, *Poems of Wisdom and Learning in Old English* (Cambridge: D. S. Brewer, 1976), 12.

32. Ibid.

33. J. Glyn Davies, "The Welsh Bard and the Poetry of External Nature: From Llywarch Hen to Dafydd ap Gwilym," *Transactions of the Honourable Society of the Cymmrodorion*, Session 1912–13 (London: Chancery Lane, 1914), 84–88.

34. Jackson, EWGP, 1.

35. Ifor Williams, *Lectures on Early Welsh Poetry* (Dublin: Institute for Advanced Studies, 1970), 39.

poems. For one thing, it is not at all clear that this poem is part of those verses frequently referred to as "Mechydd ap Llywarch,"[36] and neither is it definitely gnomic. Ford labels it a gnome in his edition,[37] but it does not clearly possess gnomic characteristics; rather, it seems to describe a winter landscape. It is essential that we be able to differentiate between a gnome and a description, as the two might serve different purposes.

Thomas Parry makes the distinction by gauging the degree of universality in the utterance: the gnome makes a statement "that is true always," and the description makes a statement "that is true only in a particular circumstance."[38] The comment "Leaves are green in spring" expresses a universal truth and is therefore gnomic, for it is "true always." To help us understand the gnome, T. J. Morgan suggests that we add a confirmatory statement in parentheses—in other words, provide a *translation:* "Leaves are green in spring, *of course, obviously.*"[39] The function of the gnome is to confirm our understanding of obvious truths. But "Bitter is the wind tonight, / It tosses the ocean's white hair" is a description, because the use of the word "tonight" makes it clear that the speaker means to refer to a specific moment in time. One way, then, of gauging the gnomic or descriptive quality of an utterance is to note the use of orienting codes, a word or phrase that grounds us in a particular moment or point of view or, on the other hand, a word or phrase that clearly suggests generality.

The latter can be found in many Old English and Welsh gnomes. Two sections of verses among the Welsh, for instance, one from *The Red Book of Hergest* (see Texts no. 5) and one from *Peniarth* MS 102, are labeled *Bidiau I* and *II* because of their use of *bid*, the aforementioned imperative and/or consuetudinal form of *bod* ("to be"):

15.   Bit wenn gwylyan. bit vann tonn.
       bit hyuagyl gwyar ar onn.
       bit lwyt rew. bit lew callonn.
                           (RB: 1030.29–30)

[Let the seagull be white, let the wave be loud,
let blood be a stain on the ash-spear,
let frost be gray, let the heart be brave.]

<hr/>

36. Ibid., 27.
37. Ford, PLlH, 121.
38. A *History of Welsh Literature*, trans. H. Idris Bell, (Oxford: Clarendon Press, 1955), 37.
39. T. J. Morgan, "Canu Gwirebol," *Ysgrifau Beirniadol* 8 (1974), 20.

Compare the strikingly similar use of the verb "to be" in *Maxims II* (see Texts no. 4):

> wind byð on lyfte swiftust·
> þunar byð þragum hludast·   þrymmas syndan cristes myccle·
> wyrd byð swiðost·   winter byð cealdost·
> lencten hrimigost·   he byð lengest ceald·
> sumor sunwlitegost·   swegel byð hatost·
>
> (3^b-7)

[Thunder will be loudest at times. Great are Christ's powers.
Fate will be strongest, winter will be coldest,
spring frostiest, it will be longest cold.
summer will be brightest, sun will be hottest.]

The use of this form of the verb in English identifies the gnomic function of these verses, according to T. J. Morgan, who remarks that *bid* in the Old English appears to mean "is by nature"[40] (I have translated it as the futuric that it is), whereas *bit* in Welsh carries an imperative sense, or a connotation of "resolve" that can only be translated using the present indicative and some confirmatory expression like "of course."[41] Following Morgan, Jackson gives us *bid amlwg marchawg*: "the *real* knight needs to be conspicuous." This meaning, as a number of scholars have pointed out, is supplied in the Old English by the verb *sculan*, "to be destined to," "to have to," "to be in the habit of."[42] In *Maxims I* it ascribes function to a thing:

---

40. Ibid., 20.

41. EWGP, 62.

42. Chadwick and Chadwick, in *Growth of Literature*, 1:380ff., write that *sceal* means "is indispensible to," "is to be," "must be." Stanley Greenfield and Richard Evert note the inconsistent interpretation of this word by various scholars ("*Maxims II*: Gnome and Poem," in *Anglo-Saxon Poetry: Essays in Appreciation for John C. MacGalliard*, ed. Lewis E. Nicholson and Dolores Warwick Frese. [Notre Dame: University of Notre Dame Press, 1975], 346). "Does the term have a prescriptive or a descriptive function?" they ask. Paul Beekman Taylor writes that it expresses "what *should* be, how things *should* function. . . . the *sceal* maxims comprise a sort of handbook on ritual: descriptions on the one hand of the rituals of nature which, being of God's provenance, are out of man's control, and, on the other hand, description of the rituals of men which are heroic obligations" ("Heroic Ritual in the Old English Maxims," *Neophilologische Mitteilungen* 70 [1969], 388).

FORST sceal freosan   fyr wudu meltan
eorþe growan   is brycgian
wæter helm wegan   wundrum lucan
eorþan ciþas.

(EB2: 73–76ᵃ)

[Frost freezes, fire consumes wood,
earth grows, ice makes a bridge,
water wears a helmet, wondrously locks up
the seeds in the earth.]

Elsewhere, it clearly expresses resolve:

gearo sceal guþbord   gar on sceafte
ecg on sweorde   ond ord spere
hyge heardum men   helm sceal cenum
ond a þæs heanan hyge   hord unginnost

(202–5)

[The war-shield must be ready, the spear-head on the shaft.
The edge on the sword, and the point on the spear.
Courage in a brave man, a helmet must be on the hero,
And (to him) of cowardly spirit always least treasure.]

Another confirmatory marker in the Welsh gnomes is the word *gnawd*, as a noun meaning "custom," "nature," and as an adjective, "usual," "customary," "typical," "normal." These verses are referred to as the *gnodiau*, and the pattern *gnawd* XY means "It is an attribute of X to be Y"[43]

5.   gnawt gwynt or mynyd. gnawt meryd y mro.
      gnawt kael to yggweunyd.
      gnawt arlaeth maeth dyn creuyd.
      gnawt deil agwyeil agwyd.

(RB: 1031.13–14)

[Typical wind from the mountain. Typical a fool in the country.
Typical to get thatching in moorland.
Typical the rearing of a cleric on milk.
Typical leaves and saplings and trees.]

43. EWGP, 51.

We might also find a gnomic tag in the word *gorwyn* of another series of verses in the *Red Book* but it is not one that describes a general condition *per se*. Translated by Jackson as "delightful," its literal meaning is "very white," "radiant," or "beautiful." But in reading these verses as gnomic we run into a problem. Sententious statements abound ("Nature is stronger than education"), and we even have a clearly gnomic marker in verse 5 ("Typical upon the feeble [are] anxieties"), but the first verse exhibits what looks like orienting language:

> Gorwyn blaen onn. hirwynnyon vydant·
> pan dyuant ymblaen neint.
> brongwala hiraeth y heint.
>
> (1033.1–2)
>
> [Radiant the tips of the ash; tall, bright they are
> *where* (when?) they grow at the head of the glens.
> A heart full of longing (leads) to sickness.]

Does this mean that the ash trees that grow at the head of the glen and no others are tall and bright? Or does it mean ash trees that customarily grow at the head of the glen are tall and bright? We might be splitting hairs here, but the statement verges on the descriptive rather than the gnomic. There seems to be a ghost of a reference in *pan* ("when," "where") and Jackson calls these verses "semi-gnomic,"[44] perhaps because their images serve no apparent purpose beyond that of decorative, obvious comments. We might compare them with the *Llym Awel* verses of *The Black Book* (see Texts no. 6), which feature hardly any gnomic utterances among their nature descriptions but which have been classified as gnome by Ford and Morgan, included with the verses on "Mechydd ap Llywarch" by A. O. H. Jarman, cut to ribbons by Ifor Williams, and scoffed at by J. Glyn Davies for their "inconsistencies."

The frequent references to "today" seem to mark the poem as descriptive rather than gnomic; their repetition makes it sound oddly like a weather report:

> 14c.   oer divlit. yr eluit hetiv.
>
>   ["Cold, raw the land today."]
>
> 16c.   garv mir glau a uit hetiv.
>
>   ["Rough the seas, there will be rain today."]

44. Ibid., 3.

Likewise, the hyperbolic comments about the frozen grass, so hard that a man could stand on the blades, describe a particular circumstance rather than a universal condition. The "cries" of the wind (or of seabirds) before the hilltops in stanza 2 come close to depicting a "scene," especially following the marvelously alliterative line about the waves. It seems as though the poet is indeed trying to recall to us the sensations of winter, not merely utter gnomic observations.

We do find our standard "human gnomes" as the poem progresses, and for this reason, perhaps, the entire poem has been looked upon as gnomic:

7c.   Kadir yscuid ar yscuit glev.

["Fine the shield on the shoulder of the brave."]

10c.   meccid llvwyr llauer kyghor.

["A coward fosters many councils."]

13c.   ir nep goleith lleith dyppo.

["Despite any evasion, death will come."]

15c.   dricweuet llyvrder ar gur.

["cowardice is an evil thing in a man."]

The poem ends, I believe, in stanza 21 with the return to the opening line ("Shrill the shouting wind"); Jackson adds to it four more stanzas from the following poem, and both Williams and Jarman see it as part of a long poem addressed to Mechydd ap Llywarch. But the elaborate ornamentation with the excessive alliteration suggests that we have here a closing formula, as described in an earlier chapter, and the repetition in *breit orseuir allan* of one of the statements at the beginning also suggests closure. The poem, then, gives us descriptions of winter interspersed with gnomes about cowardice. It is less a gnomic poem, if we follow the strict definition set forth by Parry, and more a medieval *descriptio* of nature. If it is to be attached to the following verses about Mechydd ap Llywarch, then the nature images might serve to emphasize the theme of cowardice in battle (as well as link it with the saga-*englynion*), just as the summer images in *Claf Abercuawg* help offset the isolation and misery of the protagonist. In this respect, the images create a mood. But the use of formula, type-scene, reliance on general characteristics, appeal to proverbial wisdom and figura, and blithe disregard for physical and temporal consistencies mark this poem as belonging to a medieval tradition of poetry, and these are also the features that offended J. Glyn Davies when he came to it expecting a naturalistic description of a particular day in winter. It describes *generalized* winter, but its images have every appearance of striving to create a sensory impact.

The Gnome as Exemplum

If the original purpose of the gnome is not to create a sensory impact but an intellectual one, then this motive is perhaps the hardest for a contemporary reader to accept. T. A. Shippey speaks of the "undeniable charm" of the Anglo-Saxon *Maxims* and also of their "unimaginable purpose."[45] We would like to root out the aesthetic function of *sententiae* and make them into comprehensible images that speak to us today, and if they do so successfully, then who are we to deny this very real by-product of reading these poems? Nevertheless, the preoccupation with *exempla* and proverbial wisdom puts gnomes in a firm medieval tradition that took satisfaction in placing things of the world into categories. The tradition stretches back to antiquity with the apothegms of Aristotle, the wise sayings of Isis, and the proverbs of Solomon.

Suggestions that the early Welsh and English gnomes were little more than metrical exercises or "models for alliterative composition"[46] have been debated vehemently by scholars wishing to find in them a more dignified purpose. But the *exemplum* or "model" of either a proper poetic form or a proper mode of behavior, or both, had its own dignity and status in the Middle Ages. Exercises by bright students were held in a certain esteem, and games or contests were considered fit to record. The *Hisperica Famina* is probably a collection of contesting scholars,[47] and recently it has been suggested that the "Gwarchanau" of *Canu Aneirin* are "teaching poems" intended to display metrical and prosodic forms.[48] Jackson expresses a more fundamental basis for the gnomic poems:

45. Shippey, *Poems of Wisdom*, 12.

46. Blanche Williams, GPAS, 109.

47. See P. Grosjean, "Confusa Caligo: Remarques sur les *Hisperica Famina*," *Celtica* 3 (1956), 35–37. For more extended commentary as well as a translation, see Michael W. Herren, ed. and trans., *Hisperica Famina: The A-Text, A New Critical Edition with English Translation and Philological Commentary* (Toronto: Pontifical Institute of Medieval Studies, 1974).

48. See Kathryn A. Klar, "What are the *Gwarchanau*?" in *Early Welsh Poetry: Studies in the Book of Aneirin*, ed. Brynley Roberts (Aberystwyth: National Library of Wales Press, 1988), 111.

They are expressions of a desire for classification, for having the world with its chaotic variety formulated in an intelligible way; it is a step from the very primitive state in which man feels himself over-whelmed by a mass of unrelated phenomena to one in which he is beginning to co-ordinate them and find his own place in relation to them.[49]

This explanation strikes one as artificial: "primitive" or otherwise, human beings do not need gnomes to help them find their place in the world; nothing seems more like a "mass of unrelated phenomena" than the gnomes themselves, which decidedly do *not* show relationships, either between natural objects or between human being and natural object, outside of putting them together in a list. I suspect that whatever the putative origins of the gnome and whatever grounding it has within the medieval predilection for moral instruction and sententia, the Welsh and English works remaining to us have developed some highly stylized features that invite examination from an aesthetic basis. Their juxtapositions amount to a kind of artistry and display their own peculiar sense of connection.

The Gnome as Poem

In search of this saving artistry, R. MacGregor Dawson attempts to find a "logical pattern" within *Maxims I* and *II* declaring them to be "mnemonic arrangements in sequences built up by multiple association of ideas, either through meaning or sound."[50] He goes through both sets of poems showing how one image or idea could have inspired the next, declaring that lines 12[b] through 26[a] in *Maxims I* show a train of thought based on association:

	he us geþonc syleð
missenlicu mod	monge reorde
feorhcynna fela	fæþmeþ wide
eglond monig	eardas rume
meotud aræde	for moncynne

---

49. Kenneth Jackson, ECNP, 136–37.
50. R. MacGregor Dawson, "The Structure of the Old English Gnomic Poems," JEGP 61 (1962), 15.

    ælmihtig god   efenfela bega
    þeoda ond þeawa   þing sceal gehegan
    frod wiþ frodne   biþ hyra ferð gelic
    hi á sace semaþ   sibbe gelærað
    þa ær wonsælge   awegen habbað·
    Ræd sceal mid snyttro   ryht mid wisum
    til sceal mid tilum   tu beoð gemæccan
    sceal wif ond wer   in woruld cennan
    bearn mid gebyrdum   beam sceal on eorðan
    leafum liþan   leomu gnornian

                [He (God) gives us thought,
    different temperaments, many tongues.
    Many living races far and wide
    are on many islands, broad lands
    the Lord decreed for mankind,
    Almighty God, equally many
    people and customs. A meeting will
    a wiseman hold with wisemen. Their thought is similar.
    They always settle disputes, advise peace,
    which wretched men before have disrupted.
    Advice must go with wisdom, justice with wisemen,
    the good with the good. Two should be mated.
    A man and a woman must bring into the world
    A child through birth. A tree must on earth
    lose its leaves; its branches mourn.]

The train of thought is as follows: God bestows various gifts on man, the most important of which is wisdom. The notion of wisdom leads us to the mention of good counsel in line 18, which in turn leads us to the idea of good men keeping company together in line 23ª. In 23ᵇ, this idea is followed "by a suggestion that it is man's destiny to move in pairs, and the train of thought progresses to the idea of man and wife and their offspring."[51] Dawson then surmises that mention of a birth suggests the idea of death, expressed in the image of the dying tree in line 25ᵇ, and after a minute discussion of other associative connections in *Maxims I* and *II*, he concludes somewhat weakly (and presumptuously) that his system "is the only way to account for the

51. Ibid., 16.

logical pattern to be found in the Exeter and Cotton Gnomes. . . . [that] it is not, perhaps, a good pattern for a poem, but it is an adequate one, and is far more satisfactory than the total absence of form which many critics feel to be characteristic of these poems."[52]

Once more we are faced with an *apologia* for an absence of "unity" in medieval poetry. The connections that Dawson finds in lines 23 and 25 of *Maxims I* may be aural rather than logical, though. The poet had to maintain alliteration with *t* and *b*, and the logical link may have been secondary. One wonders if it is profitable to look for logical links in gnomic poetry, where the form and the subject matter are so strictly stylized. Morgan notes the apparent meaninglessness of one of the lines cited above from the *gnodiau*: "Typical are leaves and saplings and trees." This line appears to be padding, he tells us, but it contains an early example of *cynghanedd sain* (*gnawt deil a gwyeil a gwyd*) and has obviously been included for aural purposes.[53]

This stance seems to put us back in league with the critics who dismiss the gnomes as "little more than metrical exercise," showing the "crudeness" that comes of a "stilted, copybook purpose."[54] One wants to find a reason for their inclusion in manuscripts that also contain some of the finest poems in medieval English and Welsh poetry. The urge to defend the "unity" and aesthetic soundness of the Anglo-Saxon and Welsh gnomes is understandable, but I do not think they should be judged by other poems that show other rhetorical purposes. In *The Seafarer* and *Claf Abercuawg* a philosophic or religious stance is forwarded and a mood carefully cultivated which the images of nature somehow underscore. Their inclusion of gnomic elements to this end is better understood the more we seek to understand the gnomic poems themselves from the standpoint of medieval aesthetic thought, especially among the Welsh poems, where the function of the nature image—either as gnome or description—is so ambiguous.

As I have tried to show in the previous chapter, metrical and prosodic requirements may have played a large part in affecting connections, and this feature in itself should be given more credit as a highly effective artistic principle of organization. For our purposes we might be able to approach the artistry of the gnomic poems (and consequently the nature references in some of the other poems) from two standpoints, one examining visual connection

---

52. Ibid., 22.
53. Morgan, "Canu Gwirebol," 92.
54. EWGP, 98.

and the matter of "point of view," and the other stressing contextual connection and the matter of cultural associations. In so doing, we might be better able to isolate some of the differences between Old English and Early Welsh poetry.

The first theory stresses the place of the gnomes within a medieval aesthetic of modularity and accretion where disjunction, juxtaposition, the flattening of perspective, and the stylization and removal of natural objects from their customary contexts are a norm in the visual arts and find their counterparts in the treatment of time and space in the verbal arts. Description was subordinate to category and moral lesson in the medieval insular gnome, but one of its requirements may have been the very absence of connectedness that has caused critics grief. Perhaps one of its purposes was to present the things of the world in a "patchwork-quilt" fashion,[55] breaking up the "hegemony of artificial perspective" as part of the philosophy peculiar to it which stresses universal as opposed to individual vision. The second theory invites us to regard certain natural references as contextually programmed, by which I mean that their connection in the gnomes and elegies with sententious statements about human affairs was dependent on their having some kind of cultural meaning, an understanding on the part of the audience that sea and sadness go together. The natural reference would trigger an association that has no explicit grammatical expression. This theory has the advantage of explaining how gnomic images appear in non-gnomic poems, as they do so often in the Welsh.

These two approaches are not mutually exclusive, and, in fact, are fundamentally related in that they examine the same general problem—that of connection and orientation—from two different angles: The one examines the level of "concreteness" that links one image with the next, and the other examines the level of "explicitness" that unites one idea with the next. It should be stressed that the Welsh and English gnomes are not strictly alike in character and that they differ in degrees of explicitness and expansion in much the same way that their other poems do. Chapters 5 and 6 will address these two approaches separately.

55. Morgan, "Canu Gwirebol," 23: "fel plentyn wrth edrych ar effaith *kaleidoscope* y cwilt yn gyfan" ["like a child looking at the kaleidoscopic effect of a patchwork quilt"].

5

The Vanishing Point:
Deixis and Conjunction

For religious man, every existential decision to situate himself in space
in fact constitutes a religious decision.
　　　　　　　—Mircea Eliade, *The Sacred and the Profane*

gwelais wedy cad kolut ar drein
("I saw after battle bowels on thorns.")
　　　　　　　—Cynddelw, *Lament for Owain Gwynedd*

In the last chapter I suggested that hypotaxis confers a hierarchy of relation-
ships on the grammatical statement in much the same way that a point of
view affects the description of imagery. The analogy can be extended to the
visual properties of perspective in painting. A painter gives the illusion that a
scene is being viewed from a specific point in space by foreshortening objects:
the lines of the receding buildings come together on the horizon at the
"vanishing point," and it is when this principle was rediscovered in medieval
painting that we have a movement away from Carolingian linearity, the
beginnings of the Renaissance, and the increasing dominance of the picture.
The Old English and Early Welsh gnomes juxtapose images that in everyday
experience would not be juxtaposed, and in this sense they have neither a
point of view nor a deictic center; both have vanished (or resisted develop-
ment) along with a hierarchic system of grammatical relationships. This
mode would significantly affect how we view their sense of connections.

Seeing and Knowing in the Gnomes

Nicholas Howe writes that "the catalogue could be used for a variety of encyclopedic and poetic purposes because it corresponds to a certain vision of experience, or pattern of thought, which values plenitude and diversity."[1] Lynn Remly locates the origin of Anglo-Saxon gnomic poetry within an ancient tradition of the celebration of the sacred, which, she writes, "has to do with what is preeminently real. A perception of the things that are has the effect of revitalizing the perceiver, for in the presence of the sacred, man is also curiously aware of partaking of its power as well as being overtaken by it."[2] Mircea Eliade examines the religious dimensions of spatial heterogeneity:

> Revelation of a sacred space makes it possible to obtain a fixed point and hence to acquire orientation in the chaos of homogeneity, to "found the world" and to live in a real sense. The profane experience, on the contrary, maintains the homogeneity and hence the relativity of space. No *true* orientation is now possible, for the fixed point no longer enjoys a unique ontological status; it appears and disappears with the needs of the day.[3]

This "fixed point," though, is not to be found in the subjective point of view in the way that it is privileged in modern thought. Subject ceases to be, and it ceases to "see"—at least in ways that have deictic orientation—when it partakes in the hierarchies of sacred space, and it is in the context of this statement that I would like to examine the English and Welsh gnomes, along with the placelessness of the sufferers in the elegies.

In a close reading of *Maxims II* (see Texts no. 4), Stanley Greenfield and Richard Evert probe the notions of perception in the Anglo-Saxon gnomes by suggesting that the purpose of the poem is to show how "true wisdom ultimately reveals the limitations of human knowledge" by contrasting "the unknowability of the state of heaven with the relative knowability of conditions on this earth."[4] The opening "establishes the essential perspective of the

---

1. *The Old English Catalogue Poems, Anglistica* 22 (Copenhagen, 1985), 17.
2. "The Anglo-Saxon Gnomes as Sacred Poetry," *Folklore* 82 (1971), 149.
3. "Sacred Space and Making the World Sacred," in *The Sacred and the Profane: The Nature of Religion*, trans. Willard R. Trask (New York: Harcourt, Brace and World, 1959), 23.
4. Stanley B. Greenfield and Richard Evert, "*Maxims II*: Gnome and Poem," *Anglo-Saxon Poetry: Essays in Appreciation for John C. MacGalliard*, ed. Lewis E. Nicholson and Dolores Warwick Frese (Notre Dame: University of Notre Dame Press, 1975), 340.

poem" by referring to the "marvelous work stones," built by giants that can be "seen from afar." This image "prepares us for the final mention of the *sigelfolca gesetu*, the extraterrestrial locale which cannot be described."[5]

Far from being a random compilation, the poem is an artful and pleasing creation that connects seemingly unrelated things through the clever device of beginning a statement in the *b*-verse and ending it in the following *a*-verse, an element of which alliterates with something in the next *b*-verse. "Thus the poet imposes upon a set of semantically disconnected statements a pattern within which syntactic and rhythmic expectations create a highly satisfying sense of aesthetic order in the multiform diversity of the experiences of life."[6] Ordering the poem is the implicit contrast between knowable and unknowable things, earthly experience and heavenly mysteries, reinforced in this last section by the contrasting references to things above, and things below.[7]

While I reviewed in the last chapter some of the arguments against endowing the "mental image" with any kind of textual chartability, one is still free to look for evidences of an *intention* to offer a picture to the hearer's imagination. It is trickier with the gnomes, given their nature, but I suggest that the bird in the air, the salmon in the pool, the hill on the earth, the star in the sky, and the cattle on the ground might be thought of as "images" that call to mind a contrast in spatial areas while they reinforce the age-old gnomic wisdom of all things in their proper places. Perhaps part of the pleasing and even sought-after effect of the poem is this incongruity that creates a conceptual montage effect. While our ear is treated to aural harmonies, our mind's eye is directed now here, now there, now up, now down, and it brings into focus, if ever so briefly, certain tangible details of the gnomic referent:

> Eofor sceal on holte·
> todmægenes trum. . . .   Darod sceal on handa·
> gar holde fah·   Gim sceal on hringe·
> standan steap and geap·
>
> (19b–20a, 21b–23a)
>
> [A boar must be in the wood,
> strong of toothmight . . . A spear must be in the hand,
> a shaft decorated with gold.   A gem must on the ring
> stand high and wide.]

5. Ibid., 353.
6. Ibid.
7. Ibid., 350.

To insist that the gnomic referent never has any imagistic force is to deprive these and the Welsh gnomes of much of their charm. How can we derive pleasure from "Let the puppy be snarly" (Texts no. 5) if we don't recognize in it something we have seen and heard? In *Maxims II*, the *a*-verse appears to expand on a physical detail of the object named in the previous *b*-verse, but to call these references "descriptions" is to invest them with too much specificity, for they do, after all, point to conventional and therefore universal attributes; nevertheless, visual properties of these objects are frequently alluded to and the poem begins with a reference to seeing. Colors are mentioned: the gold on the javelin (line 21ᵃ), the flood-gray river (line 31ᵃ), the green hill (line 35ᵇ); and we are made to note the characteristic movement of some animals: the bird sports or sweeps (*lacan*) through the air, the salmon glides (*scriđan*) with the trout. Knowledge is the theme of this poem, which, "coupled with a movement from consideration of the *visibilia* of the earthly experience to the *invisibilia* of the heavenly, gives the poem its unity."[8] Seeing in medieval thought is closely related to knowledge; our knowledge of the world derives from what we can see of it; our ignorance of God's realm derives from what we cannot see of it.

In fact, its "seeing" resembles in many instances the kind of vision described by Alcuin, Augustine, Ambrose, and Boethius, which affixes wings to the mind and lifts us up out of a mortal, singular station on earth:

> Pennas etiam tuae menti, quibus se in altum
> tollere possit, adfigam, ut perturbatione
> depulsa sospes in patriam meo ductu, mea
> semita, meis etiam vehiculis revertaris.
>> Sunt etenim pennae volucres mihi,
>> quae celsa conscendant poli;
>> quas sibi cum velox mens induit,
>> terras perosa despicit . . .
>> Boethius, *De consolatione philosophiae*[9]

> [For I shall affix wings to your mind by
> which it can lift itself; so that, all
> disquiet banished, you may return safely

8. Ibid., 340.
9. Liber 4, pr. i, m. i.

to your homeland by my guidance, my path,
and also by my conveyance (says Philosophy).
> For my wings are swift
> That they may ascend to the lofty skies;
> When the speedy mind has put them on
> It despises the hated lands . . .]

Man's likeness to God lies not in his body but in his soul, "because of the soul's power to range throughout the world in thought," to make absent things present to itself.[10] Peter Clemoes proposes Alcuin's *De ratione liber* as a probable source for *The Seafarer*, with its admiring description of the *mens* or *animus* which is

> Of such mobility that it does not become inactive even when it is asleep, of such speed that at one moment of time it surveys the sky and, if it wishes, flies across seas, traverses lands and cities, in short, by thinking, it, of itself, sets before its view all things it chooses, however far and wide they may be removed. And yet some people marvel if the divine mind of God keeps all parts of the universe simultaneously and always present to it—God's mind which rules all things, everywhere present and everywhere whole—when strength and power of the human mind shut up within a mortal body is so great that it cannot be restrained at all, even by the confines of this heavy and sluggish body to which it is tied, from having the free power of thinking without tolerating rest.[11]

The *anfloga* in *The Seafarer* might be an actualization of *maria pervolet* ("it flies across seas") in Alcuin's text "whose wording would have given [the poet] a powerful nucleus around which to crystallize his portrayal."[12] P. L. Henry argues that *The Seafarer* is influenced by the Celtic connection of birds and souls.[13] Other sources are scriptural and patristic, and the generally widespread belief throughout medieval Christian tradition that the soul

---

10. Peter Clemoes, "Mens absentia cogitans in *The Wanderer* and *The Seafarer*," in *Medieval Literature and Civilization: Studies in Memory of G. N. Garmonsway*, ed. Derek A. Pearsall and R. A. Waldron (London: Athlone Press, 1969), 67.

11. Ibid., 63–64.

12. Ibid., 68.

13. P. L. Henry, EECL, 137–49.

leaves the body in the visible form of a bird.[14] Nevertheless, "seeing" is a talent of the Celtic poet, and it *is* knowledge:

> The Irish *fili* . . . connects with Welsh *gweled* "to see": *gweledydd* "a seer," and there is a strong probability that the second element in *derwydd*, the Welsh for *druid*, is connected with the *vid-* in Latin *video* "I see," cf. the Greek οἶδα, "I have seen," then "I know," and the Welsh *gwyddbod*, *gwybod* "to know," literally "to be in a state of having seen." The poet was a man who saw. Over and over again in our early poetry the bard sings *gwelais*—"I have seen." The poet was a seer. From the same root comes the English *wit*, and the *wise* man is so called because he has seen and knows.[15]

Along similar lines, Maria Tymozsko suggests that the disconnected images in *Cetamon*, a poem attributed to the seer-figure Finn, come out of a native Celtic tradition of poetic and supernatural vision.[16] "The poem," she writes, "gives a vision of the world in all its details, a vision not accessible to the mortal eye at one place or one moment in time."[17] She notes that the story in which the poem features tells us that Finn composed it to prove his *eicse*, his "divination of wisdom,"[18] but what she effectively reveals is the organizing principle behind the gnomes. If we adopt her theory, then, the Old English line "grief is wondrously tenacious, the clouds glide" is not a mere non sequitur dictated by the demands of alliteration; it shows us an expanded view in which natural and human experience, no matter how unlike or physically separate, have a continuity that is not grasped by the single point of view. It obliterates the quotidian perspective that colors one's understanding of the

---

14. Clemoes, "Mens absentia," 69, cites *The Life of Saint Gregory*, written by a Whitby monk in the late seventh century, "in which it is related that Paulinus's soul 'migrated to the heavens, when he died, in the form of a white bird. . . .' The author is likely to have taken his precedent from Gregory's *Dialogues*—a book well known to him—where it is told that the soul of a certain Abbot Spes at his death issued from his mouth in the form of a dove and, after the roof had parted miraculously, flew off into the heavens." Possessing vision and being carried off by a bird is a common motif in early and late medieval literature, as Paul Beekman Taylor and I argue in our article "In the Grasp of the Falcon: Re-reading the *Corpus Christi Carol*," *Assays* 6 (1991), 93–109.

15. Ifor Williams, *Lectures on Early Welsh Poetry* (Dublin: Institute for Advanced Studies, 1970), 7.

16. Maria Tymocsko, " 'Cetamon': Vision in Early Irish Seasonal Poetry," *Eire-Ireland* (1983), 17–39.

17. Ibid., 25.

18. Ibid., 22.

universe and one's place in it and puts human joy and woe together with leaves and saplings and trees.

Deixis and Medieval Point of View

Whatever its origins in an indigenous style of verse, this "vanishing" point of view in early English and Welsh imagery is reinforced by a medieval aesthetic that privileges the general over the particular and that is bolstered by complex theological underpinnings. Grammatical point of view, as we understand it today, is expressed by the linguistic term *deixis*, meaning "pointing," or "indication," especially as it indicates the relationship of objects in space and time as they are oriented with respect to the speaker.[19] Certain adverbs and pronouns—"this," "that," "here," "there," "now," "then"—show the spatial and temporal location of objects as perceived from a specific standpoint or from a particular moment. Tenses operate deictically, as does person, obviously, and some prepositions that depend on a personal point of view, such as "beyond," or "behind," "in front of," or "to the left of." The use of such deictic terms is a significant part of "perspective": it has obvious bearing on both verbal narrative and visual art because it is interested in a sensorium in which the observer and/or hearer can partake along with the speaker. It is vital to the concept of poetry as "discourse"—an exchange between author and real or imagined hearer—and this kind of *deixis* was an important element in the development of Renaissance art, in which the patron's specific point of view was actively cultivated.

Literature manufactures a world that becomes "immediate" to its readers and hearers by the controlling powers of its creator. *How* immediate it becomes to us, or *how* lifelike, is again dependent on the creator and his purpose and on the rules by which he works. It is possible to look for deictic

19. Emile Benveniste was one of the first to employ the term *deixis* ("Structure des relations de personne dans le verbe," *Bulletin de la Société de Linguistique* 126 [1946], 1–12). See also Umberto Eco, *A Theory of Semiotics* (Bloomington: Indiana University Press, 1976), 115–21, and John Lyons, "Deixis, Space, and Time," in his book *Semantics* (Cambridge: Cambridge University Press, 1977), 2:636–724, and especially Charles Fillmore, "Towards a Descriptive Framework for Spatial Deixis," in *Speech, Place, and Action: Studies in Deixis and Related Topics*, ed. Robert J. Jarvella and Wolfgang Klein (Chichester: John Wiley, 1982), 31–60. More work needs to be done with the use of deixis in literary discourse; its implications for semiotics, gender studies, and psychoanalysis seem fruitful.

markers in poetry in order to gauge the evocative quality of poetic images, to see the extent to which a poet has tried to make his images visually and emotionally immediate to his hearers. Carolingian art and the study of the relationship between the visual and verbal arts in the European Middle Ages has provided us with a number of clues as to the status that was granted this kind of *deixis*. Art historians have generally distinguished between the "classical" and "barbaric" modes: the one, writes Charles W. Jones, incorporates a "love of rotundity, space enclosure, perspective, organic unity, sublimity, and monumental naturalism," which he attributes to the Carolingian admiration for classical antiquity,[20] and the other incorporates "abstract linearity . . . of flat surface in plastic art; of episodic, chronographic narrative in literature; of articulated rather than fluent plain song in music," which he attributes to influence by Hiberno-Saxon and Philistine art.[21] He notes René Huyghe's comments about Barbaric art, which "finds its accomplishments not in statuary but in ornament. It is no longer concerned with space as such. . . . Geometry replaces the naturalism of observed reality. Line supplants volume."[22] The Carolingian artists negated the Aristotelian principle that a work of art is like a living organism with a centered design that derives its beauty from its function, and they imposed instead a numerical abstract upon reality, which was to mirror the order and rationality of God's universe.[23] One can locate this concern for abstraction and number in the Christian "imitation" of God—*similitudo*, "likeness without identity."[24] Modulation reduces things of nature to a numerical order: the module is the building block of order. Separation is sought after, as well as a linearity of design, not the uninterrupted continuity that would suggest the pagan preoccupation with a "natural" and therefore godless world. Christian eschatology informs the treatment of time in early medieval Latin narrative such that discrete events can be linked vertically to Divine Providence.[25]

Scholars of Old English in particular have compared Anglo-Saxon poetic structure to the structural interlace and juxtapositive, modular quality of

20. Charles W. Jones, "Towards a Carolingian Aesthetic: Why Modular Verse?" *Viator* 6 (1975), 312.

21. Ibid., 312–13.

22. In *Larousse Encyclopedia of Byzantine and Medieval Art* (1963), cited by Jones, "Carolingian Aesthetic," 312.

23. Edgar de Bruyne, *Etudes d'esthètique médiévale* 1 (Bruges: Tempelhof, 1946), 1–108.

24. Jones, "Carolingian Aesthetic," 317.

25. Eric Auerbach, "The Arrest of Peter Valvomares," in *Mimesis: The Representation of Reality in Western Literature*, trans. Willard R. Trask, (Princeton: Princeton University Press, 1945), 73–74.

insular decorative art.[26] Peter Schroeder suggests that we look to medieval decorative patterns for clues to the structure of Old English narrative, where the artist "rearranges space, annihilates spatial relations, pulls objects from their natural context and creates a new, 'unnatural' but dynamically patterned context in which to place them."[27] He declares that "space in the visual arts is analogous to time in poetry,"[28] that events in the Anglo-Saxon poem *Exodus* are shown "simultaneously" and that our efforts to locate a chronological unfolding of events are thwarted. Here is his translation of a passage recounting the destruction of the Egyptians in the Red Sea:

> The folk was frightened, the flood terror came to their miserable souls, the sea threatened death, the mountain slopes were bedewed with blood, the sea spewed gore, noise was in the waves, a slaughter-mist arose.[29]

This might seem to present events "simultaneously," but our confusion arises primarily from the fact that the Old English poet has omitted a *þonne* between the two clauses ("the sea threatened death" / "the mountain slopes were bedewed with blood"), and another editor might have attempted to suggest the break (and the connection) with a colon. *Þonne* ("then," "next") is a deictic marker which orients events within a continuum of time, but the montage of images here is not really occurring simultaneously; the relationship is expressed through a juxtaposition instead of a conjunction.

We have seen numerous instances in Old English poetry where the omission of a grammatical "pointing" word will produce the ambiguity that bothers us; but for every conjunction that is omitted in one Anglo-Saxon poem, it is just as often supplied elsewhere, sometimes in overabundance, as in *The Seafarer*. It is true that the Anglo-Saxon poems differ in style and logical development, that some show more influence by a Latin periodic grammar, but this question of the linear, modular, and abstract quality of Old English verse is far from being resolved, especially as we have more satisfying exam-

---

26. See Paul Beekman Taylor, "The Structure of Völundarkviða," *Neophilologus* 47 (1963), 228–36; John Leyerle, "The Interlace Structure of *Beowulf*," *University of Toronto Quarterly* 37 (1967), 1–17; Richard A. Lewis, "Old English Poetry: Alliteration and Structural Interlace," *Language and Style* 6 (1973), 196–205; Peter Schroeder, "Stylistic Analogues between Old English Art and Poetry," *Viator* 5 (1974), 185–97; Carol Braun Pasternak, "Stylistic Disjunctions in *The Dream of the Rood*," *Anglo-Saxon England* 13 (1984), 167–86.

27. Schroeder, "Stylistic Analogues," 187.

28. Ibid.

29. Ibid., 148.

ples of the stylization of image and time in the poetry of the Welsh. Of course one's critical stance is largely dependent on what one uses as a means of comparison, and I am here reading the Old English through the lens of the Welsh. Theories about the modular and disjunct qualities of the Old English are by no means invalidated, but they ought to be put in perspective with other medieval traditions, those which carry the disjunctive and abstract style to an extreme. Welsh scholar Gwyn Williams has also found an analogy in Celtic decorative patterns for what is happening in the Welsh poems:

> The absence of a centred design, of an architectural quality, is not a weakness in Old Welsh poetry, but results quite reasonably from a specific view of composition. . . . Aneirin, Gwalchmai, Cynddelw and Hywel ap Owain were not trying to write poems that would read like Greek temples, or even Gothic cathedrals, but rather, like stone circles, or the contour-following rings of the forts from which they fought, with hidden ways slipping from one ring to another. More obviously, their writing was like the interwoven inventions preserved in early Celtic manuscripts and on stone crosses, where what happens in a corner is as important as what happens at the centre, because there often is no centre.[30]

This analogy is more appropriate to the Old English gnomes than it is to the Old English narratives, for the Maxims have no center, no vanishing point, whereas the narrative poems have the ordering imposition of a plot which disguises the "insular" underpinnings of Anglo-Saxon aesthetics. In light of the other stylistic exigencies that combine to make Old English poetry what it is, it is doubtful that analogies between the visual and the verbal arts are entirely satisfactory. Elsewhere I have expressed doubt that comparing the treatment of space in manuscript illuminations to the treatment of time in the narratives is efficacious, precisely because of the hierarchic nature of argument or chronology that confers centers and points of view.[31] When compared to the Welsh poems, one sees in retrospect a real concern on the part of many Old English poets, including the authors of The Seafarer and The Wanderer, for chronicity, continuity, the ordering of events within a temporal continuum, the ordering of images within a visual plane, and the relationship of an ego to an external sphere of influence.

30. *The Burning Tree: Poems from the First Thousand Years of Welsh Verse* (London: Faber and Faber, 1956), 15.
31. Sarah L. Higley, "Forcing a Gap: The Stylistics of 'Amputation' in *Marwnad Llywelyn* by Gruffudd ab yr Ynad Coch," *Viator* 19 (1988), 251–54.

This concern extends as well to many modern-day medievalists: Phillip Damon shows a decided prejudice in favor of troubadour poetry over the Goliardic Latin lyric, exhibiting the customary modern preference for the image to the catalogue, the personal observation to the public formula.[32] Both the troubadour lyric and the medieval Latin lyric make use of a nature preface that introduces expressions of love or other personal emotion. In exploring the possibility of Arabic influence on troubadour poetry, Damon contrasts the Latin lyricist with the Provençal and charges the former with "schematizing nature" by aiming at "an unorganic, almost anti-sensuous *catalogue raisonné* instead of at an image":

> The pictorial details of his lyrics are usually listed in a bald series joined by such correlatives as *et . . . et, nunc . . . nunc, iam . . . modo.* His vocabulary of description is almost entirely limited to a small number of conventional generic terms and abstract epithets. Verbs of perception are, with very few exceptions, impersonal. Birds are heard, flowers are seen, and breezes felt; but the poet's lyric ego never enters the scene to hear, see, or feel them. . . . The poet's own reactions to the scene are carefully kept separate from his description of it. Indeed, one of the primary effects of the Latin nature introduction seems to lie in the abrupt *chute* from a rigidly impersonal introduction to an assertively personal exposition of the poet's condition.[33]

Citing from the *Carmina Burana,*[34] he writes that although the goliards "often rose above the level of [their often] mediocre performances . . . the

---

32. Phillip Damon, *Modes of Analogy in Ancient and Medieval Verse* (Berkeley and Los Angeles: University of California Press, 1961).

33. Ibid., 303.

34. Ibid., 304:

> Sevit aure spiritus
> et arborum
> come fluunt penitus
> vi frigorum
> silent cantus nemorum
> nunc torpescit ver solo
> fervens amor pecorum;
> semper amans sequi nolo
> novas vices temporum
> bestiali more.
> [The wind blows harshly, and the leaves have dropped from the trees because of the cold's might; the songs of the birds are stilled. Now the beasts, fervent only in spring, are sluggishly unamorous. But I, the constant lover, refuse to follow the changing seasons after their fashion.]

invariable tendency of the medieval Latin lyric, from first to last and from best to worst, was to keep the poet outside the scene he described. Nature seems to be presented as a public fact rather than a personal experience, as a concept rather than a percept."[35] In contrast, the nature introduction of the troubadour *canso* exhibits a subjectivity unrivaled in early medieval European verse:

> The imagery is ordinarily presented as something seen, heard, and felt by the poet. Even the more or less hardened formulas emphasize the personal perception and response so conspicuously absent from the medieval Latin and popular lyrics: "Bel m'es quan . . . ," "Lancan vei . . . ," "Be m'agrada . . . ," "Er ai gran joi que . . . ," "Be'm platz quan."[36]

This formula, "When I see" or "I take delight in," emphasizes the visual or sensational quality of the images, and they underscore the poet's physical relationship to the things he describes. Thus, they have deictic function.

Damon's preferences for the Provençal over the goliard—so undisguisedly expressed in his choice of diction ("mediocre performances," "invariable tendency," "hardened formula," "bald series")—should be familiar to us by now, and they bespeak yet again the deep-seated modern insistence that poetry express subjectivity. One could note, however, that the use of the first person in these vernacular poems is every bit as conventional as the "public percepts" of the Latin poems—a point Damon concedes; their repeated avowals of first-person point of view do not, however, cultivate what Peter Clemoes calls "audience perspective"[37]—a feature that becomes more prominent in late medieval and Renaissance literature, but which is largely lacking in the poems that we are examining at present.

Perspective in the Old English Poems

In his article "Action in *Beowulf* and Our Perception of It," Clemoes raises an issue important to literary studies of *deixis* without marshaling any of the

---

35. Ibid., 305.
36. Ibid., 306.
37. Peter Clemoes, "Action in *Beowulf* and Our Perception of It," in *Old English Poetry: Essays on Style*, ed. Daniel G. Calder (Berkeley and Los Angeles: University of California Press, 1979), 147.

linguistic and pragmatic arguments that he could have, and that is the ex-
plicit inclusion of the reader (or hearer) within the point or points of view
being presented. His argument is a simple one with complex implications: he
compares the treatment of point of view in *Sir Gawain and the Green Knight*
to the embarkation passage in *Beowulf*. The passage from *Gawain* occurs
toward the end when Bercilak's servant points out the way to the Green
Chapel:

> Til hit watz sone sesoun þat þe sunne
>   ryses þat tyde.
> Þay were on a hille ful hyȝe,
> Þe quyte snaw lay besyde;
> Þe burne þat rode hym by
> Bede his mayster abide.
>   (2085–90)

Clemoes writes that "the poet has placed the two men, freshly emerged from
a dense wood, on a snowcovered hilltop at sunrise. *To our mind's eye* they are
silhouetted there when Gawain experiences his moment of truth. We appre-
hend him at the center of a *sharply focused image. We see* the two men in
their setting as they cannot see themselves" (italics mine).[38]

He contrasts this use of "audience perspective" with that in lines 210b–11a
of *Beowulf*, as the hero is about to set forth with his men for Denmark:

> fyrst forð gewat;   flota wæs on yþum,
> bat under beorge.   Beornas gearwe
> on stefn stigon,—streamas wundon,
> sund wið sande;
>
> [In a while it went forth, floater was on waves,
> boat under headland. Soldiers ready,
> on prow mounted, currents roiled,
> sea against sand.]

The audience, however, has no particular point of view with respect to the
boat. "There is no feature in this description which specifically directs it
towards us."[39] Direct address to an audience is rare in Old English and

38. Ibid., 148.
39. Ibid.

limited to the homily; the voice of the poet "remains the voice of traditional corporate wisdom,"[40] even that which asserts experience from its own perspective, as in the poems of lament. "But no Old English narrator ever explicitly invites us, the audience, in our imagination to see and hear happenings for ourselves, to be on the spot and have our own spectator's relationship to events," as does the chorus of Shakespeare's *Henry* V when it asks the audience to picture the departure of the King's ship.[41]

True enough; the Old English poems are not self-consciously discursive in this sense, not even in the way that certain ballad-romances are in later centuries ("Herken lordyngys þat ben trew . . .").[42] Yet Clemoes raises a problematic issue in his assertion that "to our mind's eye" Gawain and his guide are "silhouetted" on the mountain top or that "we apprehend him at the center of a sharply focused image," seeing them "as they cannot see themselves." This would appear to invite challenge from a whole battalion of specialists on the mental image. The way a reader perceives images in a text is deeply subjective and unchartable. All we have to the matter at hand are deictic markers that would signal our optical involvement in a described scene—nothing else. A poem is not like a videotape, and my mental image of this scene was very different from Clemoes's: I was situated on the mountain top with Gawain and his guide (for my habit when I read is to locate my perspective in that of the character who perceives, and whose point of view is given lesser or greater delineation according to stylistic custom). "Þe quyte snaw lay besyde"—this preposition *beside* is not an informative deictic, and there are no clues in the text indicating where the snow or the sun or the mountain or the two men are in relationship to me as I project myself into the scene. Other readers, more influenced by cinematic techniques, might well convert third-person narratives into film shots, as Clemoes seems to do. In *Beowulf*, deictic clues are rare, but the coastguardsman sees the ship coming in to the harbor, and we share his point of view (229–54ᵃ). It is more difficult to do so with Grendel's final raid of Heorot, where we see him see the hall that he approaches (714–16ᵃ), then his eyes standing forth "most like flames"—but the analogy with cinematic techniques is inadequate; the more approximate pictorial analogy is that of an Anglo-Saxon illustration (like *The Sacrifice of Isaac*)[43] in which one might see spread out across the page (or

40. Ibid., 150.
41. Ibid., 151.
42. Ibid., 149.
43. London, British Museum, MS *Cotton Claudius* B. iv, fol. 38r. In this illustration one starts at the bottom left corner of the picture and follows Abraham and his son up the mountain, where at

carved into the side of a reliquary) the depiction of Grendel's approach in one frame; in another his entrance at the door with eyes standing forth like flames; in another the sleeping men, Beowulf with one eye open. As viewers, we are outside the scene, if a graphic arts analogy is required, and this is the "audience perspective" that Clemoes misses mentioning. An audience then would most likely associate verbal and visual telling as we do today; but no amount of speculation will reveal whether or not they located their imagined points of view within that of the character performing an action.

The speaker of *The Wife's Lament* locates herself in a specific time and place and tells her story from this standpoint:

> ic þæt secgan mæg
> hwæt ic yrmþa gebad   siþþan ic up [a]weox
> niwes oþþe ealdes   no ma þonne nu
> (EB2, p. 152, lines 3^b–5)

> [I can tell that,
> what I endured of miseries   since I grew up,
> new or old,   never more than now]

Words like *heonan, her, þissum, londstede* show a spatial point of view, and words like *ærest, þa, eft, nu,* and *þonne* show a temporal point of view where we, presumably, are to regard things along with her:

> *ærest* min hlaford gewat   *heonan* of leodum
> ofer yþa gelac   hæfde ic uhtceare
> *hwær* min leodfruma   londes wære·
> *ða* ic me feran gewat   folgað secan
> wineleas wrecce   for minre weaþearfe·
> ongunnon [þæt]   þæs monnes magas hycgan
> þurh dyrne geþoht   þæt hy todældan unc
> þæt wit gewidost   in woruldrice
> lifdon laðlicost   [ond] mec longade·
> het mec hlaford min   *her* heard niman

---

each stage the same characters are depicted doing different things in different parts of the story. In the top right-hand corner we have the intervention of the angel of God just as Abraham is about to slay his son. This mode of pictorial representation is so common throughout the Middle Ages (in manuscript illustrations, carvings on caskets, reliquaries, and crosses) that it would seem to provide the most useful analogy with narrative images and the lack of "audience perspective."

ahte ic leofra lyt   on *þissum londstede*
holdra freonda   forþon is min hyge geomor·
ða ic me ful gemæcne   monnan funde
heardsæligne   hygegeomorne
mod miþendne   morþor hycgendne
bliþe gebæro   ful oft wit beotedan
þæt unc ne gedælde   nemne deað ana.
owiht elles   *eft* is *þæt* onhworfen
is *nu*   swa hit no wære
freondscipe uncer   s[c]eal ic *feor ge neah*
mines fela leofan   fæhðu dreogan

(lines 6^a–25^b)

[*First* my lord went *hence* from (his? our?) people
over tossing of waves. I had dawn-care
where my lord could be on earth.
Then I went forth seeking service,
friendless exile, because of my woeful need.
That thing the kinsmen of the man began to plot
through secret thought that they could separate us
so that we two lived most far in the world
in greatest enmity and I suffered longing.
My lord bade me *here* to take lodging.
I had in *this land* few beloved ones
loyal friends. Therefore is my heart sad(.)[44]
when (*then?*) I found my true-mated man
unblessed, mournful-minded,
hiding his heart, thinking upon crime(.)
(W)ith blithe demeanor(.) (F)ull often we two boasted
that nothing else would part us except death alone.
That has changed *since.*
Now it is as if our love were not.
Far and near I must endure the hostility of my beloved.]

With the description of the earth cave, we switch to the present tense,
which would seem to indicate that the narration is proceeding from this place

---

44. The beginnings and endings of statements are frustratingly ambiguous in this and the follow-
ing three lines, and the meaning of the poem and the chronology of its events are of course utterly
dependent on them.

and this moment in time and that the speaker is able to contrast her present
solitary situation with that of imagined distant lovers:

> heht mec mon wunian   on wuda bearwe
> under actreo   in *þam* eorðscræfe·
> eald *is þes* eorðsele   eal ic *eom* oflongad·
> *sindon* dena dimme   duna uphea
> bitre burgtunas   brerum beweaxne
> wic wynna leas   ful oft mec *her* wraþe begeat
> fromsiþ frean   frynd *sind* on eorþan
> leofe lifgende   leger *weardiad*
> *þonne* ic on uhtan   ana *gonge*
> under actreo   geond *þas* eorðscrafu
> *þær* ic sittan *mot*   sumorlangne · dæg
> *þær* ic wepan *mæg*   mine wræcsiþas
> earfoþa fela   forþon ic æfre ne *mæg*
> *þære* modceare   minre gerestan·
> ne eallas *þæs* longaþes   þe mec on þissum life begeat
>
> (lines 26ª–41ª)

[One bade me dwell in a wooded grove
under (an? the?) oak tree in *this* earth cave.
Old is *this* earth hall; I am all oppressed with longing.
Dim are valleys, hills high,
bitter fortress enclosures, with briars overgrown,
dwellings empty of joy. Full often *here* oppressed me cruelly
the departure of my lord. There are lovers on earth
living lovingly, sharing a bed,
while I at dawn go alone
under oak tree through *these* earth caves(.)
There (where) I must sit the summerlong day(.)
There (where) I can weep my exile-journeys,
my many hardships. For I can never
find rest from *that* (the) anxiety of mine,
nor from all *that* (the) longing which afflicted me
in *this* life.]

Demonstrative pronouns are notoriously ambiguous in Old English, and it
is not clear that the demonstrative (*þære modceare*), which was to become our

definite article, had as yet developed the deictic and anaphoric distinction of modern English "this" and "that." "The" and "that" in Old English are almost invariably synonymous, it would seem, "this" (ðeos) being marshaled when more specifically deictic signification is desired; translators should refrain from assigning anaphoric sense to the demonstrative unless the context makes it clear that a distinction is being made. In fact, the deictic situation in *The Wife's Lament* is obscure; it is unclear, for instance, whether the oak tree is meant to be a specific one or one of many; absence of an article does not necessarily indicate indefiniteness. And some translators put a break after line 36, regarding *þær* in lines 37 and 38 as an anaphoric adverbial:

> *There* I must sit the summerlong day;
> *there* might I weep my miseries.

This interpretation has the effect of making the speaker seem to step back suddenly and view herself from a distance, rather like poetic "astral projection." The gnomic closure of the poem has a similar effect, wherein specifics are replaced by generalities and close-ups by objects seen at a distance:

> a scyle geong mon   wesan geomormod
> heard heortan geþoht   swylce habban sceal
> bliþe gebæro   eac þon breostceare
> sinsorgna gedreag   sy æt him sylfum gelong
> eal his worulde wyn   sy ful wide fah
> feorres folclondes   þæt min freond siteð
> under stanhliþe   storme behrimed
> wine werigmod   wætre beflowen
> on dreorsele   dreogeð se min wine
> micle modceare   he gemon to oft
> wynlicran wic   wa bið þam þe sceal
> of langoþe   leofes abidan·

(lines 42ᵃ–53ᵇ)

[Ever must a young man be mournful-minded,
hard the thought of his heart; likewise he must have
blithe demeanor, also the breastcare,
a multitude of constant sorrows, whether it be that upon himself
    depend
all his worldly joy or whether it be that very far,

an outcast from his distant homeland that [it is?] my lover sits
under a stone cliff, befrosted by storm,
weary-minded friend, with water drenched
in dreary hall, he suffers, my friend,
much care; he remembers too often
more joyful dwellings. Woe is him who must
endure longing for the beloved.]

As Old English periodic sentences go, the long one above is among the
most difficult and ambiguous. Even were we to know exactly what gnomic
wisdom is being expressed here, the generalities give way, at an indeterminate
point, to a strangely empathic vision (one presumes) of the speaker's beloved,
who suffers a plight not unlike her own, except for the fact that his is attended
by the conventional images of winter instead of those of summer. We have
seen how winter imagery serves as a stereotypical symbol of distress and
loneliness in Old English verse, and the reference to the "summerlong day"
may be equally conventional in its suggestion of weary duration. It could be
argued, however, that the summer setting, along with repeated mention of
the oak tree and the high occurrence of *deixis* in general are descriptions of a
particular place and situation. This notion cannot be proved and is perhaps
unlikely; however, the fact remains that the author has tried to make the
scene as visually and emotionally immediate to his or her audience as possi-
ble and is careful to delineate relationships. In other words, the landscape has
been fleshed out.

We might note the use of *deixis* in some of the other poems: *The Ruin*, for
instance, presents "a scene viewed from a complex series of perspectives
covering a vast range of time" that illustrates its predominant theme of muta-
bility.[45] First, the differing tenses signal "a contrast in the observer's mind
between past and present. The *wealstan* exists in the present tense of the
poem, but the past is brought sharply into the context of the present through
the reminder that this wall is *gebræcen.*"[46] A further contrast is made with the
visual scope of the observer, who notes the gray and red lichen on the wall
but continually juxtaposes such minutiae with "an expanding view stretching
back through human history."[47] As an exercise in deictic orientation, the

45. Daniel G. Calder, "Perspective and Movement in *The Ruin,*" *Neuphilologische Mitteilungen*
72 (1971), 443.
46. Ibid.
47. Ibid.

poem offers an intriguing problem, for while it abounds with pointing language which serves to emphasize the contrast between this present heap and that former palace (*þæs wealstan*, line 1; *þæs wag gebad*, line 9; *forþon þas hofu dreorgiað*, line 29; *þæs teaforgeapa*, line 30; *þær iu beorn monig*, line 32; *þæt wæs hydelic*, line 42; *þær þa baþu wæron*, line 46), there is no mention of the first person, no appeal to the personal emotion or reflection we so often find in other Anglo-Saxon poems on this subject. However, one can almost follow the direction of the observer's eye as he takes in the ruined building; one seems to walk with him into the dilapidated courtyard and imagine the place as it used to be. *Wrætlic is þæs wealstan*, we are told, and our eyes are directed to the fallen roofs and the crumbling towers in line 3 and then to the "broken gate" in line 4, a sequence which suggests that we are outside the edifice. The poet brings us closer—*hrim on lime* ["frost on the lime," line 4b]—and even closer still: *oft þæs wag gebad / ræghar ond readfah* ["Often this wall endured, lichen-gray and red-stained," line 10]. The speaker then goes on to contemplate its design, which leads him to imagine the unknown architect, which in turn leads him to reconstruct in his mind's eye a scene as one might have found it within the castle walls at an earlier time:

> beorht wæron burgræced   burnsele monige
> heah horngestreon   heresweg micel
> meodoheall monig·   · mon · dreama full
>   (lines 21–23)

> [Bright were townbuildings, many bathhalls
> high pinnacles, much host-noise,
> many a meadhall full of man joys.]

When we return to the site of the ruin, we find that the speaker has gone inside: *forþon þæs hofu dreorgiað / ond þæs teaforgeapa* ["therefore are these courts dreary, and this arch of stone . . ." lines 29b–30a]. Without once referring to self, the speaker of *The Ruin* nevertheless describes a scene from a very particular point of view that we are expected to share; the act of observation is oddly transferred to the imaginary nobleman of the past, who once looked upon a scene of opulence where now lie heaps of broken roofwork—observed, it is implied, by the speaker himself:

                    tigelum sceaded
hrost beages rof   hryre· wong gecrong
gebrocen to beorgum·   þær iu beorn monig
glædmod ond goldbeorht   gleoma gefrætwed
wlonc ond wingal   wighyrstum scan
seah on sinc on sylfor   on searogimmas
on ead on æht   on eorcanstan·
on þas beorhtan burg   bradan rices·
                                (lines 30^b–37^b)

[From tiles parts
the roost strong of ring, place shrank with decay
broken to mounds. There once many a man
gladminded and goldbright, gleamingly adorned,
proud, wine-swollen, shining in armor,
looked upon treasure, upon silver, upon crafted gems,
upon wealth, upon possessions, upon precious stones,
upon this bright city of broad kingdom.]

Notice how the imaginative impulse of the speaker has caused the deictic reference to change in this last line; no longer is the city of the past "that once bright city"; it is *"this* bright city," as though he has called forth a palpable vision. We saw such a deictic shift in *The Wife's Lament*, only it took us in the opposite direction, away from a personal orientation into the remoteness of gnomic commentary where things are viewed from afar. Here the impersonal view takes on a personal orientation; this dramatic shifting between here and there and between now and then illustrates the Anglo-Saxon preoccupation not only with dynamic contrasts but with relationships among those contrasts.

The Seafarer abounds with *deixis*. The message of the poem, or one of its major messages, is the counsel it gives us to put ourselves and our lives in relationship to God and to the world and to put the world into perspective with God's order. The poem has been regarded as disjointed, confused, haphazard, associative, and ambiguous, as we have seen, but such views taken of it derive primarily from its first half. The second half, which does not receive nearly so much attention, is lucid, clear, to the point, didactic, and not so interesting, perhaps, but like the speaker in *The Wife's Lament*, the speaker of *The Seafarer* seems to step out of his mortal, limited human perspective and lose himself in Christian wisdom expressed through gnome. It becomes increasingly clearer, as the poem progresses, that the images of seafaring are to be regarded in retrospect as *exempla* of the ascetic life which firmly controls the fluctuations and worldly desires of the soul. This understanding of them in no way diminishes their immediacy as images of real seafaring, but in the abstracting process of the poem they do a dissolve, to use a film term, and are replaced by the lesson. Following is a step-by-step analysis of this process (see Texts no. 1, for the poem in full).

The Seafarer begins with the position of the speaker on land, recalling his grueling adventures at sea, and struggling with his conflicting desires about a future voyage. The word "there" recurs frequently, establishing his present physical distance from this experience and also establishing our position with him looking out to sea and back in time. These deictic markers continually emphasize one's station within the world in relationship to things present or past, near or distant, and they stress one's ability to affect or be affected by the world. This world has specific, palpable impact on the mariner:

> þær mec oft bigeat
> nearo nihtwaco   æt nacan stefnan
> þonne he be clifum cnossað   calde geþrungen
> wæron mine fet   forste gebunden
> caldum clommum   þær þa ceare seofedun
> hat[e] ymb heortan   hungor innan slat
> merewerges mod.
>
> (lines 6ª–12ᵇ)

> [*There* often befell to me
> the narrow night-watch at prow of ship
> *when* it knocks against cliffs; by cold pinched
> were my feet frost-bound
> by cold fetters; *there* cares sighed
> hot around heart, hunger gnawed inside
> the seaweary spirit.]

Furthermore, he is eager to impress on us the distance he felt from his home and his friends, and he uses a device that is found as well in *The Wanderer*, the ironic replacement of his dear absent friends and their remembered laughter with the presence of seafowl and their harsh cries. This shock of "immediate" reality which distances all imagined reality by the force of its concreteness is perhaps most deftly handled in *The Wanderer*: the man dreams that he is kneeling before his beloved lord only to wake up to find the seabirds before him. In both poems, the poet strives to inspire a physical as well as an emotional empathy in his hearers, and he goes to lengths to manipulate the painful contrast between things present and things absent, things in the immediate foreground and things not.

I have already examined in some detail the startling use of *forþon* in line 33[b], which introduces a contradictory idea. The problem for us with this poem is that the high degree of deictic orientation, or the placement of objects into perspective with the speaker—in other words, the "immediate" quality of its images—masks the highly rhetorical and stylized impulse behind it which seeks to offer us a kind of dialectic between the active and contemplative life. The almost perfect split in the poem has created a good deal of confusion too; the first half dwells on the horrific aspects of seafaring and barely hints at the speaker's firm Christian faith, and the second half never once refers back directly to seafaring in a way that would explicitly fortify the relationship between the two halves. It is no wonder that critics thought it comprised two separate poems, but this division and change also seems to result from the dialectic structure of the argument. The man who lives for the world and the man who lives for God are seen together in one soul, and the tension in the poem hinges on the choice that a man of divided feeling must make. He chooses to live for God, and this choice gives birth to a new type of discourse in which he reveals his wisdom to us. M. Rieger, with great perspicacity, saw it as a dialogue,[48] which in a sense it is, but not between an old man and a youth. Rather, the poem is "dialogical" in the Bakhtinian sense in that it is double-voiced—hence its ambiguity.

Lines 1–34[a] stress the repugnance felt by the mariner towards his seafaring life—the loneliness, the pain, and the suffering that he fears. This section is a long one, and its vividness is deliberate. The poet means us to understand the full implication of going to sea, and he strives to heighten our awareness with a formulaic expression of contrast which he repeats twice: "the man who abides happiest on earth does not know this (his own wretchedness) [lines 12[b]–13]; "He little knows—he who has experienced life's pleasures in town, of adversities few, proud and flushed with wine—how, weary, I had to endure the tracks of the sea [lines 27[b]–30]." Then, lines 34[b]–38 switch abruptly in the famous disjunction to an expression of desire for an ocean voyage urged

---

48. M. Rieger, " 'Der Seefahrer' als Dialog hergestellt," *Zeitschrift für deutsche Philologie* 1 (1869), 334.

on him by beating thoughts which in the previous lines take the form of beating hailstones. Lines 39–43 return us with another ambiguous *forþon* to the sobering aspects of seafaring, the constant fear of the unknown which no man of the world can fully conquer. In this passage, perhaps, we find the first hint of the spiritual significance of the sea. Lines 44–52 fall into step with this argument, seeming to continue the thought, but change subtly to suggest that enthusiasm for seafaring obliterates worldly concerns, that, in fact, the pleasures of the earth urge the eager, adventurous mind to the challenge of seafaring. In lines 53–57, the other voice counters with an opposing concept, using an ambiguous coordinating conjunction (*swylce:* "likewise"? "also"? "on the other hand"?). The cuckoo warns him of ill, and the blithe, prosperous and flabby man swollen with wine puts in a third appearance along with the formula noted above: "The fortunate man knows this not: what those endure who lay their tracks of exile furthest [lines 55b–57]." In lines 58–64, the ambiguous *forþon* introduces the transitional passage of the poem. The speaker finally rejects this last argument and sends his thoughts over the sea. This passage exhibits an interesting example of *deixis:* the spirit becomes disembodied while the bodily eye watches it recede into the distance and come back (*cymeð eft to me*). It is hard to tell at this visionary moment whether the *anfloga* (line 62b) is his returning spirit or an actual bird that adds its voice to the speaker's own eager desires. It is perhaps both; most certainly, though, it is the antithesis of the cuckoo.

After this stunning image, the poem launches into a whole new gear; description is replaced by gnome, and, as in *The Wife's Lament*, it is almost as if the speaker's psychic projection has removed all mortal perspective from him. *Forþon me hatran sind / Dryhtnes dreamas þonne þis deade lif / læne on londe*, says the seafarer: "For God's joys are hotter to me than this dead life," and sure enough, "dead" to us are earth's natural details, and we see them no more in the way that we have. Nevertheless, the second part of the poem comments didactically upon ideas half-suggested in the first part, and asks us to view its images in retrospect: the spiritual significance of springtime, the cuckoo, and the wine-swollen landlubber are summed up in the *contemptus mundi* of lines 66b–102, which conclude with the image of a man strewing his brother's grave with gold. A repeated pattern in these lines is formed by the temporal contrast between things as they are now and things as they will be on the Day of Judgment and by the spatial contrast between our situation *here* and our future situation *there* in God's more "immediate" reality:

ne mæg þære sawle   þe biþ synna ful
gold to geoce   for godes egsan
þonne he hit ær hyded   þenden he her leofad·
(lines 100–102)

[For the soul which is full of sins, gold cannot be an aid before the
terror of God *when* he has *formerly* hoarded it *when* he was alive *here.*]

Likewise, line 106 seems to address the man with "fat" on his soul, aptly
embodied in the image of said landlubber: *dol bid se þe him his dryhten ne
ondræded / cymed him se dead unþinged* ["foolish is he who fears not his
Lord; death comes to him unawares"]. This statement also recalls lines 40–43
of the previous section: *Forþon nis þæs modwlonc mon ofer eorþan . . . þæt
he a his sæfore sorge næbbe / to hwone hine Dryhten wille* ["There is no proud
man on earth . . . that never has anxiety in his sea voyage about what the
Lord will do to him"]. Line 107, then, puts most of the previous images of
wretchedness into new perspective: *eadig bid se þe eaþmod leofad cymed him
seo ar of beofonum* ["Blessed is he who lives wretchedly; to him comes grace
from heaven"]. The conflicting images of the man on shore and the man at
sea gain new significance in the context of this lesson, but most telling is the
following gnomic utterance in line 109:

stieran mon sceal strongum mode   ond þæt on staþelum healdan

["One must restrain a strong mind and hold it within bounds" or:
"One must control with a strong mind and keep it within bounds"]

This statement echoes almost word for word the line from *Maxims I* (line 51).
There, "steering" or "controlling" is seen in close connection with the image
of a storm at sea, held back by the sturdy walls. Likewise, the diction of *The
Seafarer* forcefully controls the images and ideas of the speaker; where he
seems to get too involved in the painful reality of the life at sea he alters the
terms of the image, making it fade into symbol. Always he is concerned with
location, for it is important where we stand in relationship to this life and the
next. The last part of the poem emphasizes this relationship repeatedly in
deictic terminology:

Uhton we hycgan   hwær we ham agen
ond þonne geþencan   hu we þider cuman
ond we þonne eac tilien   þæt we to moten
in þa ecan   eadignesse
þær is lif gelong   in lufan dryhtnes
                                        (lines 117–21)

[Let us consider *where* we have a home,
and then think how we shall come *there*,
and then we should also strive to attain
to *that* blessed eternity *where* life springs
from the love of the Lord.]

Perspective in the Welsh Poems

The principal dynamic in both *Claf Abercuawg* and *Can yr Henwr* (Texts nos. 2 and 3) is contrast, manipulated by a juxtaposition instead of a grammatical explanation. Some Old English poems, as we have seen throughout the course of this study, make use of adversative asyndeton; but in the elegies, at least, there is much more syntactic conjunction than anything to be found in the Welsh. The highly formal and repetitive structure of the Welsh poems of lament imposes a pattern which seems to replace grammar. Temporal and spatial contrasts are conveyed by the arrangement of the lines. In the first two lines of the *englyn* we hear of events in the past or of phenomena at a certain remove from the speaker, and in the final line there is a reference to the speaker's present condition and emotional state that most often clashes with the image presented in the previous lines. The effect is a kind of exaggerated parataxis wherein a dialectic of sorts is created: two separate comments create a new fusion, and much of the impact of the verse is contextual, implied. Such poetry can be dazzlingly evocative in its understatement, and in poems like *Claf Abercuawg* and *Can yr Henwr* the images of nature have their original affective force. Though there is a prominent "point of view" in these poems, it is expressed through tense and verbs of perception rather than through the tight spatial indicators of "here" and "there." Like the troubadour poets Damon praises, the speaker of *Claf Abercuawg* frequently alludes to his personal perception of a thing:

8a.   Neus e[n]deweis i goc ar eidorwc brenn.

[I listened to a cuckoo on an ivy-covered tree.]

9a–b.   Yn y vann odywch llon dar.
         Yd e[n]deweis i leis adar.

[On the peak over the vigorous oak
I have listened to voices of birds.]

27a–b.   Kigleu don drom y tholo
          vann y rwng gra[ae]n a gro.

[I heard the heavy roar of the surf
loud among sand and gravel.]

The problem for modern readers arises only when we try to relate these poems to the gnomic and quasi-gnomic poems that precede them in *The Red Book*, where we apparently have no protagonist and consequently, it would seem, no point of view. There is little question that they are related in some way; many of the same stereotypical nature references occur there as they do here, especially in *Gorwyn Blaen*, which comes before *Claf Abercuawg* in the manuscript, and to which it is probably some kind of preface. In the *Gnodiau* we have the very same englyn that appears in *Can yr Henwr*:

Y deilen a dreuyt gwynt.
gwae hi oe thynget.
hen hi. eleni y ganet.
                    (RB: 1031.24–25)

[The leaf which the wind whips away;
alas for her fate!
Old she, born this year.]

In the context of "The Song of the Old Man" (stanza 14), this verse has a poignancy and metaphoric significance that is lost, however, in the context of the gnomes. Either the poems of lament are borrowing nature references that are originally gnomic and adapting them to their purposes, or the gnomic poems have excerpted the nature references from their original context of lament. This latter theory seems plausible partly because of the

odd and occasional emergence among the gnomic poems of a personal
statement:

> Glaw allan gwlychyt vyg gwallt.
> (RB: 1032.32)

> [Rain outside; it wets my hair.]

> Eiry mynyd hyd kyngrwn.
> llawer a dywedeis os gwnn.
> anhebic y hafdyd hwnn.
> (RB: 1028.20–21)

> [Mountain snow, hunched the stag.
> Much have I said, I know;
> unlike the summer's day, this.]

> Gorwyn blaen brwyn. kymwyn biw.
> redegawc vyn deigyr hediw.
> (RB: 1033.37–38)

> [Radiant the tops of rushes, tame the cattle;
> flowing my tears today.]

Even so, we must still ask how the nature images could become so detach-
able, so highly stereotypical and categorical, that they would seem to be so
evocative in the Llywarch-Hen corpus and yet recede into the distance in the
gnomes. The answer might lie in the discrete structure of the lines themselves
within the englyn and their formulaic contribution to the rhyme and the meter
of the whole verse. Except where the speaker actively mentions physical percep-
tion of his surroundings ("I have heard a cuckoo on an ivy-covered branch"),
the external images and the internal feelings are at a curious remove from each
other in Claf Abercuawg. There is a reference to cuckoos singing and a refer-
ence to the speaker's sorrow, and one infers that his grief over his condition is
sharpened by so much vitality and natural beauty all around. The connection
is not explicitly stated, except, perhaps, in stanza 7 where the speaker says of
the cuckoos that his heart finds it wretched that "those who heard them do not
hear them also." For the most part, though, the juxtapositions set up an ironic
contrast between inner and outer weather, and rarely do we see the Sick Man
actively involved in the world around him—except to hear. And this is signifi-

cant. Hearing clearly takes precedence over seeing in these verses. The speaker hears cuckoos, dogs barking, the heavy roar of the surf on the sand. We find it hard to imagine his position in relationship to the cuckoos; these are given specific locations—on flowering branches, on ivy-covered trees, on the top of the strong oak; but the speaker could be anywhere—inside or out, lying down or walking around, sitting before the shelter mentioned in stanza 20. The speaker of *The Wife's Lament* is more specific about her own physical presence in the poetic landscape than is this Welsh speaker. Like hers, his gaze (if you can call it that) goes everywhere: the white hilltops, the wet streams, the cold moon, the wide wave, the gray top of the mountain, the fragile tips of the ash. Essentially, he is everywhere, and as the poem progresses the images become increasingly removed, it seems, from his point of view. As in both *The Seafarer* and *The Wife's Lament*, they become increasingly gnomic in their appeal to category and typicality:

22.   Alaf yn eil meil am ved.
       nyt eidun detwyd dyhed.
       amaerwy atnabot amyned.

[Cattle in a shed, a cup for mead.
Strife is not the wish of the fortunate.
The compass of understanding is patience.]

The protagonist of *Can yr Henwr* is much more visible to us primarily because he is described: "I am old, I am alone, I am deformed, cold" (stanza 17), and in stanza 13 he is shown moving about feebly in a world that surrounds him with its hostile vitality—although from the impersonal gnomic point of view:

Dyr gwenn gwynt gwyn gne. godre
gwyd dewr hyd diwlyd bre.
eidyl hen hwyr y dyre.

[Certain (broad?) the laughter of the wind, white the vision of the edge of the wood; bold the stag, hard the hill,
feeble the old man, slow his ascent.]

In both poems, however, the skillful use of juxtaposition and contrast effectively calls to mind the great "elemental indifference" by which Shippey explains the meaning of the famous juxtaposition in *Maxims II: Wea bið wundrum clibbor, wolcnu scridad,* line 13 (Grief is wonderfully tenacious. The clouds roll).[49] It is the natural analogy in its essential form, and it approaches the *gnomic* in its depiction of the inexorable way of things which man, especially the poor *diriaid,* the "unlucky, perverse one," cannot alter.

This fatalistic outlook is reinforced by poetic style and by the organization of images. There is simply less syntax of control than that exhibited in *The Seafarer* and *The Wanderer,* and, consequently, there is a cynicism and a fierce pathos in the Welsh poems that is blunted in the English by explanation. If hypotaxis means the placement of ideas in a hierarchic relationship to each other and if parataxis means placing unlike ideas next to each other and giving them equal stress, then we might see how the differences we have been noting in syntactic connection extend to the imagery of man and nature in both Old English and Welsh poetry of lament. The imagery of the Welsh poems is subtly different from that of the English elegies. Dazzling and vivid, it comes to us in pieces which do not have a clear physical relationship to the sufferer nor even to sacred fixity. The sufferer can neither affect the spaces of the world nor hold at bay the annihilating threat of the noisy and empty sea. Natural and human phenomena together are laid next to each, flattened out, and made universal and for this reason it is hard to tell the gnomic statement from the description. The intrusion of the one into the other blurs the distinctions between the sacred and the secular, contributing powerfully to their ambiguity.

On the other hand, the imagery of the Old English elegies more clearly suggests the speaker's station inside the landscape and his wandering throughout it, a characteristic especially suited to a poetry that insists on the subordination of life in this world to a life in the hereafter. The syntax of subordination in *The Seafarer* shows a world that can be put into perspective by the human spirit just as words and ideas can be shaped into relationships by the scops. The outlook expressed by the Llywarch-Hen poet finds suitable expression in a poem where the absence of connection and the abstractness of the imagery suggest the inability of the will to modify the human condition. The following chapter will deal with the contextual overtones of certain key images in Old English and Welsh that establish this difference even more clearly.

49. T. A. Shippey, *Poems of Wisdom and Learning in Old English* (Cambridge, England: D.S. Brewer, 1976), 14.

6

The Third Thing:
Context as Connection in
Gnomic and Nature Poetry

"This side" and "beyond" are faint repetitions of the dialectics of
"inside" and "outside." . . . Man's being is confronted with the
world's being.
— Gaston Bachelard, *The Poetics of Space*

Anthropologist Edward T. Hall examines the linguistic confusion that arises
among cultures which do not share a context that fills in discursive gaps.[1]
"Context" he defines as information that is assumed and therefore not ex-
pressed on a verbal level but that nonetheless gives essential dimension to the
linguistic "code."[2] The "contexting process" allows us to "pay attention to the
right things";[3] it acts as a screening process which "provides structure for the
world and protects the nervous system from information overload."[4] Each
culture decides what it will relegate to assumed knowledge and what is to be
emphasized or pointed out. Meanwhile, Hall provides us with another set of
terms for describing the distinctions I have been trying to illuminate: a "high-
context communication" is one where "most of the information is either in

1. Edward T. Hall, *Beyond Culture* (Garden City, N.Y.: Anchor Press, Doubleday, 1976).
2. Ibid., 35.
3. Ibid., 74.
4. Ibid.

the physical context or internalized in the person, while very little is in the coded, explicit, transmitted part of the message." A "low-context communication" is where "the mass of the information is invested in the explicit code."[5] Cultures use both modes, but some are more highly contextual than others, such as Asian cultures which have developed over centuries a body of assumed information and whose "simple messages" are rife with implication. More diffuse and fragmented societies in which a high premium is put on personal privacy and individual endeavor—such as the German and the American cultures—prefer to communicate more explicitly. Misunderstanding of semiotic diversities has made itself felt in all areas of interpretation, both sociopolitical and literary.

Like any communication, poetry requires a hearer as well as a speaker to make the communication complete, and it also requires a context to give meaning to the communication. Context is the most important "third thing" in the understanding of written texts, and the most elusive because it is so often metalinguistic. The very nature of ancient codices tends to obliterate much of it:

> Licgende beam læsest groweð
> > *(Maxims I*, line 148)

[A fallen tree grows least]

> Werig sceal se wiþ winde roweþ
> > (line 186ᵃ)

[Weary is he who rows against the wind]

These might be aphorisms which comment on human behavior—the fruitlessness of sin, perhaps, for the one, and wasteful endeavor for the other— but as literal statements they are bafflingly obvious; scores of statements of this type among the English and Welsh gnomes possess even fewer proverbial implications. T. A. Shippey writes that "proverbs in the end consist of 'statement plus context,' and once the context is lost, the point is also."[6] "Less depressing," he observes, is the possibility that "modern terminology is simply inadequate for describing ancient practice."[7]

5. Ibid., 79.
6. T. A. Shippey, *Poems of Wisdom and Learning in Old English* (Cambridge: Derek Brewer, 1976), 13.
7. Ibid.

I suggest that an explanation lies somewhere between these two alternatives. Certain images may have been charged with a significance that would clarify the link between *wea biđ wundrum clibbor* and *wolcna scriđađ*, but this link may not have been nearly so systematic as that provided by a proverb, nor would it have the precise meaning expressed by a proverbial metaphor. It may instead depend on a deep-rooted reception of the natural world of which the gnomic poems make a kind of ceremony. Each image might strike an associative chord which carries the weight of a complex ethos and philosophy that has built up over centuries, and has not seen the necessity for self-explanation. In addition, we might regard the accompanying laments, or poetic fragments, as possessing what some scholars refer to as "latent narrative," where the context, well known to its audience, is concealed beneath the emergent tips of the poem like an iceberg.[8]

Context in the Old English Poems

One recurrent imagistic association in Old English is that of dawn and something sinister. *Uhtan*, a debatable word, presumably refers to the early hours of the morning, before the sun has risen. It is at this time that the wanderer and the forsaken wife feel their deepest depression and sense of loneliness:

> oft ic sceolde ana   uhtna gewhylce
> minre ceare cwiþan
>
> (*The Wanderer*, EB1:8–9ª)
>
> [Often I had, alone, every dawn, to bewail my care.]

8. Paul Zumthor, "Les Narrativités latentes dans le discours lyrique médiéval," in *The Nature of Medieval Narrative*, ed. Minnett Grunmann-Gaudet and Robin F. Jones (Lexington: French Forum, 1980), 39–55. See also Eugene Vance, *Mervelous Signals: Poetics and Sign Theory in the Middle Ages* (Lincoln: University of Nebraska Press, 1986), 101, who makes some inquiring remarks pertinent to my own study: "Must a story be told or 'written out,' " he asks, "in order to be called a story? If a story is not told or written out, but latent or repressed, is the repression of the story *part* of that story?" By "latent narrative" in the *trouvère* lyric, he means "quite simply that the lyric performance proffers to its audience a set of implicit roles whose interaction is sufficient to generate a complete story, even though that story is not through-composed in *trouvère* lyric as linear narrative." He acknowledges that this critical realm has not yet been adequately explored in studies of narrative.

> frynd sind on eorþan
> leofe lifgende   leger weardiað
> þonne ic on uhtan   ana gonge
> (*The Wife's Lament*, EB2:33ᵇ–35)

[There are lovers on earth living in affection, sharing a bed, while I at dawn walk alone.]

Elsewhere in *The Wife's Lament*, it appears in part of a compound—*hæfde ic uhtceare* (7ᵇ)—and in *Resignation B* we find yet another compound:

> him bið a sefa geomor
> mod morgenseoc
> (lines 95ᵇ–96ª)

[his heart is ever sorrowful, his mind morning-sick]

Given the wide range of this associative connection, mere mention of dawn might carry foreboding implications in other poems, as in the strange reference in *Beowulf* to the blithe-hearted black raven that "announces Heaven's joy" to the victorious people of Heorot (lines 1801–2). The use of different compounds in *uhtceare* and *morgenseoc* suggests that we have a real association, not one that arises from the need to satisfy an aural or metrical requirement. We should be mindful of this problem in our assessment of associative links: the connection of life with death that R. MacGregor Dawson points out between *gebyrdum* and *beam* in line 25 of *Maxims I* may have come about by alliteration, a difficulty to which he admits.[9] Our efforts to find contextual or associative connections are complicated by the fact that this poetry follows strict phonetic conventions, as the whole of Chapter 2 sought to point out. That an association may have existed apart from this requirement is harder to prove, but if we look at the section in *Maxims I* where trees and human birth and death occur side by side, we find what might be a more purely associative link in the next line, where no alliteration is required:

> beam sceal on eorðan
> leafum liþan   leomu gnornian
> fus sceal feran   fæge sweltan

9. "The Structure of the Old English Gnomic Poems," JEGP 61 (1962), 15, 20.

ond dogra gehwam   ymb gedal sacan
middangeardes

(EB2: 26ᵇ–30ᵃ)

[A tree on earth must lose its leaves, its branches mourn. The ready
man must set forth, the doomed must die, and every day must deal
with departure from this earth.]

We have the association of a tree and aging in another juxtaposition, again
unassisted by alliteration:

sele sceal stondan   sylf ealdian
licgende beam   læsest groweð·

(157–58)

[The hall must stand, and itself grow old. The fallen tree grows least.]

In both examples, the sense of spiritual development enters in some way, first
with the tree that must grow bare and the "ready man" who "struggles"
(*sacan*) with his departure, and second, with the image of the aging building
and the fallen tree. Dawson surmises that the link between these lines is
suggested by the connotations of *beam* as "column," "pillar," or "joist,"[10]
while the more obvious association is yielded by the contrast between "stand-
ing" and "lying" and their respective connotations of "living" and "dead." A
thing must grow old to develop in wisdom or character, and the image of the
hall standing and aging has perhaps given the following image of a standing
tree that grows larger as it ages, but least when it has been felled. Likewise,
faithless and false-hearted men, as the verses state a few lines later, have
"felled" themselves by their own wickedness, and do not grow in God's grace.
In *Maxims II*, however, Faith will spring up within the righteous like a
flourishing tree:

treow sceal on eorle·
wisdom on were·   wudu sceal on foldan·
blædum blowan·

(32ᵇ–34ᵃ)

[Loyalty must be in a warrior, wisdom in a man. A wood must
blossom on the earth with foliage.]

10. Ibid., 19.

The alliterative connection is there, to be sure, as is the paranomasia with *treow* and *wudu*, but the frequency of this association of trees with human growth, especially the growth of wisdom or virtue, is too persistent to dismiss as merely aural or metrical. Perhaps for this reason the speaker in *Resignation B* contrasts his condition with that of a flourishing tree, and without an alliterative connection:

> nu ic me sylf ne mæg
> fore minum wonæhtum   willan adreogan ·
> wudu mot him weoxan   wyrde bidan
> tanum lædan   ic for tæle ne mæg
> ænigne moncynnes   mode gelufian
> (EB2: 103^b–7)

[I cannot myself now perform my desire (that of going on a journey of exile?) because of my poverty. The wood can grow, abide its fate, shoot forth twigs. I, because of disgrace, cannot love in my heart anyone of mankind.]

He is a *licgende beam*, incapable of the development he yearns for, and he expresses it with what Claes Schaar would call "adversative asyndeton," and Brooke-Rose a "bald juxtaposition." But explicit connecting diction was not needed in a comparison so common, and one that has a firm basis within Christian wisdom literature.[11]

Space does not allow a detailed discussion of all the contextual associations that surround so many of the stock images in Anglo-Saxon. "Space," however, is an important feature in the context of the outcast in a wilderness setting, especially those that contrast inside and outside. In Chapter 5, I examined the formal expressions of a subjective point of view and its relationship to the sacred and secular world. To extend that discussion, I will here examine some important natural images and their associations with subjectivity: the storm with anguish and chaos, the storm with the mind, thought with something hard, and all of the above with the "virtues of control, dominance, the tight grip."[12] Anguish comes from being outside the walls of society,

11. See for instance Psalm 92:12–15. The Gospel of John yields, of course, the most famous Christian analogy of spiritual growth or death (15:4–6): "I am the vine, you are the branches. He who abides in me, and I in him, he it is that bears much fruit. . . . If a man does not abide in me, he is cast forth as a branch and withers" (Revised Standard Version).

12. Shippey, *Poems of Wisdom*, 15.

comfort from being inside God's order, a self-enclosed unit that can repel bad weather. These images may be compared with the corresponding Welsh treatment of the heart as something soft, as something made raw and penetrable, oppressed by the overloud sounds of birds, ground to a pulp in the wash of wave against gravel, exposed to the withering surround of profane and unprotective space.

The Hard Mind in Old English

Cultures differ in the linguistic emphasis they give to one sense over another, and it is this developing interest in the "sensorium" over the past thirty years or more that has given rise to a host of studies in metaphor, linguistics, philosophy, and cognitive science,[13] and a particular interest of late in Old English "heart" and "mind" terms and their semantic distinctions.[14] Both the Welsh and the English had a tactile way of dealing with thought, mind, heart, and their mental and emotional processes. The Old English writers come to grips with hard ideas as they would with an opponent, and the hard/soft dichotomy has important cultural and intellectual implications. That which is soft is penetrable, that which is hard is impenetrable and capable of penetrating what is soft. The martial associations are obvious: pain is hard, pleasure is soft; valor is hard, cowardice is soft; willpower is hard, lack of willpower is soft.

The storm and its associations with anguish and chaos occur repeatedly in

13. Walter Ong defines the sensorium as the use of the senses in language as a conceptual apparatus to define the universe (*The Presence of the Word: Some Prolegomena for Cultural and Religious History* [New Haven: Yale University Press, 1967], 3). Marshall McLuhan sees the invention of the printing press as moving the word from the realm of the oral to the realm of the visual (*The Gutenberg Galaxy: The Making of Typographic Man* [Toronto: University of Toronto Press, 1962]); Michael Reddy suggests that we view the process of communication in physical terms: ideas are objects put into containers or "conduits" and sent from one party to the next ("The Conduit Metaphor," in *Metaphor and Thought*, ed. A. Ortony [Cambridge: Cambridge University Press, 1979]). George Lakoff and Mark Johnson extend Reddy's thesis in their book *Metaphors We Live By* (Chicago: University of Chicago Press, 1980) and add a host of other metaphoric orientations that permeate English idiom, such as the notion of "argument as war."

14. See Michael Phillips's dissertation, "Heart, Mind, and Soul in Old English: A Semantic Study," University of Illinois at Urbana, 1985; M. R. Godden, "Anglo-Saxons on the Mind," in *Learning and Literature in Anglo-Saxon England: Studies Presented to Peter Clemoes on the Occasion of his Sixty-fifth Birthday*, ed. Michael Lapidge and Helmut Gneuss (Cambridge: Cambridge University Press, 1985), 271–98.

Anglo-Saxon poetry. In *Andreas* it clearly holds symbolic meaning, in that the torments the saint suffers in prison come to him in the form of "gray battlestalkers," the harsh, lacerating onslaught of the elements which the warrior nevertheless withstands, "bold and hard in endurance":

Þa se halga wæs   under heolstorscuwan
eorl ellenheard,   ondlange niht
searoþancum beseted.   Snaw eorðan band
winter geworpum.   Weder coledon
heardum hægelscurum,   swylce hrim ond forst,
hare hildstapan,   hæleða eðel
lucon, leoda gesetu.   Land wæron freorig
cealdum cylegicelum,   clang wæteres þrym
ofer eastreamas,   is brycgade
blæce brimrade.   Bliðheort wunode
eorl unforcuð,   elnes gemyndig,
þrist ond þrohtheard   in þreanedum
wintercealdan niht.   No on gewitte blon,
acol for þy egesan,   þæs þe he ær ongann,
þæt he a domlicost   dryhten herede,
weorðade wordum,   oððæt wuldres gim
heofontorht onhlad.

(VB: 1253–69[a])

[Then the holy man was under the shadow of darkness,
the valiant nobleman, all night long
cunningly besieged. Snow bound the earth,
downcast with winter; weather cooled
with hard gusts of hail; likewise, rime and frost,
gray battlestalkers, locked up the home of warriors,
the settlement of people. The lands were frigid,
with cold icicles the might of the water crept
over the seas, ice made a bridge
over the black flood-paths. Blithe-hearted dwelt
the fearless man, mindful of his courage,
bold and hard in endurance under duress
throughout the winter-cold night. By no means was he muddled in mind,
frightened by the terror, for from the time that it first began,

so that he (might) ever praise the Lord most gloriously,
he worshiped with words, until the gem of glory,
heavenly radiant, unclosed.]

Eric Stanley, scoffing at early scholars who were troubled by the inappropri-
ate weather in Ethiopia, identifies the storm as symbolic of a mood.[15] But he
misses, I believe, an important connection between the will and the storm as
entities doing battle: both are physically *hard*, and it is not merely the "effect
of misery" that is foremost in the poet's mind so much as the effect of contest.
Andreas is cunningly besieged; like an assailant, the storm rains blows upon
him which he, God's warrior, deflects with faith and song.

As an extended metaphor for spiritual conflict (the winter storm is missing
in the sources available to the poet), this passage seems only a little more
elaborate than that to be found in *Resignation* A, wherein the speaker prays
for assistance from God when the storm should come against his spirit in the
form of demons that tempt him at death:

> forlæt mec englas seþeah
> geniman on þinne neawest   nergende cyning
> meotud for þinre miltse   ðeah ðe ic mana fela
> æfter dogrum dyde   ne læt þu mec næfre
> deofol seþeah
> þin lim lædan   on ladne sið
> þy læs hi on þone foreþonc   gefeon motan
> . . . .
> forstond þu mec on gestyr him   þonne
> storm cyme·
> mynum gæste ongegn
> (EB2: 49b^b–60^a)

[Let angels nonetheless
take me into thy presence, redeeming King,
Lord in thy mercy; although I have done

---

15. The winter scene in a poem that presumably has its setting in the Middle East created some
early confusion. Kenneth Brooks declared in his edition (*Andreas and the Fates of the Apostles*
[Oxford: Clarendon Press, 1961], 107) that "the description of the cold winter night proves that
Mermedonia is not the name for Ethiopia." Stanley objects to this literal interpretation of figurative
landscapes; he sees in it an elaborate metaphor for the physical and mental torments that the saint
suffers in prison ("Old English Poetic Diction and *The Wanderer, The Seafarer,* and *The Penitent's
Prayer,*" *Anglia* 73 [1955], 440).

> many sins in (my) days, never let the devil
> lead me, thy limb, on the hateful journey,
> lest they in their original plan should exult. . . .
> Stand by me and restrain them when the storm
>   comes
> against my spirit.]

Old English literature is filled with the hard arrows of Satan as emblems of temptation, the fortress of the soul as symbol of spiritual strength—images taken from Paul's famous letter to the Ephesians about "the armor of God." Certain Old English storms function similarly, although in a much less structured allegory: their hard hailstones very often depict the anguish of a mind or heart literally battered by external but especially internal and spiritual forces. Those who are to withstand them must have in the most physical sense hard minds to counter them.

We should reinstate this tactile quality of the Anglo-Saxon word *heard*. Too often, translators have lost the original meaning in their translations; hence our "brave under helmet" for *heard under helme*, where the important alliteration is sacrificed. Anglo-Saxon warriors are *hard* in poetry. They resist the blows of the enemies like steel. Like steel they cut through their opponents. Our word "brave" derives from a vulgar Latin term meaning "wild" and "savage"—only approximate in meaning. There are three general meanings for *heard*: (1) Passively resistant, impenetrable; said of objects and found frequently in the riddles, often countered by the antonym *hnesce*, "soft"; it refers as well to that which is difficult, not easily mastered or surmounted, or which presents an obstacle: a hard word, a hard problem. (2) Aggressively resistant and penetrating, said frequently of warriors, and under which fall our modern translations: "intrepid," "brave," "strong," "bold," "hardy." (3) A large category meaning "unpleasantly resistant": "harsh," "severe," "bitter," "cruel" (*heard dogorrimum*, "bitter days"; *heard wite*, "cruel torment"). The word is often used to translate Latin *durus*, which has the same general semantic range; of course they all share the general meaning of resistant. Hardness is that which if pushed will not yield. As an adverb, "hardly" in modern English has come to mean "barely." "Hardy," as in "stalwart," comes from Norman French *hardi*, from the verb *hardir*, "to harden," to make hard or bold, and it has cognates in West Germanic and Gothic *hardjan* and in Old High German *hartjan*. All come from Old Teutonic **hardus*, corresponding to pre-Teutonic **kartus*, "power."

Heard frequently modifies the aforementioned "heart" and "mind" words in Old English. Recent studies have attempted to separate and analyze the

perplexing and often overlapping meanings of *hyge, sawol, mod, heorte, sefa, hreðer,* and *fehrð,* especially as they reveal metaphors of containment, disclosure, and the gathering and sending forth of thought. Briefly and quite omissively, the arguments are these: Both *hyge* and *mod* gloss Latin *mens* and *animus,* both *hyge* and *mode* seem capable of emotion, both are separate from a conscious ego or self which speaks in the first person; *mod* occurs about ten times more frequently than *hyge; hyge* has associations with "intention," "resolve" and "will" (its related form being *hycgean* and *gehygd,* for which reason it is often translated as "courage"). The heart, the breast, and the *hreðer,* of uncertain meaning, are terms that describe locations for thought and emotion. Much admonition in Old English is directed at keeping the *mod* or the *hyge* within their containers, controlling the thoughts that want to overflow the *hreðerlocan,* or in keeping out destructive external elements and admitting beneficial ones. The stance of the individual human being toward the world in Anglo-Saxon is essentially agonistic in nature: one is a contestant not only with hard or inexorable external forces, but with gnawing and surging internal forces. *Mod* or *hyge* is often seen to well up in the heart like fire or hot water, as in *Beowulf,* where Hrothgar "continually seethed with sorrows" [*swa ða mælceare   maga Healfdenes / singala seað* ines 189–90), or as in *Solomon and Saturn,* where fate wells up like a storm
/ave and is kept down by a clear mind:

> Solomon cwæð:
> "Wyrd bið wended hearde,   wealleð swiðe geneahhe;
> heo wop weceð,   heo wean hladeð,
> heo gast scyð,   heo ger byreð,
> and hwæðre him mæg wissefa   wyrda gehwylce
> gemetigian,   gif he bið modes gleaw
> and to his freondum wile   fultum secan,
> ðehhwæþre godcundes   gæstes brucan."
>   (ASMP: 437–43)

> [Solomon said:
> Fate is hard to alter. Often it wells up powerfully.
> It causes weeping; it piles up woe;
> it wounds the spirit; it bears the years.
> And nevertheless the wise mind can mitigate
> those things of Fate if he is clear in his mind
> and seeks help from his friends,
> and furthermore enjoys the Holy Spirit.]

In *Maxims I* it is mind that is the storm wave in need of being controlled or steered:

> styran sceal mon strongum mode·   storm oft holm gebringeþ
> geofen in grimmum sælum   onginnað grome fundian
> fealwe on feorran to londe   hwæþer he fæste stonde
> weallas him wiþre healdað   him biþ wind gemæne
>
> (EB2: 50–53)

> [One must control with a strong mind (or: "one must control a strong
>   mind"), the sea often brings
> a storm, the ocean in grim times, the dark waves attempt
> an onslaught from afar upon the land, however ("to see whether") it
>   stands fast,
> the waves hold them back, they share the wind.]

Here storm is shown as something over which man can willfully exert power, like the wall holding back the waves. Almost the selfsame statement is made in *The Seafarer*, only it does not supply the immediate connection with the storm as does the other. The first half of the poem, though, more than makes up for the missing image:

> stieran mon sceal strongum mode   ond þæt on staþelum healdan
> ond gewis werum   wisum clæne
>
> (EB2: 109–10)

> [One must control with a strong mind (or: "one must control a strong
>   mind"), and hold it within bounds, and (he must be) true to men and
>   in his ways pure.]

This line seems to give a whole new dimension to the theme of *The Seafarer*, and those who argue for a symbolic interpretation of the poem are vindicated by the highly associative nature of its images. The speaker is shown to be a man in turmoil, torn between desire and fear, impulsiveness and caution, in love with the ascetic and godly life, and yet loath to give up the comforts of the happy existence on shore. Anglo-Saxon philosophy as it is expressed in the gnomes urges us to find our niche, to make up our minds, to quell turmoil or indecisiveness; and thus the battle of the seafarer with the elements has symbolic as well as literal significance: it shows him getting command of his priorities. Thought, mind, or will as something hard and compelling seems to be a pervasive Anglo-Saxon metaphor and is expressed in one of the most famous lines in *The Battle of Maldon*:

> Hige sceal þe heardra,   heorte þe cenre,
> mod sceal þe mare,   þe ure mægen lytlað.
> (ASMP: 312–13)

> [Courage (lit. "mind") shall be the harder, heart the keener, spirit the greater as our might grows less.]

Given this context, then, it might be possible to make some sense of the perplexing transition in line 33ᵇ of *The Seafarer*:

> nap nihtscua   norþan sniwde
> hrim hrusan bond   hægel feol on eorþan
> corna caldast   forþon cnyssað nu
> heortan geþohtas   þæt ic hean streamas
> sealtyþa gelac   sylf cunnige
> (31–35)

Here again is Shippey's translation of this passage:

> The shadow of night grew dark, it snowed from
> the north, frost bound the earth, hail fell
> to the ground, coldest of grains. // So the
> heart's thoughts impel me to make trial
> myself of the deep currents, the salt waves'
> tumult.[16]

His use of the Latinate word "impel" obscures the impact and physicality of the original *cnyssað* in line 33ᵇ, which not only alliterates with *corna caldast* but suggests the action of hailstones "beating" upon the speaker in the form of his thoughts. Were we to translate the passage in the following way the connection might be clearer:

---

16. Shippey, *Old English Verse* (London: Hutchinson University Library, 1972), 69.

The shadow of night grew dark; it snowed from the north;
frost bound the ground; hail fell to earth,
coldest of kernels. Thus beat now
my heart's thoughts (on me) (or: "thus beat thoughts upon my heart")
    that I make trial myself
of the high seas, the salt waves' tumult . . .

Here the thoughts of his heart pelt him like hailstones pelting the earth; the same verb is used to describe the ship that "knocked" against the cliffs (*þonne he be clifum cnossað*). Ironically it is the storm itself that drives him to take on the storm again, seeming to plant the seeds of the thought in his imagination just as it sows the earth with the "coldest of kernels." His heart is pummeled from without and within, a feature which suggests that the entire sea voyage might be an extended analogy of the hard mind coming to grips not only with the hard forces of the world but with the hard longing for asceticism and God that is stronger than the longing for pleasure. John Vickrey makes a convincing case for interpreting the sea voyage as the life of the sinner,[17] drawing upon the figurative images of the storm given us by Gregory in his *Dialogues*:

> ic eom gecnyssed mid þam stormum þære
> strangan hreohnesse in þam scipe mines modes
>
> [I am beaten by the storms of the harsh
> tempest in the ship of my mind]

Vickrey's important contribution lies in recognizing the storm as an image of spiritual contest, and he cites other Old English and Anglo-Latin sources for this "nautical image."[18] Seen in this light, the Seafarer is the opposite of the Wanderer, who shelters his thoughts in his *breosthord* as if they were too tender to expose to the hardness of the world and fate. The conflicts of *The Wanderer* have been frequently dwelt upon, especially the images of closure and disclosure in the figures of the hidden heart and the open ruin:[19] the

17. John Vickrey, "Some Hypotheses Concerning *The Seafarer*: Lines 1–47," *Archiv für das Studium der neueren Sprachen und Literaturen*, 219 (1982), 57.

18. Ibid., 48 and passim; see *King Alfred's West-Saxon Version of Gregory's Pastoral Care*, Part 2, ed. Henry Sweet, EETS, o.s. 50 (London: Oxford University Press, 1871; rpt. 1958), 403: *Ða sint to manienne ðe hiera lichoman synna onfunden habbað, ðæt hie huru æfter ðæm scipgebroce him ða sæ ondræden* ["Then it is to admonish those who have endured the sins of the body that soon after the shipwreck they are fearful of the sea"].

19. See Julian Wasserman and S. L. Clark, "The Imagery of *The Wanderer*," *Neophilologus* 63.2 (1979), 291–96.

speaker's desire to disclose his *modsefa* at the same time that he binds it within his *ferðlocan* echoes his desire to seek his lord although he has buried him within the darkness of the earth. The thoughts that need to be thus sheltered are described as "weary" and helpless:

> Ne mæg werig mod   wyrde wiðstondan
> ne se hreo hyge   helpe gefremman.

The Seafarer might have been intended as an answer to the problem posed in the former poem. Both might serve as mirror images to one another. The Wanderer speaks from the vantage point of one who is in exile, thinking back on his former life among men. Emerging from his dream of his dead lord, he looks to the flock of seabirds in efforts to find an old familiarity, but his *mod* is driven inward in disappointment to search fruitlessly for the ghosts of the past. The Seafarer speaks from the vantage point of one who has returned and who thinks back on his "exile": his *hyge* is able to burst free of his *ferðlocan* and is driven out over the sea. The cry of the "lone-flyer," as something hard, "whets" his desire to cut the strings that bind him to the familiar world of humanity and to return, instead, to the sea. Both poems gain meaning in their shared context with each other, playing off vibrant images and their rich coherency of implication.

Context in the Welsh Poems

It is harder to find this coherency of implication among the nature references in the Welsh than it is in the English. First, there is nothing equivalent for Welsh scholars like the *Concordance to Old English Literature* to facilitate semantic studies. The issue of the boundaries between poems is more vexing, and the formula that is so clear-cut in the English (hard storm/hard mind) is diffuse and contradictory in the Welsh. For the Sick Man of Abercuawg, the entire world is an irritant. Wintry images afflict in the preceding gnomic verses, but in the planctus it is the vigorous life of spring and all its manifestations that run roughshod over the raw heart or mind of the leper. First, however, let me speak of the gnomes.

The English gnomes are more explicitly didactic than the Welsh, and their expansive style encourages associations. The Welsh gnomes are not "wandering" in the way that the English gnomes are; rather, they are kaleidoscopic, and look as though they have been excerpted from a context which would have given them a clearer meaning. We find some of the same phrases repeated in different combinations: "the stag is thin," "reeds are withered," "a wave breaks." It is clear that a tight network of formulas and sound patterning governs them; where they occur in the poems associated with Llywarch Hen they are more contextually illuminating because of the presence of a protagonist who seems to react to them.

A few *englynion* from the gnomic poems seem to show an understandable association between image and idea, where the link is a standard association of cock's crow and human rejoicing:

> Bit goch crib keilyawc. bit annyanawl y lef
> o wely budugawl.
> llewenyd dyn duw ae mawl.
> (*Bidiau*, RB: 1030.1–2)

> [Let the cock's comb be red, spirited his voice
> from a bed of exultation.
> The joy of man, God praises it.]

The subject of the following *englyn* from *Bidiau I* (see Texts no. 5) bears a marked resemblance to some of the gnomic comments of *Maxims I* and *II*:

> Bit amlwc marchawc. bit ogelawc lleidyr.
> twyllyt gwreic goludawc.
> kyueillt bleid bugeil diawc.
>
> (1030.11–12)

> [Let the knight be public, the thief skulking.
> A woman deceives a rich man.
> A wolf befriends the lazy shepherd.]

> sceomiande man sceal in sceade hweorfan   scir in leohte geriseð
> (*Maxims I*, EB2: 66)

> [A man doing shameful things must walk in shadow; it is fitting that
> the shining be in the light.]

þeof sceal gangan þiestrum wederum·   þyrs sceal on fenne
  gewunian·
ana innan lande·   ides sceal dierne cræfte·
fæmne hire freond gesecan·   gief heo nyle on folce geþeon
þæt hie man beagum gebycge·

(Maxims II, 44^b–45^a)

[A thief must walk in dark weathers; a demon must dwell in the fen
alone in the land; a woman must with hidden craft,
a maiden, seek her lover if she does not want it
to succeed among her people that one
may buy her with rings (i.e., "that she be marriageable"?)]

Wineleas wonsælig mon genimeð him wulfas to geferan fela fæcne
  deor

(Maxims I, EB2: 146–47^a)

[The friendless unfortunate man must take wolves as companions to
  himself, treacherous beasts.]

Here, the rather obvious dichotomies and their metaphoric extensions are
that virtue is visible, vice keeps to the shadows like the wolves. In one of the
verses from *Eiry Mynydd* ("Mountain Snow") we have what might be a
proverb:

Eiry mynydd coch traet ieir
bas dwfyr myn yt leuir.
chwenneckyt meuyl mawreir.
(RB: 1029.22–23)

[Mountain snow, red the feet of hens.
Shallow is water where it babbles;
Disgrace increased by big words.]

There seem to be a number of comments among the gnomes about the
"shallowness" of too much talk—*nac adef rin a lauar* [Do not confess a secret
to a babbler (RB: 1032.25)], *a mwyalch ar y nyth / a chelwydawc ny theu vyth*
[A blackbird on its nest and a liar are never silent (RB: 1032.26–27)], *gnawt o*

benn direit teruysc [typical is disturbance from the mouth of the *diriaid* ("unlucky, perverse one") (*Kalan gayaf*, RB: 1031.37–38)]—and thus the reference to the babbling water might be metaphoric. Elsewhere, however, we find little or no connection at all between lines, and it is almost as if the collectors aimed at a kind of disjunction or contrast between references. This attitude might be that of the frustrated modern reader who has lost the contextual matter that gives dimension or irony to the images.

If we examine whole sections of verses, we sometimes find a repeated theme, as, for instance, that of "cowardice" in the *Llym awel* verses of *The Black Book* (Texts no. 6), which has caused scholars to group them with the Llywarch cycle. In *Eiry mynydd* the tenor of most of the sententious comments is negative, and this mood seems to be consonant with the images of winter that fill the poem: trees bending before the wind, wind whistling over the roofs of towers, the ice with its gray beard, the withered reeds, and in almost every stanza the stag—swift, roaming, leaping, swimming, hunched, thin and bent, seeking shelter in the valley, in the rushes, in flight, but always solitary. The pervasiveness of this image suggests that it is meant to remind us of human loneliness, and the human gnomes that it introduces emphasize isolation, wretchedness, age, and the paltry and malicious spirit summed up in the complex Welsh word *diriaid* ("difficult," "unlucky," "mischievous," "perverse one"), generally countered by *dedwydd* ("blessed," "fortunate," "happy"):[20]

> hwyr hen hawd y ordiwes
> *(Eiry Mynedd*, RB: 1028.11)

> [slow the old man, easy to overtake him.]

20. For discussions of the use of *dedwydd* and *diriaid*, see Kenneth Jackson, EWGP, 53–54, where he comments that *dedwydd*, "happy," glosses L. *beatus*, and *diriaid* seems not to mean "wicked," but rather "mischievous," "wrong-headed," "the perverse sort of person who is not really vicious but who cannot help making a mess of things." Rowland, EWSP, 30–31: ". . . The natures of the *dedwydd* or *diriaid* . . . form one of the major preoccupations of Welsh wisdom literature. . . . There seems to be an element of predetermined destiny underlying the concept as in RB 1192 *Mae ef diryeit oe eneityaw* ('He is *diriaid* from birth') or in the often-quoted *Nyt reit y detwyd namyn y eni* ('the *dedwydd* has only to be born')." These terms could be compared to OE *dol* ("foolish") and *eadig* ("blessed"); cf. *The Seafarer* (lines 106ª, 107ª): *dol biþ se þe him his dryhten ne ondrædeð* ["foolish is he who does not dread his Lord"] . . . *eadig bið se þe eaþmod leofaþ* ["blessed is he who lives humbly"]. These terms, Welsh and English, together raise a subtle question: Is the man *diriaid/dol* because of his actions, or does he act unwisely because he is *dol/diriaid*? The syntax of *The Seafarer* is ambiguous, as I have noted, and it not only raises an issue with which medieval religious philosophy was deeply concerned (the reconciliation of God's omnipotence and man's free will), but it affects our readings of these poems.

gnawt gan bob anauus gwyn

(1028.33)

[Typical is complaint from every wounded one.]

gnawt pob anaf ar di[r]eid

(1029.3)

[Typical each pain upon the *diriaid*.]

meckyt llwuyr llawer adoet

(1029.17)

[The coward nurses many a hurt.]

trydyd troet y hen y ffon

(1029.19)

[A third foot to the old one is his stick.]

diryeit ny mynn gwarandaw

(1029.21)

[The *diriaid* does not wish to listen.]

The attractiveness or unattractiveness of the images seems to have little effect on the tone of the sententious comments. The *Gorwyn blaen* ("Lovely the Tops") verses still exhibit mostly negative commentary and a preoccupation with longing. In short, the gnomic and nature poems that precede *Claf Abercuawg* and *Can yr henwr* in *The Red Book* overwhelmingly stress the dismal and unpredictable aspects of life. They set the stage, too, for the message in those poems associated with the Llywarch-Hen figure about the misery of old age, ill health, and a father's remorse over the proud attitude that sent his sons to their death.

As in the Old English poems, the Welsh poems contain key images which seem to inspire certain associations. A possible use of associative metaphor might be found in stanza 22 of *Claf Abercuawg*, and it would depend on our understanding the images of the shed, the bowl, and the boundary as containers:

Alaf yn eil meil am ved.
nyt eidun detwyd dyhed.
amaerwy atnabot amyned.

[Cattle in a shed, a bowl for (around?) mead.
not the wish of the *dedwydd* (the "lucky," the "blessed") for strife.
the compass of understanding: patience.]

These images only seem to reinforce the fact that the speaker has no protective circle within which he can feel secure; instead, he has the vacuous and annihilating expanse of wilderness all around him. He is exposed, and in the next stanza we get the famous line about the sea: "I have heard the heavy roar of the sea, / Loud among the sand and gravel." The emphasis on sound and touch, far outweighing that of sight, is remarkable in these poems. Earlier we hear the lonely sound of dogs in the wilderness, but it is the sea that seems to be most often associated with vulnerability, grief, and weariness. Sea and waves are almost always accompanied by a comment about sadness and strife:

Tonn tyruit toit eruit.
pan aut [ant?] ky[n]vrein ygovit.
Gwen gwae ryhen oth etlit.

(RB: 1037.39–40)

[A wave thunders, breakers cover
When warriors go off to battle
woe to the old man who grieves for thee.]

Dymkyfuarwydyat unhwch dywal
chwerw blwng chwerthin mor
ryfel dorvlodyat.

(RB: 1039.14–15)

[Unhwch the fierce would say to me,
Bitter, harsh the laughter of the sea:
battle-tumult.]

Bit wenn gwylyan. bit vann tonn.
bit hyuagyl gwyar ar onn.
bit lwyt rew. bit lew callonn.

(*Bidiau*, RB: 1030.29–30)

[Let the seagull be white, let the wave be loud,
let blood be a stain on the ash-spear,
let frost be gray, the heart bold.]

rac hwyeit gwesgereit tonn.
pybyr pwyll pell oual ym kallon.
                    (*Gorwyn Blaen*, RB: 1033.17–18)

[Before the ducks breaks the wave,
thought valiant; long the care in my heart.]

            chwerthinat tonn.
ny chel grud kystud kallon.
                    (*Gorwyn Blaen*, RB: 1033.20)

[Laughing the wave,
the cheek does not hide the affliction of the heart.]

            ehalaeth
tonn. gwiw callon rac hiraeth.
                    (*Claf*, Texts 2, st. 14b–c)

[Wide the wave, withered the heart with longing.]

o ebyr dyhepkyr tonn.
peuyr pell chwerthin om kallon.
                    (*Claf*, st. 19b–c)

[From estuaries flows a shimmering wave.
Laughter is far from my heart.]

kigleu don drom y tholo.
vann y rwng gra[ae]n a gro.
krei vym bryt rac lletvryt heno.
                    (*Claf*, st. 27)

[I have heard the heavy roar of the surf,
loud among the sand and gravel.
Raw my heart with sorrow tonight.]

Many of these connections are facilitated and perhaps governed by the rhyme with *tonn* ("wave") and *callon* ("heart"), or *tonn* and *onn* ("ash spear"). In *Bidiau II*,[21] however, we have the connection between sea and misery without the rhyme:

> Bid gwyrdd gweilgi; bid gorawen tonn;
> bid cwyn pob galarus,
> bid aflawen hen heinus.
>
> (EWGP: st. 5)

> [Let the sea be green; let the wave be exultant (lit: "over-*awen*," i.e.,
>   "inspired")
> let the sick one be plaintive,
> let the old and ill be unhappy.

A wave crashing suggests tumult and destruction. In modern Welsh, and perhaps in medieval Welsh too, as the first verse in *Bidiau II* illustrates (see the example below), *ton* can mean both "wave" and "broken." It is curious how frequently the double meanings of words are played upon in these verses; elsewhere, tumult and chaotic noise are juxtaposed with references to oppression, sadness, or incapacity, often with a deft use of double meaning or sound-play:

> Ton tra thon toid tu tir.
> goruchel guaetev rac bron banev bre
> breit allan or seuir.
>
> (*Llym awel*, Texts 6, st. 2)

> [Wave after wave covers the land.
> Very shrill are the shrieks (of wind? of seagulls?)
> Before the peaks of the hill;
> one can scarcely stand up outside.]

> Bid gogor gan iar; bid trydar gan lew,
> bid ofal ar a'i car;
> bid ton[n] calon rac galar.
>
> (EWGP: st. 1)

---

21. Originally found in the sixteenth century *Peniarth* MS 102; the edition is Jackson's EWGP, 35–37).

[Let there be cackling from the hen,
clamor from the brave;
let there be care on him who loves him,
broken (*ton*) the heart with grief.]

Commotion is frequently associated with the *diriaid*, which gives complex
and disturbing dimensions to *Claf Abercuawg*:

gnawt o benn dirieit teruysc
  (*Kalan Gaeaf*, RB: 1031.37–38)

[typical is commotion (tumult, riot, disturbance)
from the mouth of the *diriaid*]

Hir nos gordyar morua.
gnawt teruysc yg kymanua.
ny chytuyd diryeit a da.
  (*Baglawc Bydin*, 1032.16–17)

[Long the night, very loud (or sad) the salt-marsh;
typical is commotion in the assembly;
the good and the *diriaid* (i.e., "the bad")
do not agree.]

Interestingly, *dyar* can mean both "loud" and "sad," perhaps reinforcing the
association of tumult and chaos with depression. Loud laughter is also given
negative connotations, it seems, and a wave is frequently spoken of as
"laughing":

am gwymp hen chwerdit gwen gwas.
  (*Kalan Gaeaf*, 1031.44)

[When the old man stumbles, the fair youth laughs.]

gnawt gan rewyd rychwerthin.
  (*Gorwyn blaen*, 1033.44)

[Typical with the wanton is too much laughter.]

bit haha bydar.
  (*Bidiau*, 1030.19)

["Ha-ha"ing is the deaf man.
Or: "eh?-eh?"ing is the deaf man.]

bit chwannawc ynvyt y chwerthin.
(Bidiau I, Texts 5, st. 12b)

[Let the fool be prone to laughter.]

chwerthinat tonn.
ny chel grud kystud kallon
(Claf, st. 27b–c and Gorwyn, 1033.20)

[Laughing the wave; / the cheek does
not hide the affliction of the heart.]

The Raw Heart in Early Welsh

As in the Old English elegies, sense in the Welsh poems of lament operates on a similar metaphoric or figurative basis. The seeming non sequiturs have a link in the *sensorium*: the mind is raw, the heart brittle, the will feeble, and as such it cannot support the weight of the joyful, indifferent world. Like the insubstantial souls in Lewis's *The Great Divorce* who are pierced by a single grass blade, the speaker in *Canu Llywarch Hen* and the related poems makes use of an image of bruisedness, tenderness, which is squashed by the vitality of life, power, and youth.

Under it, the feeble, the wretched, the old, the redundant, and the ill are worn away to nothingness. A predominant theme in these Welsh gnomes and poems of lament is the battle for survival, the strife between predator and prey—the stag that is hunted, that must find shelter, the wolf that lurks, the old man who is overtaken, laughed at when he stumbles, wasted by disease, shunned by other members of society, "an enemy of men below, an enemy of God above"—and the plentiful references to the vicious nature of the world add keenly to the tone of cynicism and startling cruelty that permeates these poems. Gnomes and plaint poems are speckled throughout with the imagery of something brittle being crushed under the weight of something heavier or with the juxtaposition of hardness and softness:

gwychyr gwynt gwyd migyein.

(Gorwyn blaen, RB: 1034.20)

[Fierce the wind, trees bent (or: "shaking").

cwynuanus gwann, diffwys allt

(Baglawc Bydin, 1032.32–33)

[Plaintive the weak, rough the hillside.]

ryseiw gur ar vn conin.

(Llym awel, Texts 6, st. 1c)

[A man could stand on a single stalk.]

crin calaw caled riv

(Llym Awel, st. 14)

[Withered the reeds, hard the slope.]

gwesgyt gwawn grawn yn y wreid

(Bidiau I, st. 8c)

[Gossamer binds (presses?) grain in root.]

Bit grwm bydar. bit trwm keu.
esgut gorwyd yg kadeu.
gwesgyt gwawn grawn yn y adneu.

(Bidiau I, st. 9)

[Let the deaf be hunched, an enclosed ("empty"?) thing heavy,
let the horse be swift in battles;
gossamer binds (presses?) grain deposited.]

. . . dewr hyd diwlyd bre.
eidyl hen hwyr y dyre.

(Can yr Henwr, Texts 3, st. 13)

[bold the stag, hard the hill,
feeble the old man, slow his ascent.

briuhid tal glan gan garn carv culgrum cam

(Llym awel, st. 21c)

[the edge of the bank breaks under the
hoof of the thin, bent, crooked deer]

medal migned kalet riw.
rac carn cann tal glann a vriw.

(Gwen a'i Dad, RB: 1037.15–16)

[Soft swamps; hard the hill;
the stream's bank breaks with the horse's hoof.]

This last image is found in the dialogue between Llywarch and his son Gwen (*Gwen a'i Dad*, RB: 1037.9–16) and serves to fuel the taunt directed by the father toward his son. Gwen says to his father Llywarch: "I will not lose your honor [lit. "face"], battle-ready man. / When the brave gird themselves for the border, / I will bear distress before I yield." Llywarch says with skepticism: "A wave runs along the shore. / By chance does resolution break. / (Under) battle cover, typical is flight with braggarts." Gwen says: "I have what I speak of. / Spears will shatter where I shall be. / I won't cry out nor shall I flee." His father says: "Soft the swamps; hard the hill. / The stream's bank breaks with the horse's hoof. / A promise not performed is no promise." These insertions of nature imagery from the surrounding gnomic poems have been regarded by many scholars as space fillers; but if we think of them as metaphors, a meaningful discourse begins to unfold: Llywarch accuses his son of not being able to "hold up" under the onslaught of battle. Swamps are soft but the hill is hard (*kalet*). He is not resilient: he is like a stream's bank that breaks under the horse's hoof. [22] This image gains in meaning when we find in *The Gododdin* and other panegyric poems numerous kennings for chieftains who are "ramparts" to their people, "pillars," "anchors," "breastplates," "shields," and other objects of durability. A frequent term in *The Gododdin* is "rock": a warrior is a rock against the onslaught. These warriors, like the English ones, are *hard*. But there are fewer metaphors in Welsh for hard minds. The words *colwed* and *bron* appear in *The Gododdin* and are translated as "heart" by

---

22. Rowland, EWSP, 208–9. Rowland notes as well the metaphoric strength of hard and soft here: Is Gwen "to be hard or soft, evident or concealing himself in war? . . . Bold exteriors can mask a shallow interior. The thin, overhanging edge of a bank looks as firm as the rest but quickly breaks under pressure."

Kenneth Jackson;[23] the latter clearly means "breast." *Calon* is the Welsh word for "heart," the organ within the breast. In *The Gododdin*, it would seem, no great distinction is made, as in English, between the emotional faculty and its house within the body. Heart *is* breast; both are courageous, generous, and fierce.

Nevertheless, heart and mind are given peculiar emphasis in *The Songs of Llywarch Hen*, which brings me to my main point of comparison. "My mind (*bryd*) yearns to be sitting on a hill," says the speaker in the first stanza of *Claf Abercuawg*. "And yet it moves me not." Whereas in the heroic poems the man is his heart—his organ of generosity and ferocity—the leper is divorced from his mind. It can yearn; like *mod* it has its emotions that, as in the Old English, are often curiously separate from the individual; it can have resolve—like *hyge* in Old English. But like the one in *The Wanderer*, this mind is weary, impotent. It is in this poem that we have the reference to the mournful cuckoos that has inspired so much comment among comparative scholars. It seems no coincidence that the sad cuckoo whose song admits bitter sorrow into the breast in Old English should crop up in these Welsh poems but nowhere else outside *The Exeter Book*. Here comparison ends with *The Seafarer*: there is no hard resolve in the Sick Man stanzas, no whetting of the will, no Christian consolation, only grief expressed over lost vigor. The loud song of the cuckoo is continually juxtaposed to the feebleness and illness of the speaker, and in fact the word "loud," *dyar*, has the secondary meaning of "sad," as does the word *oer*, "cold." Consider again these verses and their wealth of associations:

> Very loud [very sad] the birds, streams wet,
> moon shines, cold [sad] is midnight.
> Raw my mind from the torment of illness.

> Very loud [very sad] the birds, wet the beach,
> bright the sky, broad the wave,
> withered the heart from longing.

23. *The Gododdin: The Oldest Scottish Poem* (Edinburgh: University Press, 1969), wherein he translates *nyt didrachywed colwed drut* (CA: A.20) as "not undestructive was [your] fierce heart" (124); for *chynon lary vronn* (CA: A.36) he translates "Cynon of the generous heart" (p. 131); but also *callon ehelaeth* (CA: B.26), "of generous [lit. 'wide'] heart" (107). The heart can have dimensions. We have already seen the withered heart in *Canu Llywarch Hen* juxtaposed ironically to the wide or generous sky. In CA: A.24 we find the word *arch* ("ark, coffer, chest") standing in for the "trunk, body, waist, side or breast" (GPC): *ytoed wryt ene arch*, "there was courage in his breast" (Jackson, 126).

I heard heavy roar of waves,
Loud [sad] among sand and gravel.
Raw my mind from sorrow tonight.

Branching the top of the oak,
Bitter the taste of the ash.
Sweet the cow-parsley, laughing the wave;
the cheek does not hide the hurt of the heart.

This last stanza is most telling, and abounds with sensorial details. The bitter taste of the ash offsets the sweet taste of the cow-parsley, the laughter of the wave offsets the weeping heart. The expansive top of the oak tree opens up to the heavens, but the countenance fails to keep the heart's sorrow secret. Throughout these verses runs the motif of a wound exposed, not unlike the open ruin in *The Wanderer*, which offsets and threatens the closed heart of the speaker in the first half of the poem.[24] The word *crai* ("raw") is an intriguing one in connection with the mind. Three times the speaker declares that fever, sickness, or sorrow has rendered his mind *crai*, a word that has an array of definitions: "new, fresh; raw, crude, bare and rough; severe, sad; or clear and pleasant." It is what bread is when it is leavened, what cloth is when it is threadbare, what meat is when it is uncooked. Simply to translate "sad" (which definition is obviously taken from its context here) is to ignore the sensorial extensions that enrich it. *Crai* seems to have the meaning of exposed, made sore or worn, so that when the speaker says, "I heard the heavy roar of waves / loud among the sand and gravel. / Raw is my mind from sorrow tonight," it is almost as if the mind, the *byrd*, has been rolled around in all that merciless gravel. The sea, because it is loud, is sad, hurtful. Because it is heavy, it is sad and hurtful, too. *Trwm* in Welsh, as does *hefig* in Old English, has the extended meaning of "sad, mournful" for obvious reasons. And, interestingly, our old cliché, "the broken heart," nonexistent in Old English, is an established formula in Early Welsh:

vyg callon neur dorres
penn a borthaf am porthes.
(*Urien Rheged*, RB. 1039.44–1040.1)

[My heart is broken.
I carry a head that carried me.]

24. Wasserman and Clark, "Imagery of *The Wanderer*," 293.

The Contexts of Space

Medieval space is an enormous and unwieldy image, in itself a book-length topic. The distance that the speakers put between themselves, the world, and the wilderness they describe has varied enormously. We have heard the distant barking of dogs and scrutinized the minute shades of lichen on walls. We have examined it from the standpoint of expressed subjectivity and *deixis*, the presence of an ego regarding a world wherein he or she is the center—or not the center. We have looked at the human world from afar, watched it being diced into generalities, brought in close or held at arm's length by grammatical, poetic, and imagistic ploys. We have felt the spaces between the lines and the silences—*ellwch tawellwch*—between the words themselves. And with these various lepers, exiles, pilgrims, and cast-off men and women we have been made to feel their fragility on the one hand and their stoicism on the other.

It might seem that in this chapter I have divided space into binary oppositions—space as it reveals weakness (the soft), space as it reveals strength (the hard)—and have unfairly assigned these "bad" and "good" characteristics to the Welsh and the English respectively. One might charge me with having done the same in this matter of point of view—image as it reveals a dominating hierarchy of deixis, image as it reveals multifaceted vision or lack of point of view. I agree, rather, with Gaston Bachelard that "unless one is careful [the dialectic of inside/outside] is made into the basis of all thoughts of positive and negative,"[25] and I urge the importance of abandoning preconceived notions of bad and good. I should like to examine the uses of space from the standpoint of the pilgrim and the exile: One is an active seeker of the Kingdom of God, moving willfully through externals, turning its hardships into a spiritual physic; the other is an exile by default, confined to a bitter place, bludgeoned by the sharp world. The one is on the outside looking into the Kingdom of God; the other is on the inside looking out through the prison bars of his or her own malady and sorrow. Or he is on the outside looking into the wrong inside—a secular world from which circumstances have excluded him. The question of importance here is whether or not either speaker recognizes the unhelpfulness of the interior he or she longs for, and how explicitly this recognition—this translation between self (inside) and circumstance (outside)—is made for the reader.

Space has many uses and contexts in medieval poetry. There is space and

---

25. *The Poetics of Space*, trans. Maria Jolas (Boston: Beacon Press, 1969), 211.

the lover, where nature takes on an intimate and joyous quality as we have seen it briefly in the poems of troubadour and goliard; and space and the discarded or separated lover, where nature is harrowing, a constant reminder of one's lack and the love that is elsewhere, behind closed doors, involving other people. There is space and the warrior, where waves and skulls break in time with each other, where every bending tree is a reminder of one's duty, of the ground one must hold or cover. And there is space and the non-warrior or sick man, where birds and barking dogs are distant, a sore reminder of one's noninvolvement in the world of activity. "Outside" in *The Seafarer* is treated ambiguously: it is something to fear and to covet. The speaker envies and is scornful of the man in the city who inhabits the wrong interior. Separation from the bad inside makes the outside a channel to yet another "inside," but a better one: the sea leads us out and away from these secular confines into the unimaginable interior of God's Kingdom. Exteriors in *The Wanderer* are more clearly inimical; the speaker's thoughts continually return to a longing for interiors, only to find them turned inside out in the imagery of the open ruins.

The gendering of space is an intriguing critical theme of late,[26] but the identification of the public outside with the masculine "active" and the private inside with the feminine "passive" reduces the subtleties in these medieval poems to categories that are too facile. In medieval thought, the Kingdom of God is modeled after the societal structure of the tribe, clan, or *duguth*, whose very survival depended upon an inside structure to which all privileged belonged. Contemporary feminist Claudine Herrmann argues for the masculine experience of appropriating and dividing space into hierarchies and the feminine experience of finding power and refuge in unsystemized space.[27] She draws her inspiration from Simone Weil, who wrote that "not to exert all the power at one's disposal is to endure the void."[28] These modern musings may seem anachronistic, but they offer interesting applications to the poems and interpretations we have been examining. Medieval Christianity in general

26. There has been much critical discussion of the gendering of public and private space, primarily by scholars of modernism. For a smattering, see the anthology edited by Susan Merrill Squier: *Women Writers and the City: Essays in Feminist Literary Criticism* (Knoxville: University of Tennessee Press, 1984).

27. "Feminine Coordinates: Space and Time," in *The Tongue Snatchers*, ed. and trans. Nancy Kline (Lincoln: University of Nebraska Press, 1989), 113–34.

28. *Gravity and Grace*, trans. Arthur Wells (New York: Putnam, 1952), 56, 55; cited by Herrmann, *The Tongue Snatchers*, 115.

insists upon a deific Patriarchy of systematized space—Eliade's structure of the Sacred—and it has produced insular poems that show an obsession with place and placelessness and what active or passive deeds will help set one right. And yet it has also produced a number of poems wherein the speakers seem not only to endure but to revel in the void—the structure of the Secular—and even to reject the conventional systems of Christian doctrine.

Medieval Christianity, especially medieval insular Christianity, is hardly a monolithic, single system; every modern scholar can find in it something to emphasize. To be sure, the exile in nature and his state of spiritual or poetic privilege is undoubtedly a strong Christian theme, but it bears the seeds of certain pre-Christian practices. P. L. Henry and Jenny Rowland call upon the many instances in Celtic and Anglo-Saxon literature wherein a hostile wilderness serves to test one's patience and spiritual strength. Rowland's point— that leprosy was seen as a spiritually healing condition—forms the basis for her support of the primarily penitential coloring of *Claf Abercuawg*. By this she means that it fits into a wide variety of medieval insular literature about nature and privation, much of which was written by and/or about men and women of the Christian God. The suffering of Suibne Geilt in the wilderness speaks powerfully of salvation through sorrow and madness in Old Irish literature.[29] There are the Old Irish verses uttered in *The Old Woman (or Nun) of Beare* which resemble both *The Sick Man* and *Song of the Old Man* in tone and subject matter, verses in which the speaker laments the loss of her beauty, of fair arms that are now too bony and thin for the boys to see.[30] *The Old Woman* adds what is "missing" in the Welsh poems, a confidence that her physical ebb will result in a spiritual flood: "My flood; / it is well my loan was preserved. / Jesus, Mary's Son, saved it / so that I am not sad at ebb."[31] The speaker uses natural imagery in more obvious symbolic ways than it is used in the Welsh poems we have examined: the ocean is her youth and old age at high and low tide; her "cloak" is her body, as is the lichen on an old tree.

Devotional nature poems abound in Irish where the hermit's isolation in nature is self-imposed. Consider these verses from the famous song of St.

---

29. *Buile Shuibhne* ["The Frenzy of Suibne"], ed. J. G. O'Keefe, *Irish Texts Society* 12 (London: David Nutt, 1913). See also Pádraig O Riain, "A Study of the Irish Legend of the Wild Man," *Eigse* 14 (1971–72), 179–206.

30. Kuno Meyer, ed. *Liadain and Curithir* (London: D. Nutt, 1902). For a recent translation, see Ruth P. Lehmann, *Early Irish Verse* (Austin: University of Texas Press, 1982), 49–53.

31. Lehmann, *Early Irish Verse*, 53.

Columba, who eschews human systems and takes refuge in the variegated
expanses of open space:

> Mellach lem bith i n-ucht ailiun
>   for beind cairrge,
> co n-aicind and ar a menci
>   féth na fairrge . . .
>
> Co n'aicind a trácht réid rindglan,
>   ní dál dubai,
> co cloisind guth na n-én n-ingnad,
>   seól co subai . . .
>
> Co n-aicind a helta ána
>   ós lir lindmar,
> co n-aicind na míla mara,
>   mó cech n-ingnad.
>
> Co n-aicind a traig 's a tuli
>   ina réimim;
> co mbad hé m'ainm, rún no ráidim,
>   "Cúl fri hÉirinn."
>
> Co n-am-tísad congain cride
>   ic a fégad;
> co rocóinind m'ulcu ile,
>   annsa a rélad.]32
>
> [It seems to me delightful on the breast of an island
> at the peak of a crag
> so that I may see the multiple
> face of the ocean . . .
>
> That I may see its smooth shore, clear points of land,
> no gloomy meetings;
> that I may hear the voice of wonderful birds,
> a joyous strain . . .
>
> That I may see its excellent flocks of birds
> above the great watery ocean;

32. Ibid., 109.

that I may see its huge creatures,
greatest of marvels;

That I may see its ebb and its flood
in its running,
so that this should be my name, a secret that I speak:
"Back [turned] toward Ireland";

That repentance of heart might come to me,
looking at it;
that I may lament my many evils,
difficult to make them known;][33]

On the other hand, there is the theme of the Wildman of the Woods, in which an involuntary ordeal in the wilderness confers poetic vision and prophecy on the sufferer.[34] Suibne Geilt ("Sweeney the Wild") is traditionally miserable in the wilderness. Driven insane by the curse of Saint Ronan in punishment for his sins (or, in other traditions, by the cries at the battle of Mag Roth), Suibne "lived in trees, grew feathers and talons and shunned mankind."[35] He is restored to society by the blessing of Saint Mo Ling and "shares his natural experiences with his fellow humans through the medium of poetry."[36] Another exile inhabiting the liminal and therefore "unsystematized" area between tribal communities or *túatha* is Finn the *fenníd* (champion, outlaw, and poet) whose encounter in the wilderness with otherworldly experiences (particularly the "salmon of wisdom") gives him second sight. Besides the nature poetry attributed to Finn, many of the poems uttered in the Fenian tradition are mantic and frequently obscure.[37] The origin of the Celtic nature poem is unclear; Kenneth Jackson argues for a tradition native to the Celts;[38] Robin Flower suggests that it was introduced by literate Irish

---

33. Ibid., 38–39.
34. Kenneth Jackson speaks of the madness of two notable poets and prophets of related tradition: Suibne in Irish literature and Myrddin in Welsh (ECNP, 111); see also Robert D. Scott, *The Thumb of Knowledge in Legends of Finn, Sigurd, and Taliesin* (New York: Publications of the Institute of French Studies, 1930); Nora K. Chadwick, *Poetry and Prophecy* (Cambridge: Cambridge University Press, 1942); Joseph Falaky Nagy, *The Wisdom of the Outlaw: The Boyhood Deeds of Finn in Gaelic Narrative Tradition* (Berkeley and Los Angeles: University of California Press, 1985); and Lehmann, *Early Irish Verse*, 64–77, for a brief discussion of Suibne and his poetry.
35. Lehmann, *Early Irish Verse*, 68.
36. Nagy, *The Wisdom of the Outlaw*, 30.
37. Ibid., 27.
38. ECNP, 149–75.

monks into poems about exiles and pilgrims.[39] Possibly pre-Christian in origin, it offers an alternative to sacred masculine space, its subjects not only enduring but finding strength in the void. The pertinent issue, writes Joseph Nagy, is "the traditional connection of [nature poetry] with 'outlandish figures,' who live outside or on the periphery of human society and thereby, in some mysterious way, become inspired to compose verse about their natural environment."[40] Nagy's study particularly addresses the threshold nature of these characters who mediate between the Otherworld and the human world in the way of a shaman.[41] He comments on the shabby and leprous condition of these mantics, and he tells the story of the great poet Senchán Torpéist,[42] who is accompanied on his journeys by a mysterious *gilla* ("servant"), "leprous and dressed in rags." When Senchán is challenged by a woman to finish the poem she begins, it is the leper who responds, after which he is transformed into a handsome youth and vanishes. The story ends with *dubiam itaque non est quod ille Poematis erat spiritus* ("and so there is no doubt that he was the spirit of Poetry").[43] Nagy writes: "It is clear that the various poets we have examined—poets who live outside society, compose nature poetry, and are characterized as impoverished or diseased—have exceptionally great poetic knowledge and exercise great poetic power in the stories in which they appear, even though they are peripheral figures and are engaged in seemingly peripheral genres of filidecht ['poetry']."[44]

Could the speaker of the Llywarch-Hen corpus, including *The Leper of Abercuawg*, be a latent poet rather than a latent penitent? Claims to poetic prowess are no more evident than penitential utterances, but that has not deterred scholars from arguing for the latter reading. Welsh poetry does have its literary equivalent to Suibne Geilt in the figure of Myrddin, poet and prophet, who laments his madness and his wretched life of exile in the *Afallanau* and *Oianau* of *The Black Book*,[45] in terms reminiscent of Llywarch or "The Sick Man":

39. *The Irish Tradition* (New York: Oxford University Press, 1947), 41.

40. *Wisdom of the Outlaw*, 31.

41. Ibid., 25.

42. In Kuno Meyer, *Sanais Cormaic: An Old-Irish Glossary*, #1059, in *Anecdota from Irish Manuscripts* 4, ed. Osborn Bergin et al. (Halle: 1912).

43. Ibid., 32.

44. Ibid., 33.

45. *LLyfr Du Caerfyrddan*, ed. A. O. H. Jarman (Caerdydd: Gwasg Prifysgol Cymru, 1982), 26–35.

Ojan a parchellan. nud glas minit
tenev vy llen imi nyd llonit.
lluid yw. vy bleit nim treit guendit.

(BBC: 128–30)

[Hail, piglet. The mountain is green.
Thin my cloak, it is not enough for me.
Gray is my hair, Gwendydd does not visit me.]

"In some ways," writes Jackson, "the life of the hermit and that of the exile or madman lurking in the wilds must have been alike; and though the essential characters of the two groups of poetry . . . can easily be distinguished, sometimes the distinctions are blurred." One can understand scholars' desire to fix the restless verses of *Claf Abercuawg* within a reassuring genre of medieval Christian "penitential poetry." It gives a necessary perspective to the ugliness of illness, age, and solitude. Without it, life is meaningless, *diriaid*. However, in the broad picture, all conditions in medieval literature lead to the necessity of penitence, and when given such wide parameters, "penitential" literature is a meaningless category. Critically speaking, sameness is less interesting than difference, and the problem with flattening poetry under such broadly based generic categories is that it collapses important intertextualities. It is important that *The Sick Man* verses leave open the dreadful question of what the forces hostile to man and his salvation can do to one. Will it turn one into God's chosen, or will it turn one into a monster? The repeated juxtaposition of *dedwydd* and *diriaid* throws the issue of the Sick Man's attitude into an important ambivalence where the matter of being within the right interior becomes crucial. It is also important what counsel is given or withheld in poetry, what is relegated to private or public discourse. The heroic and the confessional or penitential are public acts; they subsume the private perspective in a larger one. To be sure, the act of penance has its element of the private in utilizing a withdrawal from society, a spiritual and personal calling to God, but its lessons are public. Why should the Welsh verses withhold these lessons if they are truly penitential?

One could argue that in their silence they invite rumination and comment. They invite us to fill in and explicate, to take the appropriating masculine stance toward literary and spiritual mysteries. But one could also argue that the author(s) of *The Sick Man* and accompanying verses was more interested in complaining vividly about the uncooperative *world* than in contemplating the *topos* of mutability or Christian struggle, a stance that is reinforced to brilliant effect in the grammar and imagery of nonrelationship. He revels in the heterogeneous void, enriching his text with his ambiguities. Speaking of ambiguities, then, I turn to a discussion of the uncooperative *word* and the topic of intentional obscurity.

PART III

THE PRIVATE CONNECTION

7

Intentional Difficulty in
Early Welsh Poetry

Feminine pleasure has to remain inarticulate in language, in its own
language, if it is not to threaten the underpinnings of logical operations.
—Luce Irigaray, *This Sex Which Is Not One*

Keluyd kelet y aruaeth
("The skillful, let him conceal his design.")
—*Eiry Mynyd*

Here I enter into perilous space.

Poetic obscurity is of immense interest to discourse analysis, reader re-
sponse theory, sign theory, and other modes of inquiry that examine episte-
mology, the relationship of text and reader/hearer, and the ideological and
cultural underpinnings of notions of language in literature.[1] The very term
"obscurity"—not to mention "*intentional* obscurity"—privileges clarity by
reading absence into its opposite. In poetry, writes George Steiner, "multiplic-
ity of meaning, 'enclosedness,' are the rule rather than the exception. . . .
Lexical resistance is the armature of meaning, guarding the poem from the
necessary commonalities of prose."[2] In *After Babel* Steiner repeatedly stresses

1. For a fruitful discussion of literature as linguistic "deviation," see Derek Attridge, *Peculiar
Language: Literature as Difference from the Renaissance to James Joyce* (Ithaca: Cornell University
Press, 1988).
2. "On Difficulty," in *On Difficulty and Other Essays* (Oxford: Oxford University Press, 1972,
1978), 21.

the element of "translation" in all speech currents that are only "partially congruent," even those within the same idiom.[3] How much more difficult, then, are our attempts to interpret medieval Welsh poetry, where bad textual transmission, special bardic vocabulary, and lost context widen the gulf that already stretches across the centuries? And what, finally, are we to do with the obscurantist impulses of much Welsh poetry whereby the speaker seems to *intend* to conceal, to leave unspoken, to hint at darkly?

Difficulty in Early Welsh Poetry

Up to this point I have been talking about a natural kind of "difficulty" in Welsh poetry—an unquestioned assumption that it is not the purpose of a poem to disclose all its message in verbally explicit terms, nor is it to progress from point A to point B with the logical connection that prose discourse offers. But I have yet to speak of this rationale as "difficult" in the sense suggested above. A quality seems to emerge in some Welsh poems which suggests that the poet's purpose is not only not to be apprehended instantaneously by an untrained mind but that his utterances are agonistic in intention, meant to defeat his spiritual and poetic competitors. In a number of poems and dialogues, especially those uttered by the persona of Taliesin or Myrddin (Merlin), metaphors for inspiration are martial. Poetry is warfare between poetic contenders—titles from the cryptic *Book of Taliesin*[4] yield "Battlefield of Bards"[5] and "Hostile Alliance"[6] (if we can even translate these phrases accurately)—and like the *Hisperica Famina* they are full of bellicose imagery.[7] In *Preideu Annwn* ("The Spoils of the Otherworld") inspiration is

3. George Steiner, *After Babel: Aspects of Language and Translation* (London: Oxford University Press, 1975).

4. *The Book of Taliesin: Facsimile and Edition*, ed. J. Gwenogvryn Evans (Llanbedrog: Issued to Subscribers Only, 1910).

5. *Buarth Beird* (BT 7.12–8.20). The meaning of *buarth* is uncertain: In a note on *buarthaw* in 7, 45, Ifor Williams and J. E. Caerwyn Williams cite the meaning given in *Geirfa Barddoniaeth*: "to pen, to fold, to herd, ? to plunder (*preiddio*)," and submit that *buarth*, like *ysgor* and *creu*, might denote "a battlefield, a battle-enclosure." *The Poems of Taliesin* (Dublin: Institute for Advanced Studies, 1975), 91.

6. *Angar Kyfyndawt*, BT 18.25–23.8; Texts no. 8.

7. From *The Hisperica Famina: I. The A-Text, A New Critical Edition with English Translation and Philogical Commentary*, ed. and trans. Michael W. Herren (Toronto: Pontifical Institute of Medieval Studies, 1974), 65–65:

> What texts do you recite
> and what rhetor do you adhere to?

seen as a raid on *Caer Sidi*,[8] and throughout these poems, poetry itself is depicted as something acquired with difficulty and therefore of difficult access to the hearer. Discussions of intentional difficulty in poetry, however, have been limited mainly to modern literature, perhaps owing to the assumption that it is only in modern thought that we have a basic distrust in the signifying power of language. To quote Steiner again, the concept of the "lacking word" is characteristic of modern poetry: "It divides a literature essentially housed in language from one for which language has become a prison."[9] From the dawn of Western literature until the time of Mallarmé, he writes, "poetry and prose were in organic accord with language." He acknowledges the "deliberate obscurities and subversions" of language in Pindar and the medieval lyric, but for the most part, he says, poetry "moved with the grain of speech" up until the "second half of the nineteenth century. There it breaks down abruptly. Goethe and Victor Hugo were perhaps the last poets to find that language was sufficient to their needs."[10]

The kind of syntactical subversion that Steiner addresses is located in a growing cynicism about the public nature of language that lies at the core of contemporary philosophy. But the tactical difficulty of ancient poetry has a different genesis: the divine nature of the letter, the codified and unutterable word of divinity, and, by extension, all privileged writing, all inspired speaking. To an extent that Steiner does not admit, poets long before Mallarmé were moving against the "grain of speech."[11] From the Scriptural, Apocryphal and Gnostic texts to the Indic and Arabic mystic poetry, from the

---

Thus do I challenge the adroit wrangler to a verbal duel,
to engage in rhetorical gymnastics with eagerness.
For previously I contended against three athletes:
I slaughtered helpless warriors,
punished powerful peers,
and brought down stouter giants in the fray.

8. BT 54.16–56.13. The title *preideu annwn*, added in a later hand to the manuscript, describes the events of the poem but could also be a metaphor for the poetic process, so often seen as a physical acquisition throughout Indo-European poetry. The speaker is a warrior and a voyager who wrests it from the Otherworld, here depicted as a fortress whose descriptive epithet changes in every stanza: "Caer Sidi," "Caer Vedwit," "Caer Rigor," "Caer Golud." The speaker appears to deride readers, not warriors, who are deficient in knowledge.

9. *After Babel*, 176.

10. Ibid., 177–78.

11. Mary Louise Pratt explodes the traditional distinctions made between "poetic" and "non-poetic" language ("The Poetic Language Fallacy" and "Natural Narrative: What is Ordinary Language Really Like?" in *Toward A Speech Act Theory of Literary Discourse* (Bloomington: Indiana University Press, 1977), 3–37, 38–78. See also Attridge, Introduction to *Peculiar Language*, 1–16.

Hisperica Famina of seventh-century Ireland to the *ulaṭbāṃsī* of Kabir[12] we find ample evidence of arcane vocabulary, secret contexts, tangled words; in short, private languages that questioned the assumption from the start that word and world could be connected for the uninitiated—or the fallen.

Classical and medieval language theory is fraught with ambivalence over the sufficiency of language to express not only one's needs but the True. Plato's *Cratylus* introduces the best-known dispute over the natural or conventional nature of words and their efficacy or fallibility,[13] a problem that was to plague Augustine, who identifies language as a product of postlapsarian humanity, an arbitrary, agreed-upon system that has been severed from its original relationship with God.[14] Defective, subject to lying and false augury, it is empowered only by the Incarnation, making theology and scriptural authority possible. In the account of his acquisition of language and later conversion in his *Confessions*, Augustine "illustrates the function of the spoken and written word as media of revealed wisdom," as Marcia Colish writes, and concludes with a "schematic outline of the various uses of redeemed speech."[15]

Where medieval Welsh obscurity (or outsiders' conceptions of it) might fit in with these intellectual concerns over language is indeed a curious problem; in its pre-Christian origins it might reflect an older sacral relationship between word and nature. Whatever the case may be, no discussion of the disjunction of images or of the associative or poetic logic in Welsh is complete without an examination of the hermetic elements in Welsh poetry so carefully preserved for us in *The Book of Taliesin* and other late medieval and early Renaissance Welsh texts. The number of references to obscure Celtic speaking is noteworthy, and they span a range of various genres and tones:

> The Gauls are terrifying in aspect and their voices are altogether harsh; when they meet together they converse with few words and in riddles, hinting darkly at things for the most part and using one word when they mean another.[16]

12. "Upside-down language," part of a long poetic and epigrammatic tradition in India of intentionally obscure or paradoxical discourse. For a splendid treatment of this philosophy, see Appendix A by Linda Hess in *The Poetry of Kabir*, trans. Linda Hess and Shukdev Singh (San Francisco: North Point Press, 1983), 135–61.

13. In *The Dialogues*, trans. B. Jowett (Oxford: Clarendon Press, 1953), 3:50–106.

14. *On Christian Doctrine*, trans. D. W. Robertson, Jr. (New York: Macmillan, 1987), 60–61.

15. *The Mirror of Language: A Study in the Medieval Theory of Knowledge* (New Haven: Yale University Press, 1968), 20.

16. Diodorus Siculus, V.32, trans. C. H. Oldfather, Loeb Classical Library, ed. T. E. Page et al. (Cambridge: Harvard University Press, 1939), 177.

Diodorus Siculus here describes a pagan people whose obscurity is a locus for power. So, too, is that of the poet-magician Gwydden, labeled "The Abstruse" (*Gwydden Astrus*) in *Culhwch ac Olwen*, an early Arthurian tale from *The Mabinogion*. [17] Obscurity is later treated more ambiguously by the author of *Breudwyt Ronabwy*, who describes in a rather comic scene a group of bards come to recite songs which no one can understand, except that they are in praise of Arthur. [18] Still later, in a poem included in the sixteenth-century prose tale by Elis Gruffydd, Taliesin admonishes the bards of Maelgwn for their ignorance of his esoteric utterances:

> ni wyddoch chwi yn ddau
> ddaalld y peth a gaan y min mav
> na dosbarth diau
> hrwng y gwir a'r gav. [19]

> [Truly you do not know
> the meaning of what my lips sing,
> nor the veritable distinction
> between the true and the false.]

The bards' confusion is understandable. Prior to this accusation, Taliesin charges them not to be arrogant unless they know "the name for *rimin*, and the name for *ramin*, and the name for *rimiad*, and the name for *ramiad*."[20] Not content with this humiliation, he makes them say *blerwm blerwm* with their fingers on their lips when they go to recite praise poems to their king. Taliesin's rantings are contextually unintelligible, but make strange claims for his identification with scriptural figures which he mingles with figures from Early Welsh mythology:

> A myui a wn hennwau'r seer
>   o ogleedd hyd awsder;

---

17. *Kulhwch ac Olwen*, in *The Text of the Mabinogion and Other Welsh Tales from the Red Book of Hergest*, ed. John Rhys and J. Gwenogvryn Evans (Oxford: Issued to Subscribers Only, 1887), 111.

18. *Breudwyt Ronabwy*, ed. Melville Richards (Caerdydd: Gwasg Prifysgol Cymru, 1948), 20.

19. Elis Gruffydd, *Ystoria Taliesin*, National Library of Wales, MS. NLW 5276D, in Patrick K. Ford, *Ystoria Taliesin* (Cardiff: University of Wales Press, 1992), 81. This book came out a few weeks before my own went to press. See Ford's introduction for similar discussion of Taliesin's background and history.

20. *Hanes Taliesin*, 80.

Myui a vum ynghaer Vidion
  ynhittreggramatton;
Myui a vu[m] ynn y Gannon
  pan laas Apsalon;

. . .

Myui a vum ar vann krog
  Mab Duw Duw drugarog;
Myui a vum dri chyuynod
  mewn karchar Arianrhod;

. . .

Myui a nerthais Voesen
  drwy dwr Aurddonen;
Myui a vum ar yr wybren
  gida Mair Vadlen;
Myui a gefais awn
  o bair Keridwen;[21]

[I know the names of the stars from North to South.
I was in the fortress of Gwyddion in the Tetragrammaton.
I was in the canon when Absalom was slain.
I was upon the top of the cross of the merciful Son of God.
I was three periods in the prison of Arianrhod.
I supported Moses through the water of Jordan.
I was in the sky with Mary Magdalene.
I received inspiration from the cauldron of Cerridwen.]

These later references do not rule out an older tradition of poetic obscurity. References to Taliesin are scattered throughout the thirteenth-century *Gododdin*, one of the most important attributions being the preface to the "Gwarchan Maeldderw," a notoriously difficult poem for which it is said that Taliesin won a prize.[22] The *Book of Taliesin* is filled with texts of a

---

21. *Hanes Taliesin*, 77–78. Part of the unintelligible nature of these claims rests in the distortion of Scripture; that is, Moses would have been upheld in the river Nile, not the Jordan, and it would have been Mary, the Mother of Jesus, not Magdalene, that Taliesin shared the sky with. Even so, it is difficult to know exactly what the speaker means when he claims to be in the "canon" when Absalom was slain. The blithe mingling of biblical and Celtic mythology is characteristic of these types of poems.

22. *Eman weithyon e dechreu gwarchan maelderw. Talyessin ae cant ac a rodes breint idaw. kemeint ac e odleu e gododin oll ae dri gwarchan yng kerd amrysson* ["Here at last begins the Gwarchan Maeldderw. Taliesin sang it and honor was given to him, in as great a quantity as for the

character similar to that in Gruffudd's work—"Could Lycophron or the sybils be so elaborately incomprehensible?" exclaims Sharon Turner of the *Preideu Annwn*[23]—and the language of the poems contained in it might be older than the manuscript itself.[24]

Difficulty in the Welsh falls into two major categories. (1) There is the relatively commonplace difficulty of the "courtly" poetry which uses an arcane vocabulary and a convoluted syntax, such as we find with the *gogynfeirdd* ("not-so-early bards"). It might be compared to the difficulty of skaldic verse, where one's knowledge of poetic vocabulary and "kennings" make the poem more or less intelligible, or to the difficulty of the *trobar clus* of the troubadours, where understanding depends on a private courtly context. Poetry of this sort is panegyric and eulogistic, and its difficulty is largely syntactic and lexical in nature. (2) Then there is that of the "vatic" traditions of poetry, so well represented in the Early Welsh, which make obscure references to supernatural or antiquarian lore. Here we find prophecies, and also a kind of bardic flyting where the *vates* or *sywedydd* ("wiseman") or *drui* ("wizard," "druid") makes a display of his powers with the intention of dazzling, confusing, and impressing his hearers with his visionary knowledge. Poetry of this sort is self-declamatory, and its difficulty is contextual. It might be compared to any kind of vatic poetry, such as the Delphic oracular utterances, or verses that the Greeks called "dithyrambic," and it frequently takes the form of enigmata.[25]

---

verses of the entire *Gododdin* and the three *gorchanau* in the poetic competition."] *The Book of Aneirin*, MS Cardiff 1, 28. A. O. H. Jarman omits this poem from his translation of *The Gododdin* on the grounds that the matter is not pertinent and the text "has hitherto defied all attempts at elucidation" (*Y Gododdin: Britain's Oldest Heroic Poem* [Llandysul: Gomer Press, 1990], lxvii).

23. Sharon Turner, *History of the Anglo-Saxons* (London, 1828), 3:634, 636.

24. D. Simon Evans, *A Grammar of Middle Welsh* (Dublin: Institute for Advanced Studies, 1976), xxi. Evans follows the accepted opinion and places the BT in the thirteenth century. Marged Haycock argues in her doctoral dissertation for its being later (*Llyfr Taliesin: Astudiaethau ar rai Agweddau*, Aberystwyth, 1983), 1–48. Of *Preideu Annwn* she writes that she can find nothing "genuinely and convincingly archaic" about it (p. 7), presumably countering John T. Koch's suggestion that the use of deponent verbs indicates early composition ("Clywanhor, Gwydanhor, Gwydyanhawr," *Bulletin of the Board of Celtic Studies* 31 [1984], 87–92.) This is a moot point: Those who want to make *The Gododdin* or any other text "earlier" than it is point out its archaisms and reconstruct sixth-century Brythonic paradigms for its language; those who want to make it "later" than it is point out the "archaizing" tendencies of the *gogynfeirdd* and pooh-pooh reconstructions. Both stances have been taken with regard to *The Gododdin* and *The Book of Taliesin* alike. It is doubtful that the notion of deliberate poetic obscurity sprang up full bloom in fourteenth-century Welsh thought, and I suggest that since references to it are numberless it had earlier origins.

25. For a lucid catalogue of the various functions of early Western poets, see *The Role of the Poet in Early Societies* by Morton W. Bloomfield and Charles W. Dunn (Cambridge: D. S. Brewer, 1989),

More to the point, certain Celtic poems are comprised of lists of natural forms that the speaker takes or has taken—"I am wind on the sea . . . I am a salmon in a pool"—where he appears personified as Nature, Wisdom, or one who has harnessed the powers of the natural world. The Welsh tradition, especially as we find it in *The Book of Taliesin*, has roots within a pre-Christian concept of the poet who calls upon a secret language that links him with the unknowable forces of the cosmos. The easily assimilated Christian values with their concern for empowered language would account for the numerous scriptural identifications that seem to introduce so much contradiction into these poems. And when two types of difficulty are combined—an obscurity of vocabulary and syntax and an obfuscation of context—we have something resembling glossolalia. Failure to understand the bard's rantings signals a spiritual as well as an intellectual deficiency in hearers: "I do not reward the ruler's little men of letters," charges Taliesin in *Preideu Annwn*,[26] where ignorant monks, unlearned in the superior lore of the druid, are so many howling dogs. Taliesin's song, however, is "endowed" by Christ.[27]

Among both types of obscure poem we find the juxtaposition of elements without explanation, the natural difficulty with which this study has been concerned. The recognition of an intentional type of difficulty might give us a new handle on this natural difficulty, as well as offer us insight into concepts of visionary poetry in Wales and the effect of *awen* ("inspiration") on poetic connection. An examination of a later type of poetry, such as that produced by the *gogynfeirdd*, shows the direction poetry took in the hands of poets who admired and imitated earlier bards, including Taliesin and Aneirin.

The Difficulty of Court Poetry

The author of *The Dream of Rhonabwy* aims a barbed comment at court poets:

especially their comments about the nature of oracular poetry in "Wisdom Genres and Types of Literature": "Obscurity or ambiguity is a well-known feature of prophecy, and lack of exactitude can obviously be a blessing to the prophet's reputation" (142). This attribution of difficulty to the poet's self-defensive measures makes a certain amount of sense, but it doesn't explain the strong aura of intentional obfuscation in certain of the Taliesinic revelation discourses, and I have to disagree with their conclusion that "the audience and the utterance shared with the poet in the total poetic complex."

26. *Ny obrynafi lawyr llen lywyadur*, BT.55, 13–14. A line subject to much interpretation and caviling.

27. Ibid., 56.4–5, 13.

Ac ar hynny nachaf veird yn dyvot y datkanv
kerd y Arthur. Ac nyt oed dyn a adnapei y
gerd honno, namyn Kadyrieith ehun, eithyr y
uot yn uolyant y Arthur.[28]

[And thereupon, behold, bards coming to recite a song to Arthur.
And there was not a man who could understand that song, but for
Cadyrieith himself, except that it was in praise of Arthur.]

Since this comment comes after a kaleidoscopic and dreamlike sequence of
events which gives the story its general air of comedy and confusion, we
cannot be certain whether the author is praising or satirizing the bards.[29] It
might have been a matter of course among the Welsh that court poetry was to
present difficulties to the ordinary hearer—especially poetry recited in other-
worldly places—and that it was a mark of one's intellectual and class merit to
understand it; hence the man named Cadyrieith, "mighty speech," is a
privileged hearer. "Whatever we may think of the origin of the tale of
Rhonabwy," writes T. Gwynn Jones, "we have probably in the words quoted
evidence of a Welsh prose writer of the twelfth or thirteenth century as to the
unintelligible character of the bardic composition of his own day."[30]

Jones here refers to the poetry commonly ascribed to the *gogynfeirdd* ("not-
so-early bards") of the twelfth and thirteenth centuries, somewhat later than
the elegies we have been studying; these poets looked back to and perfected
techniques found in the *cynfeirdd* ("early bards"), including Taliesin. A num-
ber of other scholars have commented on this matter of cultivated obscurity.[31]
Referring us to the medieval term *gravis* ("difficult"), J. Lloyd-Jones speaks of
the deliberate archaisms of the *gogynfeirdd*, who found in the earlier bards
not only their archaisms but their "dominant exemplars, the patterns of

28. *Breuddwyd Ronabwy*, ed. Melville Richards, 20.
29. See especially Thomas Parry, *A History of Welsh Literature*, trans. Idris Bell (Oxford: Claren-
don Press, 1955), 84; John Bollard, "Troddodiad a dychan yn *Breudwyt Ronabwy* [Tradition and
Satire in *The Dream of Rhonabwy*]," *Llen Cymry*, 13 [1983], 160; and, for an examination of failed
language, my article "Perlocution and Perlection in *The Dream of Rhonabwy*: An Untellable Tale,"
Exemplaria 2.2 (1990), 527–62.
30. T. Gwynn Jones, "Bardism and Romance," in *Transactions of the Honourable Society of the
Cymmrodorion*, Session 1913–14 (London: 64 Chancery Lane, 1915), 205–6.
31. John J. Parry, for one, locates the satire in rivalry between the classes of poets. He surmises
that the jibe aimed at the bards is leveled by "a minstrel of the lower class," namely, the author of the
story; a real courtly audience, accustomed to this poetry, would have "understood it well enough"
("The Court Poets of the Welsh Princes," *PMLA* 67 [1952], 513).

excellence for their own craftsmanship." "Nothing," writes Jones, "distinguishes their poetry . . . more than this prepossession, which represents a conscious design to maintain their craft as an esoteric art."[32]

Deliberate opacity on the part of other non-Celtic poets has already been looked into by Edgar de Bruyne, who divides medieval poetry of the Roman Empire into the Attic and Asiatic styles first characterized by Quintilian.[33] Myrddin Lloyd uses de Bruyne's argument to shed light on the *gogynfeirdd* poets, who, like the authors of the *Hisperica Famina*,[34] preferred the strange word to the plain one and who deliberately convoluted syntax for the sake of producing as ornate and as artificial a poetry as possible.[35] J. Caerwyn Williams gives us samples of the *sangiadau* ("chevilles," or "sidesteps") and the *torymydroddion* ("intercalations") of the *gogynfeirdd*, by which they intertwine sentences "so that a few words of one are followed by a few words of another."[36] Here is his very literal translation of a poem listed in the *Myfyrian Archaeology*:

> Dygnaf, Duw eurnaf, diwarnawd dyngddu,
>   fu ddoe gan dri llu, ddogn o drallawd
> Dwyn eurwas difas defawd diweccry
>   i dy dirwely daear waelawd.

> [God, excellent lord, most dire on a pressingly gloomy day was yesterday by three hosts—enough tribulation—the bearing of an excellent youth, thoughtful, not frivolous in manner, to the final bed abode on earth bottom.][37]

Williams contrasts the style of the *gogynfeirdd* with that of the prose period in "(i) its unusual word order; (ii) its frequent use of compound words and composite phrases; (iii) its compactness: it seems to eschew wherever possible

32. J. Lloyd-Jones, "The Court Poets of the Welsh Princes," *Proceedings of the British Academy* 34 (1948), 171.

33. Edgar de Bruyne, *Études d'estèthique médiévale* (Bruges: Tempelhof, 1946), 1:108.

34. Michael W. Herren, ed. and trans. *Hisperica*. In his introduction, Herren includes a section on "The Hisperica Famina and Irish Culture," wherein he suggests that the " 'Hisperic craze' was a self-conscious attempt to create a specialized diction based upon Latin that could be used for non-Christian themes" and that it makes use of a kind of "hieratic language that would be accessible only to the few" (43).

35. "Esthetig yr oesoedd canol," *Llen Cymru* 1:153–68, 220–38.

36. *The Poets of the Welsh Princes* (Cardiff: University of Wales Press, 1978), 57.

37. Ibid., 57–58.

the use of what grammarians sometimes call accessory or subsidiary words, e.g. the definite article and prepositions, and even to shun the use of the finite verb in favour of the verb noun."[38] One might compare such techniques, and especially the use of *sangiadau*, to the elaborate "braiding" of phrases to be found in tenth-century *Drátkvætt* poetry of Iceland, which is combined with an elaborate system of *kenningar* or metaphors and which deliberately sets out to obfuscate.[39] Like the *gogynfeirdd*, the skalds composed for a select and educated audience, and difficulty, which was intentional, lay not merely in convoluted word order and obscure kennings but also in hidden contexts. As Roberta Frank writes, "*Drátkvætt* and the settlement of Iceland are . . . both products of a culture that did not waste syllables, where the shapes of stillness, of what is not uttered, had their own meanings."[40]

Contextual Difficulty and the Inspired Poet

Many *gogynfeirdd* poems have the poetic unexpectedness that we have observed in the earlier Welsh poems; J. Caerwyn Williams speaks of "the gogynfeirdd habit of following an associative rather than a sequential logic to extremes:"[41]

> Moch dywreawc huan haf dyfestin.
> maws llafar adar mygyr hear hin.
> mi ytwyf eur ddetyf diofyn yn rin.
> mi ytwyf llew rac llu lluch vyg gortin.
> Gorwylyeis nos yn achadw fin.
> Gorloes rydyeu dyfyr dygen ureitin.
> Gorlas gwellt didrif dwfyr neud yessin.
> gordyar eaws awdyl gynneuin.
> Gwylein yn gware ar wely lliant.
> lleithyryon eu pluawr, pleidyeu etrin.
> Pellynnic vyg khof ag kynteuin.
> yn ethrip caru kaerwys vebin.

38. Ibid., 45.
39. An excellent example can be found in Roberta Frank's book, *Old Norse Court Poetry: The Drátkvæt Stanza* (Ithaca: Cornell University Press, 1978), 50–51.
40. Ibid., 23.
41. *Poets of the Welsh Princes*, 37.

pell o uon uein. yduyti dwythwal werin.
essmwyth yssyt ynn asserw gyfrin.
yt endeweis eneu yn echlyssur gwir
ar lleueryt gwar gwery y lein.
ac ar lles ywein hael hual dilin.
dychysgogan lloergyr rac vy llain.

(LlH: 16.1–18)

[An early rising sun, summer hastens;
pleasant the speech of birds, fine smooth weather;
I am of golden nature, fearless in battle,
I am a lion, my onrush a flash before the host.
I watched at night, keeping a border;
ford waters bubbled in the Dygen Breiddin.
Bright-green the wild grassland, the water fair;
loud the nightingales' familiar song,
gulls playing on the surface of the sea,
damp their feathers, clamorous their ranks.
far away is my memory with early summer,
because I love a Caerwys maiden.
Far from little Anglesey, are you (and from its) lively folk;
carefree under the secret shelter of the ashtrees.
I listened to lips in a true retreat,
to the gentle words of a maiden-fawn,
and to the advantage of generous Owain, fine fetter;
the English tremble before my sword.]

This poem, entitled *Gorhoffedd* ("praise," "boast") and attributed to the poet Gwalchmai, goes on for more than a hundred more lines; there is only one other poem extant, that by Hywel ap Owein, to bear this title. The *Gorhoffeddau* pose something of a literary problem in that we do not know whether they are vestiges of a genuine genre, characteristics of which we should be looking for in other poems. In addition, their focus is unclear. Both have martial and amatory elements, but for whom they were writing and in what context is unknown. Their titles may have arisen from the perception of these poems as uniquely self-reflexive; their composers were warriors and statesmen—Hywel was son to the king that Gwalchmai served and may even have been tutored by Gwalchmai—who, being poets, had no need of other poets to sing their own praises; hence the private aura of both poems. J. Caerwyn Williams declares that the one by Gwalchmai "defies analysis on account of its seemingly disjointed character,"[42] surely a peculiar exaggeration, as this feature is one displayed prominently in the poetry of Llywarch Hen. Williams reminds us that the term *gorhoffedd* means "exultation" as well as "boasting," and suggests that the disjointedness in the train of thought may be a manifestation of exuberance.[43] This point is important in view of my subsequent inquiry into the poetry of *The Book of Taliesin*. The word *gorhoffedd* can be broken down into two elements—a noun (*hoffedd*) meaning "delight" or "pride," and an intensifying prefix (*gor-*) that carries the same force as *ver-* in German: "over," "much." "Exultation," then, is a fairly close rendering of the meaning of this word, which seems to express an emotion that carries one away with rapture and pride, wherein one sees the fundamental relationship between love and war—"the awareness at the same time of contrary seasons and passions."[44]

In the *Gorhoffedd* of Hywel ab Owain Gwynedd, this exultation is more obviously directed at the speaker's homeland than it is in Gwalchmai's poem, but they have in common the abrupt and unexplained juxtaposition of natural imagery and emotional declaration:

> Tonn wenn orewyn a orwylych bet.
> gwytua ruuawn bebyr ben teyrnet.
> caraf trachas lloegyr lleudir goglet hediw.
> ac yn amgant y lliw lliaws callet.
>
> (LlH: 315, 1–4)

> [A foaming white wave washes over a grave,
> the tomb of Rhufawn Pebyr, chief of monarchs.
> I love today the great hatred of the English: the open land of the
> North,
> and the multitude of growth on the border of the Lliw.]

As in *Canu Llywarch Hen*, this link may be explained by an overarching context of associations, but here the sea, despite its connection with the grave, is more obviously linked with patriotism than with sadness and loss. The use of the natural analogy may be intended to impart what the Welsh

42. *Poets of the Welsh Princes*, 37.
43. Ibid., 38.
44. Gwynn Williams, *The Burning Tree: Poems from the First Thousand Years of Welsh Poetry* (London: Faber and Faber, 1956,) 13.

called *awen*, "poetic inspiration" (from IE *an*, "breath"), almost always seen as a force that the poet gathers into himself from without and that seems to take him out of himself. The poet becomes the world about which he utters verses, and his poem expresses an expansion and disconnectedness that is unsurpassed in the aretalogies of nature found in Gnostic, Pythagorean, and certain Celtic traditions. It is to these that I turn in a discussion of Taliesin.

Taliesin and the Revelation Discourse

In his *Description of Wales*, Geraldus Cambrensis describes the trance and ecstatic recitation of poetry by a group of Celtic diviners:

> Among the Welsh there are certain individuals called *Awenyddion* who behave as if they are possessed by devils. You will not find them anywhere else. When you consult them about some problem, they immediately go into a trance and lose control of their senses, as if they are possessed. They do not answer the question put to them in any logical way. Words stream from their mouths, incoherently and apparently meaningless and without any sense at all, but all the same, well-expressed; and if you listen carefully to what they say you will receive the solution to your problem. When it is all over, they will recover from their trance, as if they were ordinary people waking from a heavy sleep, but you have to give them a good shake before they regain control of themselves. . . . They seem to receive this gift of divination through visions which they see in their dreams.[45]

We might dismiss this account as an interesting but essentially trivial aspect of Welsh custom were it not for the fact that there is substantial representation in Welsh and Irish literature of the poet who utters prophecies in obscure and compelling verses. "Vaticinatory" poetry has been assiduously collected and is primarily associated with the legendary figures of Taliesin and Myrddin ("Merlin").[46] More extreme in its wild associations are what I call the Celtic "aretalogies" or "revelation discourses": these are a litany of assertions in the first person about the varied and paradoxical forms taken by the speaker or the

45. Gerald of Wales, *The Journey Through Wales, and the Description of Wales*, trans. Lewis Thorpe (Harmondsworth: Penguin Books, 1978), 246–47.

46. See, for instance, the *Armes Prydein o lyfr Taliesin* ["The Prophecies of Britain from *The Book of Taliesin*"], ed. Ifor Williams, (Caerdydd: Gwasg Prifysgol Cymru, 1955).

places to which he or she has traveled.[47] The Old Irish "Song of Amargain" in *Lebor Gabala Erinn* ("The Book of the Takings of Ireland") provides a splendid example:

> Am gaeth i m-muir.
> Am tond trethan.
> Am fuaim mara.
> Am dam secht ndirend.
> Am seig i n-aill.
> Am der grene.
> Am cain lubai.
> Am torc ar gail.
> Am he i l-lind.
> Am loch i m-maig.
> Am bri a ndae.
> Am bri danae.
> Am gai i fodb. (feras feochtu)
> Am de delbas do chind codnu.[48]

> [I am wind on the sea.
> I am a storm wave.
> I am ocean's roar.
> I am a seven-antlered stag.
> I am a hawk of the cliff.
> I am a dewdrop.
> I am a fair body.
> I am a boar for valor.
> I am a salmon in a pool.
> I am a lake in a plain.
> I am a word of their poetic art.
> I am a word of skill.
> I am a spear in cutting which pours out savagery.
> I am a god who makes antlers for the head.][49]

47. My article "The Mouthful of the Giants: Words and Space in Indo-European Revelation Discourse" (in *De Gustibus: Essays for Alain Renoir*, ed. John Miles Foley et al. [New York: Garland Press, 1992]), 266–303, explores this genre more fully.

48. "Amargain's Song," in *Lebor Gabal Eren* ["The Book of the Takings of Ireland"], ed. R. A. S. MacCallister (Dublin: Irish Texts Society, 1938), 5:110–11.

49. Daniel F. Melia, trans., in *Sources and Analogues of Old English Poetry, 2: The Major Germanic and Celtic Texts in Translation*, ed. Daniel G. Calder et al. (Cambridge: D. S. Brewer, 1983), 105.

The Book of Taliesin contains very disparate material: eulogies to Urien Rheged, a historical leader of the sixth century; elegies to other nobles; religious and scriptural poems; prophecies; one riddle; and a handful of curious poems boasting of poetic inspiration, supernatural knowledge, and shapeshifting, which give lists of revelations similar to those in "Amargain's Song." They all revolve around the shadowy sixth-century character of Taliesin, mentioned in Nennius along with Talhaearn and Aneirin as a historical poet.[50] Like Virgil, this Taliesin acquired the reputation of a magus and loremaster,[51] and he is shown in a number of dialogue poems pitting his wisdom against that of Merlin and other seers;[52] he appears as "Telgesinus" in Geoffrey's *Vita Merlini*, where his role, as summarized by Basil Clarke, is to be "the vehicle for some traditional scientific information included for entertainment-education,"[53] which is to say that he answers questions put to him by Merlin about the mysteries of the cosmos in the popular medieval "dialogue genre."[54] Merlin is gifted with like knowledge, but he differs from the character of Telgesinus in being a prophet. In other traditions, Taliesin takes on this role as well, and like Amargain of Irish tradition he is wont to declare his oneness with the universe in numerous aretalogies. Compare the following excerpt from *The Book of Taliesin* to "Amargain's Song":

> wyf kerdolyat. wyf keinyat claer.
> wyf dur wyf dryw wyf saer wyf syw.
> wyf sarff wyf serch yd ymgestaf.
>
> . . .
>
> Wyf kell wyf dell wyf datweir llet.
> wyf llogell kerd wyf lle ynnyet.
>
> (BT: 7.17–19, 8.1–2)

---

50. Nennius, *Historia Brittonum*, ed. F. Lot (Paris: 1934), 201: *Tunc Dutigern in illo tempore fortiter demicabat contra gentem Anglorum. Tunc Talhaern Tat Aguen in poemate claruit: et Neirin et Taliessin et Bluchbard et Cian, qui vocatur Gueinth Guaut, simul uno tempore in poemate Brittannic claruerunt.* "Then Eudeyrn at that time was fighting valiantly against the people of the Angles. Then Talhaern, 'Father of Inspiration [*awen*]' was renowned in poetry; and also Aneirin, Taliesin, Bluchbard and Cian who is called *Gueinth Guaut* [Williams: "Wheat of Song"?] were at the same time renowned in British poetry."

51. See Juliette Wood, "Virgil and Taliesin: The Concept of the Magician in Medieval Folklore," *Folklore* 94 (1983), 91.

52. See *Ymddiddan Myrddin a Thaliesin* and *Ymddiddan Taliesin ac Ugnach ap Mydno*, ed. A. O. H. Jarman, in *Llyrf Du Caerfyrddin* (Caerdydd: Gwasg Prifysgol Cymru, 1982), 1–2, 75–76.

53. *The Life of Merlin: Geoffrey of Monmouth's Vita Merlini* (Cardiff: University of Wales Press, 1973), 217.

54. *Vita Merlini*, lines 737–940 and 1179–1253, in Clarke, 92–103, 114–21.

[I am a poet; I am a brilliant singer;
I am steel; I am a druid; I am a builder; I am a magi.
I am a serpent; I am love by which I devour myself (?).
. . .
I am a story; I am a jewel; I am the gatherer of space (?).
I am a dwelling of song; I am a place in commotion (?).]

The poems of this sort in *The Book of Taliesin* are traditionally referred to as the "mythological" poems because of their presumed relationship to the shapeshifting legends of "Gwion Bach" in later literature, and they have been treated as little more than curiosities. Taliesin's history resembles that of the Irish Finn and the "salmon of wisdom," and it is so recounted by Elis Gruffudd in the sixteenth-century manuscript *Hanes Taliesin*.[55] Made to tend the cauldron of knowledge prepared for the witch's ugly son Afagddu, Gwion Bach accidentally ingests three drops of the potion, which burn his thumb. He puts his thumb in his mouth and is granted prophetic wisdom. Knowing that Cerridwen intends to kill him, he flees from her in the shape of a hare; she pursues in the shape of a hound; he and she take various shapes by land, water, and air until he disguises himself as a grain of wheat in a granary, which Cerridwen (turned hen) picks out and swallows. Nine months later, she is delivered of the infant Taliesin, whom she puts into a coracle and tosses into the sea. Elphin rescues the lad, and later, when Elphin offends King Maelgwn of Gwynedd and is thrown into prison, Taliesin contends on his behalf by confusing and shaming the king's bards with a recitation of the aforementioned boasting poems that they cannot understand.

The serious regard with which medieval redactors viewed and set down the kaleidoscopic powers of Taliesin has not been widely shared by critical scholarship. Ifor Williams and J. E. Caerwyn Williams's edition of *The Poems of Taliesin*[56] excerpts only those poems which seem to be associated with the historical personage mentioned in Nennius, that is, the court poet to Urien Rheged of *The Book of Taliesin*. The mantic poems get passing

---

55. *Hanes Taliesin* (Elis Gruffydd, Peniarth MS 6209E). See Juliette Wood, "The Folklore Background of the Gwion Bach Section of *Hanes Taliesin*," *Bulletin of the Board of Celtic Studies* 29 (1982), 621–34, as well as Patrick Ford's transmission of "The Tale of Gwion Bach and the Tale of Taliesin," in *The Mabinogi and Other Welsh Tales* (Berkeley and Los Angeles: University of California Press, 1977), 159–81.

56. *The Poems of Taliesin*, ed. Ifor Williams and J. E. Caerwyn Williams (Dublin: Institute for Advanced Studies, 1968).

mention in their introduction,[57] the only complete, up-to-date translation and commentary of the manuscript being the 1983 dissertation by Marged Haycock,[58] who bridges the gap between the historical and mythological figure in the medieval *persona* of Taliesin, capable of being both praise poet and Bard of Elphin. Haycock makes it clear that the emergence of the mythological noises of that "other" Taliesin (*bum hwch bum bwch. bum syw bum swch. bum ban bum banhwch. bum gawr ymrythwc*)[59] in *Canu y Meirch*, an otherwise respectable poem about famous steeds, need not give the puzzlement that it did to Ifor Williams.[60] "The main advantage of the existence of such a multi-lateral character as Taliesin," she writes, "is that he is a handy focus for so many various traditions; like an elastic band, the *persona* has the ability to stretch out, surround, and enchant them."[61]

Nonetheless, the critical world has not hastened to usher *The Book of Taliesin* into the fold, something which says more about contemporary than about medieval concepts of canonicity. There is the pervasive problem of the text: the fourteenth-century manuscript contains material that is much older; how old, we cannot tell, but a fair amount of textual corruption has been transmitted, making translation agonizingly difficult, especially in those poems which draw from already obscure tradition. The mantic discourses are tedious, their statements seemingly as banal as they are unintelligible, rarely rewarding the efforts of translators with meanings that one can be sure of. Exceptions go to the published translations made by Patrick K. Ford[62] of "Kat Godeu" ("Battle/Army of Trees") and by Marged Haycock[63] of *Preideu Annwn*, both of these beautiful and compellingly intricate although cryptic, poems. Then there is the fact that enthusiastic yet misguided study has been made of Taliesin

57. Ibid., xiv–xviii.

58. *Llyfr Taliesin: Astudiaethau ar rai agweddau* ("The Book of Taliesin: Studies of Certain Aspects"), Diss., Aberystwyth, Wales, 1983. This work has not, to my knowledge, been published in book form. For those who read modern Welsh, it is an invaluable and painstaking examination of the meter, style, and vocabulary of the texts in the BT, and it offers translations and commentaries upon all the poems.

59. "I was a pig; I was a buck; I was an excellent [one]; I was a ploughshare; I was a peak; I was a boar; I was a shout in the tumult."

60. Williams and Williams, PT, xxiv.

61. Haycock, LIT, 51: *Prif fantais bodolaeth cymeriad mor amlweddog a Thaliesin yw ei fod yn ffocws hwylus i gynifer o draddodiadau amrywiol. Fel band elastig, mae'r persona a'r medr i ymestyn i'w cwmpasu a'u huno.*

62. "Cad Goddeu," in Ford, *The Mabinogi*, 183–87.

63. "Preiddeu Annwn and the Figure of Taliesin," *Studia Celtica* 18/19 (1983–84), 54.

in the late nineteenth and early twentieth centuries, much of it growing out of a romantic fascination for the *primeval*. Taliesinic scholarship suffered regression when Robert Graves based his study of Gnostic and cabalistic interpretations of Celtic poetry on spurious translations of *Kat Godeu* and "Amargain's Song." Despite the fact that *The White Goddess* is an effective and complex examination of the mythic underpinnings of poetry, his study was spurned by scholars not only because he took a casual attitude toward translating these Middle Welsh texts but because in so doing he proposed a "magical language" derived from an ancient matriarchy usurped by a patriarchic language of "logic."[64] In its emphasis on a "feminine" and "Dionysian" discourse of riddle and disjunction as opposed to a "masculine" and "Apollonian" discourse of clarity and connection, his book must have hit just about every irritable nerve in traditional anglocentric circles. Regardless of its dated aspects, though, it looks ahead to some of the keenly Dionysian notions in contemporary theory that argue for pluralities, opacities, margins, gendered discourse, canon revision, relativism, and a reevaluation of the prevailing ideologies of power.

Arguments for the Indo-European origins of poetic practice have, however, met with resistance because there seems to be a covert association of such approaches with popular interest: Dumézil, Joseph Campbell, anthropology, folklore, and feminism are subtly allied with the public, the romantic, the uncredentialed (by those who don't know much about them). The scholar looks to his Latin source materials and the "most authentic" bardic traditions; the dilettante collects his coffee-table books about druids. The idea of an ecstatic, or worse, a shamanic Welsh poet stirs up the same critical discomfiture, partly because of its reductive tendencies (shamans were being identified everywhere), partly because scholars are still rejecting, late in the twentieth century, the Romantic notion of the inspired poet. Any discussion of reader-response theory in Taliesin threatens to tread on the traditional byline about "uninvited audiences" insisted upon by Morton Bloomfield and Charles Dunn, who are still banishing Thomas Gray's "The Bard" and setting us straight about "primal poetry."[65] It is also hard to forget the disgust expressed by Kenneth Jackson in his passionate tirade against romantic concepts of the Celtic mind as

64. *The White Goddess: A Historical Grammar of Poetic Myth* (New York: Farrar, Straus and Giroux, 1966), 9–10.
65. "Primal Poetry and the Modern Audience," in *The Role of the Poet in Early Societies*, 150–66.

something mysterious, magical, filled with dark broodings over a mighty past; and the Irish, Welsh and the rest as a people who have direct contact with a mystical supernatural twilight world which they would rarely reveal to the outsider. The so-called "Celtic Revival" of the end of the last century did much to foster this preposterous idea. A group of writers, approaching Celtic literatures (about which they usually knew very little, since most of them could not read the languages at all) with a variety of the above prejudice conditioned by the pre-Raphaelite and Aesthetic movements and their own individual turns of mind, were responsible for the still widely held belief that they are full of mournful, languishing, mysterious melancholy, of the dim "Celtic Twilight" (Yeats's term), or else of an intolerable whimsicality and sentimentality.[66]

Jackson goes on to say with indignation that a Welshman cannot publish a collection of the most realistic and cynical short studies "without some reviewer tracing in them the evidences of Celtic mysticism,"[67] and he declares that the most outstanding characteristic of Celtic poets is "their astonishing power of imagination."[68] He also reminds us of Whitley Stokes's comment that Irish literature is "strong, manly, purposeful, sharply defined in outline, frankly realistic, and pitiless in logic."[69] These protests suggest that it is not so much the mysterious or the visionary that bothers Jackson as their connotations of affectation or effeminacy. Especially noisome to opponents of the Second Medievalism are interpretations that take too much pleasure in the text as mysterious and Other, which, like forbidden lovers, try to penetrate its secrets and spread them around exuberantly, sentimentally, without benefit of orthodox scholarly training. Studies of an anthropological or folkloric nature have flourished in Old Irish scholarship, but little study has been made of very similar features in *The Book of Taliesin*.[70] Second-guessing Taliesin is

66. *A Celtic Miscellany: Translations from the Celtic Literature* (Harmondsworth: Penguin Books, 1979), 19–20. Compare this tirade to the more sardonic response of Patrick Sims-Williams in "The Visionary Celt: the Construction of an Ethnic Preconception," *Cambridge Medieval Celtic Studies* 11 (1986), 71–96, which has all the barely disguised contempt of a minority being romanticized and made other by a majority.

67. Jackson, ibid., 20.

68. Ibid.

69. Ibid., 19.

70. Nora Chadwick has investigated the shamanic elements of the Irish *imbas forasnai* in her article by that name (*Scottish Gaelic Studies* 4 [1935], 97–135); so, too, have American scholars Joseph Falaky Nagy in his study of the Finn cycle ("Shamanic Aspects of the Bruidhean Tale," *History*

indeed a dangerous proposition. One can find in his tangled words what one wants to find, and almost everything has been found. This is their special nature: they lure us so effectively into surrounding them with our desires—even when we try to ignore or dismiss them.

Identifying Taliesin's "invited" audience seems a fairly arid and fruitless exercise; more interesting are the responses he has elicited in the uninvited, and early Celtic poetry has inspired a long history of scrutiny. Caesar,[71] Strabo,[72] Diodorus Siculus,[73] Valerius Maximus,[74] and other Latin writers refer to the belief on the part of the Gaulish druids in "reincarnation," mistakenly likening it to Pythagorean doctrine, which taught that a soul was rewarded by being released from the body and punished by being reborn in the bodies of animals or plants, thus made to undergo a cycle of metempsychosis until the sin was expunged. In Fragment 115 of his *Expiations*,

---

of Religions 20 [1981], 302–22) and Daniel F. Melia in his work on Irish saints ("Law and the Shaman Saint," in *Celtic Folklore and Christianity: Studies in Memory of William W. Heist*, ed. Patrick K. Ford (Center for the Study of Comparative Folklore and Mythology; Santa Barbara: McNally and Loftin, 1983), 113–28). For its most recent applications in Old English, see Stephen Glosecki, *Shamanism and Old English Poetry, The Albert Bates Lord Studies in Oral Tradition*, 2 (New York and London: Garland, 1989). Welsh scholars have been loath, it seems, to turn similar attention to *The Book of Taliesin*, primarily because by the time the BT was due for reexamination in the mid-eighties, this critical approach had seen its heyday; Patrick Ford speaks of the "archetypal poet" of Welsh tradition (*The Mabinogi*, 17–21), and more forthrightly for the shamanic underpinnings of the Llywarch figure in PLlH, 58–62. His article "The Death of Aneirin" (*Bulletin of the Board of Celtic Studies* 34 [1987], 41–50), explores the "dark school" of bardic poetry, the ritual confinement in Welsh tradition by which students were "initiated" and expected to compose, which is described by O. J. Bergin as "a relic of some rite or ceremony of divination handed down from pagan times" (*Irish Bardic Poetry: Texts and Translations*, ed. David Greene and Fergus Kelly [Dublin: Institute for Advanced Studies, 1970], 9). Objection to the study of shamanism in European literature usually dwells on its derivation from certain Asian religious rites (Jere Fleck, "The 'Knowledge-Criterion' in the *Grimnismál*: The Case Against 'Shamanism,' " *Archiv for Nordisk Filologi* 86 [1971], 49–65). The real objection, especially to proponents of the "native" theory of Welsh poetic origins, is to the *Dumézilian*; an approach which along with Indo-European studies and studies of the shaman threatens to open the door to popular culture and "armchair anthropologists." So despite Sims-Williams's polite sneer at altericization, there remains a critical atmosphere which subtly reinforces Welsh alterity, exempting it from any comparisons or critical approaches that aren't strictly linguistic or historical.

71. Julius Caesar, *The Gallic War*, 6.14., trans. H. J. Edwards (Cambridge: Harvard University Press, 1952), 339.

72. Strabo, *Geography*, 4.4.4., trans. Horace Leonard Jones, Loeb Classical Library, ed. E. Capps (Cambridge: Harvard University Press, 1923), 245.

73. Diodorus Siculus, V.28, in Loeb Classical Library, 171.

74. Valerius Maximus, II.vi.10, cited by Alfred Nutt in "The Celtic Doctrine of Rebirth," in *The Voyage of Bran Son of Febal to the Land of the Living*, ed. Kuno Meyer (London: David Nutt, 1897), 2:109.

Empedocles tells us that liars and murderers "shall wander thrice ten thousand weary years, far from the blessed, / And be born through time in various shapes of mortal kind."[75] Efforts to treat Pythagorean doctrine as direct source material for the Celtic aretalogies have never gained much credence. One Irish poem hints at an ordeal of metempsychosis undertaken to punish sin,[76] but most of the Celtic texts, including the Welsh poems, offer no such punitive picture of their shapeshifters, whose litany of forms seems to describe a series of paradoxes rather than reincarnations. Nor are the speaker's declarations a by-product of pantheism, as was popularly thought, but rather, as Alfred Nutt puts it, a kind of "pan-wizardism":

> . . . a belief, not in the immanence of deity, so that all shapes are but manifestations of one essence, but in the all-might of the soothsayer and spell-wright, who is superior to, and who can control and overrule the forms in which life, animate or inanimate, manifests itself.[77]

This "wizard," in whom "everything has been found," might be an offshoot of the various personae of Wisdom that we see throughout early Indo-European and Middle Eastern hermetic traditions who are invariably identified with the multifaceted dimensions of natural and human phenomena— the unendurable and unsystematized Void. These speakers surpass "vision" in their claims and become what they "see." Sophia, Isis, Viṣṇu, Hari, Odin, Widsid—all of these speak to us in the form of aretalogies, literally a vaunting of virtue (arête), or revelation discourses that reveal the polyvalent nature of their divinity. These discourses take the form of the aforementioned catalogue of different esoteric names, shapes, contradictory properties, or impossible places to which the speaker has traveled, and are generally uttered in the first person. Hierarchies and systems are irrelevant; multiplicity is all. The Gnostic text "Thunder, Perfect Mind" bears an interesting resemblance to some of the Welsh aretalogies:

75. Empedocles, *The Expiations*, trans. William Ellery Leonard (Chicago: Kegan, Paul, Trench, Trubner, 1908), 55.

76. See *Tuan mac Cairill* in *Lebor Gabala Erenn*, ed. MacCallister, 3:43, 81. The prose story, however, gives the usual outcome of such ordeals (*Scel Tuain maic Cairill do Finnen Maige Bile inso sis* ["Tuan mac Cairill's Story to Finnen of Moville here below"] (in Appendix A of *The Voyage of Bran Son of Febal to the Land of the Living*, Kuno Meyer, 2:293, 300): After relating his various transformations as stag, boar, hawk, and salmon, and his ingestion by the wife of King Cairill, who gave birth to him as a human, Tuan declares that he knew "all that was done in Ireland in that time" and that he was "given prophetic knowledge" (*ogus robsa faith*).

77. "The Celtic Doctrine of Rebirth," in *The Voyage of Bran*, 2:121.

Do not be ignorant of me.
For I am the first and the last.
I am the honored one and the scorned one.
I am the whore and the holy one.
I am the wife and the virgin.
I am the mother and the daughter.
I am the members of my mother.
I am the barren one and many are her sons.
I am she whose wedding is great,
and I have not taken a husband.
    . . .

I am the one whom you have pursued,
    and I am the one whom you have seized.
I am the one whom you have scattered,
    and you have gathered me together.
    . . . .

Hear me, you hearers,
    and learn of my words, you who know me.
I am the hearing that is attainable to everything;
I am the speech that cannot be grasped.
I am the name of the sound
    and the sound of the name.
I am the sign of the letter
and the designation of the division.[78]

We find it as well in the *Bhagavad-Gita* in Viṣṇu's self-declaration to Arjuna:

I am the soul, Gudakesa,
    That abides in the heart of all beings;
I am the beginning and the middle
    Of beings, and the very end, too.

I am the wind of purifiers,
    Rama of warriors,
I am the dolphin of water monsters,
    Of rivers I am the Ganges.
    . . .

---

78. "The Thunder, Perfect Mind," trans. Charles W. MacRae, in *The Nag Hammadi Library*, ed. James M. Robinson (San Francisco: Harper and Row, 1978), 271, 272, 276.

Of creations the beginning and the end,
  And the middle too am I, Arjuna;
Of knowledges the knowledge of the over-soul,
  I am speech of them that speak.

Of syllables (letters) I am the letter A,
  And the dvandva of compounds,
None but I am immortal Time,
  I am the Ordainer (Creator) that faces in all directions.

I am death that carries off all,
  And the origin of things that are to be;
Of feminine entities I am Fame, Fortune, Speech,
  Memory, Wisdom, Steadfastness, Patience.[79]

Angar Kyfyndawt

Attempts to explicate this poetry can easily go awry. If you ignore
traditional lore, you're a fool. If you approach the material as a
scholar, pulling long lists of meanings out of your pocket, you're a
fool. If you don't have an intimate, immediate understanding of the
poem, you have nothing. If you report your personal interpretation,
why should anyone believe you?[80]

So writes Linda Hess of the Indian poet Kabir and his "upside-down lan-
guage." She could just as well be writing about Taliesin, to whom we are all,
professional or amateur, rank fools. One could wish, mired in one's an-
glocentrism, that the Taliesinic rhapsodies were so apparently translatable as
Viṣṇu's song. Angar Kyfyndawt, the companion piece to Kat Godeu in The
Book of Taliesin, has been reproduced and translated to the best of my
abilities in Texts no. 8, but holes nevertheless remain. Its title means either
"Cruel Confinement" or "Hostile Alliance," depending on whether one takes
kyfyndawt to be Modern Welsh cyfyngdod ("straitness, confinement")[81] or

79. Bhagavad-Gita, trans. and ed. Frank Edgerton (Cambridge: Harvard University Press, 1977),
chap. 10, vs. 19–20.
80. The Bijak of Kabir, 135.
81. Haycock prefers the second meaning because the first, she says, is not attested in the GPC
before the seventeenth century (LIT, 101). This is not proof, however, that the word as it is found in

kyfundawt ("union, alliance"). This kind of lexical ambiguity permeates the poem at all levels, so that almost every line is susceptible to two or three different interpretations; their original obscurity may well have contributed to mistakes made by the scribe. In fact, we see in it the many layers of confusion and misreading as a scribe copied what was perhaps a copy of something taken down in a fog. From this standpoint, the text is an intriguing testimony to the state of being between languages ("A Cruel Confinement"): it mixes archaic with later Welsh; it has little regard for metrical regularities; it is full of neologisms, casual about syntax; it seems to omit words, perhaps whole passages; it has long strings of statements that are almost simplistic in their clarity, followed by verses of such obscurity that there seems to be no hope of unraveling them. It is not clear that they were meant to be unraveled. Whoever the patron was who commissioned this book, he was apparently interested in all of Taliesin's multifarious forms, including his powers of obfuscation. Joyce Hill addresses this kind of medieval fascination for the "list" that almost completely escapes modern sensibilities. In her study of the Old English *Widsið*, similar in some respects to this Welsh poem, most of the spurious claims would have been lost on their hearers, but this was beside the point: "By the tenth century at least, part of the poem's appeal lay in the total impression created by the catalogues, rather than in the evocative force of each allusion in turn; . . . the audience did not and could not understand every apparent allusion, and . . . the poem was included in the Exeter Book more because of its seemingly encyclopaedic nature than because it repre-sented the Germanic bard's stock-in-trade."[82] I suspect this understanding may account for the appeal of something like *Angar Kyfyndawt*. At the very least, the text is fascinating in its portrayal of an artifact caught between orality and literacy: What may have meant something to select hearers in its original spoken context becomes reified on vellum, its opacity compounded the more it is copied, the more it manifests its separation from the original text in the form of "corruptions." Word becomes thing, powerful even in its blankness, and this, I suspect, is why this aspect of Taliesin has been of little interest to traditional interpretive study, preoccupied as it is with origins and reconstructions.

By modern standards, *Angar Kyfyndawt* is unacceptably long and ram-

---

Llyfr Taliesin does not have this meaning; it merely suggests that the lexicographers could not definitely assign it this meaning, given its contextual paucity. As I point out in Texts no. 8, the root *cyfyng* ("narrow," "confined") goes back at least as far as the thirteenth century.

82. "Widsið and the Tenth Century," *Neuphilologische Mitteilungen* 85 (1984), 305.

bling, and its demarcation from the following poem is not clear, despite the designating titles. It begins with a bardic challenge and a request that the speaker receive a prize or a gift for his song. The context appears to be the imprisonment of Elphin by Maelgwn and Taliesin's poetic plea for his release, but many more obscure allusions to Celtic mythology and other esoterica are included. The futility of translation as well as the uncooperativeness of a text can hardly find a better model, as there is so little contextual evidence and so many unattested words and compounds that the translator is prevented from arguing for an interpretation or offering an emendation. Appeals to dictionaries are largely unhelpful, as the lexicographers must have encountered the same kind of difficulties in assigning meaning, and it is no wonder that the punctilious translator has been reluctant to deal with poems where one's authority is always put at risk, one's translation always full of question marks and parenthetical asides.

Nevertheless, several things emerge from this maelstrom. The speaker is empowered, despite the unintelligibility of his poem. He knows important sources: Talhaearn is another poet-seer, known by Nennius as "the Father of Awen." *Annwfyn*, the mythological region identified with this property, is the Welsh version of the Celtic Otherworld or land of the gods; it presents a genuine ambiguity that has been preserved in the meaning of the word: *dwfyn* can mean either "world" or "deep," and, like many Welsh prefixes, *an*- can be either a negative or an intensive. *Annwfyn* then means either "unworld" or "very deep" (or *both* "unworld" and "very deep"). After the spread of Christianity, it was confused with hell, naturally enough, but here it seems to be the fount of Gwion's *awen*—"from the Deep it will come" (line 14). The speaker takes on the persona of Gwion (Taliesin before his birth from the goddess Cerridwen), and further references to Afagddu and Elphin suggest that the context for this poem is Maelgwn's court and the confusion of his bards. Throughout the speaker emphasizes in a contentious manner his identity as lore-master and his knowledge of esoterica. The opening challenge is traditional; it is a ritual boasting or flyting. Charles Plummer points out that the competitions between druids and clerics replaced a native tradition of competitions among druids themselves and that each faction tried to best the other with obscure wisdom.[83] The speaker hints at withholding wisdom because of flagging generosity on the part of those for whom he sings (cf. lines 5–6: "The bountiful one[s] who may refuse me, who [or "what he"?]

---

83. *Vitae Sactorum Hiberniae* (Oxford: Clarendon Press, 1910), 1:clxvii n. 2.

may give, it will not come to him through the language of Taliesin"; lines 14–17: "It is Gwion who speaks; from the deep it will come; it would make from the dying living, and it is impoverished" [i.e., it is unremunerated? unappreciated? unempowered? misunderstood?], or "foreign" [i.e., abstruse? unintelligible? God-given?]; lines 61–62: "that which a brother might ask, no one would know from me"). The arrogant power of the poet-seer is evident throughout the poem, and it is almost as if the text mocks our efforts today with its insistent allusions to its own private nature. As a genre, this seems quite the opposite of the *quaestiones* or catechisms of medieval literature, where answers are given to inquiries. While a genre of dialogue poetry flourishes in Middle Welsh, the poems of Taliesin seem to block dialogue and thwart any kind of response.

A remote possibility is that it is "parodic." Both Mikhail Bakhtin and Julia Kristeva talk about the "carnivalesque" in medieval writing.[84] In finding the earliest roots of the novel in medieval origins, Bakhtin describes the European linguistic experience as one poised between languages: one that centralizes and unifies, the other that decentralizes and stratifies.[85] Thus do we find the *cento* and the *Cena Cypriani*, texts that are made up of the rearranged fragments of other texts (usually sacred) and trotted out for times of prescribed laughter and festival.[86] "Heteroglossia," the unsuppressed interplay of multitudinous meanings and contexts, is allowed free rein at carnival, though in normal circumstances language is kept strictly monologic by authorities in control of meaning. Kristeva remarks that the "transgression of linguistic, logical and social codes within the carnivalesque only exists and succeeds, of course, because it accepts another law."[87] This description applies accurately enough to the mythological texts of Taliesin (which appeal to a bardic code that transcends clerical learning) even if the parodic or the carnivalesque do not; whatever the nature of the garbled texts of Taliesin, they are "monstrous" in the original meaning of the Latin word *monstrum*, "prodigy," "portent," that which "shows," from L. *monere*, "to warn." Pieced together from fragments of scriptural Latin, biblical mythology, and Welsh arcana—the speaker himself being

84. Mikhail Bakhtin, *The Dialogic Imagination*, trans. Caryl Emerson and Michael Holquist (Austin: University of Texas Press, 1981), 51–83; Julia Kristeva, *Desire in Language: A Semiotic Approach to Literature and Art*, trans. Thomas Gora, Alice Jardine, and Leon S. Roudiez (New York: Columbia University Press, 1980), 70–71.

85. Bakhtin *The Dialogic Imagination*, 67.

86. Ibid., 69–70.

87. Kristeva, *Desire in Language*, 71.

made up of the various elements of the world—both Taliesin and his texts are "monsters" in Isadore's understanding of the term.[88] They admonish, they berate, they display themselves, they prophesy, they point to wisdom we cannot fully understand. The relationship of this kind of poet to the wild man, the hermit, and the leper will presently be more evident.

Nature and the Visionary Poet

Much of the rest of *Angar Kyfyndawt* is made up of the now familiar aretalogies, where many of the shapes claimed by the poet are natural things: "I was a blue salmon, / I was a dog, I was a stag, / I was a roebuck on the mountain" (lines 226–28). In the passage where he speaks of being swallowed by the "red-clawed hen," in whose womb he passed "nine nights as a lad" (lines 245–48), he obviously alludes to the tale of Gwion Bach, and Ifor Williams ascribes all such verses to the same source. But they continue into the next poem (*Kat Godeu*), where they seem to have a much wider context:

> Bum yn lliaws rith
> kyn bum disgyfrith. . . .
> bum geir yn llythyr.
> bum llyfyr ym prifder.
> bum llugyrn lleufer
> blwydyn ahanher. . . .
> bum hynt bum eryr.
> bum corwc ymyr.
> bum darwed yn llat.
> bum dos ygkawat.
> bum cledyf yn aghat.
> bum yscwyt yg kat.
> bum tant yn telyn

---

88. Isidore of Seville, "On Man and Monsters" (from Book 9 of the *Etymologiae*), *The Medical Writings*, trans. William D. Sharpe, Transactions of the American Philosophical Society 54.2 (1964), 51–52. For this connection between monstrosity and prophecy, I am indebted to Eve Salisbury's yet unpublished paper, "Re-membering Origins: Gower's Monstrous Body Poetic," in which she explores the related themes of stylistic disjunction and prognostication in the *Vox Clamantis*.

lletrithawc naw blwydyn.
yn dwfyr yn ewyn.
bum yspwg yn tan.
bum gwyd yngwarthan.
nyt mi wyf ny gan
keint yr yn bychan.

(BT: 23.9–10, 12–20)

[I was in a multitude of forms
before I was let loose. . . .
I was a word in a letter.
I was a book in the beginning.
I was lanterns of light a year and a half. . . .
I was a course, I was an eagle.
I was a coracle in seas.
I was a bubbling in drink.
I was a drop in a shower.
I was a sword in the grasp.
I was a shield in battle.
I was a string in a harp, enchanted for nine years.
In water, in foam.
I was a spark in fire.
I was wood in (?).
I am not one who does not sing;
I have sung since I was small.]

Declarations of oneness with the elements of nature and the world are often accompanied by declarations of knowledge of the secrets of nature as well. Long passages introduced by *gogwn* ("I know") occur in *Angar Kyfyndawt:* I know the expanse, / I know when it vanishes, / I know when it fills, / I know when it pours, / I know when it ebbs away, / I know what creatures are under the sea" (lines 178–84). This preoccupation with knowing or being a part of nature brings us to a crucial point: One of the most important aspects of the Celtic poet-seer is his function as mediator between the world of human beings and the unpredictable world of nature. Certain pagan practices involving the *ollav* ("poet") survived until the sixteenth century in Ireland, including inauguration rituals in which the poet would hand the prince his rod or wand, "which symbolized his mystic union with the land, with growth and fertility."[89] A poet's satire was to be deeply feared, as he could sever a ruler from the powerful forces of the natural world. The link between poetry and nature as we find it in the early divinatory poets has an important bearing on the study of the natural analogy, in that whole sections of these texts are strongly reminiscent of the gnomic poems we have already examined in detail; it is possible that the two forms are cousin to each other. With the nature poems we have statements of wisdom about natural forces, and with the visionary poems we have statements about the personifications of nature in the form of the speaker himself—I am wind; I am sea; I am fire—who shows his knowledge in a litany of sententious utterances. "I know why milk is white, why holly is green, why a billy goat is bearded" is not so far removed from the more gnomic "milk is white, holly is green, the billy goat has a beard." Both are arranged in lists; both employ a kind of panoptic imagery. In Taliesin's aretalogies, however, the use of deixis is paradoxical in that the first person is without center. The speaker is not in relationship to everything, he *is* everything. The natural analogy is thus turned on its end, and there is no gap between speaker and world. The gap is rather between speaker and hearer.

For this reason, then, the juxtapositive quality of these poems is out of bounds. It far exceeds that of any of the other poems we have looked at. There is also a marked emphasis in these texts on an ordeal of some sort. The poet has status as a passive vessel to which things are done, challenging our conventional concepts of the distinctions between power and powerlessness. He boasts repeatedly that he has died, been buried, imprisoned, engulfed, swallowed, penetrated, transformed, reborn, and received into the Otherworld, a repository of poetic inspiration. Armed with these advantages he harangues other poets with his discourse of enclosedness. The poet's passivity is an appropriation of a particularly feminine power, by which he becomes penetrable, mutable, and earthen, through which he gives birth to impenetrable words. In other contexts, his suffering exacts something from him. Thus does Merlin describe himself in the *Vita*:

> Raptus eram michimet quasi spiritus acta
> sciebam preteriti populi predicebamque futura.
> Tunc rerum secreta sciens volucrumque volatus
> stallarumque vagos mous lapsusque natantum,

89. James Carney, *The Irish Bardic Poet* (Dublin: Dolmen, 1968), 11.

id me vexabat naturalemque negabat humae menti
districta lege quietem.[90]

["I was taken out of my true self, I was as a spirit and knew the history
of people long past and could foretell the future. I knew the secrets
of nature, bird flight, star wanderings and the way fish glide. This
distressed me and, by a hard law, deprived me of the rest that is
natural to the human mind."][91]

To argue that *The Sick Man of Abercuawg* has its generic roots in a tradition
of poetically inspired "outlaws," "lepers," and hermits in Celtic tradition
would be to fall into the traps set by the penitential argument: it is not strongly
supported in the text, nor does it present the whole picture.[92] This poem,
however, has a compelling dialogic quality, the power to suggest many differ-
ent layers and directions. The connection of the pre-Christian seer and poet
in Ireland with "outlawry," with wilderness, illness, and a life outside the
conventions and protection of society has been argued by Joseph Falaky Nagy
in his study of the Fenian tradition.[93] The mantic poet of Ireland found
strength and wisdom in straitened circumstances, in being "in-between," in
operating on the fringes, in contact with the natural and spiritual world. It is
no wonder that Christian poetry, especially that produced by clerics, found a
voice within a native Celtic tradition of inspiration and power acquired in a
natural setting. The Aeschylean notion of "wisdom through suffering" is an
ingrained Indo-European concept,[94] and many of the seers and poets of Irish

90. *Vita Merlini*, lines 1161–66, in Clarke, 113.
91. Clarke, *Vita Merlini*, 114.
92. In *Gwen a'i Dad*, Llywarch refers to his *awen*: *Neut atwen ar vy awen / yn hanuot. cun
achen. tri gwyd oric elwic awen* RB: 1037.12–13 ["I know by my *awen* / we come from fine stock. /
One has remained a precious time, O Gwen!"]. Ford relies on this reference to argue for the
relationship of the Llywarch figure to a tradition of poetic inspiration (PLlH, 61). Rowland objects
(EWSP, 513), citing the GPC's alternate definition of *awen*: "desire, inclination, mind, genius."
Besides its appearance in the *Red Book*, the earliest citation given by the GPC is from *Peniarth* 5.60a:
Ar m(archawc) yna a gymerth awen (cupiens) milwryaeth o newyd yndaw ["the desire for warfare
seized the knight anew"]. But Rowland's "I know in my heart" does little justice to the quality of
seizure or possession that the word seems to convey. Such quibbles are reductive; I offer that Llywarch
is referring to his jawbone (GPC *awen* 2.2: *asgwrn gen; asgwrn grudd*): "I know by my jawbone / that
we come of good stock." After all, he is Llywarch "the constant talker." The possibility that all three
meanings of the word might be in operation is attested by the Welsh fondness for paranomasia.
93. "Finn, Poet, and Outsider," in *The Wisdom of the Outlaw: The Boyhood Deeds of Finn in
Gaelic Narrative Tradition* (Berkeley and Los Angeles: University of California Press, 1985), 17–40.
94. See Olga Aranovsky, "On the Interpretation of 'Knowledge by Suffering' in Aeschylus's
'Agamemnon,' " *Journal of Indo-European Studies* 6 (1978), 244.

tradition are also leprous and "mad," as is Suibne Geilt, who, in punishment for his sins, is forced to live the life of a wild-man, from which he emerges crazy, hairy, and gifted with song. In a peculiar poem from *The Gododdin*, Aneirin drew the poetic inspiration known to Taliesin "of skillful declamation" from his confinement "under the feet of maggots."[95] In close contact with earth, death, and the forces of nature, the pre-Christian Celtic poet grew strong, even "monstrous." He is hardly Gray's bard with flowing cape, certainly no gentleman reclining desultorily on a couch, as Aneirin states in the *Gododdin*, and Patrick Ford examines the tradition of his physically abhorrent or deformed aspects.[96] Whatever his many manifestations, the image of the aggressive and iconoclastic Celtic poet persisted well into Christian times, to which the many debates between clerics and druids attest, along with the challenges made of ignorant monks in *The Book of Taliesin* by an arrogant bard intent on withholding the meaning of his enigmas.

The Leper and the Seer

Claf Abercuawg is enigmatic enough. Like an extra key, it won't fit any of the available locks: it is neither of a piece with the saga *englynion* about Llywarch, nor is it clearly "heroic," as Ford claims, nor an obvious model for *The Seafarer* as Pilch claims, nor as explicitly penitential as Rowland wants it to be. To summon up once and for all the accursed "penitential" argument, I would like to suggest that the context of the gnomes, quasi-gnomes, and laments in the first part of the Red Book, along with their half-given utterances, their silences, their lists, their montages and patchwork-quilt effects, might be the debris of a tradition of wisdom far older than Celtic Christianity. To be sure, they are heavily secularized; wisdom, both Christian and pre-Christian, has been subsumed in the plaints of quotidian society, which could explain the eloquent inarticulateness of *Claf Abercuawg*. Its apparent gaps might be due to the phenomenon of the "shifting dominant," as Roman Jakobson defined it,[97] wherein "elements which were originally secondary

95. See Ford's discussion of this poem in "The Death of Aneirin" (note 70 above).

96. "The Blind, The Dumb, and The Ugly: Aspects of Poets and Their Craft in Early Ireland and Wales," *Cambridge Medieval Celtic Studies* 19 (1990), 27–40.

97. Roman Jakobson, "The Dominant," in *Readings in Russian Poetics: Formalist and Structuralist Views*, ed. Ladislav Matejka and Krystyn Pomorska (Cambridge: MIT Press, 1971), 85: "In the evolution of poetic form it is not so much a question of the disappearance of certain elements and the

become essential and primary" and the primary ones "subsidiary and optional."[98] Thus a tradition that might have had as its "dominant" a tradition of wisdom and suffering in a natural setting has given way to a dominant of lamentation in the Llywarch and related poems. Spiritual consolation and the lessons of penance are written into it in some texts, but not in others; for it is not so much that all these poems about outcasts adrift in a natural world derive from a genre of penitential literature as that the penitential element was so easy to insert.

This shifting dominant could likewise explain the "irrelevant" nature references in some of the other poems. Nature is marshaled by the poet-seer in a demonstration of his powers and sought out by the voluntary hermit as a setting more suitable to his spiritual needs than the city. Far from being in tune with nature, however, both Llywarch and the leper (if tradition must see them as separate) are cut off from it, as they are from everything else, including the community and the youth for which they long. The leper is an involuntary hermit and a demoted seer, outside the controlling order of the things he can see but cannot command. Neither can he make any claims to special knowledge or spiritual power. Everyone moves with the tides of the season except him. He is fallen in the Christian hierarchy as well, for the Christian interpretation follows the same parallels in compassionately tracing the demise of a man whose understanding has broken down. Seeing has become dark, *awen* has become a vehicle of madness and sorrow.

Perhaps, then, the concept of the "lacking word" that marks modern literature and has become its prison house lies at the core of the leper's dilemma; despite his vivid and affecting plaints, language does not ultimately work for him. He cannot utter a prayer in an oratory, cannot make the explicit leap from sinner to penitent, cannot openly repent of his sin of despair or give or find consolation in saving words. Likewise, nature has ceased to signify in any meaningful way; it has become an "irritant," its birdsong scrapes his raw heart, its tides rake him with his own sadness. But then language works most effectively for him in conveying its inefficacy in its fallen state. Deformed, dissolving before our eyes, the leper-seer shows forth and warns readers against the monstrous sin of despair.

Less tolerant of such incoherent ends, the English coat their wisdom literature and their images of nature with more obvious didactic layering,

---

emergence of others as it is the question of shifts in the mutual relationship among the diverse components of the system."

98. Ibid.

which gives most of their plaint poems a different texture from the Welsh and a relative sense of verbal plenitude. This is not to say that they do not have a discourse of obscurity. It is harder to unearth, though, as the final chapter will show, with the exception of one entirely enigmatic and powerful poem: *Wulf and Eadwacer.*

8

Clarity and Obscurity
in Old English Poetry

gleawe men sceolon gieddum wrixlan
("Wise men should exchange sayings.")
—*Maxims I*

Old English poetry is not without its difficult texts. Its lists and catalogues of poetic feats such as are found in *Widsið* and *Deor* elevate the task of the Old English poet to magic proportions much like that of the Celtic poet. Old English has its aretalogies, too, mainly to be found among the riddles and the Solomonic dialogues that celebrate arcana. My focus in this final chapter will be on certain riddles, particularly the strange poem *Wulf and Eadwacer*, where nature, planctus, and enigma come together in ways that run counter to the usual Anglo-Saxon predilection for clarity and all that is *undyrne*.

"The First Riddle of Cynewulf"

"What is easily torn that never was joined?" The answer: "our song together." Or: "our utterance together." Or: "our riddle together."

Is this a riddle? And is one or all of these the answer? The penultimate line of *Wulf and Eadwacer* (see Texts no. 7) may figure as a warning to anyone who seeks to attach an interpretation to it. For every explanation of the poem that is offered, there is a rebuttal or a counterexplanation waiting to undermine it. Because of its placement in *The Exeter Book* at the head of a section of riddles and because of its enigmatic and disjunct quality, similar to that of many of the enigmas, critics of the nineteenth century referred to it as "the first riddle of Cynewulf."[1] Despite its later identification as a lament, I shall treat it here as an introduction to my discussion of riddles and obscurity in Old English.

Frederick Tupper found runes in *Wulf and Eadwacer;*[2] various explanations were proposed,[3] which, however, ignored its obvious strain of lament. Since Henry Bradley's identification of the poem as a dramatic monologue spoken by a woman torn between two sexual relationships—her illicit union with "Wulf" and her marital union with "Eadwacer"[4]—interpretations of the poem have focused on deciding whether the three epithets designated in the poem refer to the same or different men, or on ascribing the problem of its obscurity to a tradition now lost to us.[5] It must be emphasized that the

1. See W. W. Lawrence, "The First Riddle of Cynewulf," *PMLA* 17 (1902), 247–61, and Frederick Tupper, "The Cynewulfian Runes of the First Riddle," *Modern Language Notes* 25 (1910), 235–41.

2. See note 1.

3. H. Patzig solved it as "millstone" in "Zum ersten Rätsel des Exeterbuches," *Archiv.*, 155 (1923), 204, and Moritz Trautman solved it as "riddle" in "Cynewulf und die Rätsel," *Anglia* 6 (1883), 158.

4. Henry Bradley, review of Morley's *English Writers*, 2, *Academy* 33 (1888), 197.

5. In his review (see note 4), Bradley remarks that it seems to be a fragment of some lost longer poem and Kemp Malone ("Two Old English *Frauenlieder*," *Comparative Literature* 14 [1962], 108; rept. *Studies in Old English Literature in Honor of Arthur G. Brodeur*, ed. Stanley B. Greenfield [Eugene: University of Oregon Press, 1963], 106–17) suggests that the poem either comes out of a prose narrative interspersed with dramatic verse (much the same kind of solution proposed for the poems of Llywarch Hen), or it had a specific context, now vanished, which at the time needed no direct allusion. In this respect, he concludes, it more closely resembles popular poetry than formal courtly or learned poetry. Interpretations of *Wulf and Eadwacer* are many and varied: Bradley's "two men" theory has been challenged on several fronts. John C. Adams argues that the figures of Wulf and Eadwacer are the same, *Eadwacer* being a "vitriolic" epithet ("*Wulf and Eadwacer*: An Interpretation," *Modern Language Notes* 73 [1958], 4), as does Stanley Greenfield ("*Wulf and Eadwacer*: All Passion Pent," in *Hero and Exile: The Art of Old English Poetry*, a tribute to Stanley B. Greenfield, ed. George H. Brown [London: Hambledon Press, 1989], 185–194); Richard F. Giles interprets *Eadwacer* as an address directed by the speaker to herself ("*Wulf and Eadwacer*: A New Reading," *Neophilologus* 65 (1983), 468–72; non-human interpretations have argued for an exchange between two dogs (W. J. Sedgefield, "Old English Notes," *The Modern Language Review* 26 [1931], 74–75), a charm to remove wens (Donald K. Fry, "*Wulf and Eadwacer*: A Wen Charm," *Chaucer Review* 5 [1971], 247–63), and more than one scholar has argued for a relationship between a woman and her

overriding response of scholars to this poem is a need to make sense of its troubling gaps. Some have looked upon it as foreign in origin, a translation of a lost Norse poem,[6] or a reference to Signy's destruction of her cowardly son in *The Volsunga Saga*.[7] What becomes clear as we grapple with this most uncooperative text is that it cannot be translated *unless* we come to it with a preconceived reading.[8] This conundrum, I have argued, is an aspect of all translations, but especially so of this one: the language is more ambiguous than that of any other Old English poem of its length. Numerous words have multiple meanings, and the brevity of the poem does not offer enough cohesive information to clarify their correct use. Its obscurities are similar in kind to those of *Angar Kyfyndawt*—lexical ambiguity and incoherent context make it impossible to test any one interpretation against another. *Lac*, for instance, can mean "sport," "gift," "offering," "sacrifice," or even "skirmish" or "battle." It is unclear what is being given to the speaker's people. Since the next few lines seem to express concepts of warfare and defeat, most translators have chosen to interpret the first line as a statement about easy victory. Nevertheless, the meaning of the second line is again dependent on our understanding of the first line and also of two highly ambiguous words— *apecgan* and *þreat*—which can make it refer either to a hostile reception (a*d*ecgan) of an invasion (*on þreat cymeð*) or friendly (or hostile) reception of a man come into peril. Either interpretation affects the meaning of the first line retroactively: it is like fiddling with a Rubik's Cube. The laconic statement of the refrain—*ungelic is us*—could easily modify the following statement as well as the preceding, and in retrospect the absence of the dual form here in a poem which ends on a dual note (*uncer giedd geador*) does not permit us to see the phrase as a reliable reference to the two lovers. The question of "who" is a beastly problem in this poem.

Another complicating factor lies in the high incidence of *hapax legomenon* and/or scribal error. The words *dogode, reotugu,* and *beaducafa* appear seldom or never in other poems, and, again, there is little contextual informa-

son (Dolores Warwick Frese, "*Wulf and Eadwacer*: The Adulterous Woman Reconsidered," *Notre Dame English Journal* 15.1 [1983], 1–22; Marijane Osborn, "The Text and Context of *Wulf and Eadwacer*," in *The Old English Elegies: New Essays in Criticism and Research*, ed. Martin Green [Rutherford: Associated University Presses, 1983], 174–89).

   6. W. W. Lawrence, "The First Riddle of Cynewulf," *PMLA*, 247.

   7. Henry Schofield, "Signy's Lament," *PMLA* 17 (1902), 262.

   8. Alain Renoir in "*Wulf and Eadwacer*: A Non-Interpretation" (*Franciplegius: Medieval and Linguistic Studies in Honor of Francis Peabody Magoun, Jr.*, ed. Jess Bessinger and Robert F. Creed [New York: New York University Press, 1965], 147–63) observes that hardly anyone can translate the poem without interpreting it, and one's interpretation is bound to bias one's translation.

tion to help us understand how they are used here. Finally, deictic reference is hopelessly ambiguous. The words that point to a specific location—*þæt*, *þonne*—are more unhelpful here than ever in Anglo-Saxon poetry. "Wulf is on an island, I on another," proclaims the speaker. "Fast is *that* island [*which* island?*] surrounded by fen. / Bloodthirsty men are there on *that* isle [*which* isle?]" Obviously, our understanding of the events of this poem depends on our knowing whether it is Wulf or the speaker who is trapped on a boggy and treacherous island with bloodthirsty men. Arguments for both interpretations are equally convincing.

The final obstacle for interpretation is that the poem exquisitely portrays a complex and intriguing psychology, and a range of emotions that is unequaled in the other elegies. For this reason, *Wulf and Eadwacer* is far more interesting than any of the Taliesin enigmas in its hints of a very real human dilemma, but none the clearer. Like them, it offers a peculiar kind of shapeshifting whereby Wulf becomes the battle-ready man, then perhaps the "Property Watcher," and then perhaps a skulking animal; with the development of the "hwelp" that the wolf bears to the woods we have the unsettling suggestion that both Wulf and his lover have turned into animals of a sort and produced a "cub." The fact that a human child is spoken of in such bestial terms is provoking enough, and it is hard to determine what tone the speaker is taking toward her baby— whether it is even a baby at all or merely a figure of speech: the "poem," "riddle," "saying," "utterance," or "song" that is torn apart.

We have seen how "difficulty" in later Welsh court poems was looked upon as an attribute, especially as it de-emphasized explicit statement and empha-sized ornamentation and select details. In the mantic poems about poetry, difficulty was requisite. Did Anglo-Saxon poets regard their poetry similarly? Does *Wulf and Eadwacer* come out of a suppressed Anglo-Saxon tradition where, as in the Welsh, it is the prerogative of the poet to keep things hidden or to present them with alternative interpretations? In short, how self-conscious is the hermetic nature in *Wulf and Eadwacer*? Its hermetic nature is one of its principal pleasures for contemporary readers, and *Wulf and Eadwacer* remains one of the most popular poems in the classroom, one of the most frequently analyzed.

Old English Riddles

The riddles in *The Exeter Book* provide us with telling examples of the manner in which enigma and craftsmanship were combined in ways considered pleasing to the English, and from them we may learn something about English attitudes toward the cryptic in poetry. The runic riddles offer themselves most immediately in this capacity because the ancient Teutonic alphabet known as "runes" has long been associated with secrecy and the occult— so much so that *run* came to mean "secret" or "mystery" in Anglo-Saxon, if it did not already have this meaning in the original Germanic.[9]

Presumably, a runic riddle was addressed to an audience in which only a select few were *rynemen,* or experts in these letters; otherwise the difficulty of the riddle would have been scouted. That the difficulty of the runic riddles mattered, and is in fact boasted of in *Riddle 42,*[10] is important evidence that the English shared with the Welsh, at least on some level, a delight in making a game of privileged information. The solution to the following riddle is "Cock and Hen" (*Hana and Hæn*):

Ic seah wyhte	wrætlic twa
undearnunga	ute plegan
hæmedlaces	hwitloc anfeng
wlance under wædum	gif ðæs weorces speo[w]
fæmne fyllo	ic on flette mæg
þurh runstafas	rincum secgan
þam þe bec witan	bega ætsomne
naman þara wihta	þær sceal nyd wesan
twega oðer	[ond] se torhta æsc
an an linan	acas twegen
hægeles swa some	hwylc [þ]æs hordgates
cægan cræfte	þa clamme onleac
þe þa rædellan	wið rynemenn
hygefæste heold	heortan bewrigene
orþoncbendum	nu is undyrne
werum æt wine	hu þa wihte mid us
heanmode twa	hatne sindon

(EB2: 138)

9. Joseph Bosworth and T. Northcote Toller, *An Anglo-Saxon Dictionary, Based on the Manuscript Collections* (Oxford: Clarendon Press, 1898), 804: "*run:* a whisper (*runian*), hence speech not intended to be overheard," "confidence, counsel, consultation . . ." "a mystery," "a secret"; "that which is written with the idea of mystery or magic"; "a rune, a letter." Interestingly, the word *runa* is used to mean "secrets" in the Irish poem *Imram Brain* ("The Voyage of Bran," stanza 52, trans. Kuno Meyer, [London: David Nutt in the Strand, 1895]), and in the Welsh we have *gweith keluyd yw kelu rin* (RB: 1031.33; "The work of the skillful is to hide a secret") where, if this is a borrowed word, the change in spelling reflects the Welsh pronunciation of *u* as [I].

10. The numbering of the *Exeter Book* Riddles has been in some dispute. I follow W. S. Mackie's numbering in *The Exeter Book,* vol. 2 (London: Early English Text Society, 1934).

[I saw two wondrous creatures
unsecretly playing outside
at the "marriage game"; Whitelocks will receive—
proud under garments (if in this work she succeed)—
her female fullness. I in the hall can
through runic letters tell men
who know books both names
together of those creatures. There must be Need,
another of two, and the bright Ash,
one on a line; two Oaks
and similarly Hails, which unlock
the clamps of the treasure chest by the craft of a key,
that which the riddle kept mind-fast
from runemen, hidden from [or "in"?] the heart
with cunning bonds. Now is unsecret
to men at wine how those creatures by us,
two commonplace ones, are called.]

In his comparison of the enigma to a treasure chest which he unlocks for others, the riddler reveals two things: (1) that the riddle is like a beautiful artifact to be marveled at for its intricate ornamentation and (2) that the treasure is of difficult access. The vocabulary in this little poem attests to both concepts: *wrætlic* (marvel), *hordgates* (difficulty), *cægan cræfte* (key's craft), *bewrigene* (secret, hidden), and *orþuncbendum* (marvel, difficulty). There is one further word, not appearing here but used in *Riddle 60* in connection with runestaves (at which I will look presently), that sums up the character of this riddle and that is *searo*: "cunning, skill, art, device, trick, treachery, trappings, clever contrivance." The speaker of this riddle is boasting of his clever contrivance, but one has the sense that the real emphasis of his poem, despite its many references to difficulty, is on revealing secrets, not keeping them.

First, he immediately informs his listeners/readers that the answer is to be given with runes that spell the name of the subject. Second, as much as he talks about "clamps" and holding secrets "mind-fast" and "hidden from the hearts" of runemen, he stresses his own solution of the riddle. As though he were the guesser instead of the riddler, he boasts of having "unlocked" the chest and made of the secret "no secret" to men at wine. This last comment may be a wry echo of the opening image of two barnyard fowl making no secret of their *hæmedlace*, which in its homeliness is about as far removed from mysteries as can be. The riddle is a kind of joke, especially if we look upon the talk of unlocking treasure chests with keys as a kind of sexual innuendo not unknown to Anglo-Saxon clerics and riddlers.

There is another layer of ambiguity in the poem, in that it hints intriguingly at an intentional manipulation of the contradictions inherent in a transitionally literate society. Besides making us wonder whether it conceals or reveals, the poem also makes us ask whether its difficulty (or revelation) was meant to be maintained on the visual or the aural level. For whom was it originally intended? Those who *heard* it or those who *read* it? Writing out the runes in their special code introduces a new graphic difficulty to those skilled in letters. To those for whom the written code no longer holds any secrets, the runic code reinstates the mysterious look of writing. But this mysteriousness can operate on the aural level as well, in that the clever listener must not be flummoxed by the mysterious sounds of recitation but must be able to distinguish the names of the runes from ordinary words; it is a matter of knowing which would have been considered more difficult for the Anglo-Saxon interlocutor. *Riddle 42* is perfectly ambiguous. Its references to recitation (*ic on flette, werum æt wine*) are as numerous as its references to literacy (*þam þe bec witan, an an linan*), but most telling is the fact that the scribe has chosen to write out the names of the runes rather than record their signs, when the preferred practice in *The Exeter Book* is the other way around.

We could interpret this in several ways: The scribe could not remember the runic symbols and has given us a transcription of what was dictated to him. Thus it was meant to be heard and to conceal. Or the scribe intended to deceive an audience of readers familiar with runic symbols who would be misled into thinking that the runes were references to trees instead of letters. Thus it was meant to be read and to conceal. Of course, this trick would constitute the primary mode of deception for those *hearing* the poem. With some of the other runic riddles it is hard for readers today to locate the difficulty where the method is so baldly described to the guesser: *Nu ic haten eom / swa þa siex stafas sweotule becnaþ.* "Now I am called as those six letters clearly betoken," declares the speaker in *Riddle 24*, giving us the letters that spell *higora*, "magpie." In *Riddle 23* the speaker tells us that *ago[b]* is his name spelled backwards (*agof is min noma eft onhwyrfed*) and goes on to describe a bow (*boga*). In a transitional oral society, the challenge for hearers is to turn language into a visual code which "betokens" or "reverses" its pattern.

On the other hand, if the difficulty of the runic riddle is more visual than aural, if it is primarily a literate trick (like a rebus or an anagram), then it is unrecitable; its spoken names would give away the runes which, because they contain the sounds that they stand for, are more easily identified than their arbitrary graphic symbols. Therefore, disguising the runic code in "commonplace" letters might constitute the true riddle in this text. It is this that the riddle has kept "mind-fast" from runemen by the craft of his "key," not the commonplace fowls. The speaker has made obvious (*undyrne*) what the convention normally conceals. He has deciphered, spelled out (literally!), and turned visual code into the seamlessness of heard language. This revelatory impulse seems to prevail in Old English.

Almost all who seek to define the riddle recognize it as a manipulation of a verbal deception, but they agree that the answer is part of its pleasure. A riddle without its solution is incomplete; so Aristotle implies in his comparison of riddle and metaphor:

> Most smart sayings are derived from metaphor, and also from misleading the reader beforehand. For it becomes more evident to him that he has learnt something, when the conclusion turns out contrary to his expectation, and the mind seems to say, "How true it is! but I missed it." . . . And clever riddles are agreeable for the same reason; for something is learnt, and the expression is also metaphorical. [11]

Francis Gummere locates the possible origin of the European riddle in what we know as the "kenning";[12] in a similar vein, Frederick Tupper stresses the relationship of the riddle to metaphor and mythological personification.[13] "Hardly a riddle is without its elements of metaphor," he declares, and points us to *Riddle 11* of Symphosius, where Flood and Fish are presented as "noisy house and quiet guest."[14] Ian Hamnett reinforces this notion in his comment about riddles:

> The "point" of the riddle does not depend on the respondent's ability to solve it—clearly almost impossible if the answer is not already known—but in the recognition of a subtle, even far-fetched congruence between items that when ordinarily regarded might seem to be either antithetical or at least disjoined. [15]

11. *Rhetoric*, III.xi.6 (1412a), trans. John Henry Freese, *The "Art" of Rhetoric* (New York: G. P. Putnam's Sons, 1926).

12. *The Beginnings of Poetry* (New York: Macmillan, 1902), 451–52.

13. Introduction to *The Riddles of the Exeter Book* (Boston: Ginn, Albion Series, 1910).

14. Ibid., xiv.

15. "Ambiguity, Classification, and Change: The Function of Riddles," *Man* 2.3 (1967), 379–92.

To the same degree that it involves antithesis and deception, then, the riddle depends on congruity and revelation to be meaningful, and a significant difference between the Latin and the Old English riddles lies in the fact that the Latin versions provide the solutions to their enigmas in their titles. To some scholars, this feature would disqualify them as riddles. Indeed, naming the object which the riddle seeks to hide, and at the head of the poem, would seem to defeat the purpose for readers, but the Old English riddles have lost their tails with time, and there is no way of knowing whether the scribes who recorded them expected readers to guess them. Ann Harleman Stewart writes that it was essential for the reader/hearer to have known the solution to the Old English riddle in order to have taken any pleasure in its "amusing incongruity."[16] Seth Lerer caps this comment by remarking that *Riddle 42* "provokes" rather than "mystifies," "depend[ing] for its effect . . . on the heightened attention it directs toward writing itself, and on the structures of paradox, ambiguity, and self-reference framing that attention."[17]

The amount of ambiguity and deception involved in this literary game varies among the Old English texts, and I divide them into two rough categories: (1) the elaborate metaphors in which the subject is described by comparing it to something else, or is sometimes described very straightforwardly, and (2) the works of deception in which one is made to provide the wrong context for the subject. An example of the first type is found in *Riddle 3*, which describes a stormy wind:

> Hwilum ic sceal ufan   yþa wregan
> [streamas] styrgan   ond to staþe þy[w]an
> flintgrægne flod   famig winneð
> wæg wið wealle   Wonn ariseð
> dun ofer dype   hyre deorc on last
> eare geblonden   oþer fereð
> þæt hy gemittað   mearclonde neah·
> hea hlincas
>
> (EB2: 17–24ª]

[Sometimes from above I must rouse the waves,
stir up the waters and to the shore drive
the flint-gray flood. Foaming fights

16. "Kenning and Riddle in Old English," *Papers in Language and Literature* 15 (1979), 131.
17. *Literacy and Power in Anglo-Saxon Literature* (Lincoln: University of Nebraska Press), 117.

the wave with the wall. Dim rears up
the dune over the deep, dark behind it
blended with the sea comes another
such that they meet near the watermark
by the high rocks.]

Here is a superb poem about the wind at sea, but as a riddle its answer is self-evident; it is less a metaphor than a vivid description. The fact that so many of the Anglo-Saxon texts seem to be translations or derivations of Latin riddles makes it unclear whether the tradition is native to English.[18] Nevertheless, the Old English riddles are remarkably adept in their representation of common objects in a fantastic light. *Riddle 29*, about the Moon and the Sun, portrays the former as a deer (or perhaps a cow) holding the sun's stolen light between her curved horns and bounding up to build a bower in the firmament; the latter is pictured as a kind of predatory beast who lunges up from the horizon in pursuit of the animal, reclaims its treasure, and chases her westward. It is easy to see, as Gummere has suggested, how this riddle might have grown out of an epithet like "heath stepper" or "swan road." The riddle obliterates the customary relationships by which a thing is connected to the human world. In Old English, this trick is most cleverly illustrated by the so-called obscene riddles, where an onion, or a churn, or a key, or a man's shirt, along with all the details attending these objects, are presented in such a way as to suggest that they are not what they are. The disparity between the supposed and actual solution to the riddles is what makes them funny, and their implied context is what makes them obscene.

Within this general category there are a few riddles wherein the deception consists of telescoping or confusing the chronological events which identify the subject. As with the obscene riddles, these works omit an important orienting context, the passage of time, and thereby seem to give us ambiguous or contradictory information. The following is *Riddle 30*:

IC eom legbysig   lace mid winde
bewunden mid wuldre   wedre gesomnad
fus forðweges   fyre gebysgad

---

18. Craig Williamson claims that "there is no reason to believe that the Old English Riddles were based on any well-established tradition of social riddling in Anglo-Saxon England" (*The Old English Riddles of the Exeter Book* [Chapel Hill: University of North Carolina Press, 1977], 11–12). Traditions where wayfarers are given riddles to solve are well established, however, in Germanic and Celtic literature.

bearu blowende   byrnende gled
ful oft mec gesiþas   sendað æfter hondum
þæt mec weras ond wif   wlonce cyssað
þonne ic mec onhæbbe   ond hi onhnigað to me
monige mid miltse   þær ic monnum sceal
ycan upcyme eadignesse

(EB2: 120)

[I am troubled by fire (busy with fire?), I
        sport with the wind,
wound with glory, gathered by weather,
eager of the way, afflicted by flame,
a blooming grove, a burning gleed.
Often friends send me from hand to hand
so that men and women proudly kiss me.
When I rise up they bend down to me
many with joy (humility?). There I must increase
for men the growth of happiness.]

This is a confusing riddle. Efforts to find for its solution a subject which
can be and perform at one time all the things described in it have led to
farfetched suggestions.[19] The guesser is made to believe that the object is
these things all at once, and is confused by having to force many situations
into one context. Both Williamson and F. A. Blackburn have independently
recognized that the riddle plays on different aspects of wood and its different
developments within time.[20] Its resulting air of contradiction and confusion
is deliberate and adds not only to its mysteriousness but to its cadence and
beauty. Each half-line offers a new idea which, when compounded with the
others, augments the seemingly fragmented quality of the subject, and when

19. Such as Hans Pinsker's notion that it means a "snowflake" and that the "burning gleed" is the
effect of frostbite on the hand which is kissed and blown on, that it rises up as rain in order to show to
the farmer bent over his crops the joy of a prosperous season ("Neue Deutungen für zwei altenglische
Rätsel: Krapp-Dobbie 17 und 30," *Anglia* 91 [1973], 16). To fortify this interpretation, though,
Pinsker emends *legbysig* in 1a to *lyftbysig*, and *ycan upcyme* in 9a to *ywan upcymas*. This seems to be
cheating.
    20. F. A. Blackburn ("*The Husband's Message* and the Accompanying Riddles of *The Exeter
Book*," JEGP 3 [1900], 1–3) suggests that the answer is the word *beam* with its compound meanings of
"tree," "ship," "log," "cross," and possibly "harp" and "bowl." Williamson (*Riddles*, 231) believes,
rather, that "the riddle treats the various aspects of uses of a tree": "troubled by lightning, tossed by
wind, surrounded by the glory of its foliage, made one with weather. . . . From line 5 on, the tree is
presented as wood fashioned by art."

we get to the fourth line—"[I am] a blooming grove, a burning gleed"—we
appear to be dealing with the kind of magic, shapeshifting creature that we
might find in a poem by Taliesin. To a certain extent, we are; for the divine
power that is conferred on the wood by virtue of its being made into the holy
rood—both the actual "tree" on which Christ died and its symbol to which
people genuflect—heightens the mystery of the riddle and finds its best
expression in this highly artful form which also is a poetic illustration of its
implied religious message: No other power but God's can connect the uncon-
nected things of the earth and the unrelated events in time. Interestingly, the
one poetic riddle extant in Early Welsh poetry is to be found in *The Book of
Taliesin*.[21]

It is similarly the special power of the inspired poet or visionary to connect
unconnected things, to be in many places and many shapes and to deal
constantly with contradiction: "I was a teardrop in the air. . . . I was a word
in letters; I was a book in the beginning," declares Taliesin in *Kat Godeu*.
There is not so much clear evidence of "mantic" poetry in Old English as
there is in the Welsh, but several Old English poems bear marked resem-
blance to some of the Celtic aretalogies. One of these is the *Exeter Book
Riddle 40*, a fairly close translation of Aldhelm's Latin enigma entitled
Creatura:

> ECe is se scyppend   se þas eorþan nu
> wreðstuþum [wealdeð]   ond þas woruld healdeð
> . . .
>
> he mec wrætlice   worhte æt frymþe
> þa he þisne ymbhwyrft   ærest sette
> heht mec wæccende   wunian longe
> þæt ic ne slepe   siþþan æfre·
> ond mec semninga   slæp ofergongeþ
> . . .
>
> ic eom to þon bleað   þæt mec bealdlice mæg
> gearugongende   grima abregan
> ond eofore eom   æghwær cenra
> þonne he gebolgen   bidsteal giefeð·
> . . .

21. BT 36.23–37.22; given the title *Kanu y gwynt* ("Song of the Wind"), it begins with the
imperative: *Dechymic pwy yw*, "Say what it is," whereby the speaker delivers a litany of descriptions in
the first person, much like the Latin and Old English enigmas.

hyrre ic eom heofone   hataþ mec heahcyning
his deagol þing   dyre bihealdan·
eac ic under eorþan   eal sceawige
wom wraðscrafu   wraþra gesta·
                    (EB2: 1–2, 6–10, 16–19, 38–41)

[Eternal is the Lord who this earth now
rules with might, and holds this world
. . .

He wrought me wondrously in the beginning,
when he first established this creation.
He commanded me to remain awake for a long time,
that I never afterwards sleep,
and at once sleep overcame me
. . .

I am so timid that boldly can
a grim revenant frighten me
and I am braver in every way than the boar
when furious it gives ground
. . .

Higher I am than Heaven; the High King commands me
to behold secretly his secret things;
also, under the earth, I see all
of the hateful dwelling places of evil spirits.]

This poem, along with its Latin antecedent, is even more reminiscent than
are the Welsh aretalogies of the gnostic text *Thunder, Perfect Mind*, especially
in its list of contraries. One could compare it as well to the claims of Wisdom
in *Sirach*:

"I came forth from the mouth of the Most High,
        and covered the earth like mist.
I dwelt in high places,
        and my throne was in a pillar of cloud.
Alone I have made the circuit of the vault of
        Heaven, and have walked in the depths of the abyss."
                    (24:1–5)[22]

---

22. *The Wisdom of Jesus Son of Sirach*, from the Apocrypha, *The New Oxford Annotated Bible
with the Apocrypha*, ed. Herbert G. May, Bruce Metzger (New York: Oxford University Press, 1977),
129, 159.

Given the popularity of this *topos* and its association with a figure of Wisdom, we might reconsider Erika von Erhardt's interpretation of *Riddle* 73:

> IC wæs fæmne geong   feaxhar cwene
> ond ænlic rinc   on ane tid
> fleah mid fuglum   ond on flode swom
> deaf under yðe   dead mid fiscum
> ond on foldan stop   hæfde ferð cwicu
>
>   (EB2: 214)
>
> [I was a young woman, a gray-haired lady,
> and a peerless man at the same time (or: "at one time").
> I flew with birds and swam in the sea,
> dove under waves, dead among fishes
> and strode on the earth; (I) had a living soul.]

Erhardt-Siebold compares this riddle to a fragment attributed to Empedocles of Acragus, the fifth-century Greek philosopher and poet who espoused a kind of Orphic mysticism in his belief in reincarnation:

> Once I was a young man, maiden, plant,
> and mute fish cast ashore.[23]

In her subsequent article she adds considerably to her previous argument, with her discovery of the Latin version of Empedocles' fragment in Chalcidius's commentary the *Timaeus*, more likely to have been familiar to Old English clerics than Empedocles:

> namque ego iam dudam vixi puer et solida arbos,
> ales et ex undis animal, tum lactea virgo.
>
> "Once upon a time I lived as a young man, a
> strong tree, bird, creature of the waves, then
> as a chaste maiden."[24]

---

23. Erika von Erhardt-Siebold, "Old English Riddle 74 and Empedocles Fragment 117," *Medium Ævum* 15 (1946), 48.

24. Erhardt-Siebold, "A Note on Anglo-Saxon Riddle 74," *Medium Ævum* 21 (1952), 36–37.

More interesting than the possibility of conscious borrowing is the fact that an echo of Chalcidius's translation (perhaps heard read and remembered imperfectly) was identified as a riddle, or at least set among a group of English poems now generally referred to as riddles. Regardless of its source, its resemblance to the revelation discourses in Welsh and Irish is worth noting. Clearly, the riddle, the revelation discourse or aretalogy, and the mantic poems of Wisdom were "in the air," so to speak; their inclusion in various manuscripts says less that is informative about source material and more about how scribes and redactors made generic decisions: the garbled Empedocles (if that is what it is) they saw as a mystery and included it with the riddles. The Welsh riddle (again, if that is what it is) was seen as a revelation discourse and included in a manuscript about Taliesin.

The Exeter Book contains another poem important to this discussion of revelation discourse, and that is *Widsið*. The speaker in *Widsið* derives his powers as a poet from having traveled widely, been in many different courts, and visited numerous nations. Although his experiences are not of the "shape-shifting" variety of those in the *Kat Godeu* or of the bizarre quality boasted of in Gruffydd's *Hanes Taliesin*, they do exhibit a certain fantastic nature by virtue of their multitude and their grand disregard for chronology. For instance, the speaker of *Widsið* remarks that he visited the fourth-century King Eormanric and the sixth-century Ælfwine, conqueror of Italy (lines 70, 88). Of greater significance, though, is the fact that the poem is a boast, a declaration of poetic prowess where interesting and arduous experiences in a literal "Otherworld" have served to sharpen the scop's craft:

> Swa ic geondferde fela   fremdra londa
> geond ginne grund   godes on yfles
> ðær ic cunnade   cnosle bedæled
> freomægum feor   folgade wide·
> forþon ic mæg singan   ond secgan spell
> mænan fore mengo   in meoduhealle
> hu me cynegode   cystum dohten·
> (EB2: 50–56)

[Thus I traveled through strange lands,
throughout this wide world. Good and evil
I experienced there, deprived of kinsmen,
far from my folk, I served widely.

Therefore I may sing and utter a verse;
recite before the company in the meadhall
how the nobles were generous to me.]

Then follows a litany of places visited with anaphoric use of the copula as
in the *Kat Godeu* and *Angar Kyfyndawt:*

Ic wæs mid Hunum   ond mid Hreðgotum·
mid sweom ond mid geotum   ond mid suþdenum·
mid wenlum ic wæs   ond mid wærnum ond mid wicingum·
mid gefþum ic wæs   ond mid winedum ond mid gefflegum·
mid englum ic wæs   ond me swæfu ond mid ænenum·

(56–61)

Such features point to the intriguing possibility of an association of the
poet with the mantic in Old English tradition. The speaker of *Widsið* has
been taken traditionally to refer to a wandering scop's "wide-traveling"; David
Rollman suggests that the poem is a metaphor for poetry itself which is
disseminated to different peoples.[25] Ida Hollowell identifies the speaker of
Widsith as a *wodbora*, an early Anglo-Saxon term for an ecstatic.[26] Whereas
the *scop* functions as court "historian" and producer of panegyric, the
wodbora invites questions about the *fordgesceaft*, the future and the cosmos,
as does the speaker in *Maxims I* and the various Solomonic dialogues. We
have in the Norse traditions more explicit connection between poetry and the
divine powers of the gods, and even if the "powers" have been reduced in the
riddles to clever poetic contrivances, it should be recognized that both the
riddler and the mantic poet perpetrate a similar kind of deception on their
hearers: the riddler will omit important information and thereby telescope
chronology. His riddle is like a knotted net. We see the knots but not the
network of events that would orient the subject within an intelligible context.

The existence of *Widsið* raises another intriguing question about the rela-
tionship of "ordeal" to poetic insight. The speaker of *Widsið* attributes his
power not so much to magic as he does to the breadth and extraordinariness
of his experiences and to the ordeals he has endured as an itinerant poet. In
this respect we can see the connection of plaint poems to what may have been

25. "Widsith as an Anglo-Saxon Defense of Poetry," *Neophilologus* 66 (1982), 431–39.
26. "*Scop* and *Wodbora* in OE Poetry." JEGP (1979), 317–29.

a very basic concept of trial as a means by which the poet sharpens his vision. In only a few Welsh and Old English poems do we find a deliberate connection. The speaker of *Widsið* declares that he has suffered in far-off lands: "therefore" or "because" (that familiar and vague causal conjunction *forþon*) he may sing to the company in the meadhall. The aretalogies of Taliesin less explicitly imply that the poet's various transmigrations and imprisonments make him more qualified as a visionary than the other bards. Finn and Suibne in Irish tradition derive poetic and prophetic vision from their ordeals in the wilderness. Enduring for nine days the heat of two fires, Óðinn reveals his identity to his tormentor Geirrod in the *Grímnismál* in a litany of his names which strikingly resembles the insular revelation discourses. [27] It would seem that the motif of "wisdom from ordeal" is a well-attested motif throughout Northern medieval literature as well as an established Indo-European theme. A closer look at *Wulf and Eadwacer* and *The Wanderer*, with particular attention to what both poems seek to withhold or reveal, might give us a little more insight into the relationship between suffering and poetic discourse as it was perceived by Anglo-Saxon poets.

Wulf and Eadwacer is decidedly different from the riddles. The fact that it immediately precedes a section of riddles in *The Exeter Book* has caused it to be classified as one, but its element of lament suggests that the poem serves a purpose other than to make the reader guess its solution, and it is more commonly put with the elegies. If the poem expresses pain, though, we might ask why it does not do so more directly, as in *The Wanderer* or *The Wife's Lament*, why it seems to withhold information and produce confusing ambiguities in the nature of a riddle. I surmise that the answer to these questions is twofold: *Wulf and Eadwacer* presents us with a painful picture of secret love in which we can detect what might have been a tradition of lovers speaking to each other in a cryptic fashion, rather like the *trobar clus* of the

---

27. From the *Grímnismál* of *The Poetic Edda* of the *Codex Regius*, ed. Gustav Nickel (Heidelberg: Carl Winter, 1962), 66–68. "I am called X" appears to be a kind of variant of "I am X" or "I was in X"; the general structure wherein the identity of the divine is revealed piecemeal or in a series of repetitive variations remains:

Hetomc Grimr, hetomc Gangleri,	I am called Hooded; I am called Wanderer (?),
Herian oc Hiálmberi,	Ruler and Helm-bearer
Þeccr oc Þridi,	Much-Loved and Third,
Þundr oc Uðr,	Thund and Uth,
Helblindi oc Hár.	Hel (or Host?) blinder and High One.

troubadours, and what might also have been a tradition of prisoners or plaintiffs whose artful and stylized form of expression lends a profundity and even mysterious quality to their pain.

We have an example of the riddlic presentation of love in another perplexing poem called *The Husband's Message*, which has evaded classification as deftly as *Wulf and Eadwacer*. Like it, *The Husband's Message* has been seen in relationship with the riddles because of both its content and its position in *The Exeter Book* immediately after *Riddle 60, Rune-Staff*. It contains runes, although this feature in itself does not make it a riddle. There has been some debate about its connection with the preceding text, which I offer here:

<pre>
Ic wæs be sonde   sæweale neah
æt merefaroþe   minum gewunade
frumstaþole fæst   fea ænig wæs·
monna cynnes   þæt mine þær
on anæde   eard beheolde·
ac mec uhtna   gehwam yð sio brune
lagufæðme beleolc   lyt ic wende
þæt ic ær oþþe sið·   æfre sceolde
ofer meodu   muþleas sprecan
wordum wrixlan   þæt is wundres dæl
on sefan searolic   þam þe swilc ne conn·
hu mec seaxes ord   on seo swiþre hond
eorles ingeþonc   ond ord somod
þingum geþydan   þæt ic wiþ þe sceolde
for unc anum twam   ærendspræce
abeodan bealdlice   swa hit beorna ma
uncre wordcwidas   widdor ne mænden
</pre>
(EB2: 191)

[I was on the sand near the sea-wall,
at the water's edge; (I) remained in my
original state firmly; there were few
of any of mankind that there my
deserted home beheld,
and each dawn the gleaming wave
locked me in embrace; little did I know
that sooner or later I would ever
over mead speak mouthless,

vary words; that is a sort of wonder,
cunning in the hearts (or: "difficult to
the mind"?) for him who does not know such,
how the knife's point and the right hand,
a prince's thought and the point together
press me to the thing
("the purpose"? "the debate"): that I with thee might
a message for us two alone
utter boldly, so that no other men
more widely spread it, our words.]

The Husband's Message begins with what appears to be a continuation of the idea in *Riddle 60: Nu ic onsundran þe secgan wille* / [*ymb þisum*] *treocyn ic tudre aweox* ["Now I will tell you privately (how) I came forth (from this?) tree-family."]. The damage to the manuscript and further ambiguities in the text make it difficult to discern whether the speaker is the rune-staff personified or a human messenger. If the former, then one could see both *Riddle 60* and *The Husband's Message* as one long poem, for the scribe has divided the latter into three sections which modern editors have pieced together as the present poem, and, furthermore, as Paul F. Baum aptly notes, "It is unusual for a riddle to carry a secret message 'for us two alone.' "[28]

The exclusivity of this remark along with its comments about the "difficulty" (*searolic*) of the secret rune and the ignorance (*þe swilc ne conn*) of the uninitiated cause it to resemble in some respects the boasts that Taliesin makes about the esoteric nature of his knowledge, but here it is couched in a love context. The secrecy and care that attend romantic love seem to fit naturally into a riddlic frame: lovers must send each other coded messages to ensure privacy. Even if *Riddle 60* and *The Husband's Message* were intended as separate pieces, one can still see the compatibility of the love poem and the riddle or code.

If *Wulf and Eadwacer* is a love poem in this sense—and alternative interpretations have been applied to it—its riddlic tone is appropriate. The speaker communicates her pain and confusion in coded terms. The situation calls for secrecy: a woman in clandestine communication with her outcast and presumably illicit lover. Still, however, the degree of obscurity and confusion in this poem compared with the other English poems of lament, even *Deor* or the difficult *Wife's Lament*, remains unaccounted for. *The*

---

28. *The Riddles of the Exeter Book* (Durham: Duke University Press, 1963), 34.

Husband's Message discloses the very missive that the preceding riddle promises will be kept secret, if the two were thought to be counterparts to each other (the position of *The Husband's Message* immediately following the riddle reveals, perhaps, the scribe's understanding of it as a companion piece to and extension of the riddle). Either way, we have one more example of the Anglo-Saxon proclivity for expansion, clarification, and the solution of mysteries. *Wulf and Eadwacer*, however, has an elliptical nature unmatched by most other Old English poems, and an air of abrupt non sequitur resembling the Welsh poems. Celtic or Scandinavian influence has been suggested,[29] for more than one scholar has noted its "un-English" lack of forthrightness.

The Open Hoard: *Maxims* and *The Wanderer*

The *Maxims* provide us with some opinions about forthrightness, and *The Wanderer*, itself somewhat gnomic, provides us with some opinions about secrecy. The opening lines of *Maxims I*, inveighing against keeping things secret—*Frige mec frodum wordum* ["Question me with wise words"]—orders the scop:

> ne læt þinne ferð onhælne
> degol þæt þu deopest cunne   nelle ic þe min dyrne gesecgan
> gif þu me þinne hygecræft hylest   ond þine heortan geþohtas·
> gleawe men sceolon gieddum wrixlan
>
> (EB2: 1ᵇ–4ᵃ)

> [Do not keep your soul concealed,
> hidden, what you most deeply know. I will not tell you
>   my secret
> if you do not reveal your mind's treasure and your heart's
>   thoughts.
> Wise men should exchange sayings.]

Presumably we are to imagine two wisemen or poets, one issuing the other a kind of bardic challenge and yet at the same time laying down the ground

29. W. W. Lawrence, "The First Riddle of Cynewulf"; Herbert Pilch, "The Elegiac Genre in Old English and Early Welsh Poetry," *Zeitschrift für celtische Philologie* 29 (1964), 209–24.

rules: *Gleawe men sceolon gieddum wrixlan*. We have seen this term *wrixlan* used before in *Beowulf* and in the *Riddles*, both times in connection with poetry or communication, but exchange was a concept fundamental to Anglo-Saxon society. A king exchanged treasure and protection for the loyalty of his thanes; a husband extended protection and goods in exchange for his wife's faithfulness:

> cyning sceal mid ceape   cwene gebicgan
> bunum ond beagum   bu sceolan ærest
> geofum god wesan·
>
> (81–83ª)
>
> wif sceal wiþ wer   wære gehealdan
>
> (100)

[A king must buy a queen with a price:
cups and rings. both should first
be generous with gifts. . . .
a woman must keep faith with her husband.]

Likewise, "exchange" is shown in the opening passage cited above as an important aspect of counsel, and vital to any kind of meaningful communication. A little further on, we have *ræd sceal mon secgan rune writan / leoþ gesingan leofes gearnian / dom areccan dæges onettan* ("One should give counsel, write runes, sing songs, desire a friend, reckon judgment, use days productively" [lines 138–40]). Like the king bestowing treasure, the wiseman fulfills his function by being generous with the gems of his craft. The analogy made in *Riddle 42* between the speaker's verbal coffer which he will help us unfasten makes use of a prevalent metaphor in Anglo-Saxon poetry: *Widsiþ maðelode wordhord onleac* ("Widsith spoke, unlocked his word-hoard (line 1)"). In *The Seafarer* the spirit is released from its *hreðerlocan* ("heart enclosure" [line 58]) and the bitter contents of the *breosthord* (line 55). *The Wanderer* includes three references to the heart as a bound vessel (lines 11–21); attending this image of knowledge fettered we find two equally important concepts: the power to extend to others information or wisdom hard come by, and the power to keep it secret. *The Wanderer* stresses the latter and presents it as a virtue, a "noble custom," indicative of a warrior's self-control and stalwartness. The concluding lines leave us with the image of the stoic *snottor* sitting apart in secret consultation (*rune*) with his thoughts, whereby he concludes that "a man must never too quickly reveal the pain of his heart . . . unless he knows earlier how to bring about bravely the remedy" (lines 111–14).

One is not to complain aimlessly; it is better to keep silent and to seek consolation from God, where all security rests, than to entrust one's happiness to foolish and evanescent counsel. Nevertheless, we are left with the strong feeling that it is only by default that the speaker chooses to make a secret of his feelings; had he anyone in whom to confide he would have unburdened his heart gladly:

> Oft ic sceolde ana   uhtna gehwylce
> mine ceare cwiþan   nis nu cwicra nan
> þe ic him mod-sefan   minne durre
> sweotule asecgan
>
> (EB1: 8–11^b)

> [Often, every dawn, I had to lament my
> sorrow alone; now there is no one alive
> to whom I dare tell my heart openly.]

Immediately after this remark the speaker counsels himself to "hold his hoardcoffer" (line 14) according to the "noble custom" of bereaved men, but following closely upon the image of his sealed-up heart (line 19^b), we have the evocative image of the dead king, the "gold-friend," buried under the darkness of the earth in what amounts to a powerful if implicit comparison between the two concepts. Hearts and kings alike suffer interment, not so much because of the necessity of adhering to a noble custom, but because circumstances bring about the sad fact. Clearly, communication is preferable to repression in *The Wanderer*, and it is interesting that while espousing a philosophy of silence the speaker presents us with a detailed utterance of the sorrow he declares should be kept secret. The poetry itself, with its formal structures and artifices, provides a suitable vehicle with which to bare the contents of the heart, and to make of it and its vessel the artifact it is so often depicted as being. I suggest that the paradox is no paradox at all; in choosing to make of his closed heart an open declaration of wisdom gained through suffering, the speaker of *The Wanderer* chooses between private and public experience. He is generous with the gems of his craft, and it is this that puts his poem more firmly in the camp with the sermon, the confession, the "penitential lyric," and other genres that make use of disclosure and explanation.

Tearing the Text: *Wulf and Eadwacer*

In *Wulf and Eadwacer*, however, we find very little of this taste for disclosure. Although its plaint is eloquent, it is a deeply private one to which we have no privileged access, and it is couched in such bafflingly omissive and suggestive terms as to inspire a host of contradictory interpretations. In noting the departure of the poem from the "classical literary formulaic style" of Old English poetry in its use of a refrain, in its long- and short-line couplets which resemble the Icelandic *ljoþahattr* verses, and in its irregular or missing alliteration, Kemp Malone fits *Wulf and Eadwacer* into a tradition of *Frauenlieder*. These he defines as a "body of folk-poetry made up chiefly of songs, put in the mouths of women, who gave free utterance to the feelings of their hearts,"[30] and he ascribes the obscurity of *Wulf and Eadwacer* to a lost popular context: "If the poem remains obscure to us in spite of the simplicity of its language and style, this is our misfortune, not the poet's fault. He composed for an audience that knew the story behind the woman's lyric cry."[31] It may be true that *Wulf and Eadwacer* could be explained within a narrative context now lost to us, much like that of the "saga theory" and *Canu Llywarch Hen*, but Malone here implies that its present obscurity, if it is not the "fault" of the author, is an accidental by-product of its separation from this context. I prefer to remove the onus from obscurity. I suggest that the air of ambiguity and rupture was intentional, perhaps even perceived as powerful, for several reasons. The poem precedes the riddles, and manuscript context is an index to scribal interpretation; these riddles show a fascination on the part of their creators and collectors with secrets. The amount of equivocation and comment about secrecy that appears in Anglo-Saxon poetry would suggest that the issue is fraught with ambivalence. In the Riddles, of course, secrecy is more often shown in its positive aspects, for the riddler, like an artificer, controls his subject for the delectation of his audience. Secrecy is more often presented negatively in *The Maxims*, for the secretive man or woman is more often one who acts contrary to the dictates of society:

> sceomiande man sceal in sceade hweorfan   scir in leohte gerised
> (Maxims I, EB2: 66)

> [A man in shame must turn to shadows;   shining things are fitted for the light.]

30. Kemp Malone, "Two Old English *Frauenlieder*," 109.
31. Ibid.

mægen mon sceal mid mete fedan   morþor under eorþan befeolan
hinder under hrusan   þe hit forhelan þenceð·
ne biþ þæt gedefe deaþ   þonne
      hit gedyrned weorþeð·

(*Maxims I*, 114–16)

[One must feed strength with meat; put murder underground,
deep under the earth, by him who plans to hide it.
That is no decent death when it is secret.]

In the Welsh gnomes, attitudes toward secrecy are presented with more neutrality—with secrecy, as it were—veiled by their juxtapositive and seemingly less informative textual contexts:

Eiry mynyd eilion ffraeth.
gowlychyt tonneu glantraeth.
keluyd kelet y aruaeth.

(RB: 1029.6–7)

[Mountain snow, nimble the deer.
Waves wet the edge of the beach.
The skillful, let him conceal his design.]

Kalangayaf kein gyfrin.
kyfret awel a dryckin.
gweith keluyd yw kelu rin.

(1031.33–34)

[Calends of winter, fine a shared secret.
The wind as swift as a storm.
The work of the skillful is to hide a secret.]

In *Maxims II*, however, we find the thief and the unvirtuous woman side by side with the monster:

þeof sceal gangan þystrum wederum·   þyrs sceal on fenne gewunian·
ana innan land   ides sceal dyrne cræfte·
fæmne hire freond gesecean·   gif heo nelle on folce geþeon·
þæt hi man beagum gebicge·

(42–45a)

[A thief must walk in dark weather.
A monster must dwell in the fen,
alone in the land. A woman must with secret craft
seek her lover if she does not wish it to succeed among the folk
that a man has bought her with rings.]

And in *Beowulf*, of course, all that is hidden, dark, and secret is summed up by the evil forces of Grendel and his dam, the epitome of outlawry and the antithesis of societal order:

> Hie dygal lond
> warigeað wulfhleoþu   windige næssas
> frecne fengelad   þær fyrgenstream
> under næssa genipu   niþer gewiteð
> flod under foldan
>
> (lines 1357ᵇ–61ᵃ)

> [They inhabit a hidden land,
> the retreat of wolves, windy headlands
> fearful fens, where mountain streams
> go down under the darkness of cliffs,
> flood under fold.]

The appearance of the word "wolf" as a name in *Wulf and Eadwacer* is of great significance in this context, for the wolf is commonly associated in Old English literature with criminals and outcasts. His presence in Grendel's territory is proof of the savage and inhospitable nature of the mere, and as one of the three beasts of battle, he is a curiously liminal figure, often depicted as lurking on the fringes of society—feeding on the corpses of heroes, for instance, without partaking in any of the human glory that accompanies death in war. He is so depicted in *The Wanderer*, where the metaphor of the heart as closed coffer finds its monstrous extension in the exposed ruin, the bereft hall that, once the container of the *duguð*, is now a graveyard open to storms, where the corpses of men are dragged off by wolves.

The wolf, then, is an animal without *duguð*: *Wulf sceal on bearowe / earm anhaga* (the wolf must be in the woods, wretched and alone), say *Maxims II*, and the outcast deprived of human society is associated with him in *Maxims I:*

wineleas wonsælig mon   genimeð him wulfas to geferan
felafæcne deor   ful oft hine se gefera sliteþ·
gryre sceal for greggum   græf deadum men
hungre heofeð   nales þæt heafe bewinded
ne huru wæl wepeð   wulf se græga
morþorcwealm mæcga   ac hit a mare wille·

(EB2: 42, 146–51)

[The wretched man deprived of friends takes wolves as a companion,
treacherous beast. Often the companion tears him.
There must be horror for the gray one, a grave for the dead man.
It (the wolf) laments its hunger, by no means does it lament a grief.
Indeed the gray wolf does not bewail the death,
the slaughter of the kinsmen, but it ever wants more.]

Wulfesheafod was also the legal expression for an outlaw in Old English as
Edward the Confessor informs us in his Laws:

Lupinum enim caput geret a die utlagationis suae,
quod ab Anglis wlvesheved nominatur. [32]

[For he (the outlaw) wears the head of a wolf
from the day of his outlawry, which
is called "wolf's head" by the English.]

An outlaw was literally one who remained outside the protection exerted by
law, one whom others could kill with impunity as they would kill a wolf. [33]
    What all these passages tell us about the Anglo-Saxon concept of law and
outlawry is that acceptance within human society means protection. It is
vitally important to the well-being of the individual, and the hideous implica-
tion behind the law is that social order protects the citizen not merely from
external threats but from his fellow citizens. The *utlaga* is beset by beast or
man alike; he has forfeited his humanity.

---

32. *The Law of Edward the Confessor*, chapter 6.2, in *Die Gesetze der Angelsachsen*, ed. Rein-
hold Schmid (Leipzig: F. A. Brockhaus, 1858), 494.
    33. *Et tunc gerunt caput lupinum ita quod sine judiciali inquisitione rite pereunt* ["And then they
wear the head of a wolf, and therefore die lawfully without a judicial hearing."], Henry Bracton, *De
Legibus et consuetudinibus Angliae*, 159, lib. III, tr. ii, chapter 11, ed. George E. Woodbine (New
Haven: Yale University Press, 1915).

Wulf and Eadwacer vividly depicts the plight of a *wulfesheafod*, or one who has transgressed the law in some way, either by being an enemy or by committing adultery with the wife of another man. Whatever his troubles, the association of the lamented lover with an "outlaw" is strengthened by his name. Suggestions of violence fill the poem:

> Leodum is minum swylc him mon lac gife.

"It is to my people as if one gave them a gift," declares the speaker, but *lac*, an ambiguous word, also has connotations of "sacrifice," "offering," "sport," as perhaps in the slaughter of a lamb, or booty won in a contest. The line appears to be laden with ironic understatement which is enhanced by the following line where, again, the meaning is ambiguous:

> Willaþ hie hine aþecgan gif he on þreat cymeþ.

We have seen the various ways in which this line can be translated, but my preference is for taking *aþecgan* as "consume," and *on þreat cymeþ* as "come to grief"—"They will consume him should he come to grief"—because it fits with the undercurrent of bestiality in the poem. To be sure, my translation is influenced by my interpretation, but having considered other interpretations I maintain that the association of the lover with a wolf, no matter how incidental that association, strongly suggests that we are to see Wulf as solitary and vulnerable rather than reinforced by a troop (*ðreat*). The danger seems to lie in his showing his "wolf's head" to a people that hate him:

> Wulf is on eglond   ic on oþere
> fæst is þæt eglond   fenne biworpen
> sindon wælreowe weras   þær on ige
> willað hy hine aþecgan   gif he on þreat cymeþ.

It may be unclear, as I argued earlier, who is on what island, but the bloodthirsty men seem to pose more of a direct threat to Wulf than they do to his lover, and they embody as well the predatory and violent world to which the outlaw is delivered up.

Within such a world, the outcast quickly loses his humanity, as the designation "wolf's head" implies, and the images in the poem become increasingly bestial toward the end. In the last three lines, then, we find Wulf metamorphosed into an animal: the child which he has presumably begotten has become a "whelp"; he bears it to the woods, which, according to *Maxims II*, is the suitable dwelling place for wolves, and there is the distinctly sinister suggestion of some misdirected violence in the verb *toslited*, "tears." In other words, it is not the child that is getting torn apart, but the relationship and the song. Still, the image sticks with us so forcefully as to render quite convincing Schofield's interpretation of it as a reference to Signy's destruction of her cowardly son in the *Volsunga Saga*. Tearing is a wolfish act, and it is this very word that is used in *Maxims I* to describe what wolves do to people: *Ful oft hine se gefera slited.*

Things come to confusion in this poem, what with two elements being divided that never were joined in the first place. The speaker partakes as well in her lover's disorientation, and her distressed and ambivalent feelings are poignantly revealed in her comments about her relationship with the "battle-ready man" whose love she finds pleasurable and hateful at the same time. This unstable emotional stance communicates itself to the rest of the poem and affects its indirect and uncommitted expressions. Certainly, the ambiguity in the poem derives from our ignorance of what may have been accepted idioms, but words like *lac, apecgan, þreat, toslited*, and *giedd* and their multiple meanings pack a powerful emotional force. Together, they suggest through insinuation a state of affairs that is all the more menacing for not being fully explained.

Ambiguity mounts as the poem concludes. If we cannot identify the battle-ready warrior with Wulf, neither can we identify him with Eadwacer, whom the speaker addresses in the second person, nor prove that he is the *wulf* of the third person in the following line. There can also be little doubt that the devious intention of the poet is to make us think for a split second that it is the child, borne off by a wolf, that "one easily tears apart," until the final line with its explanatory note rescues us from this grisly interpretation. Even so, the meaning of this last line remains mysterious. Perhaps the most logical interpretation is to take it as a reference to the speaker's nonmarital union with Wulf, or to her loveless union with Eadwacer, but why this union should be spoken of as song, poem, or riddle (*giedd*), who fathered the "whelp," and what attitude the mother takes toward the fate of her child and its role in the destruction of her relationships are perplexing issues. All add up to the suggestion of something clandestine, sinister, out of step with the mores of society; and the secretive tone of the poem, far removed from the happy control of the riddlers, reflects the fear, shame, and despair of its speaker.

When we compare this poem of lament to *The Seafarer*, where the narrator is shown actively righting his position in the universe by putting the godly life foremost and subordinating all else to it, we see how the structure of *Wulf and Eadwacer* shows a human being cut off from the social and moral order of the world. Men become animals, and women mate with them and "tear apart" both their young and their song. This "tearing apart" could be regarded as a metaphoric expression of what is actually happening in the poem with its absence of explicit connections: it is a shredded text, its parts disjunct; it moves, jerkily and with repetitions, from the fortress to the woods. As with the Sick Man, Wulf's lover is cut off from a scriptural tradition of offering comfort through words which do not work for her: riddle, utterance, poetry itself becomes incoherent and ripped apart. Nature is seen here as inimical and dumb, and all desire lies in the severed half of the world for which God can offer no sad consolation.

On the other hand, language works splendidly for her and for the poem. Though we do not know who wrote it or for what context, it continually invites us to probe it, to ponder its dark contents, to think for a moment that it is the vessel of meaning we have made of it. But our translations, still full of gaps, display our lack of mastery. The text remains ambiguous, untranslatable, uncooperative, and deeply powerful. This may have been its intention from the start, and, as always, it leaves us adrift between languages—and worlds.

Afterword:
Between Worlds

It might seem that in pointing out the differences between the Welsh and the English elegies I have glossed over their definite similarities. I hope to have shown, however, that these texts have evolved from the confluence of many streams and thus resist our present efforts to pin a comforting rubric on them. This is not true of all medieval poems, to be sure, but is especially true of the poems in *The Exeter Book, The Red Book,* and *The Black Book,* which deal with wanderers and exiles and with double languages and worlds. One can argue passionately for penitential or secular readings, but one's argument will always depend on what features one illuminates, what traditions one compares or contrasts to them, and in what contexts one sees them.

Manuscript semiotics, for instance, offers a promising focus for interpretation, and yet it is often overlooked in these weighty studies of genre and translation. It is perhaps a moot point whether a scribe's understanding of a poem and his placement of it among other poems contributes to its "meaning"; despite its glancing mention of salvation, *Claf Abercuawg* is sandwiched between verses of a poignant secular quality, which mingle earthy and ethical observations and which insist on reminding us of the chilling physical realities of this world. This is not all they do: any mention of the secular in medieval thought has its counterpart in and inspires thoughts of salvation. The interpolations, additions, and palimpsests that characterize so many of our medieval manuscripts, that look like blemishes to modern editors and stimulate their emendative faculties, could in fact be regarded as ways in which the scribe took part in a kind of interactive discourse with the texts he copied. Is it the poet or scribe Hywel Vychan who breaks open a series of concatenated verses to pray for the Leper's soul? Is it a defect or an act of defiance and iconoclasm that leads him to smash the "chain" of spiritual despair? Does his action remove the poem from one category and put it in another—or does it, rather, emphasize it as a text in progress, a text between categories?

The Old English elegies, separate from each other in *The Exeter Book*, seem to be companion pieces and variations on a theme, perhaps an assignment set to aspiring poets: an itinerant, a sea journey, a ruined building, a memory of past glory, and the sad certainty that all things fade are dealt with in varying degrees of emphasis and didacticism in *The Wanderer*, *The Seafarer*, *The Wife's Lament*, and *The Ruin*. Read together, they show us a diversity and multidimensionality that escapes us when read separately. Put next to the Welsh, we see much more clearly how discomfited the authors of *The Exeter Book* were made by lack of closure and secrecy, how ambivalence was much more tolerated by the authors of the *Canu Llywarch Hen*. I have already addressed the tendency to translate these differences into the binary poles of "masculine" and "feminine," the "active" and the "passive." Traditional scholarship praises "the dominance of volition . . . over the powerful provocations of experience"[1] in efforts to salvage these fretful speakers from accusations of softness or indecision or from an unendurable romanticization. It seeks to dignify its lepers and lone-goers and put them in heaven. Contemporary scholarship might challenge these assumptions: secrecy and ambiguity can be the domain of the powerful; explanation or "visibility" can open traps for itself. Attempts to apologize for the incomplete or dialogic structures of a medieval text only identify one's anglocentric assumptions about language. To conflate variants into one monolithic text,

---

1. W. F. Klein, "Purpose and the 'Poetics' of *The Wanderer* and *The Seafarer*," in *Anglo-Saxon Poetry: Essays in Appreciation for John C. MacGalliard*, ed. Lewis E. Nicholson and Dolores Warwick Frese (Notre Dame: Notre Dame University Press, 1975), 213.

the reconstructed poem, is to erase a record of medieval response. It is time we stopped doing that.

I said at the outset that in this book I would be mediating between languages, Old English and Early Welsh, but I also meant the often conflicting languages of traditional and contemporary critical scholarship. Discussions of poetic clarity and obscurity are necessarily discussions of power and ideology. More than once I have suggested that the foundations of certain assumptions about reading, interpretation, translation, and the assumed disinterestedness of traditional scholarship are open to challenge because they are rooted not in a dispassionate understanding of texts "as they are," if such a thing were even possible, but in political, cultural, and personal interpretations, as are *all* scholarly readings of ancient texts. However, clarity is not intrinsically better than ambiguity; spiritual or penitential poetry is not intrinsically more medieval than secular poetry; influence by the literate Latin tradition is not intrinsically more relevant to these poems than origins within oral indigenous or Indo-European traditions—only more in vogue. Who establishes what is in vogue in scholarly circles does so from a position of power.

Recently, especially in the United States and on the Continent, a new and disturbing locus of critical power has loomed up. In the suspicion it has thrown on traditional historicity and the canon, and in the new emphasis it has given to the marginal, to the multicultural, to subjectivity, and to the shifting and elusive quality of language itself, it promises to ventilate the close quarters of traditional scholarship. Its opponents could perhaps claim that it threatens to be the next power in charge of establishing what is in vogue or damping down all textual inquiries under a philosophy of nihilism and "relativistic chaos." They can argue, with validity, that while inveighing against "totalisms" and "hegemonies" it is well on the way to erecting its own.

I should like to suggest, however, that medievalists of all genres are in an ideal position to survive as well as to contribute to the critical upheavals of the contemporary academy by mediating between the domains offered by old and new theory. Educated in the rigorous and invaluable study of languages and historical contexts bequeathed us by the preceding generation, medievalists now have the advantage of being able to speak about textuality and problems posed by reading in ever more compelling ways. More than any other type of reader, then, the medievalist should equip herself to be pluralistic; the most interesting work done in both Old English and Celtic studies has profited by straddling traditional and nontraditional approaches. Scholars of Old English have been raising eyebrows; scholars of Early Welsh in particular have everything to gain by looking elsewhere than to the traditional English Academy for valorization. And in our frank examination of the Third Thing (the focus that our various interests and perspectives give a text and that seems to disconnect us from the comforting, positivist notions of the recoverable audience) we might be able to break free of this Fourth Medievalism, so bent now on berating the Third, and shape new work well into the next millennium.

Appendix:
Selected Texts and Translations

Because not all of my audience may be trained in both languages, I have given the texts and translations of the poems to which I refer most often or where it is important to give the text in full. I hope I have fought to the best of my powers the irresistible urge to "fill in"; my point is to disambiguate as little as possible, to insulate the reader as little as possible from the alien sounds of these poems or from alternative interpretations. Consequently, these translations are literal and peculiar-sounding, and I hope they demonstrate their failure as substitutions while suggesting some of the extraordinary qualities of their originals. With the exception of a few obvious scribal errors, I have tried to reproduce the spelling and punctuation of the manuscript versions. The commentary addresses the major editorial and interpretive quibbles.

I. Laments
1. The Seafarer

MS: *Exeter Book*, fols. 81ᵇ–83ᵃ. Follows A *Father's Instruction to His Son*, precedes *The Spirit of Men*. Editions and commentary: W. S. Mackie, *The Exeter Book*, vol. 2, EETS (London: Oxford University Press, 1934), 2–9; other diplomatic edition: Benjamin Thorpe (London: Pickering, 1842), 306–13.

1ᵃ	MÆG ic be me sylfum	I can by myself
1ᵇ	soðgied wrecan	a true poem utter,
2ᵃ	siþas secgan	expeditions tell
2ᵇ	hu ic geswincdagum	how I in days of toil
3ᵃ	earfoðhwile	a time of hardship
3ᵇ	oft þrowade	often endured,
4ᵃ	bitre breostceare	bitter breastcare
4ᵇ	gebiden hæbbe	have experienced,
5ᵃ	gecunnad in ceole	known aboard ship
5ᵇ	cearselda fela	many care-abodes,
6ᵃ	atol yþa gewealc	terrible waves's welling
6ᵇ	þær mec oft bigéat	(where) there often befell me
7ᵃ	nearo nihtwaco	an anxious nightwatch
7ᵇ	æt nacan stefnan	at vessel's prow
8ᵃ	þonne he be clifum cnossað	when along cliffs it knocked.
8ᵇ	calde geþrungen	By cold pinched
9ᵃ	wæron mine fet	were my feet,
9ᵇ	forste gebunden	frost-bound
10ᵃ	caldum clommum	by cold fetters
10ᵇ	þær þa ceare seofedun	there (where?) cares sighed
11ᵃ	hat ymb heortan¹	hot about the heart.
11ᵇ	hungor innan slat	Hunger inside gnawed
12ᵃ	merewerges mod	the seaweary spirit.
12ᵇ	þæt se mon ne wat	That the man knows not
13ᵃ	þe him on foldan	for whom on shore
13ᵇ	fægrost limpeð	most fairly it befalls,
14ᵃ	hu ic earmcearig	how I, wretched,
14ᵇ	iscealdne sæ·	ice-cold sea
15ᵃ	winter wunade	in winter endured,
15ᵇ	wræccan lastum	in tracks of exile,

16ᵃ	winemægum bidroren	of hall-companions bereft
16ᵇ	. . .	. . .
17ᵃ	bihongen hrimgicelum	hung with icicles.
17ᵇ	hægl scurum fleag	Hail flew in gusts.
18ᵃ	þær ic ne gehyrde	There I did not hear
18ᵇ	butan hlimmán sǽ	but roaring sea,
19ᵃ	iscaldne wæg	ice-cold wave.
19ᵇ	hwilum ylfete song·	Sometimes wild swan's song
20ᵃ	dyde ic me to gomene	did I make for myself as a game,
20ᵇ	ganetes hleoþor	gannet's cry
21ᵃ	ond huilpan sweg	and curlew's music
21ᵇ	fore hleahtor wera	instead of laughter of men,
22ᵃ	mæw singende	singing sea-mew
22ᵇ	fore medodrince	instead of mead-drinking.
23ᵃ	stormas þær stanclifu beotan	Storms there stonecliffs beat
23ᵇ	þær him stearn oncwæð	there (where?) tern answered
	isigfeþera	them icy-feathered.
24ᵃ	ful oft þæt earn bigeal	Often eagle screamed
24ᵇ	urigfeþra	hoary-feathered.
25ᵃ	nænig hleomæga	Not any protecting kinsmen
25ᵇ	. . .	. . .
26ᵃ	feasceaftig ferð	the destitute spirit
26ᵇ	feran meahte²	could travel (console?)
27ᵃ	forþon him gelyfeð lyt	Therefore (indeed?) he little believes—
27ᵇ	se þe ah lifes wyn	he who has ever life's pleasures
28ᵃ	gebiden in burgum	experienced in town,
28ᵇ	bealosiþa hwon	of adversities few,
29ᵃ	wlonc ond wingal	proud and wine-swollen—
29ᵇ	hu ic werig oft	how I weary often
30ᵃ	in brimlade	in sea's path
30ᵇ	bidan sceolde	had to remain.
31ᵃ	nap nihtscua	Nightshadow darkened.
31ᵇ	norþan sniwde	From north it snowed.
32ᵃ	hrim hrusan bond	Frost the ground bound.
32ᵇ	hægl feol on eorþan	Hail fell on earth
33ᵃ	corna caldast	Of kernels coldest.
33ᵇ	forþon cnyssað nú	Indeed (therefore? and?) now beat (urge?)

34ª	heortan geþohtas	the heart's thoughts (or: now thoughts beat/urge the heart)
34ᵇ	þæt ic hean streamas	that I high seas,
35ª	sealtyþa gelac	salt-waves' rolling,
35ᵇ	sylf cunnige	myself experience.
36ª	monaþ modes lust	Mind's desire reminds
36ᵇ	mæla gehwylce	on each occasion
37ª	ferð to feran	the spirit to travel,
37ᵇ	þæt ic feor heonan	that I far hence
38ª	elþeodigra	foreigners'
38ᵇ	eard gesece	land seek.
39ª	forþon nis þæs modwlonc	Indeed (therefore? and yet?) there is not so proud-hearted
39ᵇ	mon ofer eorþan	a man on earth,
40ª	ne his gifena þæs god	nor of his gifts so generous,
40ᵇ	ne in geoguþe to þæs hwæt	nor in youth so bold,
41ª	ne in his dædum to þæs deor	nor in his deeds so brave,
41ᵇ	ne him his dryten to þæs hold·	nor his lord so loyal to him,
42ª	þæt he a his sæfore	that he ever about his seafaring
42ᵇ	sorge næbbe	has not had sorrow (anxiety?)
43ª	to hwone hine dryhten	as to what the Lord with (to?) him
43ᵇ	gedon wille	wishes to do.
44ª	ne biþ him to hearpan hyge·	Neither will his thought be on harp,
44ᵇ	ne to hringþege·	nor on receiving rings,
45ª	ne to wife wyn·	nor on pleasure of women,
45ᵇ	ne to worulde hyht	nor on worldly joy,
46ª	ne ymbe owiht elles	nor about any thing else
46ᵇ	nefne ymb yða gewealc·	except about the waves' welling,
47ª	ac a hafað longunge	but always has longing
47ᵇ	se þe on lagu fundað·	he who onto water sets out.
48ª	bearwas blostmum nimað	Groves take blossom,
48ᵇ	byrig fægriað	towns grow fair,
49ª	wongas wlitigað	meadows beautiful,
49ᵇ	woruld onetteð	world hastens on.
50ª	ealle þa gemoniað	All then remind
50ᵇ	modes fusne	the eager of spirit,
51ª	sefan to siþe	the heart, to a journey,

51^b	þam þe swa þenceð	for him who thus thinks
52^a	on flodwegas	on floodways
52^b	feor gewitað³	afar to depart.
53^a	swylce geac monað	Likewise (thus? however?) cuckoo reminds (urges? admonishes?)
53^b	geomran reorde	with sad voice,
54^a	singeð sumeres weard	summer's guardian sings
54^b	sorge beodeð	inviting sorrow
55^a	bitter in breosthord	bitterly into breastcoffer.
55^b	þæt se beorn ne wat	That the man knows not,
56^a	est eadig secg	fortunate man,
56^b	hwæt þa sume dreogað	what that certain one endured
57^a	þe þa wræclastas	who those tracks of exile (acc.)
57^b	widost lecgað	laid down furthest.
58^a	forþon nú min hyge hweorfeð	Therefore (indeed?) now my mind passes
58^b	ofer hreþerlocan	over heart's enclosure,
59^a	min modsefa	my spirit
59^b	mid mereflode	with flood-tide
60^a	ofer hwæles eðel	over whale's home
60^b	hweorfeð wide	passes wide
61^a	eorþan sceatas	(over) earth's expanse,
61^b	cymeð eft to me	comes back to me
62^a	gifre ond grædig	eager and greedy.
62^b	gielleð anfloga	Lone-flier yells,
63^a	hweteð on wælweg⁴	whets onto whale-way
63^b	hreþer unwearnum	the heart irresistibly
64^a	ofer holma gelagu	over seas' lake.
64^b	forþon me hatran sind	Indeed (because? therefore?) to me hotter are
65^a	dryhtnes dreamas	the Lord's joys
65^b	þonne þis deade lif	than this dead life
66^a	læne on londe	fleeting on land.
66^b	ic gelyfe no	I do not believe
67^a	þæt him eorðwelan	that for it worldlywealth
67^b	ece stondeð⁵	forever remains.
68^a	simle þreora sum	Always a certain one of three
68^b	þinga gehwylce·	in each case

69[a]	ær his tide ge[6]	before its time
69[b]	to tweon weorþeđ	becomes ambiguous:
70[a]	adl oþþe yldo	disease or age
70[b]	oþþe ecghete	or edge-hatred
71[a]	fægum fromweardum	from doomed men
71[b]	feorh ođþringeđ	takes away life.
72[a]	forþon þæt eorla gehwam	Therefore this for every man
72[b]	æftercweþendra	of those speaking afterwards,
73[a]	lof lifgendra	of the living ones, praise
73[b]	lastworda betst	is the best of memorials
74[a]	þæt he gewyrce	that he might earn
74[b]	ær he onweg scyle	before he must on his way
75[a]	fremman on foldan	through actions on earth
75[b]	wiđ feonda niþ	against foes' hostility
76[a]	deorum dædum	through brave deeds
76[b]	deofle togeanes	against the devil,
77[a]	þæt hine ælda bearn	so that Him the children of men
77[b]	æfter hergen	will hereafter honor
78[a]	ond his lof siþþan	and His praise from then on
78[b]	lifge mid englum	may live with angels
79[a]	awa to ealdre	for ever and ever
79[b]	ecan lifes blæd·	in the blessedness of eternal life,
80[a]	dream mid dugeþum	joy amidst the Heavenly Host.
80[b]	dagas sind gewitene	The days are gone,
81[a]	ealle onmedlan	all magnificence
81[b]	eorþan rices	of earth's realm.
82[a]	næron nu cyningas	There are not now kings
82[b]	ne caseras	or Caesars
83[a]	ne goldgiefan	or gold-givers
83[b]	swylce iu wæron	such as once were
84[a]	þonne hi mæst mid him	when they among themselves the most
84[b]	mærþa gefremedon·	marvels performed
85[a]	ond on dryhtlicestum	and in the most lordly
85[b]	dome lifdon·	glory lived.
86[a]	gedroren is þeos duguđ eal	Perished is all this host,
86[b]	dreamas sind gewitene	joys are departed,
87[a]	wuniađ þa wacran	the weaker men remain
87[b]	ond þas woruld healdaþ	and this world hold,

88ᵃ	brucað þurh bisgo	occupy (it) in travail.
88ᵇ	blæd is gehnæged	Glory is laid low.
89ᵃ	eorþan indryhto	Earth's grandeur
89ᵇ	ealdað ond searað	grows old and sere
90ᵃ	swa nu monna gehwylc	as now each man
90ᵇ	geond middangeard	throughout middle-earth.
91ᵃ	yldo him on fareð	Old age overtakes him.
91ᵇ	onsyn blacað	Visage grows pale.
92ᵃ	gomelfeax gnornað	Gray-haired one mourns,
92ᵇ	wat his iuwine	knows his friends of yore,
93ᵃ	æþelinga bearn	sons of noblemen,
93ᵇ	eorþan forgiefene	to earth given.
94ᵃ	ne mæg him þonne se flæschoma	Cannot, then, the flesh-cover
94ᵇ	þonne him þæt feorg losað	when the life has left it
95ᵃ	ne swete forswelgan	either swallow sweetness
95ᵇ	ne sar gefelan	or feel pain
96ᵃ	ne hond onhreran	or a hand stir
96ᵇ	ne mid hyge þencan	or with mind think.
97ᵃ	þeah þe græf wille	Although the grave (acc.) will
97ᵇ	golde stregan	with gold strew
98ᵃ	broþor his geborenum	a brother (nom.) of his born (brother),
98ᵇ	byrgan be deadum	bury him among the dead
99ᵃ	maþmum mislicum	with various treasures,
99ᵇ	þæt hine mid wille⁷	that will not go with him.
100ᵃ	ne mæg þære sawle	Cannot be to the soul
100ᵇ	þe biþ synna ful	that is sinful
101ᵃ	gold to geoce	gold as an aid
101ᵇ	for godes egsan	before the terrible power of God
102ᵃ	þonne he hit ær hydeð	when he has hoarded it formerly
102ᵇ	þenden he her leofað·	when he lived here.
103ᵃ	micel biþ se meotudes egsa	Mighty is the terrible power of the Lord.
103ᵇ	forþon hi seo molde oncyrred	Before it (because of it?) the world turns aside.
104ᵃ	se gestaþelade	He established
104ᵇ	stiþe grundas	the solid lands,
105ᵃ	eorþan sceatas	the earth's expanse

105^b	ond uprodor·	and the heavens above.
106^a	dol biþ se þe him his drihten ne ondrædeþ	Foolish is he who does not dread his Lord.
106^b	cymeð him se dead unþinged	To him comes the death unforeseen.
107^a	eadig bið se þe eaþmod leofaþ	Blessed is he who humbly lives.
107^b	cymeð him seo ar of heofonum·	To him comes the grace of heaven.
108^a	meotud him þæt mod gestaþelað	God in him that disposition establishes,
108^b	forþon he in his meahte gelyfeð·	Therefore (because?) he in his might believes.
109^a	stieran mon sceal strongum mode	One must control with a strong mind (or: one must control a strong mind)
109^b	ond þæt on staþelum healdan	and within bounds hold it
110^a	ond gewis werum	and (be) true to men
110^b	wisum clæne·	and in ways pure.
111^a	scyle monna gehwylc	Must each man
111^b	mid gemete healdan	with moderation govern
112^a	wiþ leofne	with his friends
112^b	ond wið laþne bealo·	and with his enemies (his) malice
113^a	þeah þe he hine wille	although (lest?) him he will
113^b	fyres fulne . . .	full of fire
114^a	oþþe on bæle	or on the funeral pyre
114^b	forbærnedne	(have) burned
115^a	his geworhtne wine	his well-earned friend.
115^b	wyrd biþ swire[8]	Fate is stronger,
116^a	meotud meahtigra	God mightier
116^b	þonne ænges monnes gehygd·	than the understanding of any man.
117^a	Uton we hycgan	Let us think
117^b	hwær [w]e ham agen	where we have a home
118^a	ond þonne geþencan	and then consider
118^b	hu we þider cumen	how we might come there
119^a	ond we þonne eac tilien	and then let us also endeavor
119^b	þæt we to moten	that we might (go)

120ᵃ	in þa ecan	into that eternal
120ᵇ	eadignesse	blessedness
121ᵃ	þær is lif gelong	there (where) life springs up
121ᵇ	in lufan dryhtnes	in love of God,
122ᵃ	hyht in heofonum	joy in Heaven.
122ᵇ	þæs sy þam halgan þonc	For this let there be thanks to the Holy One
123ᵃ	þæt he usic geweorþade	that He honored us,
123ᵇ	wuldres ealdor	Glory's Prince,
124ᵃ	ece dryten	Eternal Lord,
124ᵇ	in ealle tid· Amen:7	for all time. Amen.

2. The Sick Man (Leper) of Abercuawg
"Claf Abercuawg"; Ifor Williams's title

MS: *The Red Book of Hergest*, Jesus College MS. cxi. Diplomatic edition, Gwenogvryn Evans, *The Red Book of Hergest* (Llanbedrog, 1911), 1034.24–1035.44. Follows *Lovely the Tips* ("Gorwyn Blaen") in RB: 1033.1–1034.23; precedes *The Song of the Old Man* (below). Other editions, translations, and commentary: in *Canu Llywarch Hen*, ed. Ifor Williams (Caerdydd: Gwasg Prifysgol Cymru, 1935, 1978), 23–27; in *Studies in Early Celtic Nature Poetry*, Kenneth Jackson (Cambridge: Cambridge University Press, 1935), trans. on pp. 53–56; in *The Early English and Celtic Lyric*, P. L. Henry (London: Allen and Unwin, 1970), trans. on pp. 75–77; in *The Poetry of Llywarch Hen*, ed. Patrick K. Ford (Berkeley and Los Angeles: University of California Press, 1974), ed. and trans. pp. 67–75; in *Early Welsh Saga Poetry: A Study and Edition of the Englynion*, ed. Jenny Rowland (Cambridge: Derek Brewer, 1990), pp. 448–52, trans. on pp. 497–99; comm. on pp. 617–28.

1.   Goreiste ar vrynn a eruyn uym bryt.
     a heuyt nym kychwyn.
     byrr vyn teith diffeith vyn tydyn.

To be idling on a hill my mind's desire,
and yet it does not stir me.
Short my journey, barren my dwelling.

2. Llem awel llwm benedyr[9] byw.

    pan orwisc coet teglyw
    haf. teryd[11] glaf wyf hediw.

Keen the[10] wind, bare cattletrack (?)
when trees dress in fair color
of summer. Feverishly ill am I today.

3. Nyt wyf anhyet. milet ny chatwaf
    ny allaf darymret.
    tra vo da gan goc canet.

I am not agile, a host I do not keep.
I cannot go about.
While it is good with the cuckoo, let it sing.

4. Coc lauar a gan gan dyd.
    kyfreu eichyawc[12] yn dolyd.
        cuawc
    gwell corrawc no chebyd.

Talkative cuckoo sings by day
loud (sad?) songs in meadows of Cuawg.
Better a spendthrift than a miser.

5. Yn aber cuawc yt ganant gogeu.
    ar gangheu blodeuawc.
    coc lauar canet yrawc.

In Abercuawg cuckoos sing
on flowering branches.
Talkative cuckoo, let it sing for evermore.

6. Yn aber cuawc yt ganant gogeu
    ar gangheu blodeuawc.
    gwae glaf ae clyw yn vodawc.

In Abercuawg cuckoos sing
on flowering branches.
Woe, sick man (leper), who hears them constantly.

7. Yn aber cuawc cogeu a ganant.
    ys atuant gan vym bryt.
    ae kigleu nas clyw heuyt.

In Abercuawg cuckoos sing.
It is sad to my heart
That who heard them does not hear them also.

8. Neus e[n]deweis i goc ar eidorwc brenn.
    neur laesswys vyg kylchwy.
    etlit agereis neut mwy.

I listened to a cuckoo on an ivy-covered tree.
Lax is my shield-strap.
Grief for what I loved is greater.

9. Yn y vann odywch llonn dar.[13]

    yd e[n]deweis i leis adar.
    coc uann cof gan bawp agar.

On the peak over the vigorous oak
I listened to voices of birds.
Loud cuckoo, each remembers what he loves.

10.   Kethlyd kathyl uodawc
          hiraethawc y llef
       teith odef. tuth hebawc.

       coc vreuer yn aber cuawc.

Singer of ceaseless song,
     nostalgic its voice.
On a journey intent, of hawklike
     motion,
eloquent cuckoo in Abercuawg.

11.   Gordyar adar gwly[b] neint.

       llewychyt lloer oer deweint.
       crei vym bryt rac gofit heint.

Clamorous the birds, streams
     wet,
moon shines, midnight cold,
raw my mind from torment of
     illness.

12.   Gwynn gwarthaf neint deweint.
          hir[14]
       keinmygir pob kywreint.
       dylywn pwyth hun y heneint.[15]

White the tops of streams,
     midnight long.
Honored each skilled one.
I owe payment of sleep to old
     age.
(or: I deserve the reward of sleep
     in old age.)

13.   Gordyar adar gwlyb gro.
       deil cwydit divryt divro.
       ny wadaf wyf claf heno.

Clamorous the birds, gravel wet,
a leaf falls, depressed the exile.
I do not deny that I am ill (a
     leper) tonight.

14.   Gordyar adar gwlyb traeth.
       eglur nwyvre ehalaeth
       tonn. gwiw callon rac hiraeth.

Clamorous the birds, beach wet,
sky bright, broad
the wave, withered the heart
     with longing.

15.   Gordyar adar gwlyb traeth
       eglur tonn tuth ehalaeth.
       agret[16] ymabolaeth.
       carwn bei kaffwn etwaeth.

Clamorous the birds, beach wet,
broad the wave of wide motion,
what is loved in youth,
I would love it if I could get it
     again.

16.   Gordyar adar ar edrywy ard.

       bann llef cwn yn diffeith.

       gordyar adar eilweith.

Clamorous the birds on Edrywy
     Hill.
Loud the voice of dogs in the
     wastelands.
Clamorous the birds a second
     time.

17.   Kynnteuin kein pob amat
       pan vryssyant ketwyr y gat.
       mi nytaf anaf nym gat.

Maytime, fair every growth.
when warriors rush to battle
I do not go, a blemish does not
let me.

18.   Kynteuin kein ar ystre.
       pan vrys ketwyr y gatle.

       mi nyt af anaf am de.

Maytime, fair upon the border,
when warriors rush to the
battleground,
I do not go, a blemish burns me.

19.   Llwyt gwarthaf mynyd breu
           blaen onn.
       o ebyr dy hepkyr tonn.

       peuyr pell chwerthin omkallon.

Gray the mountain-top, brittle
tips of the ash.
From estuaries flows a radiant
wave.
Laughter far from my heart.

20.   Assymy hediw penn y mis.

       yn y westua yd edewis.
       crei vym bryt cryt am dewis. [17]

For me today the end of the
month
In the lodging that he left.
Raw my mind, fever has chosen
(seized?) me.

21.   Amlwc golwc gwylyadur.
       gwnelit syberwyt segur. [18]

       crei vym bryt. cleuyt am cur.

Clear the sight of the watcher,
the secure one may perform
generosity. (?)
Raw my mind, illness wastes
me.

22.   Alaf yn eil meil am ved.

       nyt eidun detwyd dyhed.

       amaerwy adnabot amyned.

Cattle in a shed, a cup around
mead.
It is not the wish of the fortunate
for strife.
The enclosure (bond?
boundary?) of knowledge (is)
patience.

23.   Alaf yn eil meil am lat.

       llithredawr llyry llon cawat.

       a dwfyn ryt berwyt bryt brat.

Cattle in a shed, a bowl around
beer.
Slippery the paths, fierce the
shower
and deep the ford. Mind brews
treachery.

24. Berwit brat anuat ober.	Treachery brews wicked work.
bydant dolur pan burer.	There will be grief when it is cleansed.
gwerthu bychot yr llawer.	Selling much for a little (Or: "selling little for much"?)
25. Pre ator pre ennwir.[19]	(?) A (cauldron) will be prepared for the wicked
pan uarno douyd dyd hir.	when God judges on the long day.
tywyll vyd geu. goleu gwir.	Dark will be the false, bright the true.
26. Rerigyl [Kerigyl? Perigyl?][20] yn dyrchiuat	A chalice (danger?) exalted,
kyrchy[ny]at kewic.	The warrior in bandages.
llawen gwyr odywch llat.	Merriment of men over beer.
crin calaf alaf yn deiliat.[21]	Reeds withered, cattle in sheds.
27. Kigleu don drom y tholo.	I heard heavy roar of waves,
vann y rwng gra[ea]n a gro.	loud among sand and gravel.
krei vym bryt rac lletvryt heno.	Raw my mind from sorrow tonight.
28. Osglawc blaen derw. chwerw chweith onn.	Branching the top of the oak. Bitter the taste of the ash.
chwec evwr chwerthinat tonn.	Sweet the cow-parsnip, laughing the wave.
ny chel grud kystud callon.	The cheek does not hide the hurt of the heart.
29. Ymwng ucheneit. a dyuet arnaf	Many a sigh comes upon me
yn ol vyg gordyfneit.	according to my custom.
ny at duw da y diryeit.	God does not allow good to the unfortunate.
30. Da y direiet ny atter.	Good to the unfortunate is not allowed.
namyn tristit a phryder.	Only sadness and anxiety.
nyt atwna duw ar a wnel.	God does not undo that which he does.

31.   Oed mackwy mabklaf. oed   The poor sickman was a youth,
           goe[w]in gyuran.   was a daring nobleman (?)
       yn llys vr[e]nhin.   in the court of the king.
       poet gywl duw wrth edein.   May God be gentle to the
                                              outcast.

32.   Or a wneler yn derwd[y].   That which (despite which?) is
                                              done in an oaken house
                                              (house of prayer)
       ystiryeit yr ae derlly.   wretched is he who reads it.
       cas dyn yman yw cas duw vry.   An enemy of man below is an
                                              enemy of God above.

3. The *Song of the Old Man* "*Can yr Henwr,*" *Ifor Williams's title*

MS: RB; in Evans, column 1036.1–44. No clear demarcation can be found from the verses following (1037.1–1039.8), which are separated by Williams and given the titles *Gwen ap Llywarch a'i Dad, Marwnad Gwen, Pyll, Beddau, Talan, Dwc,* and *Kyny* (pp. 1–8). Follows *The Sick Man (Leper)* (above). Other editions and commentary: in Williams, CLlH, pp. 8–11; in Ford, PLlH, ed. and trans. on pp. 75–83 (not separated from *The Sick Man* verses); in Rowland, EWSP, pp. 415–18, trans. on pp. 474–76, comm. on pp. 540–48.

1.   Kynn bum kein vaglawc bum.   Before I was hunchbacked I was
          kyffes eiryawc   eloquent.
       keinmygir ny eres.[22]   Honored my marvelous (deeds?)
       gwyr argoet eiryoet am porthes.   The men of Argoed always
                                              upheld me.

2.   Kynn bum kein uaglawc bum   Before I was hunchbacked, I was
          hy.   bold.
       am kynnwyssit yg kyuyrdy.   I was welcomed in the tavern
       powys paradwys gymry.   Of Powys, paradise of the
                                              Welsh.

3.   kynn bum kein vaglawc bum
      eiryan.

    oed kymwaew[23] vym par. oed
      kyn[wan].[24]

    wyf keuyngrwm. wyf trwm wyf
      truan.

Before I was hunchbacked, I was
    fair.
Foremost was my spear, it was
    first to strike.
I am hunched, I am heavy, I am
    miserable.

4.   Baglan brenn neut kynhayaf.

    rud redyn melyn kalaf.

    neur digereis a garaf.

Little crutch of wood, it is
    harvest time.
Ruddy the ferns, yellow the
    stalks.
I have rejected that which I love.

5.   Baglan brenn neut gayaf hynn.

    yt uyd llauar gwyr ar lynn.
    neut diannerch vy erchwyn.

Little crutch of wood, this is
    winter.
Men will be talkative over drink.
Inhospitable is my bedside.

6.   Baglan brenn neut gwannwyn.[25]

    rud cogeu goleu ewyn.[26]

    wyf digaryat gan vorwyn.

Little crutch of wood, it is
    spring.
Ruddy the cuckoos, audible
    their plaintive cries.
I am unloved by a maiden.

7.   Baglan brenn neut kynteuin.

    neut rud rych neut crych egin.

    etryt[27] ym edrych yth yluin.

Little crutch of wood, it is
    Maytime.
Ruddy the furrow, curly the
    sprouts.
A grief to me to look at your
    bird-beak.

8.   Baglan brenn ganghen uodawc.

    kynhellych hen hiraethawc.

    llywarch lleueryd uodawc.

Little crutch of wood, steadfast
    branch,
may you support an old nostalgic
    man,
Llywarch, the constant talker.

9.   Baglan brenn ganghen galet.

    am kynnwyss y duw diffret.

    elwir[28] prenn kywir kynniret.

Little crutch of wood, hard
    branch—
the God of protection will
    receive me—
(you are?) called a proper wood
    for getting about.

10.   Baglan brenn byd ystywell.

Little crutch of wood, be manageable,

am kynhelych a uo gwell.
neut wyf lywarch lawer[29] pell.

support me better.
I am Llywarch of long-lasting talk
(Or: "I am Llywarch from afar").

11.   y mae heneint yn kymwed.[30]
a mi om gwallt ym deint.
ar cloyn a gerynt yr ieueinc.

Old age mocks me
from my hair to my teeth,
and the shaft that the youthful loved.

12.   Y mae heneint yn kymwed
a mi. om gwallt ym danned.
ar cloyn a gerynt y gwraged.

Old age mocks me
from my hair to my tooth,
and the shaft that the women loved.

13.   Dyr gwenn gwynt gwynn gne.
      godre
gwyd dewr hyd diwlyd bre.

Certain ("broad"?) the laughter of wind, white the sight of the wood's edge. Bold the stag, hard the hill.

eidyl hen hwyr y dyre.[31]

Feeble the old man, slow his arising.

14.   Y deilen honn neus kenniret
      gwynt.
Gwae hi oe thynghet.
hi hen eleni y ganet.

This leaf the wind whips away.

Alas for her fate!
old she, this year born.[32]

15.   A gereis.i. yr yn was yssy gas
      gennyf.
merch estrawn a march glas.

What I loved while a lad is hateful to me:
A maiden, a stranger and a gray horse.

neut nat mi eu kyuadas.

Not for me are they befitting.

16.   Ym[33] pedwar prif gas eirmoet.

My four chief hateful things in my life

yn gyueruydynt yn vnoet.

have assembled upon me at once:

pas a heneint heint a hoet.

a cough and old age, sickness and sadness.

17.	Wyf hen wyf unic wyf annelwic oer	I am old, I am solitary, I am deformed, cold (sad),
	gwedy gwely keinmic.	after (once having) a bed of honor.
	wyf truan wyf tridyblic.	I am miserable. I am bent in three.
18.	Wyf tridyblic hen wyf annwadal drut.	I am bent in three, old, I am foolish,
	wyf ehut wyf annwar.	I am simple, I am uncouth,
	y sawl am karawd nym kar.	those who loved me do not love me.
19.	Nym kar rianed nym kenniret neb.	Maidens do not love me. No one visits me.
	ny allaf darymret.	I cannot get about.
	wi a agheu nam dygret.	Woe is me, that death does not visit me.
20.	Nym dygret na hun na hoen gwedy lleas llawr a gwen.	Visits me neither sleep nor joy after the slaughter of Llawr and Gwen.
	wyf annwar abar wyf hen.	I am uncouth, feeble, I am old.
21.	Truan a dynghet a dynghwyt y lywarch	A wretched fate (is) the fate of Llywarch,
	yr y nos y ganet.	since the night he was born.
	hir gnif heb escor lludet.	Long labor without release from fatigue.

II. Gnomes and Nature Poems
4. *Maxims II*

MS: Cotton Tiberius B.i. (fols. 115a–b); follows *The Menologium* (fol. 112a), precedes *The Anglo-Saxon Chronicles* (fol. 115b). Editions: in Blanche Colton Williams, *Gnomic Poetry in Anglo-Saxon* (New York: AMS Press, 1966 1914), 126–29; in Elliott Van Kirk Dobbie, *The Anglo-Saxon Minor Poems* (New York: Columbia University Press, 1942), 55–57; in T. A. Shippey,

Poems of Wisdom and Learning in Old English (Cambridge: D. S. Brewer, 1976), 76–79.

1ᵃ	CYNING SCEAL RICE HEALDAN·	A King must a kingdom govern.
1ᵇ	ceastra beoð feorran gesyne·	A fortress will be from afar visible,
2ᵃ	orðanc enta geweorc·	cunning giants' work,
2ᵇ	þa þe on þysse eorðan syndon·	those which on this earth are
3ᵃ	wrætlic weallstana geweorc·	wondrous work of wallstones.
3ᵇ	wind byð on lyfte swiftust·	Wind will be in air swiftest.
4ᵃ	þunar byð þragum hludast·	Thunder will be at times loudest.
4ᵇ	þrymmas syndan cristes myccle·	The glories of Christ are great.
5ᵃ	wyrd byð swiðost·	Fate will be strongest.
5ᵇ	winter byð cealdost·	Winter will be coldest,
6ᵃ	lencten hrimigost·	spring frostiest,
6ᵇ	he byð lengest ceald·	it will be cold longest,
7ᵃ	sumor sunwlitegost·	summer sunniest,
7ᵇ	swegel byð hatost·	the sky will be hottest,
8ᵃ	hærfest hreðeadegost·	harvest most successful.
8ᵇ	hæleþum bringeð·	To men it brings
9ᵃ	geres wæstmas·	the year's fruits,
9ᵇ	þa þe him god sendeð·	that which God sends them.
10ᵃ	soð bið swicolost·³⁴	Truth will be most treacherous. (or: "most evident")
10ᵇ	sinc byð deorost·	Treasure will be most valuable,
11ᵃ	gold gumena gehwam·	gold, to each man,
11ᵇ	and gomol snoterost·	and an old one most sage,
12ᵃ	fyrngearum frod·	wise in former years,
12ᵇ	se þe ær feala gebideð·	who of many things has experience ere now.
13ᵃ	wea³⁵ bið wundrum clibbor·	Woe will be wondrously clinging.
13ᵇ	wolcnu scriðað·	The clouds glide.
14ᵃ	geongne æþeling sceolan	A young nobleman [acc.] must
14ᵇ	gode gesiðas·	good companions [nom.]
15ᵃ	byldan to beaduwe·	encourage to battle
15ᵇ	and to beahgife·	and to ring-giving.

16ᵃ	ellen sceal on eorle·	Courage must [be] in a prince.
16ᵇ	ecg sceal wið hellme·	An edge must against a helmet
17ᵃ	hilde gebidan·	in battle endure.
17ᵇ	hafuc sceal on glofe·	A hawk must on a glove,
18ᵃ	wilde gewunian·	wild thing, remain.
18ᵇ	wulf sceal on bearowe·	A wolf must [be] in a forest,
19ᵃ	ear[m] anhaga·	wretched lone-dweller.
19ᵇ	eofor sceal on holte·	A boar must [be] in a wood,
20ᵃ	toðmægenes trum·	strong of tooth-might.
20ᵇ	til sceal on eðle·	A good man must in homeland
21ᵃ	domes wyrcean·	achieve glory.
21ᵇ	daroð sceal on handa·	A spear must [be] in the hand,
22ᵃ	gar golde fah·	a shaft decorated with gold.
22ᵇ	gim sceal on hringe·	A gem must in a ring
23ᵃ	standan steap and geap·	stand high and wide.
23ᵇ	stream sceal on yðum·	A river must in the waves
24ᵃ	mecgan mereflode·	mingle with the seacurrent.
24ᵇ	mæst sceal on ceole·	A mast must [be] on a ship.
25ᵃ	segelgyrd seomian·	the sailcloth hanging.
25ᵇ	sweord sceal on bearme·	A sword must [be] in the lap,
26ᵃ	drihtlic isern·	magnificent iron.
26ᵇ	draca sceal on hlæwe·	A dragon must [be] in a barrow,
27ᵃ	frod frætwum wlanc·	wise, proud of adornments.
27ᵇ	fisc sceal on wætere·	A fish must in water
28ᵃ	cynren cennan·	bring forth kin.
28ᵇ	cyning sceal on healle·	A king must in the hall
29ᵃ	beagas dælan·	dispense rings.
29ᵇ	bera sceal on hæðe·	A bear must [be] on the heath
30ᵃ	eald and egesfull·	old and fearful.
30ᵇ	ea ofdune sceal	A river must downward
31ᵃ	flodgræg feran·	travel seagray.
31ᵇ	fyrd sceal ætsomne·	An army must [be] together
32ᵃ	tirfæstra getrum·	a troop of glorious ones.
32ᵇ	treow sceal on eorle·	Faith must [be] in a prince,
33ᵃ	wisdom on were·	wisdom in a man.
33ᵇ	wudu sceal on foldan·	A wood must on earth
34ᵃ	blædum blowan·	blossom with flowers.
34ᵇ	beorh³⁶ sceal on eorþan·	A hill must on earth
35ᵃ	grene standan·	stand [out] green.

35ᵇ	god sceal on heofenum·	God must in Heaven
36ᵃ	dæda demend·	judge deeds.
36ᵇ	duru sceal on healle·	A door must [be] in a hall,
37ᵃ	rum recedes muð·	broad mouth of the building.
37ᵇ	rand sceal on scylde·	A boss must [be] on a shield,
38ᵃ	fæst fingra gebeorh·	firm guard for fingers.
38ᵇ	fugel uppe sceal	A bird up above must
39ᵃ	lacan on lyfte·	play in the air.
39ᵇ	leax sceal on wæle·	A salmon must in a pool
40ᵃ	mid sceote scriðan·	with trout glide.
40ᵇ	scur sceal from heofenum·	A shower must from the heavens
41ᵃ	winde geblanden·	mixed with wind
41ᵇ	in þas woruld cuman·	into this world come.
42ᵃ	þeof sceal gangan þystrum wederum·	A thief must walk in dark weathers.
42ᵇ	þyrs sceal on fenne gewunian·	A troll must in a fen dwell,
43ᵃ	ana innan land·	alone in the land.
43ᵇ	ides sceal dyrne cræfte·	A woman must with secret craft,
44ᵃ	fæmne hire freond gesecean·	a girl, her lover seek
44ᵇ	gif heo nelle on folce geþeon·	if she does not wish [it] to thrive among her people
45ᵃ	þæt hi man beagum gebicge·	that a man might buy her with rings.
45ᵇ	brim sceal sealte weallan·	The sea must with salt surge,
46ᵃ	lyfthelm and laguflod·	air and sea currents
46ᵇ	ymb ealra landa gehwylc·	around each land
47ᵃ	flowan firgenstreamas·	flow, mighty currents.
47ᵇ	feoh sceal on eorðan·	Cattle must on earth
48ᵃ	tydran and tyman·	propogate and beget offspring.
48ᵇ	tungol sceal on heofenum·	A star must in the heavens
49ᵃ	beorhte scinan·	brightly shine
49ᵇ	swa him bebead meotud·	as God bade it.
50ᵃ	god sceal wið yfele·	Good must against evil.
50ᵇ	geogoð sceal wið yldo·	Youth must against age.
51ᵃ	lif sceal wiþ deaþe·	Life must against death.
51ᵇ	leoht sceal wið þystrum·	Light must against dark.
52ᵃ	fyrd wið fyrde·	Army against army,
52ᵇ	feond wiþ oþrum·	one enemy against another
53ᵃ	lað wiþ laþe·	foe against foe
53ᵇ	ymb land sacan·	for land fighting,

54ᵃ	synne stælan·	settling conflict.
54ᵇ	a sceal snotor hycgean·	Always must a wise man think
55ᵃ	ymb þysse worulde gewinn·	about this world's strife,
55ᵇ	wearh hangian·	a thief hang
56ᵃ	fægere ongildan·	justly to atone
56ᵇ	þæt he ær facen dyde·	for that crime he earlier committed
57ᵃ	manna cynne·	against mankind.
57ᵇ	meotod ana wat·	God alone knows
58ᵃ	hwyder seo sawul sceal·	where the soul must
58ᵇ	syððan hweorfan·	afterwards pass
59ᵃ	and ealle þa gastas·	and all the spirits
59ᵇ	þe for gode hweorfað·	which before God pass
60ᵃ	æfter deaddæge·	after the day of death;
60ᵇ	domes bidað·	judgment they await
61ᵃ	on fæder fæðme·	in the Father's embrace.
61ᵇ	is seo forðgesceaft·	The future is
62ᵃ	digol and dyrne·	dark and secret.
62ᵇ	drihten ana wat·	The Lord alone knows,
63ᵃ	nergende fæder·	the saving Father.
63ᵇ	næni eft cymeð·	None again come back
64ᵃ	hider under hrofas·	hither under roofs
64ᵇ	þe þæt her for soð·	who that here truly
65ᵃ	mannum secge·	to men may describe
65ᵇ	hwylc sy meotodes gesceaft·	what may be God's plan,
66ᵃ	sigefolca gesetu·	the saints' settlement,
66ᵇ	þær he sylfa wunað·	where He Himself dwells.

5. Let the Cock's Comb Be Red
Bidiau I, Kenneth Jackson's title, from RB: Bitieu

MS: RB. Edition: Evans, 1030.1–36. Precedes *Gnawt gwynt or deheu* ("Typical Is Wind from the South;" see below) and follows *Eiry Mynydd* ("Mountain Snow"), 1028.1–1029.31. Other editions: Kenneth Jackson, *Early Welsh Gnomic Poems* (Cardiff: University of Wales Press, 1935, 1973), 33–35. His translation of his reconstruction of *Bidiau I* can be found in ECNP, pp. 69–70; this he bases on the variants found in Jesus 3, *Bidiau II* of the Peniarth MS 102 and other much later manuscripts. See also the incomplete translation by Patrick K. Ford in *Sources and Analogues of Old English Poetry II*, eds. Daniel G. Calder, Robert E. Bjork, Patrick K. Ford, and Daniel F. Melia (Cambridge: Boydell and Brewer, 1983), 95.

1. Bit goch crib keilyawc.[37] bit
   annyanawl y lef
   o wely budugawl.
   llewenyd dyn duw ae mawl.

   Let the cock's comb be red; let
   his voice be strong (natural)
   from a triumphant bed.
   Rejoicing of man, God praises
   it.

2. Bit lawen meichyeit wrth
   ucheneit gwynt.
   bit tawel yn deleit.
   bit gnawt aflwyd ar diryeit.

   Let swineherds be joyful over
   sighing of wind.
   Let the serene be beautiful.
   Let disaster be typical for the
   perverse.

3. Bit guhudyat keissyat. bit gnifiat
   gwyd.

   a bit gynnwys dillat.
   a garo bard bit hard rodyat.

   Let the debt-collector be
   accusing. Let the contestant
   be savage.
   Let clothes be close-fitting.
   Whom the poet loves is a
   glorious giver.

4. Bit avwy unbenn a bit lew.

   [Bit lew unbenn a bit avwy][38]

   a bit vleid ar adwy.

   ny cheidw y wyneb ar ny rodwy.

   Let the king be ardent and be a
   lion.
   [Let the king be a lion and be
   ardent]
   and let him be a wolf upon the
   breach.
   He does not save face who does
   not give.

5. Bit vuan redeint yn ardal
   mynyd.
   bit yngheudawt oual.
   bit anniweir annwadal.

   Let racing be swift on the
   mountain's border.
   Let care be in the mind.
   Let the fickle be unfaithful.

6. Bit amlwc marchawc. bit
   ogelawc lleidyr.
   twyllyt gwreic goludawc.
   kyueillt bleid bugeil diawc.

   Let the knight be conspicuous.
   Let the thief be skulking.
   A woman deceives a rich man.
   A wolf befriends a lazy
   shepherd.

7.	Bit amlwc marchawc. bit redegawc gorwyd. bit uab llen yn chwannawc. bit anniweir deueiryawc.	Let the knight be conspicuous. Let the horse be rampant. Let the scholar be eager. Let the false one be unfaithful.
8.	Bit grwm biw. a bit lwyt bleid. esgut gorwyd yar heid. gwesgyt gwawn grawn yn y wreid.	Let cattle be hunched. And let the wolf be gray. Lively the horse after barley. Gossamer binds (presses?) grain in its root.
9.	Bit grwm bydar. bit trwm keu. esgut gorwyd yg kadeu. gwesgyt gwawn grawn yn y adneu.	Let the deafman be hunched. Let the hollow thing be heavy. Let the horse be lively in battle. Gossamer binds (presses?) grain deposited.
10.	Bit haha bydar. bit annwadal ehut. bit ynuyt ymladgar. detwyd or ae gwyl ae kar.	Let the deafman be "ha-ha"ing. Let the rash be unstable. Let the belligerent be foolish. Blessed is he on whom one looks who loves him.
11.	Bit dyfwn[39] llynn bit lynn gwaewawr. bit granclef[40] glew wrth awr. bit doeth detwyd duw ae mawr.	Let the lake be deep. Let the spear be sharp. Let the brave be a lion's claw (?) in battle. Let the fortunate be wise; God praises him/them.
12.	Bit euein alltut. bit disgythrin drut. bit chwannawc ynvyt y chwerthin.[41]	Let the exile be foreign. Let the daredevil be contentious. Let the fool be prone to laughter.
13.	bit wylyb rych. bit uynych mach bit gwyn claf. bit lawen iach. bit chwyrnyat colwyn. bit wenwyn gwrach.	Let the furrow be wet. Let legal security be abundant. Let the sick be plaintive. Let the healthy be joyful. Let the puppy be snarly. Let the woman be poison(ous).[42]

14. Bit diaspat aeleu.[43] bit ae[44] bydin.

    bit besgittor dyre.
    bit drut glew. a bit rew bre.

Let the shriek be mournful. Let the army be (?)
Let the lecherous be fattened.
Let the brave be fierce. Let the hill be frosty.

15. Bit wenn gwylyan. bit vann tonn.
    bit hyuagyl[45] gwyar ar onn.

    bit lwyt rew. bit lew callonn.

Let the gull be white. Let the wave be loud (high).
Let blood be a stain on the ash-spear.
Let frost be gray. Let the heart be bold.

16. Bit las lluarth. bit diwarth eirchyat.

    bit reinyat yghyuarth.[46]
    bit wreic drwc[47] ae mynych warth.

Let the vegetable-garden be green. Let the beggar be shameless.
Let the (?) be in battle.
Let the woman be bad with her many shames.

17. Bit grauangawc iar. bit trydar gan lew.
    bit ynvyt ymladgar.

    bit tonn callon gan alar.

Let the hen be clawed. Let there be tumult from the brave.
Let the quarrelsome be foolish. (Or: let the foolish be quarrelsome)
Let the heart be broken with grief.

18. Byt wynn twr. bit orwn seirch.

    bit hoffder llawer ae heirch.

    bit lwth chwannawc. bit ryngawc cleirch.

Let the tower be white. Let the harness be noisy.
Let many be asking for the coveted thing.
Let the eager one be gluttonous, let the decrepit be tottering.

6. Keen the Wind

MS: *The Black Book of Carmarthan*, 89.1–93.13. Edition: A. O. H. Jarman, *Llyfr Du Caerfyrddan* (Caerdydd: Gwasg Prifysgol Cymru, 1982), 62–64, where it is given the title *Mechyd ap Llywarch*, after Ifor Williams, and combined with verses from which I believe it forms a separate unit, defined at beginning and end by the elaboration and repetition that usually mark the reciter's preface and closure. It is interesting, though, how the descriptions of nature with the odd, occasional deictic reference give way gradually to direct addresses to Llywarch's sons and companions, starting with Cynddilig in stanza 19, and continuing in the attached verses to Pelis and Mechyd. Other editions: Ifor Williams, *Canu Llywarch Hen*, pp. 27–29, where he leaves only the "substantive" material that he wants to see as part of his saga of Llywarch. Jackson, ECNP, stanzas 1–22, 30, pp. 50–53; Ford, PLlH, pp. 120–31; Rowland, EWSP, pp. 454–57, trans. on pp. 501–3.

1. Llym awel llum brin. anhaut
        caffael clid.
    llicrid rid reuhid llin.
    Ryseiw gur ar vn conin.

    Keen the wind, bare the hill,
        difficult to get shelter.
    Ford spoiled, lake freezes:
    a man could stand on a single
        stalk.

2. Ton tra thon toid tu tir.

    goruchel guaetev rac bron banev
        bre
    breit allan or seuir.

    Wave after wave covers the
        shore.
    Very shrill the shrieks against the
        hill's heights.
    One can scarcely stand outside.

3. Oer lle. lluch rac brythuch
        gaeaw.

    crin caun calaw truch.
    kedic awel. coed in i bluch.

    Cold the place of the snowdrift
        (or lake?) before winter's
        storm.
    Reeds withered, stalks broken,
    wind angry, timber in a box (or:
        the wood bald).

4. Oer guely pisscaud yg kisscaud
        iaen.
    cul hit caun barywhaud.
    birr diuedit guit gvyrhaud.

    Cold the bed of the fish in the
        shelter of ice.
    Stag thin, grass bearded.
    Short the evening, trees bowed.

5. Ottid eiry guin y cnes.
    nid a kedwir oe neges.

    oer llinnev eu llyu heb tes.

    Snow falls, white its skin.
    Warriors do not go on their
        expeditions.
    Lakes cold, their color without
        warmth.

6. Ottid eiry guin. aren.   Snow falls, white the frost.
    segur yscuid ar iscuit hen.   Idle the shield on the shoulder
                                            of the old one.
    Ryuaur gui[n]t reuhid dien.   Very great the wind, it freezes
                                            grass.

7. Ottid eiry ar warthaw reo.   Snow falls on top of the ice.
    gosgupid gint blaen guit tev.   Wind sweeps the top of the
                                            dense woods.
    kadir yscuid ar yscuit glev.   Fine the shield on the shoulder
                                            of the brave.

8. Ottid eiry tohid istrad.   Snow falls, it covers the valley.
    diuryssint vy[48] keduir y cad.   My warriors rush to battle.
    mi nid aw. anaw nim gad.   I do not go. A blemish does not
                                            allow me.

9. Ottid eiry o dv riv.   Snow falls on the hillside.
    karcharaur goruit cul biv.   The steed a prisoner, cattle lean.
    nid annuyd hawdit hetiv.   Not like a summer's day today.

10. Ottid eiry. guin goror mynit.   Snow falls, white the mountain
                                            side.
    llum guit llog ar mor.   Bare the timbers of the ship at
                                            sea.
    meccid llvwyr llauer kyghor.   A coward fosters many councils.

11. Eurtirn am cirn. cirn am cluir.   Gold rims around horns, horns
                                            around the host.
    oer llyri[49] lluchedic auir   Cold the seas, bright the sky,
    bir diwedit blaen gvit gvir.   short the evening, treetops bent.

12. Gvenin igogaur guan gaur adar.   Bees in a shelter, weak the cries
                                            of birds.
    dit diulith.[50]   Bleak the day.
    kyssulwin kewin brin coch   White-cloaked the edge of the
        gwaur.   hill, red the dawn.

13. Guenin igodo. oer agdo rid.   Bees in shelter, cold the
                                            covering of the ford.
    reuid rev pan vo.[51]   Ice freezes when it may (lit: "is").
    ir nep goleith. lleith dyppo.   Despite any evasion, death will
                                            come.

14.   Guenin ig keithiv gwirtliv mor   Bees in captivity, green-colored
                                             the sea.
       crin calaw caled riv.   Withered the stalks, hard the
                                             hill.
       oer divlit. yr eluit hetiv.   Cold, bleak the world today.

15.   Gueni[n] ig clidur rac gulybur   Bees in shelter from the damp of
          gaeaw.   winter.
       glas cunlleit cev ewur.   Pale the stubble, hollow the
                                             cow-parsley.
       dricweuet llyvrder ar gur.   Cowardice a bad property in a
                                             man.

16.   Hir nos llum ros lluid riv.   Long the night, bare the moor,
                                             gray the hill,
       glas glan guilan in emriv.   pale the shore, the seagull in
                                             spray.
       garv mir glau a uit hetiv.   Bitter the seas, there will be rain
                                             today.

17.   Sich guint gulip hint.   Dry the wind, wet the path, (?)
          kinuetlauc[52] diffrint.   the valley.
       oer callet cul hit   Cold the brush, lean the stag.
       llyw in awon hinon uit.   Flood in the river, there will be
                                             fine weather.

18.   Driccin imynit avonit igniw.   Foul weather on the mountain,
                                             rivers contending.
       gulichid lliw llaur trewit.   Flood wets the ground of
                                             villages.
       neud gueilgi gueled ir eluit.[53]   It is the sea, looking at the
                                             world.

19.   Nid vid iscolheic. nid vid eleic[54] You are not a scholar, you are
          unben.   not a gray-haired lord.
       nyth eluir in dit reid.   You are not called in the day of
                                             need.
       och gindilic. na buost gureic.[55]   Alas, Cynddilig, that you were
                                             not a woman.

20.   Kirchid carv crum tal cum clid.   The hunched stag heads for the
                                                          end of the sheltered valley.

       briuhid. ia. brooet llum.   Ice breaks, bare the countryside.
       Rydieigc glev o lauer trum.   The brave escapes from many a
                                                          skirmish.

21.   Bronureith breith bron.   The thrush ("specklebreast") is of
                                                          speckled breast,
       breith bron bronureith.   breast speckled the "specklebreast."
       briuhid tal glan. gan garn carv   The bank's edge breaks with the
           culgrum cam.   hoof of a lean, stooping, bent
                                                          stag.

       goruchel awel guaet. vann.   Very shrill the loud-shouting
                                                          wind.

       breit guir or seuir allan.   Scarcely indeed can one stand
                                                          outside.

III. *Enigmas*
7. *Wulf and Eadwacer*; Henry Bradley's title

MS: *Exeter Book*, fols. 100ᵇ–101ᵃ; follows *Deor*, precedes *Riddle I*. Editions: Mackie, *Exeter Book*, 2:86.

1ᵃ	Leodum is minum	To my people it is
1ᵇ	swylce him mon lác gife	as if one gives them sport (offering? sacrifice?).
2ᵃ	willad hy hine aþecgan	They will (wish to?) receive him (consume him? take him in?)
2ᵇ	gif he on þreat cymeþ	if he comes in a troop (comes into peril?).
3ᵃ	ungelic is us·⁵⁶	Different (not so? unlikely?) it is for us.
3ᵇ	* * *⁵⁷	* * *
4ᵃ	wulf is on iege	Wulf is on an island,
4ᵇ	ic on oþerre	I on another.
5ᵃ	fæst is þæt eglond	Fast is the (that?) island
5ᵇ	fenne biworpen	by fen surrounded.
6ᵃ	sindon wælreowe	There are slaughter-fierce

6^b	weras þær on ige	men there on (the) isle.
7^a	willað hy hine aþecgan	They will/wish to receive/consume/take him in
7^b	gif he on þreat cumeð	if he comes in a troop/into peril.
8^a	ungelice is us	Different/not so/unlikely it is for us.
8^b	* * *	* * *
9^a	wulfes ic mines widlastum	For (?) my Wulf I, with far-wandering
9^b	wenum dogode[58]	hopes suffered.
		(Or: I thought of my Wulf with far-wandering hopes).
		(Or: I suffered the wide-wandering of my Wulf with hopes)
10^a	þonne hit wæs renig weder	When it was rainy weather,
10^b	ond ic reotugu sæt·	I tearful sat;
11^a	þonne mec se beaducafa	then (around?) me the battle-ready one
11^b	bogum bilegde	laid bows (or laid his arms?).
12^a	wæs me wyn to þon	It was a pleasure to me to some degree,
12^b	wæs me hwæþre eac lað·	It was neverless also hateful to me.
13^a	wulf min wulf	Wulf, my Wulf!
13^b	wena me þine	hopes of you
14^a	seoce gedydon	made me sick:
14^b	þine· seldcymas	your seldom visits,
15^a	murnende mód	a mourning spirit;
15^b	nales meteliste	not at all lack of food.
16^a	gehyrest þu eadwacer	Do you hear, Eadwacer?
16^b	uncerne earne[59] hwelp	Our eagle (wretched? owardly?) whelp
17^a	bireð wulf to wuda	Wulf bears to the woods.
17^b	* * *	* * *
18^a	þæt mon eaþe tosliteð	That (thing) one easily tears
18^b	þætte næfre gesomnad wæs	which never was joined:
19^a	uncer giedd geador·	our song/saying/poem/riddle together.

8. *Angar Kyfyndawt*
Title: as given in the manuscript. Meaning uncertain.

MS: *The Book of Taliesin*, facsimile edition, J. Gwenogvryn Evans, ed. (Llanbedrog: Issued to Subscribers Only, 1910), fols. 18.26–23.8. The only other really reliable edition and study of this poem is in the doctoral dissertation of Marged Haycock, *Llyfr Taliesin: Astudiaethau ar Rai Agweddau* (Aberystwyth: Prifysgol Cymru, 1983), pp. 89–120. Her invaluable translation and commentary are in modern Welsh, however, and consequently of difficult access to the novice. I think it important for readers new to Welsh to see a poem that is still in the closet, as it were, for which reason I risk my own very tentative translation of this dangerous and uncooperative text.

Bard yman ymae	A bard is here.
neu cheint aganho.[60]	I sang what he may sing.
kanet pan darffo.	Let him sing when he is finished,
sywedyd yn yt uo.	enchanter, wherever he may be.
5. haelon[61] am nacco.	The bountiful one who may deny me,
nys deubi arotho.[62]	who (what he?) might give it will not come to him
trwy ieith taliessin.	through the language of Taliesin,
budyd emellin.	the wizard of manna (or: "the beneficence of manna"?),
Kian pan darfu.	Cian, when perished
10. lliaws ygyfolu.	the host of his following.
bylleith bit areith auacdu.	Until death will be the oration of Afagddu.
neus duc yn geluyd.	May he bring skillfully
kyureu argywyd.[63]	songs of accusation (or "metered songs"?).
Gwiawn aleferyd.	It is Gwion who speaks,
15. adwfyn dyfyd.	from the depths it will come (or: "with deep grief"?).[64]
gwnaei ovarw vyw.	It would make from the dying living,

	Ac aghyfoeth[65] yw.	and it is landless (foreign?)
	gwneynt eu peiron	They would make their cauldrons
	averwynt heb tan.	which boiled without fire.
20.	gwneynt eu delideu	They would make their webs
	yn oes oesseu.	for ages upon ages.
	dydwyth dydyccawt.	Passionately will be brought
	odyfynwedyd gwawt.[66]	poetry out of a poet/prophet.
	neut angar kyfyndawt.[67]	It is a cruel bondage (or: "hostile alliance"?).
25.	pwy ychynefawt.	What is its tradition?
	kymeint kerd kiwdawt	So great is the poem of a nation
	adelis awch tafawt.	that caught your tongue.
	pyr na threthwch traethawt.	Why do you not deliver an oration?
	llat uch llyn llathrawt.	Drink above bright drink (or: "lake")
30.	penillyach pawb dybydaf yna gnawt.	Every little stanza I will make there a tradition.
	dwfyn dyfu ygnawt.	Deep came the tradition.
	neur dodyw ystygnawt.	A champion has come,
	Trydyd par ygnat.	the third spear of justice.
	Tri ugein mlyned	For sixty years
35.	yt portheis i lawrwed.	I bore laurels.
	yn dwfyr kaw achiwed.	In water, shut up with a multitude.
	yn eluyd tired.	In lands of lands
	kanweis am dioed.	I had a hundred servants,
	kant rihed odynoed.	a host of glory from them.
40.	kan yw[68] yd aethant.	Since they have gone.
	kan yw ydoethant.	Since they have come.
	kan eilewyd y gant.	Song of a poet of a hundred (host?)
	Ac ef ae darogant.	and he will foretell it.
	Lladon verch liant.	Lladon, daughter of Lliant,
45.	oedd bychan ychwant	her desire was small
	y eur ac aryant.	for gold and silver.
	Pwyr byw ae diadas	Who [are] the living who poured

	gwaet yarwynwas.	blood from a fair youth?
	odit traethator	A rarity is uttered.
50.	mawr molhator.	A great one is praised.
	mitwyf taliessin.	I am Taliesin.
	ryphrydaf y iawn llin.	I can compose a correct line.
	parawt hyt ffin	It will last until the end,
	yg kynelw elphin.	my praise of Elphin.
55.	Neur deirẏghet	Prizes will be given
	o rif eur dylyet.	from the measure of gold that is due.
	Pan gassat ny charat	When it was hated it was not loved.
	anudon abrat.	Concealments and treachery.
	nu ny chwenychvat	Now he does not desire
60.	trwy gogyuec angwawt.	through an unusual hindrance.
	Agogyfarchwy brawt	That which a brother (i.e., "monastic brother") might ask,
	wrthyf ny gwybyd nebawt.	no one would know from me.
	Doethur prif geluyd.	A sage of chief craft
	dispwyllawt sywedyd.	will teach magicians
65.	Am wyth am edrywyth	about wrath, about the trail,
	am doleu dynwedyd.	about the rings ("poetic tropes"?) of a poet/prophet,
	Am gwyr gwawt geluyd.	about true poetic craft.
	kerdwn[69] duw yssyd	It is God's minstrel,
	trwy ieith talhayarn.	through the language of Talhaearn,
70.	bedyd budyd varn.	the baptism of the diviner of judgment,
	Avarnwys teithi	who judged the qualities
	angerd vardoni.	of the gift of poetry.
	Ef ae rin rodes	He and his secret gave
	awen aghymes.	immeasurable Awen.
75.	Seith vgein ogyruen[70]	It is seven score ogyruen ("inspirations"?)
	yssyd yn awen.	that are in Awen.
	wyth vgein o pop vgein	Eight score of each twenty (?),

euyd yn vn.
yn annwfyn ydiwyth.
80.   yn annwfyn ygorwyth.
yn annwfyn is eluyd.
yn awyr uch eluẏd
ymae ae gwybyd
py tristit yssyd
85.   gwell no llewenyd.
Gogwn dedyf radeu
awen pan deffreu.
Am geluyd taleu.

am detwyd dieu.
90.   Am buched ara.
am oesseu yscorua.
am haual teyrned.
py hyt eu kygwara.
Am gyhaual
95.   ydynt trwy weryt
mawrhydic. sywyd
pan dygyfrensit[71]
awel uchel gyt.
pan vyd gohoyw bryt

100.   pan vyd mor hyfryt.
pan yw gwrd echen.[72]
pan echreuwyt uchel.
neu heul pan dodir.
pan yw toi tir.
105.   toi tir pwy meint.
pan tynhit gwytheint.
Gwytheint pan tynnit.
Pan yw gwyrd gweryt.
Gweryt pan yw gwyrd.
110.   Pwy echenis kyrd.
kyrd pwy echenis.
ystir pwy ystyrywys.
ystyrywyt yn llyfreu

brass in one.
In *annwfyn* the peacefulness.
In *annwfyn* the wrath.
In *annwfyn* below the earth,
in the air above the earth
is he who knows it,
what sadness is
better than happiness.
I know the lawful grades (?)
of Awen when it awakens.
(I know) about the gift of
    payments,
about fortunate days,
about pleasant life (conduct?),
about the ages of ramparts,
about equal kings,
how long their enjoyment,
about how equal
they are throughout the earth.
(About?) a great sage
That was given (by?)
a high wind together (?).
(I know?) why the mind will be
    proud,
why the sea will be pleasant,
why the skin (?) is strong,
why the firmament is elevated,
the sun why it is (so) placed,
what the roof of the land is,
the land's roof, what (its) size.
why rage tightens (?) pulls (?)
Rage, why it pulls;
why the earth is green,
the earth, why it is green,
who composed poems,
poems, who composed (them),
meaning, who contemplated (it),
(what) is contemplated in books,

pet wynt pet ffreu.

how many winds, how many brooks,

115.   pet ffreu pet wynt.

how many brooks, how many winds,

pet auon arhynt.

how many rivers upon courses,

pet auon yd ynt.

how many rivers go,

dayar pwy y llet.

the earth, what its width,

neu pwy ythewhet.

what its density.

120.   gogwn trws llafnawr

I know about the uproar of blades,

am rud am lawr.

around a bloody (one), around a hero.

gogwn atrefnawr

I know what is ordered

rwg nef allawr.

between heaven and earth;

pan atsein aduant

whence the echoes of the void;

125.   pan ergyr diuant.

whence the noise of perdition;

pan lewych aryant.

why silver glitters;

pan vyd tywyll nant.

why a brook will be dark;

Anadyl pan yw du.

breath, why it is black;

pan yw creu auu.

why liver is bloody,

130.   buch pan yw bannawc.

a cow, why it is horned,

Gwreic pan yw serchawc.

a woman, why she is loving,

llaeth pan yw gywn.

milk, why it is white,

pan yw glas kelyn.

why holly is green,

pan yw baruawt myn.

why a billy-goat is bearded,

135.   yn lliaws mehyn.

in a multitude of places

pan yw baruawt.

why it is bearded,

pan yw keu efwr.

why the cow-parsley is closed,

pan yw medw[73] colwyn.

why the puppy is unsteady (drunk),

pan yw lledyf ordwyn.

why the sledgehammer is flat-headed,

140.   pan yw brith i yrchwyn.[74]

why the roebuck-fawn is speckled,

Pan yw hallt halwyn.

why salt is salty,

Cwrwf pan yw ystern.

Beer, why it is bitter

pan yw lletrud gwern.

why the alder is red-speckled,

Pan yw gwyrd llinos.

why the linnet is green,

145.	pan yw rud egroes.
	neu wreic ae dioes.
	Pan dygynnu nos.
	py datweir yssyd yn eur lliant.
	ny wyr neb pan
150.	rudir y bron huan.
	lliw yn erkynan
	newyd anahawr ydwyn.[76]
	Tant telyn py gwyn.[77]
	coc py gwyn py gan.
155.	py geidw ydidan.
	py dydwc garthan[79]
	gereint ar arman.
	Py dydwc glein
	o erddygnawt vein.
160.	Pan yw per erwein
	pan yw gwyrliw brein.
	Talhayarn yssyd
	mwyhaf ysywedyd.
	Pwy amgyffrawd gwyd
165.	o aches amot dyd.[80]
	Gogwn da adrwc
	cwd a.cwd amewenir mwc.[81]
	mawr meint gogyhwc.
	kawc pwy ae dylifas.
170.	Pwy gwawr gorffennas.
	pwy abregethas.
	eli ac eneas.
	Gogwn gogeu haf.
	Auydant ygayaf.
175.	Awen aganaf.
	odwfyn ys dygaf.
	Auon kyt beryt.

why rosehips are red,
(why) a woman possesses them,[75]
why the night descends,
what change is in the golden sea.

No one knows why
its sunny breast is reddened.
Color (is) evident,
a new power brings it (?),
The harpstring, what (?) complaint?

the cuckoo, what plaint, what song?

what guarding of song?[78]
what ?? may bring
Gereint upon Arman?
what brings a gem
from a hard stone?
Why is the meadowsweet sweet?
Why are crows greenish-hued?
Talhayarn is
the greatest sage.
Who attacked sin
from (out of?) eloquence of the Covenant day?

I know good and evil.
To where is smoke dispersed,
a great quantity?
Whose cup poured it out?
What lord finished?
Who preached
(about?) (to?) Eli and Aeneas?
I know (where) the cuckoos of summer
will be in winter.

It is Awen that I sing.
From the deep I bring it,
A river though it lasts ("flows"?)

gogwn ygwrhit.   I know the expanse.
Gogwn pan dyueinw.   I know when it vanishes,
180. gogwn pan dyleinw.   I know when it fills,
Gogwn pan dillyd.   I know when it pours,
gogwn pan wescryd.   I know when it ebbs away.
Gogwn py pegor   I know what creatures
yssyd ydan vor.   are under the sea.
185. Gogwn ei heissor   I know their nature,
pawb yny oscord.   each in his/their band.
Pet gygloyt yn dyd[82]   How many ?? in a day?
pet dyd ym blwydyn.   How many days in a year?
pet paladyr yg kat.   How many shafts in battle?
190. pet dos yg kawat.   How many drops in a shower?
Atuwyn[83] yt rannawt gwawt   Well does poetry divide (share?)
nwy mefyl gogyffrawt.[84]   ??
Aches gwyd gwydyon.[85]   The rush of the trees of
                                       Gwydion.

gogwn i nebawt.   I know nothing (anything?):
195. py lenwis auon   why the river flooded
arpobyl pharaon.   upon the people of Pharaoh,
py dydwc rwynnon   what ?? may bring
baran achwysson.   a rage of lawsuits,
py yscawl odef[86]   what school ??
200. pan drychafafwyt nef.   why heaven was uplifted,
Pwy uu fforch hwyl   who the support of the shroud
                                       was
odayar hyt awyr.   from the earth up to the sky,
pet byssed am peir   how many fingers around a
                                       cauldron,
am vn am nedeir.[87]   around one, around a hand,
205. pwy enw y deu eir.   what the name (is) of the two
                                       words
ny eing yn vn peir.   not got in the same cauldron,
pan yw mor medwhawt.[88]   why the sea is intoxicating,
pan yw du pyscawt.   why a fish is black,
moruwyt uyd eu cnawt.   seafood will be their flesh,
210. hyd pan yw medysc.[89]   a stag, why it is a vessel for
                                       mead,
pan yw gannawc pysc.   why a fish is scaly,

pan yw du troet alarch gwyn.

pedrydawc[90] gwayw llym.
llwyth nef nyt ystyg.[91]

215.　py pedeir tywarchen
　　　ny wys eu gorffen.
　　　py voch neu py grwydyr hyd.

Ath gyfarchaf vargat vard.[92]

　　　gwr yth gynnyd escyrn nywl.[93]
220.　cwd ynt deu rayadyr gwynt.

　　　Traethattor vyg gofec.
　　　yn efrei yn efroec.
　　　yn efroec yn efrei.
　　　Laudatu laudate iessu.
225.　Eil gweith ym rithat.
　　　bum glas gleissat.
　　　bum ki bum hyd.
　　　bum iwrch ymynyd.
　　　bum kyff bum raw.
230.　bum bwell yn llaw.

　　　bum ebill yg gefel
　　　blwydyn ahanher.
　　　bum keilyawc brithwyn
　　　arieir yn eidin.
235.　bum amws ar re.
　　　bum tarw toste.
　　　bum bwch melinawr
　　　mal ymaethawr.
　　　bum gronyn erkennis.
240.　ef tyfwys ymryn.
　　　A mettawr am dotawr
　　　yn Sawell ym gyrrawr

　　　ymrygiawr olaw.

Why the foot of a white swan is black,
?? a sharp spear,
(why) the host of heaven does not submit (bow down?),
What the four turfs (lands?),
not known their ends,
what pig, or what stag wandering.
I greet you, wise bard (or bard of the Marches?),
a man, you have bones of mist.
Where are the two waterfalls of wind?
My speech will be uttered
in Hebrew in Hebraic
in Hebraic in Hebrew.
Laudatu laudate iessu.
A second time in forms:
I was a blue salmon,
I was a dog, I was a stag,
I was a buck on the mountain,
I was a trunk, I was a spade (?)
I was a drinking horn in the hand,
I was a peg in forceps
for a year and a half
I was a speckled white rooster among chickens in Edinburgh.
I was a steed in a herd,
I was a fierce bull,
I was the miller's billygoat,
like the nourisher (?)
I was a scaly grain,
it grew on a hill,
I will be reaped, I will be placed,
into the chimney I will be driven,
I will be torn from the hand,

	wrth vyg godeidaw.	by my bagfulls,
245.	Am haruolles yiar	a red-clawed hen received me,
	grafrud grib escar.	combed foe.
	Gorffowysseis naw nos	I rested nine nights
	yn y chroth yn was.	in her womb as a lad.
	bum aedvedic.	I was fully grown,
250.	bum llat rac gwledic.	I was drink before the Gwledig,
	bum marw bum byw.	I was dead, I was alive,
	keig ydym ediw.[94]	a branch went into me,
	bum y arwadawt.	I was on sediment,
	yracdaw bum tawt.	before it I was complete.
255.	Am eil kyghores[95]	A second time I was devoured:
	gres grafrud am rodes.	the red-combed one gave me wrath.
	odit traethattor	A rarity is uttered,
	mawr molhator.	a great one is praised.
	Mitwyf taliessin	I am Taliesin,
260.	ryphrydaf iawnllin	I can compose a correct line,
	parahawt hyt ffin.	until the end shall last
	yg kennelw elphin.	my praise of Elphin.

Textual Commentary

The Seafarer

1. L. 11ᵃ *hat*. Mackie (EB2) emends to *hate*.
2. L. 26ᵇ *feran*. Mackie emends to *frefran*, "console." The loss of a half-line makes it difficult to emend; an editor's impulse is to treat the lacuna as nonexistent and to make the syntax "complete." *Ferð* could be nominative or accusative.
3. L. 52ᵇ *gewitað*. Mackie emends to *gewitan* for the infinitive sense: "thinks to depart."
4. L. 63ᵃ *wælweg*. Mackie emends to *hwælweg*, and this is the accepted emendation; an unemended reading could yield the sense "way of slaughter," i.e., "death," which has been suggested by a number of scholars.
5. L. 67ᵇ *stonded*. Mackie emends to *stondað*.
6. L. 69ᵃ *tide ge*. Read *tidige*.

7. L. 99^b *hine*. Mackie: *him*.

8. L. 115^b *swire*. Generally emended to *swiþre*, "stronger."

The Sick Man (Leper) of Abercuawg

9. 2a. *benedyr* is unattested, and metrically inconsistent. Henry (EECL) suggests "cattle-track," emending to *beudyr*, which he derives from OIr *bóthar*, "lane, track." Rowland concurs (EWSP).

10. I have tried to avoid unnecessary use of the definite article since it is as underused in the Welsh poems as it is in the Old English. Nonetheless, our modern "the" has become such a generic indicator that its omission in certain constructions troubles readers. It is important to note that *llem awel* and other such phrases are not simply nouns and modifiers (literally: "keen wind") but zero-copula constructions, better expressed in translation by "wind keen" with its distorted word order. "Keen the wind" comes closest to expressing the force of these phrases while still retaining the cadence of other similar phrases like *byrr vyn teith* ("short my journey"). I retain some flexibility in my translations here and below.

11. 2c. Williams (CLlH) declares that *teryd* means "severely ill"; Rowland writes that it has connotations of heat.

12. 4b. *eichyawc*. GPC: "high, loud, sad." Here is an instance (as I explain in Chapter 5) where loudness and shrillness are associated with sadness.

13. 9a. *llonn dar*. Williams directs us to *cynffonloni*, "to wag the tail"; thus, "shaking"? Henry has "moving," Jackson (ECNP) "rustling." Rowland prefers "strong," recalling Williams's connection of *llon* with Ir. *lónn* ("fierce," "strong," "violent," "vehement," "eager," "bold"); Ford (PLlH) has "mighty."

14. 12a–c. This *englyn* has been universally disliked by scholars because it interrupts a series of *cymeriadau* (11–16), and has suffered much revision. Williams emends to *gwynn gwarthaf [bre gwlyb] neint deweint*, modeling it after 19a; Rowland emends to *gordyar adar gwlyb neint*, modeling it after 11a.

15. 12c. A highly ambiguous line. GPC *dylyaf* can mean either "to owe" or "to deserve," and *pwyth* (according to Williams) can mean either "payment" or "reward."

16. 15c. *agret* is possibly a scribal error for *a garet*. Williams emends to *fy angerd ym mabolaeth*, "my strength in youth." Rowland favors the less radical emendation.

17. 20c. *am dewis,* "chooses me"? Williams emends to *delwis,* the third singular preterite of *daly,* "to seize," so "seized me," basing his interpretation on the variant (*delwis*) in the copy made by Thomas Wiliems in BL Addl. MS 31055 (1596), and National Library of Wales (NLW) MS 4973b, which puts "l" in the margin (see Rowland, p. 623). These, too, are editorial decisions, albeit earlier ones.

18. 21b. A highly ambiguous line. As Rowland shows, *syberwyt* comes from L. *superbia,* "pride," but in non-Christian contexts, she states, the Welsh word can mean "generosity, nobility, charity," and other virtues of the highborn. Likewise, *segur* (from L. *securus*) also has a double meaning in the Welsh: "idle, vain, unconcerned," and "safe, secure, well-off." It is hard to know what tone is being taken here. *Gwnelit* may be the impersonal subj. form of *gwneuther,* "perform, do, make," or it may be the third-singular present indicative. So: "pride is exhibited (done, performed) by the idle (i.e., the rich)," or "the nobleman exhibits generosity."

19. 25a. An apparently corrupt line. The only certain word is *ennwir,* "wicked men," and *-ator* is the future impersonal ending to a verb. Williams has *peritor peir i ennwir,* "a cauldron shall be prepared for the wicked." Rowland suggests *pr[ou]ator pre[ssen] enwir,* "this wicked world will be tried." She also suggests *[K]reator [k]re[in] enwir,* "the wicked will be made prostrate," on analogy provided by the scribal error of Peniarth MS 111 in verse 26a (*Perigyl* for RB *Rerigyl,* probably *Kerigyl;* see the verse below). This seems to be stretching the interpretation.

20. 26a. *Rerigyl* is an apparently meaningless word, most probably in error for *kerigyl,* "chalice." *The White Book* has *perigyl,* "danger."

21. 26c *deilyat.* A scribal error for *eiliat,* "sheds."

Song of the Old Man

22. 1b. *ny.* Universally emended to *vy,* "my." *eres,* a nominal adjective?

23. 3b *kymwaew.* Generally emended to *kynwaew, cyn + gwaew,* "first spear."

24. 3b Ms: *kynn wyf keuyngrwm.* Generally emended to *kynwan,* "first to strike," *cyn + gwanu,* for the sake of both the rhyme and the sense. Pen Ms 111 has *oed kynvyf* with *kynwyf* crossed out and *cynwan* written above it.

25. 6a *gwannwyn* is also the word given in Pen Ms 111 and BL Addl. MS. 31055, but *gwayanwyn* in NLW 4973a and b. Williams (CLlH) and Roland (EWSP) emend to *gwaeannwyn.*

26. 6b *ewyn*. Williams: *e gwyn*, "their meal," from *cwyn* (GPC, 2). Roland: *ynghwyn*, "their lament," following analogies offered by Pen Ms 111 and NLW 4973a, from *cwyn*, "lament" (GPC 1). Ford (PLlH): "their cry." *Goleu*, literally "light," can also mean "evident," "audible."

27. 7b *etryt*. An error for *etlid*, "grief, sorrow."

28. 9c *elwir*. Understood by Williams to be *yth elwir*, "you are called"; with precedent set by Pen Ms 111.

29. 10c *llywarch lawer*. The site of some incendiary polemic. Williams emends *lawer*, "much, great," to *lauar*, "talk," taking 8c *lleueryd uodawc* as precedent: thus his *lauar pell*, "long-lasting talk." *Pell* has spatial as well as temporal connotations, meaning either "far" in distance or "long" of time, and Ford uses its spatial sense to support his theory that the figure of Llywarch is a construction of the poet, an ancestor and revenant who thus speaks "from afar."

30. 11a *y mae heneint yn kymwed*. Williams emends to *kymwed y mae heneint* to restore the end rhyme.

31. 13c *hwyr y dyre*. *Dyreaf* in the GPC means "run, hasten, return, rise, ascend, raise, lift up, lead, conduct, straighten." Rowland suggests that it is an ironic comment on the old man's failing sexual powers, a notion that is reinforced not only by the useless "shaft" mentioned in stanzas 11 and 12, but also by the image of the stag, a common medieval symbol for lust (Rowland, "Englynion Duad," *Journal of Celtic Studies* 3 [1981], 83): "one is tempted to see a play on words with the n. *dyre* GPC 'sexual desire, lust, wantonness,' etc.: 'slowly he rises'—'slow his lust.' "

32. Like the French, the Welsh have only two genders, and while it would be more linguistically correct here to translate *hi* as "it," the sense of personification that is conferred by the feminine gender has an astonishing effectiveness in English.

33. 16a *ym*. Rowland emends to *vym* for better sense.

Maxims II

34. 10ª *swicolost*, "most treacherous." As Cassidy and Ringler write, this is "not a very appropriate epithet for *sod*"; it is generally emended to *switolost* ("most evident"), on the grounds that *c* and *t* are commonly confused (*Bright's Old English Grammar and Reader*, ed. Frederick G. Cassidy and Richard N. Ringler, 3d ed. [New York: Holt, Rinehart and Winston, 1971], 374).

35. 13ᵃ Dobbie (ASMP) emends to *weax* "wax," as "*wea,* 'grief,' is hardly defensible."

36. 34ᵇ *beorh.* Possibly *beorc,* "birch."

Let the Cock's Comb Be Red

37. 1a–c. Translations of the *bidiau* pose numerous problems. How do we translate *bit* (from the copula *bod*)? What do we do with the departures from the syntactic formula (copula + predicate adjective + noun)? Do these variations matter? Which is the noun and which the adjective in the sections that are all substantive adjectives? Are these substantives plural or singular ("the feeble," "the querulous")? Definite or indefinite? *Bit* has futuric, imperative, and consuetudinal sense. Translators have generally favored the latter and render: "Cock's comb is (usually) red." I prefer "let the cock's comb be red" because it retains the imperative sense while suggesting the futuric and the habitual. In 2b, 3a, 7b, 10a, 14a, 16b and 16c we have a reversal of pattern (copula + noun + predicate adjective) which shows that early Welsh poetical structure is flexible and prescriptions hard to establish. I do not make any distinction in my translation.

38. 4a *Bit lew unbenn a bit avwy.* Variant in Jesus 3 that Jackson favors (EWGP).

39. 11a *dyfwn.* Jackson emends to *dwfyn,* "deep."

40. 11b. RB *granclef* is senseless. Jackson has a long note surmising how the mistake could have been made (see p. 63 for his reconstruction of putative manuscript transmission), and he proposes *bit guarant leu gleu,* "The brave is a dependable lion," as an emendation. *Guarant* is a borrowing from OF *garant,* "warrant," "voucher," but does not show the expected mutation. A more native possibility might have been *crafanc leu,* "lion's claw," "talon," extending the imagery of sharpness: "Let the brave be a lion's claw."

41. 12a–b. The scribe of *The Red Book* seems to have dropped a line from stanza 12 and conflated it with stanza 13; no capital demarcates the stanzas. Jackson emends by analogy with the *bidiau* in Jesus 3 and adds *bit lwm ros, bit tost kenin* ("The moor is bare, the leek is pungent").

42. The use of nouns as adjectives seems frequent in these verses.

43. 14a *diaspat.* GPC: *diasbad,* "shriek," *aele,* "sad." Predicate adjective and subject here seem to be reversed, as in 16c, unless we have in *diasbad* an

adjectival sense, as with *gwenwyn* in 13c: "Let the mournful be shrieking, crying out."

44. 14a *ae*. Unattested.

45. 15b *hyuagyl. magl*, from L. *macula*.

46. 16b *bit reinyat yghyuarth*. The meaning of these words is unclear: Following Joseph Loth (*Revue celtique*, 42, 372), Jackson derives *reinyat* from *rhan*, "distribution," i.e., "distributor," i.e., a "ring-giver," "prince"; or from *rhain*, "stiff," i.e., a prop or a support. GPC *cyfarth* has "a barking, a baying, a holding at bay (of an animal, etc.), resistance, opposition; battle, fight."

47. 16c *bit wreic drwc*. Again, predicate adjective and subject are reversed, unless we are to read "let the bad (one) be a woman with her many shames" as in "Alas, Cynddilig, that you were not a woman." It is possible to emend to *bit drwc wreic ae mynych warth* for consistency, and possibly better scansion, but the previous line (*bit reinyat yghyuarth*) also appears to reverse the pattern—if we could be certain what it meant.

Keen the Wind

48. 8b *vy*. Rowland (EWSP) suggests omitting *vy* for metrical reasons.

49. 11b *llyri*. Rowland translates "paths," following Jackson's suggestion that *llyri* is plural for *llwrw* (ECNP). *Llyry* is given in the GM as plural for *llyr*, "sea."

50. 12b This line is incomplete.

51. 13b *reuid rev pan vo*. Rowland's translation, "Ice forms when it may," is preferable to that by Jackson and Ford (PLlH) ("It freezes when there is frost") first, because the order for their construction (*pan fo rhew*) has been disturbed by the meter; and second, because it fits nicely with the "inexorability of natural processes" capped by the final line.

52. 17a *kinuetlauc*. Rowland emends to *kiuuetlawc*, following Jackson's suggestion (EWGP): *cywethlog, cyweithl*, MW *cywaethyl*, "to contend," hence his "brawling the watercourse (?)." Rowland suggests translating "quarreling, contending." This would be hard to attach to the noun *diffrint*, which looks like *dyffryn*, "valley."

53. 18c *neud guelgi gueled ir eluit*. Ford tentatively translates this difficult line: "It is the sea—seeing the world" (PLlH). Jackson: "The world is an ocean to look upon." Rowland outlines the debate about the use of *ir* with

gueled and suggests that it could be a mistake for *yn,* thus: "It is the sea which was seen (on) the earth." More interesting is her suggestion that *gueled* could be an error for *guellt,* "The grass of the world is the sea." The flood, however, suggests that the sea has come up onto earth in places where it doesn't belong; hence, it is "seeing the world."

54. 19a *eleic.* Uncertain; Rowland finds it occurring in the BT as "gray"; Jackson gives "skulking"; Ford has "gray-haired."

55. 19a–c. This stanza may be a later interpolation drawn from the Llywarch corpus. It sounds like a typical Llywarchian remonstration and only goes to show that the boundaries between these poems are indefinite.

Wulf and Eadwacer

56. 3ª *ungelic is us.* Lacking a subject. "*What* is unlike to us?" The common understanding that this refers to Wulf and the speaker is thrown in doubt by the fact that the dual form, to be found in lines 16ᵇ and 19ª, is not used here.

57. "3ᵇ" *Wulf and Eadwacer* does not conform to conventional Old English poetic lineation, and appears to have these missing (or extra?) "half-lines" here and in lines 8 and 17.

58. 9ᵇ *dogode.* Presumably from *dogian* ("to endure?"), a *hapax,* which is why editors have preferred to emend to *hogode,* from *hycgian* ("to think on, consider"), which takes the genitive. These two half-lines admit of so many possible interpretations that it is dizzying; the juxtaposition of *widlastum* and *wenum* lure us into thinking that they are a syntactic unit when this might not be the case.

59. 16ᵇ *earne.* "eagle." Mackie emends to *earmne* ("wretched," EB2), F. Holthausen to *eargne* ("cowardly" (*Anglia* 15 [1893], 188).

Angar Kyfyndawt

60. 2 *canho.* Third-person singular present subjunctive of *canu.*

61. 5 *haelon.* GPC: *haelioni,* "generosity, bounty." Haycock (LIT): could be either singular or plural, "dyn[ion] hael, arglwydd(i)," "bountiful man/men," "lord(s)."

62. 5 and 6. Haycock, following Williams in PT xv: "a lord who refuses me will never afterwards have anything to give."

63. 13 *argywyd*. GPC: *argywedd*, "injury, harm, wrong; accusation." Also possible: *ar* + *cywydd*, a type of meter, thus "metrically"? Haycock suggests "harmoniously, melodiously" (*gân ar fydr/gân bersain*), p. 96.

64. 15 *dyfyd*. GPC: *dyfydd*: "grief, sorrow, affliction."

65. 17 *aghyfoeth*. GPC: *anghyfoeth*, "without riches, landless, without estate." Haycock assumes *anghyfiaith* (GPC: "speaking or pertaining to a foreign tongue,' "foreign," "alien") which, she says, makes better sense if the adjective refers to the utterance and not the speaker. As so little of the poem makes sense, emendation seems futile. I suspect *gair mwys* may be in operation here as it is everywhere.

66. 23 *gwawt*. GPC: *gwawd*. One of the older terms in Welsh for "poetry," cognate with OE *wod* ("mad") and ON *óðr* ("poetry"). It now has connotations of "satire" or "mockery" in ModW; in the context of these poems, the harmful or biting quality of poetry was part of its power, which Taliesin makes much of.

67. 24 *angar kyfyndawt*. The phrase to which the poem owes its title. GPC: *cyfyngdod* gives the meanings "distress, straitness, bondage"; GPC: *cyfundod* has "concord, unity, agreement, combination; federation, league, association; community, society." Haycock prefers this second meaning to the first because the first is "not attested before the seventeenth century" and translates "Hostile Alliance." Nevertheless, its root, *cyfyng*, goes back to the thirteenth century: "narrow, close, restricted, confined; straitened, distressed, hard put to, perilous, perplexing; mean, paltry, ungenerous, suspicious, bigoted; precise, exact, strict." *Angar*: GPC: "hostile, cruel." A combination of *an* ("not") + *car* ("love").

68. 40 *kan yw*. Is this a variant of *canys/kanys*? ("since," "for" "because")? *Kan* can also mean "a hundred," "a host," but it ordinarily suffixes "t" before vowels. Other early meanings are "white," "shining," or "white dog"; "song," "object of song." The poet clearly seems to be playing on the double meanings of *can* and *cant* here and in the following lines.

69. 68 *kerdwn*. GPC has no entry; Haycock suggests reading *kerdwr*, which gives us "minstrel, musician" (*cerddwr*).

70. 75 *ogyruen*. An obscure word that seems to be associated with *awen* and traditions about poetic inspiration and Kerridwen's cauldron of poetry: *gwawt ogyrwen*, in BT:33.11.

71. 97-98 *pan dygyfrensit awel uchel gyt*. According to all the authorities, *dygyfrensit* (3rd sing. impersonal) comes from *dygyfrannu* ("to give, share,

distribute," *dy+ cyfrannu*), but both GPC and G cite only this line from BT by way of example. *Gyt* ("together") and its relationship to the rest of the phrase is obscure. Haycock suggests *cyd*, "a joining," "a coupling." The conjunction *pan* has a range of functions in Middle Welsh: as a relative, "that," or a relative interrogative, "from where," "why."

72. 101 *echen*. Haycock suggests *cen* (*llinach* [*arbennig*], "special family line").

73. 138 *medw*. Haycock translates *ffwndrus*, "stumbling," and adds *llyth. yn feddw* ("literally, drunk").

74. 140 *yrchwyn*. *Wyn* is a diminutive; it seems to have been applied solely for the rhyme.

75. 146 "(why) a woman possesses them." Haycock's translation; the meaning of the verb is unclear.

76. 152 *newyd anahawr ydwyn*. The syntax here is very unclear, as is the function of the initial "y." "Its bringing"?

77. 153 *py gwyn*. The syntax here with *py* seems darkly idiomatic. It could be translated "a harpstring, why does it complain?" or "a harpstring, what *its* complaint?"

78. 155 "what guarding of song?" Haycock: *Paham y mae'n dal at ei cherdd?* ("Why does it keep to its song?")

79. 156 *garthan*. "Wall, courtyard, camp, tent, booth," according to G.

80. 165 *aches*, GPC: "sea, tide, eloquence, flow of speech." Thus also: "from the rush (onslaught?) of the Day of Covenant." It is possible that this is an error for *o achaws*: "who attacked sin *on account of* the Covenant Day?" Haycock wonders if *amot dyd* could be "Day of Judgment." *Gwyd* could also be "trees": "Whom did the trees attack in the rush of the Day of Covenant?" This interpretation is not entirely off base, considering that the following poem, *Kat Godeu*, is about an army of trees.

81. 167 *cwd a.cwd*. Haycock suggests deleting the possibly redundant *cwd a* and emending to *cwd amwehenir mwc* "to where is smoke dispersed," the sense being "where does it go when it disappears?"

82. 187 *gygloyt*. Unattested. Representing a measurement of time?

83. 190 *Atuwyn*. GPC *addwyn*, "fine, fair, shapely; good, virtuous, seemly."

84. 192 *nwy mefyl gogyffrawt*. The line is completely obscure. *Gogyffrawt* could be "great attack" (*go + cyffrawd*).

85. Another reference, it would seem, to the *Kat Godeu*.

86. 199 *odef*. Unclear. Haycock cites G. *goddef*: "course, race, behavior, form, mode; to suffer, to bear, to allow; purpose, design, plot, scheme."

87. 204 *nedeir*. GM: *neddair*, "hand."

88. 207 *medwhawt*. Possibly *meddwol* (Haycock).

89. 210 *medysc*. Possibly *medd* + *dysg* ("bowl, cup, dish"). Haycock wonders if this refers to the horns of the stag being used as a vessel for dispensing mead.

90. 213 *pedrydawc*. Haycock: some kind of compound with *pedr(y)* ("four"?); "a reference to the shape of the spear?"

91. 214 *ystyg*. GPC: *estyngaf*: "to fold, to bend, to stoop, to bow down to, to submit."

92. 218 *vargat vard*. GPC: *bargadfardd*, citing this line, offers the meaning "wise bard, sage," conjecturing that *bargad* is a compound of *bar* ("foremost") and *cad* ("wise, sharp"). G. suggests *cyffin-fardd* ("border bard," "bard of the marches"), deriving *bargat* from *bargawt*, *bargod* ("edge, border, marches").

93. 219 *escyrn*. Plural of *asgwrn*, "bone"; *nywl. niwl*, "fog. mist."

94. 252 *ydym ediw*. Haycock: "has gone into me" (if *ediw* is *ethyw*). She suggests that what is described here is the process of making beer.

95. 255 *kyghores*. The editors of GPC emend to *kyghnoes* < *cynghnoi*, "gnaw, devour," and Haycock follows suit. The emendation makes sense in context.

Name and Title Index

Abelard, Peter, 77–78
Adams, John C. 222n5
Addison, Joseph, 100–101
Aelfwine, 235
Afagddu, 203, 212
Afallanau, 182
Alan of Lille, 8, 51
Alcuin, 100n9, 105, 122, 123
Aldhelm, 232
Allen, Michael J. B., 93n82
Altman, Robert, 21
Ambrose (Saint), 122
Anderson, S. Olof, 39n26, 40
Andreas, 66, 72, 75–76, 81–82, 156–57
Andrew, S. O., 41, 42, 43, 74, 77n53
Aneirin, 54n59, 58–59, 194, 202, 218
Angar Kyfyndawt, 30, 188, 210–15, 223, 236, 284–92, 299–302
Anglo-Saxon Chronicle, 106, 271
Aranovsky, Olga, 217n94
Aristotle, 77, 98, 100, 106–7, 114, 228

Arjuna, 209
Armes Prydein, 200n46
Arthur (King), 191, 195
Attridge, Derek, 187, 189n11
Auerbach, Eric, 79n58, 126n25
Augustine of Hippo (Saint), 40n27, 122, 190
Augustine, Pseudo-, 93n83
Austin, J. L., 78n57

Bachelard, Gaston, 149, 177
Baglawc Bydin, 171, 173
Bakhtin, Mikhail, 213
Baldwin, Ralph, 41n30
Bambas, Rudolph C., 55n60
Bardic Grammars. See *Gramadegau'r Penceirddiaid*
Barley, N., 107
Bartrum, Peter C., 8n9
Battle of Maldon, 66, 87, 161
Battlefield of Bards. See *Buarth Beird*
Baum, Paul F., 239

Beddau, 268
Belanoff, Patricia, 55
Bell, Idris, 33n8, 70n23, 195n29
Benson, Larry D., 80n62
Benveniste, Émile, 125n19
Beowulf, 22, 61, 66, 72, 83, 92, 131–33, 151, 159, 241, 245
Bergin, Osborn, 182n42
Bergman, Ingmar, 21
Bessinger, Jess B., Jr., 45n41, 66n15, 223n8
Bhagavat-Gita, 209–10
Bidiau, 31, 106, 168, 171–72, 297
Bidiau I, 109–10, 164, 172, 173, 275–78, 297–98
Bidiau II, 106, 109–10, 170, 275
Bjork, Robert E., 276
Black Book of Carmarthen, ix
Blackburn, F. A., 231
Blickling Homilies, 40n27, 41
Bloch, R. Howard, 5n3, 79n59
Bloomfield, Morton W., 11, 193n25, 205
Boethius, 77, 93, 122–23
Bollard, John, 195n28
Book of Aneirin, 54n59, 193n22
Book of Taliesin, 14, 30, 63, 188, 190, 192–93, 194, 199, 202–4, 206, 207n70, 210, 218, 232
Bosworth, Joseph, 225n9
Bracton, Henry, 246n33
Bradley, Henry, 222
Breudwyt Ronabwy, 191, 194–95
Brooke-Rose, Christine, 23, 154
Brooks, Kenneth, 157
Brown, George H., 222n5
Buarth Beird, 188
Burke, Carolyn, 10n23

Cadyrieith, 195
Caesarius of Arles, 93n83
Calder, Daniel G., 88, 93n82, 130n37, 137n45–47, 201n49, 276
Campbell, Joseph, 205
Can yr Henwr, 8, 17, 20, 51, 53–54, 144–48, 167, 173, 179, 263, 268–71, 295–96
Canu Aneirin, 63–64, 114
Canu Llywarch Hen, 7, 11, 30, 33–34, 48, 52, 59, 64, 85, 88, 108, 172, 175, 199, 243, 252, 279
Canu y Meirch, 204
Capps, E., 207n72
Carmina Burana, 129
Carney, James, 216n89
Cassidy, Frederick G., 92n81, 296
Cena Cypriani, 213
Cerquiglini, Bernard, 12

Cerridwen, 192, 203, 212
Chadwick, H. Munro, 107, 110n42
Chadwick, Nora, 9, 46n44, 47, 107, 110n42, 181n34, 206n70
Chalcidius, 234–35
Chapman, Raymond, 79n57
Charlesworth, M. P., 46n44
Chaucer, Geoffrey, 58; *Canterbury Tales*, 100
Chomsky, Noam, 77–78
Claf Abercuawg, 8, 9, 16, 17, 30–31, 36–37, 47, 48–50, 53–55, 61, 82, 86, 113, 117, 144–48, 163, 167–68, 171, 172, 175, 179, 182, 183–84, 217, 218–19, 249, 251–52, 263–68, 294–95
Clancy, Joseph P., 68
Clark, S. L., 162n19, 176n24
Clarke, Basil, 202, 217n90–91
Clemoes, Peter, 100n9, 123, 130–32
Cynddylan, 59–61, 62, 70
Colish, Marcia, 190
Columba (Saint), 93, 179–81
Conybeare, John Josias, 9, 71n26
Conybeare, William D., 9n16, 71n26
Crane, L. Ben, 77n51
Creed, Robert F., 45n41, 84n71, 223n8
Culhwch ac Olwen, 191
Curtius, Ernst, 79n58
Cynddelw, 119
Cynewulf, 74, 221–22
Cynddilig, 279

Dafydd ap Gwilym, 58
Damico, Helen, 55n61
Damon, Phillip, 129–30
Davies, J. Glyn, 32, 37, 38–39, 93n84, 108n33, 112, 114
Davies, John, 101n16
Dawson, P. MacGregor, 41n30, 115–17, 152, 153
de Bruyne, Edgar, 126n23, 196
de Rijk, L. M., 77n50
Dennett, Daniel, 103n24
Deor, 47n49, 61, 66, 68, 221, 239, 282
Dialogue Between Tristan and Gwalchmai, 19, 35
Dickens, Bruce, 40n28
Diodorus Siculus, 190–91, 207
Dobbie, Elliot Van Kirk, 271, 297
Dream of the Rood, 22, 92
Dumézil, Georges, 205
Dunn, Charles W., 11, 193n25, 205
Dwc, 268

Earl, James W., 5
Eco, Umberto, 125n19

Edgerton, Frank, 210n79
Edward the Confessor, 246
Edwards, H. J., 207n71
Ehrhardt-Siebold, Erika von, 234
Ehrisman, G., 40n27
Eiry Mynydd, 165–66, 187, 275
Eisenstein, Sergei, 21–22
Elegy on Cynddylan, 59–62, 64–65, 70
Elegy on Gwen. See *Marwnad Gwen*
Elegy on Urien Rheged, 70–71
Elene, 66
Eliade, Mircea, 119, 120, 178–79
Eliot, T. S., 102n18
Elledge, Scott, 101n13
Elphin, 70–71, 203, 204, 212
Emerson, Caryl, 213n84
Empedocles, 207–8, 234–35
Empson, William, 21
Eormonric (King), 235
Ephesians, 158
Eudeyrn. *See* Outigern
Evans, D. Simon, 7n7, 8n10, 74n36,
    193n24
Evans, H. Meurig, 12n26
Evans, J. Gwenogvryn, 188n4, 191n17, 263,
    275, 284
Evert, Richard, 110n42, 120–22
Exeter Book, x
Exhortation to Christian Living, 52
Exodus (Poem), 127

Father's Instruction to His Son, 256
Fillmore, Charles, 125n19
Finn, 181, 203, 237
Fleck, Jere, 207n70
Fleishman, Suzanne, 5n3, 79n59, 85
Foley, John Miles, 80n61, 84, 201n47
Fontes Anglo-Saxonici, 93n82
Ford, Patrick K., 7n8, 8n11, 9, 26n26, 34n10,
    35, 37n15, 49, 63n7, 107, 112, 191n19,
    203n55, 204, 207n70, 217n92, 218, 263,
    268, 276, 279, 294, 296, 298–99
"Foweles in the frith," 18
Fox, Cyril, 40n28
Frank, Roberta, 197
Frantzen, Allen, 4, 5n2, 52–53, 80n61, 93n82
Frazer, Ray, 99n3
Freese, John Henry, 228n11
Frese, Dolores Warwick, 41n29, 110n42,
    120n4, 223n5, 252n1
Fry, Donald K., 81n63, 222n5
Furbank, P. N., 101n14, 102

Geirfa Barddoniaeth, 188n5
Geirrod, 237

Geoffrey of Monmouth, 202, 216–17
Geoffrey of Vinsauf, 99
Geriadur Mawr, x
Geriadur Prifysgol Cymru, x
Giles, Richard F., 222n5
Giraldus Cambrensis, 200
Glosecki, Stephen, 207n70
Gneuss, Helmut, 155n14
Gnodiau, 31, 97, 106, 145, 275
Godden, M. R., 155n14
Gododdin, 12, 54n59, 57, 58, 63, 88–89, 105,
    174–75, 192, 193n24, 218
Goethe, Johann Wolfgang, 189
Gora, Thomas, 10n23, 213n84
Gordon, Ida L., 9, 25n25, 39n26, 47
Gorhoffedd, 37, 198
Gorwyn Blaen, 145, 167, 169, 171, 172, 173,
    263
Gramadegau'r Penceirddiaid, 99–100
Graves, Robert, 13n30, 205
Gray, Thomas, 205, 218
Green, Martin, 223n5
Greene, David, 59n6, 207n70
Greenfield, Stanley B., 41, 43–44, 84, 90n79,
    110n42, 120–22, 222n5
Gregory the Great, 162
Grendel, 245
Grímnismál, 237
Grosjean, P., 114n47
Gruffydd, Elis, 191, 203, 235
Grunmann-Gaudet, Minnett, 151n8
Gummere, Francis B., 82n67, 228, 230
Guthlac, 66
Guthlac A, 75n39, 76
Gwalchmai, 19, 37, 198–99
"Gwarchen Maeldderw," 192
"Gwarchanau," 114
Gwen (son of Llywarch), 34
Gwen ap Llywarch a'i Dad, 8, 174, 217n92,
    268
Gwion, 212–13
Gwion, Bach, 203, 214
Gwydden Astrus, 191

Hahn, Thomas, 5n3
Hall, Edward T., 149–50
Hamnett, Ian, 228
Hanes Taliesin. See Gruffydd, Elis
Hari, 208
Harries, W. Gerallt, 99n7
Hartshorne, C., 26n28
Haycock, Marged, 63n11, 193n24, 204,
    210n81, 284, 299–302
"Hearth Stanzas," 70–71
Heledd, 59, 70

Henry, P. L., 9, 20, 25n22–24, 47, 48–49, 123, 179, 263, 294
Hermann, John, 5n3
Herren, Michael W., 114n47, 188n7, 196n34
Herrmann, Claudine, 178
Hess, Linda, 190n12, 210
Hill, Joyce, 211
Hisperica Famina, 114, 188–89, 190, 196
Hitchcock, Alfred, 21
Hollowell, Ida, 236
Holquist, Michael, 213n84
Homer, 80
"Hostile Alliance." See Angar Kyfyndawt
Howard, Donald, 5
Howe, Nicholas, 120
Hsu Kan, 20n3
Hugh of Saint Victor, 98n2
Hugo, Victor, 189
Husband's Message, 47, 68, 238–40
Huyghe, René, 126
Hywel ap Owein, 198–200
Hywel Vychan, 252

Imram Brain, 225n9
Irigaray, Luce, 10, 187
Iser, Wolfgang, 24, 78n56
Isidore of Seville, 100, 214
Isis, 114, 208

Jackson, Kenneth H., 9n15, 19, 34n9, 35, 36, 37, 47n44, 59n6, 70n25, 82–83, 107, 108n34, 110, 112, 113, 114–15, 166n20, 170n21, 181, 183, 205–6, 263, 275, 279, 294, 297–99
Jakobson, Roman, 218–19
Jardine, Alice, 10n23
Jarman, A.O.H., 7n7, 12, 54n59, 59n6, 73n32, 112, 113, 182n45, 193n22, 202n52, 278–79
Jarvella, Robert J., 125n19
Jesus Christ, 192, 194, 232
John, Gospel of, 154n11
Johnson, Mark, 155n13
Johnson, Samuel, 101
Jolas, Maria, 177n25
Jones, Charles W., 67n16, 79n58, 126
Jones, E. D., 73n32
Jones, E. J., 99n7
Jones, Horace Leonard, 207n72
Jones, Owen, 7n8
Jones, Robin F., 151n8
Jones, T. Gwynn, 195
Jowett, B., 190n13
Judgment Day II, 52
Judith, 92

Juliana, 46, 66
Julius Caesar, 207
Juvencus, 58–59

Kabir, 190, 210
Kahrl, Stanley J., 66n15
Kalan Gaeaf, 171
Kanu y gwynt, 232n21
Kat Godeu, 204, 205, 210, 214–15, 232, 235, 236, 301
Keen the Wind. See Llym Awel
Kelly, Fergus, 207n70
Ker, W. P., 29–30, 67n16
Kijo, Murakami, 20n4
Kintevin, 82
Kittay, Jeffrey, 85n76
Klaeber, Fr., 72n29
Klar, Kathryn, 54n59, 57n1, 63–64, 114n48
Klein, W. F., 252n1
Klein, Wolfgang, 125n19
Kline, Nancy, 178n27
Kluge, F., 39
Koch, John T., 59n6, 193n24
Kolve, V. A., 98n2, 100
Krapp, George Philip, 75n42
Kristeva, Julia, 10, 55, 68, 213
Kusatao, Nakamura, 23
Kyny, 268

Lakoff, George, 102n23, 155n13
LeMar, Virginia A., 101n16
Lapidge, Michael, 155n14
Lawrence, W. W., 66n14, 222, 223n6, 240n29
Lebor Gabala Erinn, 201, 208n76
Lehmann, Ruth P., 20n2, 179n30–31, 181n33–35
Leonard, William Ellery, 208n75
Lerer, Seth, 229
Leslie, Roy F., 40n26, 72–73
"Let the Cock's Comb Be Red." See Bidiau
Lewis, C. S., 5n5, 13, 172
Lewis, Richard A., 127n26
Lewis, Saunders, 69
Leyda, Jay, 22n8
Leyerle, John, 127n26
Life of St. Gregory, 124n14
Liljegren, S. B., 41–42
Liu, Wu-Chi, 20n3
Lloyd, Myrddin, 196
Lloyd-Jones, J., 12n26, 195–96
Llyfyr Du Caerfyrddin, 73
Llym Awel, 8, 31, 32, 62–63, 83, 106, 108–9, 112–13, 166, 170–71, 173, 174, 278–82, 298–99
Llywarch Hen, 7–8, 9, 31, 32, 34, 48, 50–52,

54, 58, 59, 70–71, 146, 148, 164, 166,
    167, 174, 182, 199, 207n70, 217n92,
    219, 222n5, 299
Lo, Irving Yuching, 20n3
Lord, Albert B., 80n61
Lord's Prayer (poem), 52
Lot, Ferdinand, 54n59, 202n50
Loth, Joseph, 298
Lovely the Tips of the Ash, 31
Lycophron, 193
Lynch, David, 21
Lyons, John, 125n19

Mabinogion, 83, 191
MacCallister, R.A.S., 201n48, 208n76
Mackie, W. S., 43, 224n10, 256, 282, 293–94,
    299
McLuhan, Marshall, 155n13
Macpherson, James, 13
MacRae, Charles W., 209n78
Maelgwn (King), 191, 203, 212
Magness, J. Lee, 24
Magoun, Francis P., 80n61
Mallarmé, Stéphane, 189
Malone, Kemp, 222n5, 243
Mark, Gospel of, 24
Marwnad Gwen, 34, 268
Mary (Virgin Mary), 192n21
Mary Magdalene, 192
Matejka, Ladislav, 218n97, 219n98
Maxims I, 45–46, 106, 110–11, 114, 115–16,
    128, 143, 150, 151–52, 160, 164–165,
    221, 236, 240–41, 243–44, 245–46, 248
Maxims II, 15, 106, 108, 110, 114, 115–16,
    120–22, 128, 148, 153–54, 164–65, 244–
    45, 248, 271–75, 296–97
May, Herbert G., 233n22
Mechyd, 279
Mechyd ap Llywarch. See *Llym Awel*
Meiser, C., 77n50
Melia, Daniel F., 201n49, 206n70, 276
Menologium, 271
Merleau-Ponty, Maurice, 15
Merlin. *See* Myrddin
Metzger, Bruce, 233n22
Meyer, Kuno, 179n30, 182n42, 207n74,
    208n76–77, 225n9
Miao, Ronald C., 20n3
Mitchell, Bruce, 43n36, 72n27
Mitchell, W.J.T., 97, 100n11–12
Mo Ling (Saint), 181
Morgan, T. J., 110, 112, 117, 118n55
Morris, E. P., 72n28
Morris-Jones, John, 58, 59n6, 64n13, 93n84
Mountain Snow, 31

Murphy, Gerald, 93n84
Myfyrian Archaeology, 196
Myrddin, 181n34, 182–83, 188, 200, 202,
    216–17

Nagy, Gregory, 81
Nagy, Joseph Falaky, 181n34 and 36–37, 182,
    206n70, 217
Nennius, 54n59, 59n5, 202, 203, 212
Newman, Randy, 21
Nichols, Stephen G., 79n59
Nicholson, Lewis E., 41n29, 110n42, 120n4,
    252n1
Nickel, Gustav, 237n27
Nims, Margaret F., 99n4
Nutt, Alfred, 207n74, 208

Odin, 208, 237
O Hehir, Brendan, 54n59, 57n1, 63–64
Oianau, 182
O'Keefe, J. G., 179n29
O'Keefe, Katherine O'Brien, 67n17
Old Woman of Beare, 51, 179
Oldfather, C. H., 190n16
Olsen, Alexandra Hennessey, 55n60, 80n61
Ong, Walter, 11n24, 80n61, 84–85, 155n13
Opland, Jeff, 83
O Riain, Pádraig, 179n29
Ortony, A., 155n13
Orwell, George, 101–2
Osborne, Marijane, 223n5
Outigern, 59n5, 202n50
Overing, Gillian, 5n3, 22, 26n28
Owain, 70–71, 198

Page, T. E., 190n16
Parry, John J., 195n31
Parry, Milman, 80
Parry, Thomas, 109, 113, 195n29
Pasternack, Carol Braun, 22, 67n16, 127n26
Patterson, Lee, 5n3
Patzig, H., 222n3
Paul (Saint), 158
Pearsall, Derek A., 123n10
Peirce, Charles S., 26n28
Pelis, 279
Penitent's Prayer, 48
Phillips, Michael, 155n14
Pilch, Herbert, 9, 47–48, 68, 85–86, 218,
    240n29
Pindar, 189
Pinsker, Hans, 231n19
Plato, 100, 190, 234
Plummer, Charles, 212
Polanski, Roman, 21

Pomorska, Krystyn, 218n97, 219n98
Porter, Catherine, 10n23
Pound, Ezra, 102
Pratt, Mary Louise, 79n57, 189n11
Pratt, William, 102
Priedeu Annwn, 63, 188–89, 193, 194, 204
Proverbs, 106, 108
Psalms, 154n11
Pughes, William Owen, 7n8
Pwyll Pendeuic Dyuet, 74n33
Pyll, 268
Pythagorus, Pythagorean, 207

Quintilian, 196

Red Book of Hergest, xi
Reddy, Michael, 155n13
Rees, Abraham, 101, 103
Remly, Lynn, 120
Renoir, Alain, 45n41, 80n61, 223n8
Resignation A, 48, 52, 157–58
Resignation B, 48, 52, 151, 154
Rhyming Poem, 85
Rhys, John, 191n17
Richards, Melville, 191n18, 195n28
Riddle 1, 282
Riddle 3, 229–30
Riddle 24, 227
Riddle 29, 230
Riddle 30, 230–32
Riddle 40, 232–33
Riddle 42, 225–29, 241
Riddle 60, 226, 238–39
Riddle 73, 234–35
Rieger, M., 39, 141
Riffaterre, Michael, 23
Ringler, Richard N., 92n81, 296
Roberts, Brynley F., 58n2, 63n11, 64n12,
    84n70, 114n48
Robertson, D. W., Jr., 54, 190n14
Robinson, Fred, 22, 43n36
Robinson, James M., 209n78
Rollman, David, 236
Roudiez, Leon S., 10n23, 213n84
Rowland, Jenny, 7n8, 9, 33n7, 49–50, 59n6,
    63n7–8, 64n12, 166n20, 174n22, 179,
    217n92, 263, 268, 279, 294–95, 298–99
Ruin, 61, 70, 71, 72, 86–88, 90, 137–39, 252
Russo, Joseph A., 81n65
Rynell, Alarik, 76, 93

Sacrifice of Isaac, 132
Salisbury, Eve, 214n88
Sbisà, Marina, 78n57
Schaar, Claes, 72n30, 74–76, 81, 154

Schmid, Wolfgang, 246n32
Schofield, Henry, 223n7
Schroeder, Peter, 6, 67n16, 127
Schucking, L. L., 40n27
Scott, Robert D., 181n34
Seafarer, The, 9, 17, 39–46, 47, 48, 49, 52–
    53, 67n17, 85–86, 93, 117, 123–24, 127,
    128, 139–44, 147, 148, 160, 161–62,
    163, 166n20, 175–76, 178, 218, 241,
    248–49, 252, 256–63, 293–94
Searle, John, 78n57
Sedgefield, Henry, 222n5
Senchán, Torpéist, 182
Shakespeare, William, 21, 101, 132
Shannon, Richard S., III, 81n64
Sharpe, William D., 214n88
Shepard, W. P., 72n28
Sheridan, James J., 51n53
Shippey, T. A., 44–46, 108, 114, 147–48, 150,
    154n12, 161, 271–72
Shûson, Kato, 20n4
Sick Man (Leper) of Abercuawg. See Claf
    Abercuawg
Sieper, Ernst, 9, 40n27, 47
Sievers, Eduard, 66, 70n24
Signy, 223, 248
Silverman, Kaja, 26n28
Sims-Williams, Patrick, 13n31, 206n66,
    207n70
Singh, Shukdev, 190n12
Sir Gawain and the Green Knight, 131–32
Sirach, 233
Skene, W. F., 7n8
Small, George W., 76n46
Smithers, G. V., 40n27
Solomon, 114, 221, 236
Solomon and Saturn, 159
Song of Amargain, 201, 202, 205
Song of Roland, 67
Song of the Old Man. See Can yr Henwr
Sophia, 208
Sources of Anglo-Saxon Literary Culture,
    93n82
Spenser, Edmund, 101
Sperber, Dan, 79n57
Spirit of Men, 256
Spoils of the Otherworld. See Priedeu Annwn
Spurgeon, Caroline, 102n22
Squier, Susan Merrill, 178n26
Stanley, Eric G., 38–39, 40–41, 103, 157
Steiner, George, 187–88, 189
Stevick, Robert D., 40n26
Stewart, Ann Harleman, 229
Stock, Brian, 77n54
Stokes, Whitley, 206

Stolz, Benjamin A., 81n64
Strabo, 207
Suibne, Geilt, 179, 181, 218, 237
Summons to Prayer, 52
Sweet, Henry, 162n18
Sweetser, Eve, 54n59, 57n1, 58n2, 63–64
Symphosius, 228

Talan, 268
Talhaearn, 202, 212
Taliesin, 7, 13n30, 14, 54, 58–59, 63n11, 188, 191–92, 194, 195, 200, 202–5, 206–7, 211–14, 216, 218, 224, 232, 235, 237, 300
Taylor, Paul Beekman, 110n42, 124n14, 127n26
Telgesinus (Taliesin), 202
Thomas of Celano, 93
Thomas, R. J., 12n26
Thomson, R. L., 74n33
Thorpe, Benjamin, 256
Thorpe, Lewis, 200n45
Thunder, Perfect Mind, 208–9, 233
Todorov, Tzvetan, 24
Tolkien, J.R.R., 13
Toller, T. Northcote, 225n9
Trask, Willard R., 79n58, 120n3, 126n25
Trautman, Moritz, 222n3
Travis, James, 57n1
Tristan, 19
Tuan mac Cairill, 208n76
Tupper, Frederick, 222, 228
Turner, Mark, 102n23
Turner, Sharon, 193
Tymocsko, Maria, 124
"Typical Is Wind from the South." See Gnodiau

Ueda, Makoto, 20n4, 23n16
Urmson, J. O., 78n57
Urien Rheged, 176, 202, 203

Valerius, Maximus, 207
van Dijk, Teun A., 79n57
Vance, Eugene, 151n8
Venantius Fortunatus, 93
Vendryès, M., 69n22
Venegoni, Charles, 4
Vercelli Book, xi
Vickrey, John, 162

Virgil, 202
Visnu, 208, 209–10
Volsunga Saga, 223, 248

Waldron, R. A., 123n10
Wanderer, The, 9, 16, 46, 48, 52–53, 67n17, 85, 86, 90–92, 93, 128, 140–41, 148, 151, 162–63, 175–76, 178, 237, 240–42, 245, 252
Wasserman, Julian, 162n19, 176n24
Watkins, Calvert, 57n1, 70n24
Weil, Simone, 178
Weiss, P., 26n28
Wells, Arthur, 178n28
Wenzel, Siegfried, 79n59
White Book of Rhydderch, xi
Whitelock, Dorothy, 40–41, 43
Widsid, 208
Widsid, 211, 221, 235–37, 241
Wife's Lament, 16, 17–18, 52, 54–55, 72, 86, 89–90, 133–37, 139, 142, 147, 151, 237, 239, 252
Wilierms, Thomas, 295
Williams, Blanche Colton, 106n25, 114n46, 271
Williams, G. J., 99n7
Williams, Gwyn, 128
Williams, Ifor, 5, 7n8, 9n22, 32, 35, 37, 54n59, 57n1, 59n5, 63n7 and 10, 108–9, 124n15, 188n5, 200n46, 203–4, 214, 263, 268, 279, 294–95, 300
Williams, J. E. Caerwyn, 19n1, 26n27, 58n3, 68, 188n5, 196–97, 198–99, 203–4
Williams, William Carlos, 23–24, 102
Williamson, Craig, 68n18, 230n18, 231
Wilson, Dierdre, 79n57
Winter's Day, 31
Wittgenstein, Ludwig, 29
Wood, Juliette, 202n51, 203n55
Woolf, Rosemary, 41n29
Wright, Louis B., 101n16
Wulf and Eadwacer, 47n49, 54–55, 61, 66, 68, 85, 220, 221–24, 237, 238, 239–40, 243–49, 282–83, 299
Wyld, H. C., 38–39

York, R. A., 79n57

Zumthor, Paul, 79n59, 84n75, 151n8

Subject Index

absence, 24, 26, 105, 123, 140–41, 249
active vs. contemplative life, 141
AESTHETICS
  Carolingian, 66–67, 85, 119, 126
  classical vs. barbaric, 126
  Hiberno-Saxon, 126
  medieval, 35, 115, 117–18, 128
  modern, 9, 39, 84, 104
  modularity, 35, 67, 79, 118, 126, 127, 128
allegory, 38, 40, 158
alliteration, 46, 57, 62–63, 66, 70, 83, 87, 89, 113, 114, 121, 152–53, 154, 158
alterity, 12, 25, 39, 103, 207n70
ambiguity, 12, 14, 16, 17, 21, 22, 23, 40, 42–43, 105, 108, 117, 127, 139, 141–42, 178, 184, 211, 212, 223, 224, 227, 229, 230, 237, 243, 248, 249, 252, 255
anagram, 227
anglocentrism, 6–7, 10, 30, 50, 74, 205, 210, 252
annwn, annwfyn, 212

anthropology, 13, 205, 206
aphorism, 24–25, 104, 107, 150
apothegm, 106–7, 114
ARETALOGY, 14, 191–92, 194, 200–203, 208–10, 214–16, 221, 232–35, 237
  definition, 208
  "revelation discourse," 200–202, 208, 235, 237
arête, 208
assonance, 62
ASYNDETON, 72, 82, 90
  adversative asyndeton, 72, 75, 81–82, 144, 154
awdl, 63
awen, 194, 200, 212, 217n92, 219
Awenyddion, 200

bit, byd (bod). See GNOME

Caer Sidi, 189
carnivalesque, 213

CATALOGUE, 14, 31, 106, 107, 120, 208, 211, 216, 218, 221
  encyclopedic organization, 120
  lists of natural forms, 194
cauldron of knowledge, 203
"Celtic Twilight," 7, 206
cento, 213
cerdd dafod, 70
cerdd dant, 70
chiasmus, 86, 87, 89–90
clarity. See explicitness under CONNECTION
concatenation, 49, 61
confession, 52, 53
conflation, 12, 13n30, 27, 37
conjunction, 14, 16, 17, 39–46, 72–73, 90, 91, 97, 127, 142, 144
CONNECTION, 4, 23–26, 37, 39, 55, 57, 70, 97–118, 121, 148, 152, 232, 249
  association, 167–68, 151
  "Celtic Connection," 46–55, 76
  contrast, 88, 139, 141, 144, 147, 166
  Cymro-English, 47
  dialectic, 144
  disjunction, 22, 67, 69–72, 79, 94, 118, 128, 139, 141–42, 166, 190, 199, 249
  dyar, 171–72, 175–76
  explicitness, 10, 13, 16–17, 24–26, 24–25, 30, 54, 74, 76, 77–79, 94, 118, 139–40, 150, 154, 221, 224, 225, 249, 253
  grammatical, 16, 17, 22, 24, 46
  hypotaxis, 70, 72, 74–76, 77, 79, 92, 97, 119, 148
  juxtaposition, 4, 14, 16, 22, 23–26, 31–32, 35, 37, 46, 70, 72–73, 74, 75, 79, 86, 88, 90, 105, 118, 119, 126, 127, 137, 144, 146, 147–48, 153, 154, 170, 175, 183, 187, 188, 194, 199, 216, 244
  loose and close relationships, 23, 36, 76
  "natural analogy," 14, 15–26, 31, 148, 199–200, 216
  oer, 175–76
  parataxis, 26, 70–71, 72–76, 79, 144, 148
  sea (in connection with "sadness"), 42, 118, 140–43, 148, 168–70, 176, 199
  subordination as it develops from parataxis, 70
  syndesis, 75–76, 91
consolation, 9, 48, 49, 86, 175, 219
consonance, 62, 66, 88, 89
contemptus mundi, 142
CONTEXT, 8, 14, 16, 90, 117, 118, 144, 148, 149–84, 188, 191, 193, 212, 229, 230–31, 236, 243, 244, 251, 254
  definition, 149

high and low context communication, 10, 149–50
cyfarwyddiaid, 83
cymeriad, 61
cynfeirdd, 54, 58–59, 93, 195
cynghanedd, 35–36, 58, 66, 117
cywyddwyr, 58, 66

dedwydd. See diriaid
DEIXIS, 14, 16, 31, 103, 119, 120, 125–26, 132, 316, 137–38, 139, 140–44, 177, 216, 224
  definite article, 136
  deictic and anaphoric distinction, 31, 136, 236
  demonstrative pronouns ("this" vs. "that"), 135–36
  in Claf Abercuawg, 144
  in The Ruin, 137–39
  in The Seafarer, 139–44
diaegesis, 10, 16
dialogical vs. monological, 37, 141, 213, 252
DIALOGUES, 141, 188, 221, 236
  dialogue genre, 39, 45, 202
  dialogue poems, 18, 202, 213
didactic, 107, 114–15, 118, 163, 202
dionysian vs. apollonian, 205
DIRIAID, 148, 166–67, 171, 183
  compared with dol/eadig in Old English, 166
  definition, 166
  direit daear, 50
  direit new, 50
  vs. dedwydd, 166, 183
discrete. See stichic
dithyrambic, 193
drui, druid, 193, 194, 205, 207, 212, 218
  druids vs. clerics, 212

eicse, 124
emendation, 10–11, 37, 60, 108–9, 212, 252
ENGLYN, 20, 23, 36, 48, 50, 54, 58–66, 69–70, 75, 83, 93, 113, 144, 145, 164, 218
  englyn penfyr, 64, 93n84
  englyn milwr, 64, 93n84
enthusiasts, 7
EXILE, 4, 15–18, 48, 52, 154, 163, 168, 177, 179, 181, 182–83, 219, 239, 251
  Old Irish ailithre, 78
  outlaw, 217, 245–247

figure, figura, 37, 39–40, 98, 100, 101, 102, 103–4, 162, 172, 224
filling in, 5, 9–10, 22, 35, 37, 44, 54, 69, 183, 255
"flyting," 212

folklore, 13, 205, 206
FORMULA, 24–25, 79–85, 92, 113, 141, 164
    as narrative device, 83
    in Old English, 80–82, 84
    in Welsh, 82–84
    oral formula, 79–81, 83–84, 85, 90
forþon (in The Seafarer), 17, 39–45, 141–42
Frauenlieder, 243

gair cyrch, 64–65
gap, 5, 9–10, 12, 23–26, 37, 38, 67, 69, 73,
    85, 90, 149, 204, 222
GENERATIVE GRAMMAR, 77–78
    deep structure, 77n53, 78
    surface structure, 77
genre, 46–53, 190–91, 198, 213, 242, 251
gloss, 11, 50
GNOME, GNOMIC, 4, 8, 14, 31, 34, 37n15, 47,
    48n49, 50, 98, 104, 105, 106–18, 119–
    25, 136–37, 140, 142, 145–47, 150–51,
    160, 163–67, 172–74, 216, 218, 240, 244
    bit, byd, biteu, 104, 107, 109–10
    definition, 106–7
    gnawd, gnodiau, 104, 111
    natural vs. human gnome, 107, 113, 166
    sculan, 110–11
    universal vs. particular, 106–14, 118, 136–
    37, 139–40
gnostic, 200
gogynfeirdd, 30, 58, 66, 69, 193, 194, 195–97
goliards, goliardic, 129–30, 178
gwarchan, 63

haiku, 20, 22, 23
hapax legomenon, 3, 223–24
hardness (defined), 158
HEART, 40, 154–55, 158–63, 170, 174–75
    breosthord, 162, 241
    bron, 174–75
    bryd, 175, 176
    buried, 242
    callon, 168–71, 175, 176
    disclosed, 162–63, 176, 241, 242
    hard, 155, 157, 158–59
    hard mind, 158–59, 161, 162, 163, 174–75
    hreðerlocan, 159, 241
    hyge, 159, 161, 163, 175
    mod, 159, 160, 161, 162, 163, 175
    modsefa, 159, 163
    raw (crai), 155, 163, 172, 176, 219
    soft, 155, 158
heteroglossia, 213

icon, 39, 98, 107
IMAGE, IMAGERY, 4, 9, 13, 14, 16, 23, 24, 30–
    31, 34, 36, 37, 38, 39, 41, 52, 87, 90, 94,
    97–118, 121–22, 126, 127, 132, 137,
    140–43, 144–48, 151, 153, 154–55, 160,
    162–64, 166–68, 172, 174, 178, 190,
    199, 216
    definition, 98
    enargia, 99, 102
    history of image, 98–104
    image and message, 41
    "imagists," 102
    mental image, 99, 100–101, 102, 103, 121,
    124, 131, 132
    montage, 22, 121, 127
incremental repetition, 70–71, 81–82
INDO-EUROPEAN, 57–58, 205
    indigenous vs. Indo-European theory of ori-
    gins, 54, 57, 63, 207n70, 253
interlace, 88, 126, 196–97
interpolation, 49, 50, 252

"latent narrative," 151
LEPER, LEPROSY, 50, 53, 175, 177, 179, 182,
    214, 252
    as healing condition, 50, 179
    lepers and poets, 217–18, 219
    lepers and seers, 218–19
LINES, 57, 67–68, 85, 93n84, 146, 243
    Old English half-lines, 68, 72, 81–82, 86,
    87, 89
    Old English hypermetric lines, 68
    Welsh poetic lines, 57, 93n84
literacy. See orality and literacy
ljoþahattr, 243
LOGIC
    associative logic, 68–69, 197
    sequential logic, 68–69, 197

"man-nature synthesis," 20–21
MEDIEVALISM
    "First Medievalism," 5
    "Four Medievalisms" (defined), 5
    "Fourth Medievalism," 5, 254
    "Second Medievalism," 5, 206
    "Third Medievalism," 5, 254
METAPHOR, 22, 23, 46, 98–99, 100, 104, 108,
    145, 151, 157, 165–66, 167–68, 172,
    174, 197, 228, 229–30, 236, 249
    dead metaphor, 101–2
    martial metaphor, 155, 157, 159, 160–62,
    188
    poetry as contest, 188, 191, 240
    poetry as raid, 189
    riddle as metaphor. See RIDDLE
metempsychosis, 207, 208
metonymy, 100
metrics, 4, 14, 59–68, 70–72, 81–82, 86, 114,
    117

Monstrum, Monstrosity, 213–14, 218, 244–45
as portent, 214

Narrative, 15, 16, 32–33, 48n49, 61, 66–79, 83–84, 90, 93, 108, 126–27, 128, 132, 134, 151, 222n5, 243
vs. lyric, 15, 68–69
"natural analogy," 4, 15, 216
nature, 14, 15–27, 30–31, 32, 34–37, 48n49, 50, 98, 106–7, 108–9, 113, 115, 117, 126, 129–30, 145–46, 148, 151, 154, 159, 163, 167, 174, 177, 179–81, 190, 199, 214–16, 217, 219, 220, 221, 249
Natureingänge, 19

Obscurity, 4, 13–14, 25–26, 187–92, 195, 204, 211, 212, 220, 222, 223, 224, 239, 243, 253
arcana, 221
glossolalia, 194
gravis, 195
hermetic, 3, 15, 190, 208, 224
intentional difficulty, 14, 184, 187, 188–94, 195–97, 211, 224, 225, 227, 229
love poems and secrecy, 237–38, 239
searo, 226, 239
secrecy, 52–53, 176, 206, 215, 225, 226, 240, 242, 243–44, 248, 252
secrecy as strength, 252
secrecy in the Old English *Maxims*, 243–45
secrecy in the Welsh maxims, 244
uncooperative text, 3, 6, 11, 14, 50, 184, 212, 223, 249, 250
visibility as trap, 252
ollav, 215
Orality, 12, 67, 76, 211
and literacy, 11, 79–87, 227–228
Ordeal, 216, 236, 237
and plaint poems, 236–237
as poetic insight, 236
as source of wisdom, 237
Otherworld, 182, 195, 212, 216, 235
outcast. *See* Exile
outlaw. *See* Exile

palimpsest, 10, 50, 252
penitence, penitential, 9, 47–51, 54, 179, 182–83, 217, 218, 219, 251, 253
penitential lyric, 6, 48–50, 51–53
Perspective. *See also* Deixis, 22, 31, 97, 105, 118, 119, 120, 125, 128, 130–49
"audience perspective," 131–33, 138
ego, 128–129
hearing, 146, 147, 150
in *The Ruin*, 137–38

subjectivity, 130, 144, 146–47, 154, 177, 253
pilgrim, 15, 43, 52, 177, 182
planctus, 8, 41n29, 86, 163, 172, 218, 219–20, 221, 236–37, 242
plurality, 41, 50, 114, 254
Poetry
as discourse, 125
Drátkvaett, 129, 197
Latin lyric, 130
Old Irish poetry, 19–20
modern concept of the poem, 12, 61
poetic initiation, 50, 207n70
reverdie, 19
Scaldic poetry, 65–66, 193
Pre-Raphaelite, 206
priamel, 37n15
"primeval," 205
prose, 32, 45, 46, 69, 93, 196–97
prosody, 37, 79, 83, 117
proverb, 31, 107, 108, 113, 114, 150–51
Punctuation
editorial, 12, 67–68, 255
pointing in Old English, 67–68
pointing in Welsh, 67–68

quaestiones, 213

reader-response theory, 78, 205
rebus, 227
refrain, 66, 243
"revelation discourse." *See* aretalogy
rhan, 58n2, 63–64
Rhetoric
apostrophe, 100
descriptio, 99, 113, 122
imitatio, 98, 126
paranomasia, 154
similitudo, 126
synecdoche, 100
tmesis, 92
Rhyme, 63–66, 85, 88–89
internal, 65, 88
Riddles, 190, 202, 205, 221–22, 224–34, 236, 237, 238–40, 241, 243, 248, 249
as kenning, 228, 230
as metaphor, 228
defined by Aristotle, 228
enigma, 193, 221, 218, 221, 224, 232
giedd, 248
runes, 222, 225, 226, 228, 238–39

"salmon of wisdom," 179, 203
sangiadau, 196–97
satire, 216
seer, 15, 124, 181, 212–13, 215, 217, 219

SEMIOTICS, 9, 14, 150, 251
  Kristeva's semiotic, 10, 55, 68
senex, 34, 51, 141, 147, 167, 172
sensorium, 125, 155, 172
sentence (definition), 77–79
"Sentimental Celt," 7, 13
shaman, shamanism, 182, 205, 206–7
shapeshifting, 202, 203, 208, 211, 214, 224, 232, 235, 237
"shifting dominant," 218–19
soul as bird, 98, 123–24, 142
SPACE, 148, 154, 177–84
  analogous to time, 88, 127, 133–36, 142, 144
  gendered, 178
  hierarchies of, 120, 178
  inside vs. outside, 6, 15, 154–55, 177–79
  sacred and secular, 6, 120, 148, 154, 179
specificity spectrum, 104–6, 107
speech act, 52, 78n57
stanza. *See also* ENGLYN, 58–67
stichic (as opposed to discrete), 17, 58, 66–67
symbolic, 10, 143, 156–57
sywedydd, 193

"Third Thing," 26, 54, 150, 254
torymodroddion, 196
TRANSLATION, 4, 10, 12, 14, 15–16, 22, 26, 29–55, 63, 69, 109, 136, 177, 188, 204, 210–11, 212, 222, 247, 249, 251, 252, 253, 255
trobar clus, 193, 237–38
troubadours, 129–30, 144, 178, 193, 238

ulatbamsi ("upside-down" language), 190, 210
UNITY, 33, 39, 41, 50, 117
  Homeric unity, 80
  in *Maxims II*, 122
unodl, 63
ut pictura poesis, 100

variants, 12, 37, 252
variation, 22, 70, 81–82
vatic, *vates*, 14, 193
vaticinatory poetry, 200
visionary, 142, 194, 206, 216, 232, 237
VISUAL, 97, 100, 117
  cinematic techniques, 21–22, 132, 140
  gwybod, 124
  seeing and knowledge, 24, 120–25
  montage, 22, 127
  visibilia/invisibilia, 122
  visual/verbal analogy, 88, 100, 102, 127–28, 133

"Wildman" theme, 181, 214, 218
WISDOM, 31, 47, 52–53, 120, 121, 124, 137, 141, 154, 203, 208, 212–13, 214, 216, 217, 218–19, 220, 234, 235, 237, 242
  wiseman, 193, 240–41
wolf, 224, 245–48
"Wolf's Head" (*wulfesheafod*), 246–47
wodbora, 236

zero-copula, 73
zeugma, 73–74, 105